A2-Level

Business

Studies

The Revision Guide

Editors:
Rachael Powers, Jennifer Underwood and Emma Warhurst.

Contributors:
Jane Barnes, P. M. Brockbank, John Grant, Peter Gray, Gemma Hallam, Jeff Harris, Jane Hosking,
Jonathan Mace, David Morris, Adrian Murray, Nagu Rao, Katherine Reed, Lynda Turner, Keith Williamson.

With thanks to Andy Park and Victoria Skelton for the proofreading.

Published by Coordination Group Publications Ltd.

This book is suitable for:

AQA, Edexcel, OCR and WJEC

There are notes at the tops of double page spreads to
tell you if there's a bit you can ignore for your
syllabus. There are also arrows like this...

AQA ONLY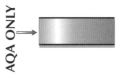

...next to the headings of content that's syllabus-specific.

ISBN: 978 1 84762 273 0

Groovy website: www.cgpbooks.co.uk
Jolly bits of clipart from CorelDRAW®
Printed by Elanders Hindson Ltd, Newcastle upon Tyne.

Contents

Marketing Objectives and Strategies

*If you can think back as far as last year, you'll remember that marketing made up a big chunk of AS. And here we are on marketing again. It's like you've never been away. Everyone should be familiar with the stuff on these pages, but don't rush or skip them — learn them properly. These two pages are for **AQA**, **WJEC** and **OCR: Marketing Option**.*

The **Role** of **Marketing** is to **Identify** and **Satisfy** customer **Needs** and **Wants**

1) Marketing ensures that the business supplies goods and services that the customer wants, in order to achieve a **competitive advantage** (see p.162) over other firms. It's **mutually beneficial** for the business and the customer — the customer gets something they like and the business achieves higher profit levels.

2) Remember, marketing covers **market research**, **market analysis**, **market planning** and the "marketing mix" — the four big Ps of product, price, promotion and place (distribution).

Objectives and *Strategies* set out *Marketing Aims* and *Directions*

1) **Marketing objectives** are what the marketing department uses to say **exactly** what it's **hoping to achieve**.

2) For many companies, the key marketing objectives are **increasing profit levels** and **gaining market share**.

3) Other marketing objectives might include **creating** and **maintaining** a strong **brand ID**, helping the company to **grow**, making sure a particular product **survives** when a rival product enters the market, or helping the business to **cut costs**, e.g. by switching from expensive television ads to a cheaper online marketing campaign.

4) Objectives can be **qualitative** (e.g. **non-numeric** plans for brand image, product quality, product development) or **quantitative** (**specific figures** for market share, sales revenue, market penetration and profitability).

5) **Marketing strategies** say who the company's **target market** is, and how they're going to use the **marketing mix** to **achieve** their marketing **objectives**. Some of the most commonly used marketing strategies are covered in more detail on the next page.

Marketing Objectives are *Influenced* by things *Inside* and *Outside* the *Business*

INTERNAL FACTORS

CORPORATE OBJECTIVES — The marketing department has to make sure its activities fit in with the company's **overall goals**. For example, if the business has set a **corporate objective** of **improving profits** in the **short-term**, there's no point in the marketing department focusing on an innovative **new product** idea that still needs to be developed and is **two years** away from being **launched**.

FINANCE — The finance department allocates the marketing department's **budget**. This affects what the marketing department is able to do. If the budget is **cut** then marketing objectives may need to be **scaled down**.

HUMAN RESOURCES — **Workforce planning** (p.92-93) identifies how many **staff** the marketing department needs. If the marketing objectives involve lots of **different activities**, the marketing department will need a **lot** of staff to get them all done. If the business has decided to **reduce** staffing levels, marketing might have to set **less ambitious** objectives.

OPERATIONS — The production department can only produce **so many** units in a certain **time** period. A marketing objective of increasing market share that involves increasing sales by giving away **free samples** in magazines will only work if production have the **spare capacity** (see p.110) to make them.

EXTERNAL FACTORS

MARKET — The **state** of the **economy** has a big impact on marketing objectives. An economic **boom** is a good time to try to increase **sales volumes** since **income levels** are generally higher. In a **recession** the marketing department is more likely to set an objective of maintaining **market share**. For more about the business cycle, go to p.129.

TECHNOLOGY — Changes in technology affect some businesses more than others. In markets where technology changes **rapidly**, the objectives of the marketing department tend to be more focused on **sales** and **price**, because new technology causes prices to rise or fall very fast. For example, the price of **DVD players** has **fallen** rapidly since the launch of **Blu-Ray™**. This isn't necessarily a bad thing — DVD players still have a high share of the market because they're now so cheap. However, it does mean that the marketing department of a DVD player manufacturer will have to reassess sales objectives and pricing strategies to ensure that they aren't left with **unsold stocks**.

COMPETITORS — The actions of competitors affect marketing, particularly in a highly **competitive** market. If a competitor is focused on **low prices**, then the marketing department may alter their objectives so customers see them as **price competitive**. For example, Tesco launched their "Real Baskets" advertising campaign in 2009, in direct response to Asda's "Saving you money every day" campaign.

Marketing Objectives and Strategies

There are **Low Cost** and **Differentiation** marketing strategies...

Low Cost

1) **Low Cost** strategy calls for the **lowest cost** of **production** for a given level of quality.
2) In a **price war**, the firm can maintain profitability while the competition suffers losses.
3) If **prices decline**, the firm can **stay profitable** because of their low costs.
4) A very **broad market** is needed for this strategy — preferably a **global** market, with huge production facilities to take advantage of **economies of scale**.

Differentiation

1) **Differentiation** strategy requires a product with **unique attributes** which consumers value, so that they **perceive** it to be **better** than rival products.
2) A unique product 'adds value' so the business can charge a **premium price**.
3) However, competitors might try to **copy** the product, or consumer **tastes** could **change**.

Of course, low cost and unique aren't always mutually exclusive...

...and **Diversification**, **Market Penetration** and **Development** strategies, too

1) **Market penetration** means trying to **increase** your **market share** in your **existing market**. E.g. if a company makes washing powder and currently has 25% market share, it might try to achieve 30% market share using **sales promotions**, **pricing strategies** and **advertising**. This strategy works best in a **growth market**. It **doesn't work well** in **saturated markets**, where demand for the product has stopped growing.

2) **Diversification** means selling **new products** to **new markets**. Diversification is a **very risky** strategy. It's used when a business really needs to reduce their dependence on a **limited product range** or if **high profits** are likely.

3) **Product development** is selling **new products** to **existing markets**. It's used when the market has good **growth potential** and the business has high market share, strong R&D (see p.116-117) and a good **competitive advantage**.

4) **Market development** is selling **existing products** to **new markets**, for example **new market segments**, or **new geographical areas**. It's particularly relevant to businesses with a **strong product** and **spare capacity** (see p.110) which can easily make lots of identical products and sell them in new areas. Market development can be **risky**, unless the firm has spotted a **clear new market opportunity**.

Marketing can be **Asset-**, **Market-** or **Product-Led**

1) **Asset-led marketing** combines **consumer wants** with the **strengths** of a firm. It's now seen as the best route to long-term **customer satisfaction** and **brand loyalty**. It helps firms ensure they're **capable** of making a product customers need before they start the manufacturing process.

2) **Market oriented** businesses start by finding out what the **customer wants**. The main benefit of this approach is that it's entirely **focused** on the **customer's needs**, so the **risk** of producing something the customer **doesn't want** is very **low**. It's also more **flexible** than asset-led marketing, and can meet **changes** in demand more **quickly**.

3) The **market-led** approach has other **risks** though — it tries to fulfil customer needs even when the firm doesn't have the right **resources** to meet them. Market-led strategies can push the firm into **new markets** where it doesn't have enough **experience**. This can end in failure, with **disappointed customers** leaving the brand.

4) **Product oriented** businesses focus on developing **new products before** they consider the **needs** of the **market**. Businesses that make **innovative products** are occasionally product-oriented, e.g. if they've developed a new type of technology they can market as the next 'must-have,' but this approach is now fairly **rare** because it's so **risky**.

WJEC ONLY

Practice Questions

Q1 Name two internal and two external factors that influence marketing objectives.
Q2 Name two benefits of a low cost marketing strategy.

Exam Questions

Q1 Jo Porter has just started up a company, Berryfruity Ltd, which makes organic blackcurrant cordial. Analyse the advantages and disadvantages of using low cost and differentiation marketing strategies. [8 marks]

Insect sellers tend to go for a locust marketing strategy...

When it comes to marketing, different companies prioritise different things. Some put the product first, others are all about customer needs. Whichever strategy they choose, it's vital to keep both factors in mind — it's pointless having a product that's easy to make but that nobody wants, or a product that everyone wants but that the firm finds hard to produce.

Marketing

*Marketing — it sounds quite creative until you realise it's all objectives and strategies. Page 4 is only for people doing **OCR: Marketing Option**, page 5 is for **OCR: Marketing Option**, **AQA** and **WJEC**.*

Marketing *can be helpful for* Other Departments...

1) Most larger businesses have a specialised **marketing department** — but marketing affects **all departments**.

2) **Market analysis** can tell the **finance** department **how much** the business is likely to make in **sales**. Market analysis tells the business how **big** the market for a product is, so they know if they can **expand** and make more profit without having to **diversify** into supplying new products.

3) Market research and analysis tells the **research and development** (R&D) department what kind of products to **research** and **design**, in order to meet **future needs**.

...*but* Not Always

Marketing objectives may **conflict** with the objectives of other departments. For example, the marketing department of a bubble bath firm might decide in June that it wants to do a "**buy one get one free**" promotion in August because they think it will **double demand** for the product. But they won't be able to meet this objective unless their **suppliers** can supply the **raw materials** in time and the **production department** is able to make the **goods** without **exceeding** its **capacity** targets (see p.110).

The Marketing Department *needs to consider* Other Factors *and* Decisions

Financial Factors

1) The marketing department has to consider the **marketing budget** — if money's tight or it's a small company, there's no point considering an expensive TV ad campaign as your marketing strategy.

2) If the company has a bad year, **unexpected budget cuts** can mean that the marketing department have to alter their objectives. Medium- to long-term objectives might need to be **scaled back** during a **recession**.

3) Also, any changes in production capacity or human resources affect the business' **strengths** and **weaknesses**, which affect the **marketing strategy** it chooses to follow.

Workforce Issues

1) A company can only **diversify** into new markets and product ranges if it has **staff** with the **right skills**.

2) This means it might need to **employ new people**. To do this, the firm must organise a successful **recruitment campaign**. It also has to be able to **afford** to pay its new staff a **suitable wage**.

Ethical Issues

More about ethics on p.136

1) Marketing departments that behave **ethically** think about **who** they're **targeting**. For example, even though companies are no longer allowed to advertise fast food products during children's TV programmes, some **sweet manufacturers** aim their **websites** at **children**. Kids who visit the website might try to **pressure** their parents into buying the product.

2) Companies might also think about the impact their marketing activities have on the **environment**. They might choose to reduce the amount of **packaging** they use in order to **reduce waste**, even if this means the product might not stand out as much to consumers.

Time and Other Constraints

1) The marketing department needs to think about **how long** it has to come up with a campaign. You can't start to plan a Christmas marketing campaign in September if it's going to take 6 months.

2) They also need to consider the **brand**. E.g. if a company is known for making soup, **diversifying** into desserts might not be successful because it just **confuses customers**.

3) Marketing departments need to think about the **competition**, especially when it comes to **pricing**. E.g. a chocolate company can't suddenly increase all their prices by 20p because customers would probably start to buy other brands instead.

"Isn't this lovely," Luke sighed. "The sun's shining, the water's warm, and I'm here with you, planning our new range of Christmas cards."

Marketing

The **Law** has an impact on **Marketing**

1) The Government regulates businesses to make sure they act in the **public interest**. It does this by passing new laws.

> Legislation = laws.

2) Legislation **protects consumers**, but it can lead to **increased costs** for firms and it may make **innovation** harder. E.g. when the **EU** proposed that it should be a **legal requirement** to **patent** all **new software**, many small companies argued that applying for patents would be so **expensive**, they'd no longer be able to afford to develop new products.

> Protectionism = placing restrictions on foreign businesses trading in your country.

3) Legislation can **open up markets**, for example the laws that opened up the utilities (gas and electricity) market in the UK, and the laws governing the EU single market. It can also **close markets** through **protectionist** measures, e.g. tariffs on imports (see p.142).

4) Legislation also protects businesses through **patents**, **trademarks** and **copyright**.

The **Law** directly affects the **Marketing Mix**

1 — Product

- Some products are **plain illegal** under UK law, e.g. handguns.
- The **Sale of Goods Act** means that goods must be "**fit for purpose**" and "**of satisfactory quality.**"

2 — Price

- **Predatory pricing** (cutting prices to force a competitor out of business) is illegal in the EU and in the US. It's difficult to **prove** that a business is trying to kill competition, though.
- Firms can't **fix prices** — they can't **agree** with their **competitors** to all charge the **same price** for a particular **item**.
- Consumers must be **told** the **price** before they buy — e.g. pubs must display drink prices.

3 — Place / Distribution

- Some products can only be sold in certain places by certain people — e.g. some medicines can only be bought with a doctor's **prescription**, not over the counter or off the supermarket shelf.
- **Licences** are required to sell some products, e.g. **alcohol** or firearms.
- **Sunday trading** is limited.

> E.g. no "prevents cancer" stickers on fruit without proof.

4 — Promotion

- The **Trade Descriptions Act** regulates promotion. Businesses can't lie about their products. They can't "bait and switch" by advertising a nice product and supplying a crummy one. Product **labelling** is regulated — for example, you can't make claims of medical benefits without proper medical evidence.
- **Offensive adverts** can be **banned**. The Advertising Standards Authority regulates adverts.
- Advertising of some products is **restricted**. **Prescription medicines** can't be advertised at all and there are very few places where **tobacco** products can be advertised. Advertising of alcoholic drinks is also restricted.
- **Advertising hoardings** need planning permission.

Practice Questions

Q1 Give one example of how marketing objectives can conflict with the objectives of other departments.

Q2 State two examples of how legislation has opened up markets.

Q3 Give three ways in which the law would affect the marketing of a new alcopop.

Exam Question

Q1 XmasDeco Ltd supply wooden Christmas decorations. Their marketing department wants to diversify into edible tree decorations. Discuss the factors that they need to consider before following a diversification strategy. [10 marks]

What's a dolphin's favourite chat-up line? 'You're fit for porpoise...'

I expect you're absolutely whizzing through these pages so far, aren't you — with a bit of luck a lot of it will be familiar from AS. Hopefully seeing it again has dragged it up from the depths of your memory and all you have to do now is refamiliarise yourself with it. Whatever you do, don't just assume you know it and flip over to the next page — revise it and revise it well.

Marketing Planning and Strategy

*So, you've got your marketing strategy. Good for you. But you're not done yet — you need to know how to put the strategy into action — you need a plan. These pages are for **AQA**, **WJEC** and **OCR: Marketing Option**.*

The **Marketing Plan** says what the **Marketing** department's **Going To Do**

1) A **marketing plan** is a document that gives details of all the **activities** that are going to take place in the marketing department to turn the **marketing strategy** into **reality**.

2) It also explains the **background** to the marketing strategy and says how **budgets** will be **spent**.

3) The information in the marketing plan is **useful** for **marketing staff**, because it lets them know **what** they'll be doing and **when**. **Other departments** use it too though. For example, if a mail order company is going to run an **advertising campaign** through the summer, the HR department might need to employ **extra staff** in the call centre to cope with the likely increase in phone calls.

All **Marketing Plans** contain the **Marketing Objectives** and **Strategy**

Marketing plans don't all contain exactly the same information. A **small business** might just produce an **informal document**, while **large businesses** usually write the marketing plan in the style of a **formal report**. Nearly all marketing plans will contain the sections listed below:

Objectives	• The marketing plan states the company's **corporate objectives**, and says how the **marketing objectives** will help to achieve them.
Budgets	• The plan contains detailed budgets with the **expected costs** of each product, department or marketing activity.
Sales Forecast	• It also says how many **sales** or how much **revenue** the business expects to make if the marketing plan is followed.
Marketing Strategies	• This section of the plan describes the **strategies** that will be used to **achieve** the **marketing objectives**.

Some companies include other sections, too — e.g. an **action plan**, saying **when** each **activity** will happen and **how long** it will take, or details of how they plan to **control** the activities to make sure everything stays **on time** and **on budget**.

The **Marketing Plan** is affected by **Internal** and **External Factors**

Internal Factors

1) The company's **product range** affects the marketing plan. For example, if they have **one** very **successful** product or already have an extremely **wide range** of products, they might not want to diversify further.

2) A successful marketing plan needs to consider the firm's **strengths** and **weaknesses** — so most marketing planners start by looking at the results of the business's SWOT analysis (see p.159).

3) A firm's marketing activities will be restricted by how much **finance** they have available.

4) **Human resources** are important too. The company needs to have staff with the right skills, or recruit some.

5) **Operational issues** also affect the marketing plan — the business needs to be sure it's capable of **producing** enough to keep up with extra demand. Otherwise, potential customers will end up **disappointed**.

6) The **current marketing mix** has an effect on the marketing plan. The business will probably want to incorporate some elements of the **existing mix** into the new plan.

External Factors

1) It's important to think about **competitors**. Firms need to consider their **competitors' sales** and **market share** and their **future plans** — if a rival is planning a TV campaign, it might be sensible for them to have one too.

2) The **state of the economy** has an impact too — if there's a economic downturn, some companies spend more on marketing, others spend less. It depends on the company and the product.

3) Companies look at the **market**. For example, the **increase** in **superbugs** created a **new market niche** — businesses started developing **personal hygiene kits** for patients to take into hospital with them.

Marketing Planning and Strategy

The marketing planning Process is Cyclical

1) **Marketing plans** give a fairly **long-term** view of what the marketing department's planning to do.

2) The plan is dependent on **market** and **environmental circumstances** remaining roughly the **same** as they were when the plan was **written**. E.g. if the plan was written in a period of economic boom, and after several months, the economy shows signs of weakening, the **plan** will probably need to be **changed**.

3) Companies need to **constantly** review what's happening in the **market** and what their **competitors** are doing, to make sure the **marketing plan** stays **relevant**. If something's **changed**, they might need to develop **new marketing objectives** and **strategies** and a **new marketing plan** so that the company can still achieve its corporate objectives. The diagram below shows how the steps of marketing planning are **cyclical**:

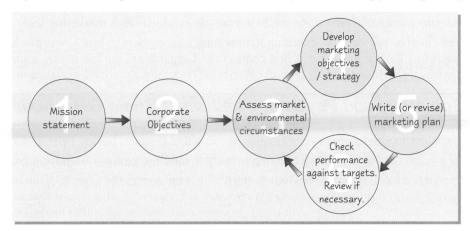

Marketing Plans can be Hard to Put into Practice

1) Having a marketing plan is great if all the **other departments** in the company are **willing** to do **what** the marketing department **wants** them to do, **when** they want them to do it. But it's not so great if, say, marketing wants the production department to print 200 000 promotional leaflets in July, but the production department knows it will be swamped with other work and won't have time to do it.

2) It's also hard to have a successful marketing plan if the company is in a market where the **circumstances change** so **fast** that the plan is **out of date** almost as soon as it's written.

3) The plan won't work if it doesn't look far enough **ahead** — it's supposed to be a **long-term** view. If marketing **confuse** short-term **tactics** with long-term **strategy**, it's hard for people to see what the **overall goals** are. And if people aren't sure what they're trying to achieve, they might **not** be very **motivated**.

4) **Bureaucracy**, or a **corporate culture** which **doesn't value cooperation**, can make it hard to have a successful plan.

Practice Questions

Q1 Give one example of how a department other than marketing might benefit from a marketing plan.

Q2 What four sections do nearly all marketing plans include?

Q3 Explain the cycle that a company needs to go through during the marketing planning process.

Exam Question

Q1 Sophie and David Barton have just set up a company selling a new variety of pink tomato and need to write a marketing plan. Discuss the internal and external factors that they will have to consider when writing their plan.   [8 marks]

Q2 Explain the difficulties that a business might encounter when trying to implement a marketing plan.   [6 marks]

Marketing planners must feel like they're going round in circles...

Whatever you're doing, it's good to have a plan, and that's especially true for revision. If you don't have one yet, grab some felt tips and paper and make one. You can waste three hours that way...ok, I'm joking, but you do have time to scribble down a quick timetable before getting back to learning the stuff on these pages — just don't colour it in...

Market Analysis and Buyer Behaviour

Market analysis is essential — it tells firms how big the market is, if it's growing or shrinking and how much of it they have. **AQA** *and* **OCR:** *Marketing Option people need* **both pages** *but* **WJEC** *people only need the* **first two subsections** *of* **p.9***.*

Businesses need to Know Their Customers — Why they buy What they buy

1) Understanding **why** a customer buys a product allows a business to **respond** to the **customer's needs**.

2) Customers go through several **stages** when they buy something: 1) **recognising** the **need**, 2) **finding information**, 3) considering **alternatives**, 4) **purchasing** the product, and 5) **evaluating** the purchase.

3) The **buying process** can involve up to six groups of people playing different **roles** — **initiators** (who suggest making the purchase), **influencers** (e.g. children, who might put pressure on the person doing the buying), **gatekeepers** (e.g. company secretaries who decide whether the salesperson gets to see the person making the final decision), **deciders** (who make the decision to buy), **purchasers** (who make the physical purchase) and **users** (who actually use the product). Being aware of all the people involved helps **marketing** know who to **target**.

4) People can be grouped by **personality** according to **how long** it takes them to **buy** a **new product**. E.g. **innovators** and **early adopters** buy the product when it **first comes out**. **Laggards** are the **last** to buy something (e.g. people who've only just bought their first mobile phone). Marketing is usually aimed at innovators and early adopters.

Economics, Sociology and Psychology all affect Buyer Behaviour

SOCIOLOGY

1) Sociology explains how **belonging** to certain **groups** can **affect** people's **buying behaviour**.

2) Examples of groups that the buyer might belong to include **families**, **clubs** or **friendship groups**.

3) Each of these groups has a **typical behaviour pattern** which **influences** the actions of the **individual**, e.g. a group of friends might all enjoy watching the same sitcom on TV. This means that when the series comes out on DVD, companies will try to convince each individual within the group to buy it.

PSYCHOLOGY

1) Psychology helps companies work out **why** people buy **certain products**.

2) Some psychologists believe people have **basic needs**, like eating and sleeping, and **higher level needs**, like creativity and self-esteem. **Basic needs** have to be satisfied before **higher level needs**. In the UK, most people can **afford** to satisfy both types of need. This might lead to poor **growth** for **goods** that satisfy **basic needs** (e.g. food) so these goods are often marketed as products that can **also** satisfy **higher level needs** like friendship and achievement — e.g. a pizza company's advertising might show a group of friends sharing a pizza.

3) It's **hard** for people to recall adverts off the top of their head, so firms use psychology to help them develop effective **point-of-sale displays** to **jog** their **memory**.

ECONOMICS

1) People can only buy something if they have enough **disposable income** to be able to **afford** it. Disposable income is the money that people have left once **tax** and **pension contributions** have been taken off.

2) **High** interest rates **discourage** people from spending. **Low** interest rates **encourage** them to spend (see p.130).

3) People's **perceptions of value** affect what they buy — this is why firms use **psychological pricing** (see p.25).

Markets are Segmented into groups of Similar Customers

Different groups of customers have different needs. **Analysing** different **segments** of a target market allows a firm to **focus** on the needs of **specific groups** within that market. A market can be segmented in several ways:

1) **Income** — **luxury products** are usually aimed at **high income** groups.

2) **Socio-economic class** — firms can segment the market based on the **jobs** people have. **Socio-economic class** is shown by a **letter**, e.g. people in socio-economic **group A** are higher managerial staff or **professional people** like MDs of big firms, or hospital consultants. **Group E** includes state **pensioners** and **unemployed** people.

3) **Age** — firms can target products at specific **age groups** — pre-teens, teens, 25-35 year olds, the over 55s etc.

4) **Gender** — e.g. chocolate companies target some bars at **women** (e.g. Flake) and some at **men** (e.g. Yorkie®).

5) **Geographical region** — some products have a **regional market** — e.g. Welsh cakes, haggis.

6) **Amount of use** — for example, **mobile phone** suppliers market differently to **heavy** and **light** users.

7) **Ethnic grouping** — new **ethnic minority** digital **TV channels** make it easier for firms to target ethnic groups.

8) **Family size** — e.g. **people carriers** are built with more seats than normal cars specifically to suit families with several children. Large "**family packs**" of breakfast cereal, loo roll etc. are aimed at large families.

9) **Lifestyle** — **busy young workers** often buy microwaveable **ready meals**, so this kind of item is often aimed at them.

Market Analysis and Buyer Behaviour

Market Analysis tells firms about Market Size and Growth

1) **Market size** is the **total sales** in the market — the **volume of sales** (**units** sold) or the **value of sales** (total **revenue**).

2) Businesses need to know if the market is **growing** (i.e. demand is increasing) or **shrinking** (i.e. demand is decreasing). The formula for market growth is:

$$\text{Market growth} = \frac{\text{New market size} - \text{old market size}}{\text{Old market size}} \times 100\%$$

3) In a **growing** market, **several** firms can **grow easily**. In a **shrinking** market **competition** can be **heavy** — there are fewer customers to go around. Firms can **diversify** or they may want to **get out** of the market altogether.

Market Analysis tells firms about Market Share

1) **Market analysis** is when a company **looks closely** at **market conditions**. It's useful for **planning**.

2) Market share is the **percentage** of sales in a market that is made by **one firm**, or by **one brand**. It's calculated using this formula:

$$\text{Market share} = \frac{\text{Sales}}{\text{Total market size}} \times 100\%$$

3) E.g., if **1 out of 4** PCs bought was a Dell, this would give Dell a **25%** market share (in terms of volume). If **£1 in every £10** spent on perfume was a Chanel purchase, this'd give Chanel a **10% market share** (in terms of value).

4) It's important to look at **trends in market share** as well as trends in sales revenue. Letting your market share go down is not good — it means that **competitors** are **gaining an advantage** over you.

> **Example:** Say the computer gaming market has grown by 15% from one year to the next. A software company would not be happy if they'd only increased their game sales by 5% from £200 000 to £210 000 — they're failing to grow at the **same rate** as the market, so their **market share** has gone down.

Market Classification means Knowing which Market you Operate In

1) **Market classification** means **identifying** a **market's characteristics**. Markets can be classified by:

- **Geography** (local, national, international)
- **Nature** of the product (agricultural, technological)
- **Seasonality** (seasonal or year-round)
- **Development** level (new, growing, saturated)
- Product **destination** (trade, private consumers)

2) Companies **don't always spot** all the **markets** they could be in — they might have been supplying a product to industrial customers for so long that they don't notice that private customers might be interested in it, too.

3) **Marketing** can also be a **problem** for firms that operate in several markets. They often need to use **different marketing activities** to target **different markets**. They also need to be able to **afford** to carry out a variety of marketing activities **simultaneously**.

Market Analysis helps companies Spot Opportunities

1) All the **tools** on these two pages help companies **work out** exactly **what the customer wants**. Many people think that knowing what the customer wants is actually **more important** than how you **promote** a **product**.

2) But although market analysis is **useful** for deciding **what to make**, and **which markets** to enter, it doesn't guarantee **success**. A lot depends on **using** the **information** that market analysis provides **effectively**.

Practice Questions

Q1 What is the formula for calculating market growth?
Q2 Give five possible ways of segmenting a market.
Q3 Give three characteristics a market could be classified by.

Exam Questions

Answer on p.184.

Q1 Calculate market share for a firm which made £985 000 worth of sales in a market worth £5 million. [3 marks]

Q2 Explain the different roles that people can play during the purchase of a product. [8 marks]

Pizza satisfies my higher level needs — it's my best friend...

Honestly, you'd think that by the time companies had finished using this lot to analyse your buying habits, they'd know you better than your mum does. On that note, here's some mumsy-type nagging — make sure you learn all the market-type calculations as well as the different market segments, customer roles and customer personalities. Why? Because I said so.

Marketing Analysis

Businesses have a lot of mathsy techniques for analysing data, and you need to know how they work.
*These two pages are for **AQA, WJEC** and **OCR: Strategic Management Unit**.*

Time Series Analysis *looks at data over* Time

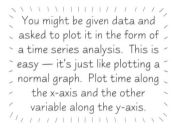

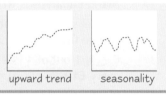

You might be given data and asked to plot it in the form of a time series analysis. This is easy — it's just like plotting a normal graph. Plot time along the x-axis and the other variable along the y-axis.

1) **Time series analysis** is used to reveal **underlying patterns** by recording and plotting data over time, for example the recording of **sales** over a year.

2) Time series analysis can be used for **sales forecasting** and monitoring **production output**. It can also be used to look for **links** between **sales** and **marketing activity** and to spot **fluctuations** in the **economy** that might indicate a boom or bust period.

3) **Trends** are the long-term movement of a variable, for example the sales of a particular product over a number of years. Trends may be **upward**, **constant** or **downward**, but there are usually **fluctuations** around the trend.

4) **Seasonal** fluctuations repeat on a **regular** daily, weekly or yearly basis, e.g. the use of electricity over a 24-hour period, or the sale of ice lollies over a year.

5) **Cyclical** fluctuations are repetitions over a **medium-term** period, often many years. The business cycle of boom and bust has a cyclical pattern.

6) **Random** fluctuations have **no pattern** to them. They also include the results of **major disturbances** like **war**, changes of government and sudden **unpredictable events** like the outbreak of foot and mouth disease.

Correlation *shows how* Closely *two* Variables *are* Related

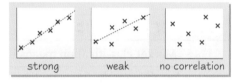

1) **Correlation** is a measure of how **closely** two variables are **related**, for example the age of employees and their productivity. Correlation may be **strong** (high), **weak**, or there may be no apparent correlation at all.

2) You can draw a **line of best fit** through a set of correlated points — the line should be as **close** as possible to **all** the **points** on the graph.

3) It's a **useful tool**, but correlation **doesn't prove** cause and effect. **Other variables** may be important — e.g. there might be strong correlation between an increase in marketing activity and ice-cream sales, but if the marketing coincided with a spell of hot weather, it's hard to say which factor had more impact.

4) If there's a **correlation** between two variables, managers might assume that the trend will **carry on**. They can **extrapolate** the graph — draw a **line of best fit** and then keep the line going to **project** the trend **further** along the **x-axis**. For example, if the graph shows the **cost** of **car repairs** against the number of **miles driven**, the line can be extrapolated to show that the **higher** the **mileage**, the **higher** the **cost** of repairs.

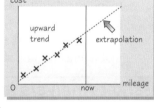

5) Extrapolation relies on **past trends** remaining **true**. Unfortunately, the **pace of change** in the market can be very fast, so extrapolations from the past don't always predict the future very accurately — it's best to use it for predicting just a **few months** ahead.

6) **Sudden unexpected events** are the biggest pitfall for extrapolation. Changes in the market due to things like **new technology** make extrapolation from past data look completely useless.

Time Series Analysis *is* Useful *for making* Short-term Plans

1) Managers can use time series analysis when making **decisions**. It's often used at the end of the decision-making process to help weigh up the **costs** and **benefits** of different courses of action, e.g. to see whether decreasing the price of a product or introducing a "buy one get one free" would have a greater impact on sales.

2) It's best to use time series analysis as a **tactical forecasting** method, e.g. to make **short-term** predictions. It's most useful in fairly **stable** environments, e.g. where the **size** of the **market** or the number of **competitors** is **unlikely** to **change** much.

Moving Averages *Smooth Out* Seasonal *and* Cyclical Fluctuations

1) Moving averages (see next page) are used to **smooth out** data which either contains **seasonal variations** or is **erratic**. The moving average **gets rid** of **fluctuations** to reveal the underlying trend. Once the trend has been isolated it can be **extrapolated** on a graph.

2) It's useful to know the general trend, but sometimes companies need a more **accurate** figure for a particular season's sales. They can calculate this by **adding** the **average seasonal variation** to the **extrapolated figure**.

Marketing Analysis

An example of *Moving Averages* — pay attention because it's *Tough*

1 Work out the sales total for the **first 4 quarters** (e.g. a whole year of business). Put it in the **4-quarter moving total** column, in the centre of the year (e.g. in between **Q2** and **Q3** of 2006).

2 Work out the total for the **next 4 quarters** (2006 Q2 to 2007 Q1), and put it in the 4-quarter moving total column, between Q3 and Q4 of 2007. **Repeat** this process for the next 4 quarters, and the next, 'til you're done.

3 Add the first two **4-quarter moving totals** together and put the answer in the **centred moving total column**, in the 2006 Q3 row. **Repeat** for the rest of the 4-quarter totals.

4 **Divide** the **centred total** by **8** and put the value in the **quarterly moving average** column in the 2006 Q3 row (bang in the **middle** of the **data** you used to calculate it).

5 **Repeat** this process for the other **centred moving totals** to get your quarterly moving averages.

6 **Plot** the quarterly moving averages on a **graph**. Always **plot** the quarterly moving average in the **middle** of the quarters that it relates to — e.g. the quarterly moving average for the **2006 Q1 to 2007 Q1** should be plotted in line with **2006 Q3**. You should end up with a fairly **smooth line**.

Year	Quarter	Sales revenue (thousand £s)	4 quarter moving total	Centred moving total	Quarterly moving average
2006	1	243			
	2	250			
	3	289	1038	2088	261.00
	4	256	1050	2117	264.63
2007	1	255	1067	2147	268.38
	2	267	1080	2160	270.00
	3	302	1080	2172	271.50
	4	256	1092	2194	274.25
2008	1	267	1102	2212	276.50
	2	277	1110	2279	284.88
	3	310	1169	2321	290.13
	4	315	1152		
2009	1	250			

You calculate a centred moving total as well as a 4-quarter moving average so that your midpoint always lines up <u>exactly</u> with a quarter. If you just used a 4-quarter moving average it would be halfway between two quarters, which wouldn't be as useful. If you were calculating the moving average for an odd number of periods, e.g. 3 months or 9 months, you wouldn't need to do this extra step.

Moving Averages can be used to *Predict Future Trends* and *Variation*

1) The **moving average** can be plotted on the same graph as the actual figures to show the **underlying trend**.

2) **Extrapolating** the moving averages line can give a clearer idea of future trends.

3) If the original data shows **cyclical** or **seasonal variation**, businesses can work out the **cyclical** or **seasonal deviation** to predict future figures **more accurately**.

4) The **cyclical** (or **seasonal**) **deviation** is the **average deviation** from the **moving average** for each period. You work it out by calculating the **average difference** between the actual figure and the moving average for each Q1. See p.177 for how to calculate averages.

5) **Cyclical/seasonal deviation** can be included in the **extrapolation** of the graph to give a more accurate idea of what will happen in the future. E.g. the cyclical deviation for Q1 in the data in the example above is −11.4, so the predicted graph would plot each figure for Q1 11.4 units under the trend line.

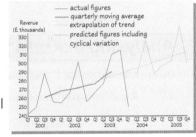

6) Moving averages can be really **useful** for businesses, but the trends they identify are only reliable if the business is operating in a **stable environment** (see opposite for more on this).

Practice Questions

Q1 What is correlation?

Q2 What is extrapolation?

Q3 What is time series analysis?

Q4 What are moving averages?

Exam Question

Q1 a) Calculate the quarterly moving average trend for the sales revenue data below (figures are in thousands). [14 marks]

2006 Q1 630	2007 Q1 621	2008 Q1 602	2009 Q1 589
Q2 567	Q2 578	Q2 550	
Q3 552	Q3 543	Q3 502	
Q4 678	Q4 600	Q4 560	

The answers to these questions are on p.184.

b) Plot the quarterly moving average trend on a graph. [4 marks]

These moving averages can reach quite a speed on level ground...

Those moving averages are hard to get your head round, but not impossible. You'll need to really make sure that you genuinely, honestly follow all the steps for calculating them. Don't kid yourself that you get it if you don't. Read the hints for each step, and you can understand it. Honest. It's doable. Don't be tempted to skip it, because it may be in the exam.

Marketing Analysis

In my day, when you wanted to draw a pie chart you had to find a protractor, a compass and a good, sharp pencil. These days, your computer can do it for you without even making a hole in the paper. This page is for people studying **AQA, WJEC** *and* **OCR: Marketing Option**, *while p.13 is just for* **WJEC** *and* **OCR: Strategic Management Unit**.

IT can be used to help Analyse Markets

Most companies use **software** to do their marketing analysis, rather than having a marketing manager do it by hand. The **advantages** of this are:

1) Doing calculations **by hand** can **take ages**. It also requires a lot of **concentration** — just one mistake affects the accuracy of the calculations and the reliability of the trends identified. By using IT, businesses can **reduce** the risk of **errors** being made.

2) Computers can **compare** moving-average trends from **different periods** at the touch of a button.

Little did Susan know that Mike was more loyal to his supermarket than he was to her.

3) Computers can process much **more data** than humans can. It would be incredibly **time consuming** for a **human** to calculate moving averages or do other kinds of time series analysis on the huge amount of data that a **large firm** generates.

4) IT can also be used to gather information for marketing analysis at the **point-of-sale**. For example, supermarket **loyalty cards** can provide information about the kinds of people who shop in a particular store or the products they're buying most often. There's more about this on p.126.

5) Lots of different companies now provide marketing analysis software. This makes it easier for a business to find a program that fits its **needs** exactly. For example, marketing analysis software allows managers to investigate **"what if?"** scenarios. They can calculate the impact of **potential changes** in expenditure or sales. The **price** of the software **falls** if the software providers are **competing** with each other on **price**.

Analysing marketing Data can be Difficult

Businesses might face **problems** when they're trying to analyse marketing data:

1) **Random variations**, more than one **correlation** in a set of data or **no** apparent **correlation** at all (see p.10) can make it hard for businesses to draw any useful conclusions from marketing analysis.

2) Buying **software** can be **expensive**. If a new version of the software is released and the business decides to **upgrade**, it costs even more money.

3) Staff need to be **trained** to use the software, which might be **expensive** and **time-consuming**. If the company **upgrades** their software at any point, further training might be needed.

4) There's a risk that having software that can deal with loads of data will lead to the company valuing the **quantity** of information over its **quality**. A business might produce lots of pretty graphs, but if nobody's drawing **conclusions** about what the **trends** mean for the company they're not useful at all.

5) Companies with lots of data might find that their **computer systems** aren't up to the job of **handling** it, e.g. if it takes too long to upload all the information. If this happens, they might have to **outsource** (see p.71) their marketing analysis to a **specialist company** or stick to analysing just a **proportion** of the available data.

Case study: Tesco Clubcard

Problem: When Tesco launched its loyalty card, Clubcard, in 1995, it took 30 hours every time they wanted to transfer the data they'd collected from their computers to the computers of the data analysis firm that interpreted it.

Solution: Tesco decided that it would be easier to interpret just some of the data and then apply their findings to the rest of the data. They agreed that the data analysis firm dunnhumby would look at 10% of the data once a week and extrapolate their findings to the other 90% of Clubcard holders. In 2007, dunnhumby introduced new software which allows them to analyse the behaviour of all Clubcard holders without relying on extrapolation.

Data Analysis

Data needs to be Presented so it's Easy to Understand

1) **Lots** of **people** are **interested** in the **data** that businesses produce. For example, the production manager might want to **compare** the absenteeism rate in his department to the rate in other **departments**. **Stakeholders** might want to see **sales data**, so they know **how the firm is doing**.

2) Data is often represented in the form of a **graph** or **chart**. The **best type** of graph or chart to use depends on the **type** of **data**.

3) **Pie charts** are used to show **market share**. Each **1%** share is represented by a **3.6°** section of the pie (because there's 360° in a circle and 360 ÷ 100 = 3.6). Pie charts are **simple to use** and **easy** to **understand**. They can be created quickly using **spreadsheets**.

Histograms use Area to represent data

1) To **read** data from a histogram, you need to **multiply** the **bar width** on the **x-axis** by the **frequency density** on the **y-axis** to work out what **frequency**, (e.g. how many) each bar represents.

2) For example, on the histogram on the right, the **0-5 bar** has a frequency density of **3 units**, so you **multiply 5** (the width of the bar or **class width**) by **3** (the **height** of the bar). In this case, 3 x 5 = 15, so 15 calls lasted between 0 and 5 minutes. **15** is the **frequency**.

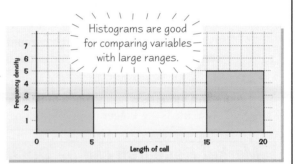

Histograms are good for comparing variables with large ranges.

3) If you're asked to **draw** a histogram, you'll be given **data** containing the **class widths** and **frequencies**. All you need to do is **divide** the **frequency** by the **class width** to work out how **high** your **bar** needs to be. So if you're told that **25 calls** lasted between **15** and **20 minutes**, you divide **25 by 5** and draw a bar **5 units** high.

Index Numbers show Changes in data over time

1) **Index numbers** are a simple way of showing percentage changes in a set of data over time.

2) Businesses take a set of data showing revenue/profits etc. over a number of years, and make the earliest year the **base year** — the value for the base year is set as 100, and the figures for the following years are shown **relative** to this figure. E.g. the table on the right shows the index numbers for revenue for an Italian restaurant.

Year	Total Revenue	Revenue Index (2003 = 100)
2003	£17 000	100
2004	£19 550	115
2005	£21 250	125
2006	£22 440	132
2007	£24 650	145

3) To work out the **revenue index** for any year, take the total revenue from that year, divide it by the total revenue in the base year and multiply it by 100, e.g. for 2006: 22 440 ÷ 17 000 × 100 = 132. The formula for this is:

Revenue index for year X = total revenue in year X ÷ total revenue in base year x 100

4) The main **advantage** of indexing is that it makes it easy to compare **trends** even if **quantities** are in **different units**.

WJEC ONLY

Practice Questions

Q1 Give three examples of potential difficulties a firm might face when analysing marketing data. *Answer on p.184.*

Q2 Last month, Wings of Steel, a budget airline, had 20 flights that arrived 0-5 minutes late, 100 flights between 5-30 minutes late and 30 flights that arrived between 30-60 minutes late. Sketch a histogram to represent this.

Q3 How do you calculate the revenue index for a particular year?

Exam Question

Q1 Peter Paulson runs a small company selling novelty mousemats. He's considering investing in software to help with marketing analysis. Explain the advantages and disadvantages of using IT for marketing analysis and say whether you think he should buy the software or not.

[12 marks]

Pie charts — they're just easier to swallow...

Some people think that histogram is just a fancy name for a bar chart. But oh no, it's a whole lot more than that. Luckily, it's simple once you've mastered it, because you really do need to understand what all these charts and numbers are showing you — if you misread the data in the exam, it's likely to cost you a good few marks. Best get learning, then.

Market Research

Every firm needs to know what people want, and how much they're willing to pay for it.
*These pages are for **OCR: Marketing Option**.*

Market Research finds out about Markets, Customers and Competitors

1) Market research analyses the **size**, **geography**, **segmentation**, and **sales potential** of markets.

2) Market research also finds out about **products** and **product development**.

3) Analysis of sales includes finding out about **sales methods**, **territories** (where things are sold), and **outlets** (the shops, catalogues or websites which do the selling).

4) **Promotional activities** can be analysed — adverts, special offers, point-of-sale displays.

5) Analysing the **economy** is also part of market research. For example, you can calculate the rate at which the economy is growing or shrinking in the same way you calculate it for a market (see p.9).

6) **Customer motivation** is an important area of market research. Businesses need to know **why** customers buy their product, why they buy **competitors'** products, and what their **perceptions** are of products on the market.

7) It's really important to research **competitors' actions** and **products**. Market research can tell you about the **competitors' market share** and about the unique selling points (**USPs**) of their products.

> The **purpose** of market research is to **reduce risk**. It's become more and more important as **business** has become more and more **risky** — the **pace of change** has increased, product development is more **costly**, globalisation means markets are **bigger** (with more consumers and more competitors), and **consumer attitudes** change frequently.

Market Research can be Qualitative or Quantitative

1) **Qualitative** research is **subjective** and attempts to find out why customers make purchasing decisions. In particular, it's concerned with customer behaviour, motivation, tastes and preferences.

2) **Quantitative** research is **factual** and consists of "how much" and "how many" type questions, e.g. "What market share does Hellman's® mayonnaise have?" "How many people buy Pop-Tarts®?".

Field Research gathers Primary Data and Desk Research uses Secondary Data

Primary Data

1) **Primary data** is information that doesn't already exist. It's collected for a specific purpose.

2) **Surveys** (face-to-face, telephone or postal), **observation** (watching customer reactions), **loyalty cards**, panel and group **discussions** and **test marketing** are used to collect primary data.

3) **Loyalty cards** (e.g. Tesco Clubcard, Nectar card) provide rewards for customers and also **collect information** about what they buy. This information is used to **target** ads and special offers to the customer's buying pattern.

4) **Panel** and **group discussions** find out about **customer attitudes** and changing **tastes** and **behaviour**. The **Delphi** technique (see p.21) assembles a panel of **experts** to discuss an issue and provide a consensus view.

5) **Test marketing** involves a **small-scale test** of a new product. This reduces costs, allows the business to learn lessons before a national launch and lets them solve any problems. But test marketing gives **competitors** a **preview** of the product — they may react by changing their marketing strategy or developing a rival product.

6) Primary data is taken from a small **sample** of the market. There's more on sampling on the next page.

Secondary Data

1) **Secondary data** is **second-hand** information, which has been gathered by someone else.

2) **Secondary data** includes data from the Department of Business, Enterprise and Regulatory Reform (BERR) and **government statistics** such as the Census and the Social Trends report.

3) **Market intelligence reports** are produced by market research organisations like Mintel and Nielsen. **Trade associations** and **trade journals** are also good sources.

Primary and Secondary market research data have Pros and Cons

Advantages of primary data	It's **targeted** at a specific issue. It can assess **buyer psychology**. It's **up-to-date**.
Disadvantages of primary data	It's **expensive**. There's a risk of **bias** if it isn't done correctly.
Advantages of secondary data	It can often be obtained for **free**. It may provide a good **overview** of the market. Secondary data is often based on **accurate**, **reliable** figures, e.g. from the Census.
Disadvantages of secondary data	It's **not tailored** to meet a specific need. **Market intelligence** reports are **expensive**. Information may be **outdated**. The original data may be biased.

Market Research

Market researchers need a Representative Sample

1) Market researchers can't ask the **whole** of a **market** to fill in a survey. They select a **sample**.

2) When they select the sample they try to make it **reflect** the characteristics of their target market. So if you're creating a **product** for **single**, **high-income women**, you'd want your **sample** to be made up of **unmarried females** with an income of over **£50 000** a year, for example.

3) A **big sample** has a better **chance** of being representative than a **small sample** — but even a big sample won't be 100% representative. There's always a **margin of error**.

4) The **size** of the **sample** may depend on how many people a **company** can **afford** to ask. If the **cash** available for research is **limited**, the **risk** of the information being **inaccurate** increases.

5) **Finance** isn't the only thing which affects the **sampling method**. It's also affected by the **type** of product or firm, the **risk** involved and the **target market**.

There are 6 Ways of Getting a Sample

Random	This is where **names** are **picked randomly** from a list of the **whole population** of interest (or pretty close — usually from the **electoral register**).
Stratified	In stratified sampling, the population is divided into **segments** called "**strata**" based on things like **age**, **gender** or **income** — for example age 18-24, age 25-34, age 35-44, age 45-64, age 65+. Names are selected at **random** from **within** each **segment** ("**stratum**").
Cluster	Often a **population** can be **broken down** into **smaller groups** (clusters), e.g. residents of individual **counties** are examples of clusters within the UK population. To carry out a cluster sample, you start by picking a **random sample** of **clusters** and then you interview a **random sample** of people from **each** selected **cluster**. For cluster sampling to be accurate, the clusters need to be as **similar** to one another as possible (in terms of population, socio-economic mix etc.). Cluster sampling needs far **less time** and **legwork** than random sampling.
Systematic	Systematic sampling involves choosing a **starting point** in the **sampling frame** (the population you're planning to survey) and **selecting every nth value**, e.g. every fifth name. There may be **bias**, if there's an **underlying pattern** in the sampling frame.
Quota	In quota sampling, the **selection** is made by the **interviewer**, who'll have a **quota** to meet — e.g. "interview 20 women between 25 and 34." It's a bit like stratified sampling, but it's **not random** — interviewers tend to pick people who look 'nice', which introduces **bias**. It's **quick** and **useful**, though.
Convenience	**New businesses** with **limited funds** often use convenience sampling, which **samples consumers** who are **most easily contacted**. **Bias** is clearly a problem with convenience sampling.

Market Research is great but it Isn't Perfect

1) **Market research** is the **most scientific way** for companies to **find out** what's happening in the **market** and what **customers** want. Effective market research **greatly reduces** the **risk** of making **expensive mistakes**.

2) However, carrying out research is usually **very expensive**, even if businesses use cheaper secondary data rather than gathering their own. Also, you **can't** just **do it once** — **market conditions change**, which means companies have to regularly carry out new market research.

3) The other **problem** is that **relying too heavily** on **market research** prevents companies from making **decisions** based on **gut feeling**. This is especially true for companies that do a lot of **quantitative research**. Having a scientific basis for all decisions might seem sensible, but a lot of **innovative products** start out as a **hunch**. Firms need to remember that often **less risk = less reward**.

Practice Questions

Q1 Give three ways of obtaining primary market research data.

Q2 Give two disadvantages of secondary data.

Q3 Name the six different types of sample and explain briefly how each one works.

Exam Questions

Q1 Define quantitative and qualitative market research. [4 marks]

Q2 Jim Smith wants to research the market for men's silk shirts. Recommend and justify a sampling method. [8 marks]

Data? But I don't fancy her...

Dipping even a toe into a market you haven't researched properly is a very, very foolish thing to do — not unlike dipping a toe into a pond full of alligators. That's why all companies should do some research, no matter how tight their budget. There is an argument for following your instincts, but best to leave that to the big guys who can afford to lose a few million.

Market Research Analysis

*Once a business has done market research, they analyse the data. There are statistical tools to help them do this — and that's what these pages are about. For **WJEC** and **OCR: Marketing Option**.*

Managers need to **Make Sense** of **Data**

1) Marketing people need to turn raw market research data into something that's **easy** for managers to use and understand. Businesses often want to know the **central tendency** of a set of data. The central tendency is another word for the **average** of a set of data.

2) **Mean**, **median** and **mode** are measures of central tendency. The **mean** is all the results added together ÷ the number of results, the **median** is the **middle** value when the figures are placed in ascending order, and the **mode** is the **value that occurs most often** in the data.

3) A **histogram** of results will often be **symmetrical** and **bell-shaped** — this usually means the results follow a **normal distribution**. A normal distribution occurs when the **mode**, **mean** and **median** of the data are all the **same**, and they all fall slap bang in the **middle** of the data.

4) Often, market researchers assume the **responses** to a particular question will be **normally distributed**. They can then use the mean and standard deviation of their sample to work out the range that they're confident the **mean** for the **entire population** would fall into. For more on standard deviation see the stuff below and on the next page.

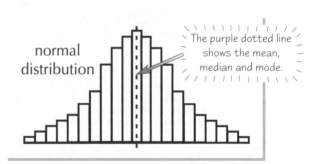

normal distribution

The purple dotted line shows the mean, median and mode.

5) **Production departments** often use **normal distribution** to ensure that **quality levels** are **consistent**. There's an example of this on the next page.

The **Standard Deviation** is a measure of how **Spread Out** your **Data** is

1) The **standard deviation** is a **really important** measure.

2) The **formula** for calculating standard deviation is: where x = each piece of data, μ = the mean, and n = the number of pieces of data.

$$\sigma = \sqrt{\frac{\sum (x - \mu)^2}{n}}$$

$\sum$ means "the sum of".

So, it's the <u>square root of</u>... (the <u>sum of</u> the <u>squares of the differences</u> between each piece of data and the mean, <u>divided by the number of bits of data</u>).

Example: The weekly sales of a product are 34, 32, 14, 25 and 24 units. The mean is $(34 + 32 + 14 + 25 + 24) \div 5 = 129 \div 5 =$ **25.8 units** per week.

Work out the standard deviation as follows:

Work out $(x-\mu)$ for each value, then <u>square</u> it, then <u>add up all the squares</u> and <u>divide by the number of values</u>, and then find the <u>square root</u>.

The variance is just the sum divided by n.

x	34	32	14	25	24			
$x-\mu$	8.2	6.2	-11.8	-0.8	-1.8	sum	variance	SD
$(x-\mu)^2$	67.24	38.44	139.24	0.64	3.24	248.8	49.76	7.05

The **Standard Deviation** of a **Normal Distribution** is very useful for **Analysis**

The standard deviation (SD) of a **normal distribution** graph is very useful for **analysis** and **problem solving**.

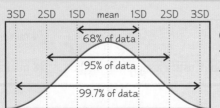

3SD 2SD 1SD mean 1SD 2SD 3SD

68% of data

95% of data

99.7% of data

One standard deviation either side of the mean = **68%** of the distribution.

Two standard deviations either side of the mean = **95%** of the distribution.

Three standard deviations either side of the mean = **99.7%** of the distribution.

These facts are true for all normal (bell-shaped) distributions.

Market Research Analysis

Check out these **Examples** of using **Standard Deviations**

Example 1: A battery lasts on average **250 hours** with a **standard deviation** of **30 hours**.
68% will last between **220-280 hours** (one SD either side of the mean),
95% will last between **190-310 hours** (two SDs either side of the mean) and
99.7% will last between **160-340 hours** (three SDs either side of the mean).

These percentages are the ones from the normal distribution graph above. Learn them.

Example 2: You can also work out the probability of one of those batteries lasting for **more than 290 hours**.

1) 290 hours is **40 hours above the mean** (250 hours). The SD is 30, so this is 40÷30 = **1.33 standard deviations from the mean**. This is called the Z score.

2) Using the Z score table for a normal distribution, we can see that a Z score of **1.33** means an area of **0.4082**.

3) **Convert** the area into a **percentage** by moving the decimal point two places to the right, e.g. **0.4082 = 40.82%**.

4) The **mean average** battery life is **250 hours**, and you've just worked out that **40.82%** of them have a life between 250 and 290 hours.

5) **50%** of them have a life of between **0 and 250 hours** So... that gives you 50% + 40.82% = **90.82%** which have a lifetime of **290 hours or less**.

6) One last simple step: 100% – 90.82% = **9.18%** have a lifetime of **more than 290 hours**.

A Section of a Z Scores Chart

Z	area	Z	area
1.22	0.3888	1.28	0.3997
1.23	0.3907	1.29	0.4015
1.24	0.3925	1.30	0.4032
1.25	0.3944	1.31	0.4049
1.26	0.3962	1.32	0.4066
1.27	0.3980	1.33	0.4082

In the exam, you'll be given the Z scores.

You can just read the Z score from the chart. For example, a Z score of 1.31 tells you 40.49% of the area under the curve lies between the mean and Z.

(How do I know that the mean is 250 hours — because the data is normally distributed, that's how. 50% of them last longer than that, 50% last less time than that.)

A final point on market research — **Surveys** always have **Errors**

1) Errors in surveys can come from **sampling errors** and **non-sampling errors**.

2) A **sampling error** is the difference between the value obtained in a survey and the true value. For example, if a **survey** concludes that people eat jam sandwiches **10 times** a month and they **actually** eat them **7 times** a month, the **sampling error** is **3**. Generally, the **larger** the sample, the **smaller** the sampling error. Sampling errors are **unavoidable** unless you can survey an entire population.

3) **Non-sampling errors** happen for other reasons. E.g. respondents may give answers to **please** the **interviewer**, they may give **socially acceptable** answers instead of their honest views, they may fail to **understand** the question, or they may fail to **return** a postal survey. Errors can also get into the data when it's being **typed up** and prepared.

She wasn't sure of the socially acceptable answer to 'Would you prefer it if I was wearing trunks?'

Practice Questions

Q1 What shape is a histogram of normally distributed data?

Q2 What is a sampling error?

Q3 What's the formula for calculating standard deviation?

Q4 What proportion of a normal distribution graph lies within 2 standard deviations of the mean?

Exam Questions

Q1 Amelia Brown sells hand-carved four-poster beds. Her weekly sales are as follows: 20, 18, 14, 12 and 24 units. Calculate the standard deviation.
Answers on p.184. [8 marks]

Q2 A kebab delivery firm has a mean delivery time of 40 minutes with a standard deviation of 7 minutes. If delivery times are normally distributed, what will the minimum and maximum delivery time be for 99.7% of kebabs? [6 marks]

It's devious, all right...

You've met standard deviation before. Remember those comforting words at AS, 'but you don't have to calculate it'? Well, maybe we should have added 'yet,' because now you do, sadly. And it's a nasty looking formula, too. Yes, it's terrifying, but terror won't get you anywhere, so get used to using that formula. Just plug the numbers in and work that little blighter out.

Marketing Decision-Making

*Ooh, thank goodness — something less mathsy. These pages about the logic behind those clever ad campaigns and new products. Page 18 is for **OCR: Marketing Option** only, and page 19 is for **all exam boards**.*

Marketing Managers use the AIDA Model to develop Promotional Campaigns

1) The **AIDA** model is used to develop promotional campaigns. It's mainly applied to **above-the-line** activities although it can be applied to below-the-line promotion (see page 29).

2) The idea behind the **AIDA** model is that **effective promotion** goes through **four stages**:

1) Awareness (or attention)	First, the advertiser aims to make the consumer **aware** of the product. To do this, advertisers try to grab the consumer's **attention**. An **amusing** or **controversial** ad campaign works well for this.
2) Interest	Next, the advertiser aims to get the consumer **interested** in the product. The ads try to **differentiate** the brand from rival brands.
3) Desire	The focus is on **persuading** the consumer he or she **wants the product**, e.g. by portraying a **desirable image** in advertising or by offering **free samples**.
4) Action	The aim now is to get the consumer to **act** and **actually buy** the product, e.g. by using **sales promotions** (like low initial price, three for price of two).

3) For the AIDA model to work, it's important to follow **all** the **steps**. There's **no point** developing a **clever ad** to get people talking if you don't eventually make it **clear** which **product** the advert is promoting. And once people **know** what the product is and **want** to buy it, you have to make sure that they can **find it** in the shops.

DAGMAR is a model for Promotion and Advertising

1) **DAGMAR** stands for **D**efining **A**dvertising **G**oals for **M**easured **A**dvertising **R**esults.

2) DAGMAR aims to **increase awareness** of the product. It's based on the idea that **customers** move through a series of **five stages** when buying a product.

Stage	Consumer	Suitable Methods of Promotion
Unawareness	**Doesn't know** about the product.	Media advertising.
Awareness	Has a **vague awareness** of the product.	Media advertising.
Comprehension	**Recognises** and **knows about** the product.	Support through product information.
Conviction	**Prefers** the product to others.	Advertising to reinforce brand differentiation.
Action	**Purchases** the product (hooray).	Personal selling.

3) The DAGMAR model uses the psychological pattern of **buyer behaviour** (see p.8). For **impulse**, or **low-value**, sales (e.g. an ice-cream) the customer may blend stages together and recognise and understand the product as soon as they're aware of it, which lets them take action quickly. For **high value** sales, the process of increasing awareness can take months.

4) Companies **combine** different **methods** of **promotion** to ensure the customer moves **smoothly** through the stages. This combination of promotions is known as the **promotional mix**.

5) Some things can **stop** the consumer from moving through the five stages — **competitor activity**, **unwillingness** to buy and **memory lapses** can all slow things down.

Businesses analyse their current situation using SWOT

SWOT stands for **strengths**, **weaknesses**, **opportunities** and **threats**. It's a tool that allows a business to consider both **internal** and **external** factors. It tells managers **where the business is** in terms of its strengths and weaknesses, and the opportunities and threats that the market currently offers.

1) The business must identify its **strengths** and **weaknesses** in a **factual** and **objective** way. For example, a bakery's strengths might include the fact that it's the only place in town that offers freshly made sandwiches. A weakness might be that it's located down a dark, dingy side alley, away from other shops.

2) The **external** environment provides the **opportunities** the business wants to exploit and the **threats** that might prevent success. So the bakery would see the opening of a new call centre with 500 employees as an opportunity, but the introduction of a low price lunch menu by a local restaurant as a threat.

3) SWOT lets the business know where it has a **competitive advantage** (see p.162) over its rivals.

Strengths
Weaknesses
Opportunities
Threats

Marketing Decision-Making

*This page is for everyone — **OCR: Strategic Management Unit, AQA, Edexcel** and **WJEC**.*

Ansoff's Matrix *is used for* Strategic Decisions

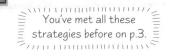

1) **Ansoff's matrix** is used when a firm's **objective** is to **grow**. It shows the **strategies** that can be used to **achieve growth** according to how **risky** they are, which helps managers make decisions about which strategy to use.

2) The **advantage** of Ansoff's matrix is that it doesn't just lay out potential strategies for growth — it also forces market planners to think about the **expected risks** of moving in a certain direction.

3) One **disadvantage** of the matrix is that it fails to show that **market development** and **diversification** strategies also tend to require **significant change** in the **day to day workings** of the company.

4) **Product development** is less risky, but it works best for firms that already have a strong **competitive advantage** (see p.162).

5) **Market penetration** is the **least risky** strategy of all — so **most firms** opt for this approach.

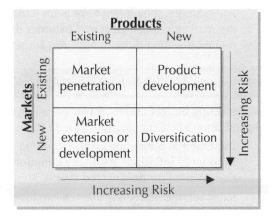

6) Some people believe that Ansoff's matrix **oversimplifies** the **options** available for growth. For example, **diversification** doesn't have to be **completely unrelated** to what the business does currently. It might be a **safe option** to diversify by moving into your **supplier's business**, as you know there's a **guaranteed market** for that product.

There are *Fewer Strategies* for *Expanding into* International Markets

1) **Not all** the **strategies** that are shown on the matrix are **suitable** if a company wants to **expand abroad**.

2) If a company chooses to **grow internationally**, this means it's entering a **new market**. So you can only use one of the strategies that involves **new markets** — either **market extension / development** or **diversification**.

3) It's **safest** and **most common** for companies expanding internationally to use a **market extension** or **development** option. For example, **fast food restaurants** tend to use this option — KFC® first opened in the USA in 1952 and then extended their market by opening in the UK in 1965.

4) In theory, companies could also use a diversification strategy when expanding into international markets. But, because **diversification** is a **risky** strategy and **expanding internationally** is **already risky**, it's **very unlikely** that a firm would decide to launch a completely new product in a foreign market that's also completely new to them.

5) It's more common for a firm to expand overseas either by **exporting** goods or by allowing a **foreign firm** to produce their products under **licence** (e.g. someone else makes the product, but it's the original company's name on the packet). The manufacturer then pays the licence holder a set amount for every product sold.

Practice Questions

Q1 What are the four stages of the AIDA model?

Q2 What are the five stages of DAGMAR and what types of promotion are used at each stage?

Q3 What four things does a SWOT analysis allow a business to consider?

Exam Question

Q1 Louisa and Bob McKenzie run a company that makes organic porridge. The product has been doing well in the UK and Louisa and Bob are considering launching it internationally. Explain what kind of strategy they're most likely to use, giving reasons for your choice. [6 marks]

Ansoff's Matrix — bet Keanu wouldn't want to star in that one...

Expect lots of bad jokes with a matrix theme over the next few pages — it was (unsurprisingly) the first thing that popped into my head. As far as the tools on these pages are concerned, AIDA and DAGMAR tell marketing departments how to lure the customer in, while Ansoff's Matrix and SWOT give a neat summary of current and future possibilities. Clever, huh?

Marketing Budget & Sales Forecasting

*The marketing budget specifies the finances available for spending on marketing activities, and contains sales targets. Sales targets aren't plucked out of thin air — they're based on a forecast. The next three pages are for **AQA** and **WJEC**.*

Marketing Departments do a **Marketing Audit** before Setting a Budget

1) Firms often do a **marketing audit** before they set a marketing budget. This allows them to find out what's **changed** with their **customers** and **competitors** since the last budget.

2) For example, they might have gained **market share** since the last budget or they might have lost some of the market to a competitor. **Customer demographics** (see p.136) might have changed, e.g. the target market might be getting older or have less disposable income.

Marketing Budget **Part One:** **Expenditure** Budget

The **marketing budget** comes in **two parts**. The **first part** tells the marketing department how much they can afford to **spend** on marketing activities. One of these methods is generally used to work out how much money is available:

1) **Incremental budgeting** involves adding a **small additional amount** to the **previous year's allocation**, to take account of **inflation**. It's a very **common** method, because it's **easy** to **understand** and easy to **do**. However, it doesn't plan for **unexpected events**, so it can leave the firm unable to respond to new opportunities or threats.

2) **Sales-related budgeting** allocates marketing spending based on the **sales revenue** that the product will generate.

3) In **task-based budgeting**, **marketing tasks** are **costed out** and finances shared out accordingly.

4) "**Competitor parity**" budgeting means matching **competitor spending**. It's **difficult** to **work out** what your competitors are spending on their marketing. Businesses don't tend to base their budget 100% on competitors — competitor action is likely to affect the expenditure budget a bit, though.

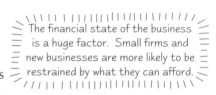
The financial state of the business is a huge factor. Small firms and new businesses are more likely to be restrained by what they can afford.

Marketing Budget **Part Two:** Marketing **Objectives**

1) The second part of the marketing budget contains the **targets** that the marketing department is aiming to meet, e.g. **increase sales** of a particular product by 15%.

2) The budget also gives the s**ales targets** that need to be met in order to achieve the marketing objectives. Businesses set their sales targets by looking at past figures and **extrapolating** (see next page).

3) Sales targets also depend on **market conditions** — the **business cycle** and **competitor** actions can affect demand.

4) The **financial position** of the business and the **expenditure budget** are a factor. Spending a lot on marketing a product means that you'd expect it to **sell** pretty well.

Budget Setting has its **Pitfalls**

1) It's best to **consult with managers** when setting the budget. Staff **resent** not being involved in setting targets.

2) On the other hand, staff shouldn't have too much control over budget setting, because they'll set targets that are **easily reached**, or ask for more money than they need so that they won't **overspend**. Managers' **egos** are a factor as well — managers may see a large budget as an indicator of **status**.

3) Preparing budgets can be very **time consuming**, especially when there's lots of negotiation.

4) Basing an **expenditure budget** purely on **financial position** has its drawbacks. It means that the business spends a **lot** on marketing when sales are **high**, and **less** on marketing when sales are **low** — when it needs it **most**.

5) With **incremental budgeting**, managers may be tempted to spend the **whole budget** to make sure they get at least the same amount in next year's budget. This isn't a cost-effective way to behave.

Marketing Budgets need to be **Justified** by the **Product**

1) Budgets need to be justified in relation to the finances available, and the likely **return**. A product with a **high predicted rate of return** will earn itself a **bigger expenditure budget**.

2) **Product portfolio analysis** and the **Boston matrix** (see p.27) are used to determine which products should be supported by extra spending and which "milked" to provide revenue for other marketing activities.

3) The **product life cycle** (p.26) is a useful model. Marketing expenditure is likely to be high during the **launch** and **growth** phases of a product, or when **extension strategies** are being used.

Marketing Budget & Sales Forecasting

Sales Forecasting aims to Predict the Future

1) **Sales forecasting** predicts the **future sales** of a product. This allows managers to set **sales targets**. Sales **performance** can be measured against those targets.

2) Sales forecasts allow the **finance** department to produce **cash flow** forecasts — once they know how much the business is expected to sell, they can work out how much money is expected to come in.

3) Sales forecasts also allow **production** and **human resources** departments to prepare for the expected level of sales. They can make sure that they have the right amount of machinery, stock and staff.

Backdata and Extrapolation are Quantitative techniques for Forecasting Sales

1) **Backdata** is **data from the past**. Sales backdata from last year can be used to predict likely sales for this year. Managers look for trends in the data and **extrapolate** them forward. Moving averages and other methods of time series analysis (see p.10) help to identify trends in sales backdata.

2) Extrapolation (see p.10) is a great way of predicting sales as long as trends stay **constant**. When there's a major upheaval in the market (rare, but it does happen), extrapolation can produce **misleading figures**.

3) Managers also use **market research data** to predict future sales.

4) **Test marketing** can be used to provide sales forecasts. The product is launched within a limited geographical area. Test marketing gives **accurate data**, and should be a **reliable** indicator of wider **demand**. Managers can **learn lessons** from the test marketing exercise and apply them to the full scale national launch.

5) On the other hand, test marketing allows **competitors** to see the product before the full launch.

Qualitative methods include Intuition, Brainstorming and the Delphi Method

Qualitative techniques call for **human judgement**. They're particularly important when there **isn't** much **data**.

1) **Intuition** is the **feeling** of a **particular individual** about how well a product is going to sell. The individual usually **knows** lots about the **product** in question — they might be in charge of **product development**, for example.

2) Some companies also ask their **sales staff** about their **hunches** because they're in **constant contact** with **customers** and know which **products** are **selling well**. However, it's also important to consider **factors** that your **sales team** might not **know about**, like the arrival of a **new competitor** or a **downturn** in the **economy**.

3) **Brainstorming** is when a **group** of people are asked to give as many **ideas** about something as they can in a **fixed** period of **time**. It's often used when a company is planning to **change** its **strategy** in some way and wants to find out what impact the change will have on sales, e.g. what will be the effect of launching a new website?

4) It's also possible to forecast sales based on **experience**. This means considering the **life cycle** of other, **similar products** that are **already available**. It's especially useful for **new firms** who don't have any **backdata**.

5) **Panel consensus** methods involve a panel of experts discussing an issue until they reach an agreement about it. It's more accurate than just asking one person for their views, but still carries a big risk of error.

6) The **Delphi method** is a bit like a panel consensus method, but **not quite** the **same**:

> **The Delphi Method — here's how it works....**
>
> 1) The **Delphi** method asks questions to a **panel of experts** in order to predict **future** market **trends**. The idea is that you get better prediction from **human experts** than from extrapolating trends.
>
> 2) The firm asks each expert **individually** for their opinion of what'll happen in the market. The experts' answers are **anonymous**. The firm puts the experts' opinions together in **summary** form, and sends the summary back to all the experts for their **comments**. The firm then summarises the comments and sends them out a second time for **further comments** and views. They repeat the process until they've all come to a **similar conclusion**.
>
> 3) Because the original responses are **anonymous**, and each expert is asked questions **individually**, the experts won't be **swayed** by reading what the leading industry guru, or their arch-enemy, has to say.
>
> 4) The process of repeatedly summarising and asking for more comments is supposed to lead the experts towards a **consensus** view that they all agree on.

"Never mind next year's sales — ask me how my feet got like this."

Marketing Budget & Sales Forecasting

Quantitative Techniques have Advantages and Disadvantages...

Advantages

1) Quantitative forecasting is usually quite **accurate** as many **trends** are **consistent** over time.

2) Quantitative forecasting follows **set methods** — so you know how you've arrived at a particular forecast.

3) It's easier to **persuade** senior managers that **sales targets** are **realistic** if they're based on **scientific methods**.

Disadvantages

1) A quantitative forecast assumes that the **future** will follow the **same patterns** as the **past**. It might turn out to be completely **irrelevant** if a **random event** occurs which causes **sales** to be massively **higher** or **lower** than they've been in **previous years**.

2) It's **hard** to do for a completely **new business** or **product** — there's **less backdata** to work from.

...and, surprise surprise, so do Qualitative Techniques

Advantages

1) A basic qualitative forecast can be provided **quickly**, **easily** and **cheaply**.

2) It's better to use qualitative methods of forecasting if the **factors** influencing sales aren't **easily quantifiable**, e.g. changes in fashion.

3) Qualitative techniques are useful if it's a **new product** or if **trends** in the product's sales have recently **changed** — e.g. if it seems to have entered another stage in the product life cycle.

4) Some managers might feel **more comfortable** working from a prediction provided by a **human** rather than generated by a **computer package**.

Disadvantages

1) Panel consensus methods, like the Delphi method, can be very **time consuming**.

2) If forecasts are made from hunches, there's a risk that a manager might forecast low sales to make **targets easier** to reach. On the other hand, they might be **too optimistic** and **overestimate** the number of sales.

3) Qualitative forecasting can leave the person who made the forecast **vulnerable** — they might be **held responsible** if their forecast turns out to be wrong.

Practice Questions

Q1 Explain the four ways budgets can be allocated.

Q2 Give three potential problems with setting budgets.

Q3 How do sales forecasts help other departments?

Q4 What is the Delphi method?

Q5 Give two advantages and two disadvantages each for quantitative and qualitative sales forecasting.

Exam Questions

Q1 Gary Snowdon is setting next year's budget for his firm. He plans to use the incremental method. Explain to him what the disadvantages of using this method might be. [8 marks]

Q2 Sue Roberts has been selling cashmere dog blankets for a year. She wants to forecast sales for the year to come, but hasn't decided whether to use a quantitative or qualitative method. Explain which method you think it would be best for her to use, making sure you justify your decision. [12 marks]

More dodgy film ideas — how about 'The Hunch Backdata of Notre Dame'

Bet you got to the end of the last page and thought we'd forgotten to give you any words of wisdom to finish it off. But no, here it is, in all its glory, purely for your learning pleasure. Well, as much pleasure as you can possibly squeeze out of the fact that you now need to learn all the stuff on budgets and techniques that's been covered on the last three pages. Urgh.

The Marketing Mix: Price

*Changes in the price of a product affect the level of demand for that product. Businesses can calculate how much demand for their products will change if they change their price — helpful for picking a pricing strategy. This lot is for **AQA**, **WJEC** and **OCR: Marketing Option**, and it could come in handy for the **OCR: Strategic Management Unit** too.*

Price Elasticity of Demand shows how Demand changes with Price

1) **Price elastic** products have a **large percentage change in demand** for a **small percentage change in price**.

2) **Price <u>in</u>elastic** products are the opposite — there's a **small percentage change in demand** for a **big percentage change in price**.

$$\text{Price elasticity of demand} = \frac{\%\ \text{change in quantity demanded}}{\%\ \text{change in price}}$$

Example: A price **rise** of **10%** results in a **30% reduction** in demand.

$$\text{Price elasticity of demand} = \frac{-30\%}{+10\%} = -3$$

Price **elastic**, because the price elasticity of demand is **more than 1** (ignoring the minus sign).

Example: A price **reduction** of **20%** results in a **5% increase** in demand.

$$\text{Price elasticity of demand} = \frac{+5\%}{-20\%} = -0.25$$

Price **inelastic**, because the price elasticity of demand is **less than 1**.

This is called the elasticity coefficient

3) Price elasticity of demand is **always negative**, so ignore the minus sign. An **increase** in **price** causes a **fall** in **demand**, and a **fall** in **price** causes an **increase** in **demand**.

4) If the price elasticity of demand is **exactly 1**, the product is **unit elastic** — the change in the quantity demanded is **the same** as the change in price. If the price elasticity of demand is **greater than 1** (ignoring the minus sign), the product is **price elastic**. If the price elasticity of demand is **less than 1**, it's **price inelastic**.

Price Elasticity affects Revenue and Profit

1) **Sales revenue = price** of product × **quantity sold**. Price elasticity shows how price affects sales revenue.

2) If demand is **price elastic**, a **price increase** will make **sales revenue go down**. The **% decrease in sales** will be **more** than the **% increase in price**.

3) If demand is price **inelastic**, a rise in **price** will make **sales revenue go up**. The % decrease in sales isn't big enough to offset the % increase in price.

Price change	PED more than 1 (elastic)	PED equal to 1	PED less than 1 (inelastic)
Increase in price	Sales revenue decreases	Sales revenue doesn't change	Sales revenue increases
Decrease in price	Sales revenue increases	Sales revenue doesn't change	Sales revenue decreases

4) If demand is **price elastic**, a firm can **increase revenue** by reducing price, which then greatly increases the number of sales. **But profit = revenue – cost**, and more sales often mean **higher costs**. The **profits** will only increase if the **rise in revenue** is **more** than the **rise** in **costs**.

5) If demand is **price inelastic**, increasing the price will make **sales go down slightly**, but **sales revenue go up**. Because there are **fewer sales**, there are **lower costs**. This means that there's **more profit**.

This table shows how price changes affect sales revenue.

Example: A company makes scarves and sells them for £11. Annual sales are 9600 scarves. Recently, they trialled a new £1.10 price increase and found that the product's elasticity coefficient is –2.5. Calculate the change in annual revenue if they permanently increase the price to £12.10.

Current revenue: £11 × 9600 = £105 600

% change in quantity demanded: 10% change in price × 2.5 elasticity coefficient = 25% decrease

25% of 9600: 9600 × 0.25 = 2400

New sales: 9600 – 2400 = 7200

New revenue = 7200 × £12.10 = £87 120

Change in revenue: £105 600 – £87 120 = £18 480 decrease in revenue.

"Yes, but if you ignore the minus sign, we've actually increased sales by £10.5 million."

The Marketing Mix: Price

It can be *Hard* to *Work Out* price elasticity of demand

1) Estimating price elasticity of demand is **difficult** because price isn't the **only** factor affecting demand. An increase in demand for ice cream could be partly down to **hot weather** and a good **advertising** campaign.

2) Businesses use **primary market research** (see p.14) to ask people what the **maximum** price they'd pay for a product is. This gives an idea of the relationship between **price** and **demand**. **However**, surveys can be **unreliable** (people generally say they'd like things a bit cheaper than they would actually be willing to pay).

3) The values used in price elasticity calculations may be wrong. The calculations are often based on **estimates** of percentage change in price and demand, or on **unrepresentative** data — the market may have **changed** since the data was collected.

Price elasticity of demand *Depends* on *Ease* of *Switching Brands*

1) If a consumer can **easily switch** to a **competitor** product, the demand will be **price elastic** when there is a **rise in price**. Customers will buy the **competitor's product** instead.

2) Businesses try to **differentiate** their products to create **brand loyalty**. **Loyal** customers won't switch even if the price goes up, so this makes the demand **less** price elastic.

3) It's easier for customers to switch if they can **compare prices** and find cheaper alternatives. The **internet** makes it easier to switch and **increases price elasticity**.

4) People tend not to switch to alternatives in the **short term**. They **take time** to get **fed up** with a product.

5) **Product types** tend to be **price inelastic**, but individual **brands** tend to be **price elastic**. For example, **petrol** sales are **inelastic** because all cars need fuel. The sales of an **individual company's petrol** are **elastic** because motorists can easily go to a **cheaper filling station**.

Income Elasticity of *Demand* shows how *Demand* changes with *Income*

When people earn **more money**, there's **more demand** for some products.
Funnily enough, there's **less demand** for other products.

$$\text{Income elasticity of demand} = \frac{\%\text{ change in quantity demanded}}{\%\text{ change in real incomes}}$$

Example: A **rise** in real income of **10%** results in a **5% increase** in demand.

$$\text{Income elasticity of demand} = \frac{+5\%}{+10\%} = +0.5$$

> Change in <u>real income</u> means change in income, taking into account how prices have changed (usually increased) over the same period (this is <u>inflation</u> — see p.130).

1) **"Normal goods"** have a **positive income elasticity of demand** that's **less than 1**. This means that as **income rises**, the **demand** for normal goods **rises** — but at a **slower rate** than the increase in income.

2) **"Luxury goods"** have a **positive income elasticity of demand** which is **more than 1**. This means that the **demand for luxury goods** grows **faster** than the increase in income.

3) In a business sense, **"inferior"** goods are cheaper, 'value' products — taking a **coach** instead of the **train**, for example or eating a **cheaper supermarket value brand** of baked beans instead of a **premium brand** of beans. Inferior goods have a **negative income elasticity of demand** — demand falls when **income rises** and **demand rises** when **income falls**.

Elasticity helps a business make *Choices*

1) **Price elasticity** helps a manufacturer **decide** whether to **raise** or **lower** the price of a product. They can see what might happen to the sales, and ultimately what will happen to sales revenue.

2) It's useful for choosing a **pricing strategy** (see opposite for more on this). For example, if a product is **price inelastic**, it's not worth considering **penetration pricing** because the low initial **price** won't increase **demand**.

3) **Income elasticity** helps a manufacturer see what'll happen to sales if the **economy** grows or shrinks.

The Marketing Mix: Price

Competition-Based Pricing sets price based on Competitors' Prices

1) **Price makers** or **price leaders** set the price, and other businesses follow. Market leaders often use this strategy.

2) Competition reduces prices. In very competitive markets, **buyers dictate the price**, and sellers have to **take whatever price** the buyer is willing to pay — e.g. milk producers selling to supermarkets are **price takers**.

3) **Destroyer pricing** or **predatory pricing** is when a business **deliberately lowers prices** to force another business **out of the market** — e.g. in **price wars** some companies cut the price of their own brand goods to incredibly low levels. It's **illegal** if its intended to destroy smaller or weaker firms. Predatory pricing is a **gamble** — the predatory business usually makes a **loss** on the product. They either need to be making enough profit on other items to **cover** the **loss**, or their rival needs to go out of the market pretty darn quick so the price can go up again.

Cost-Based Pricing uses Production Costs to work out Price

1) **Full-cost-based** or **cost-plus pricing** takes direct and indirect costs of production into account, and adds a **fixed percentage** called the **mark-up**. *See p.42-43 for more on costing.*

2) **Marginal pricing** or **contribution pricing** sets the price to be more than the **variable costs** per unit. The price of each unit makes a **contribution** towards the **fixed costs**. If there are **enough sales**, the product will make a **profit** — even if it's only selling for a tiny bit more than the variable costs. This means that firms can lower prices temporarily, and can offer special low prices for special orders. *Fixed costs = machines, rent, etc.*

3) **Absorption pricing** allocates a **proportion** of the **fixed costs** to each unit, so the price is based on the **variable costs** per unit plus a slice of **fixed costs** per unit. It's called **absorption** pricing because the price of each unit **absorbs** part of the **fixed costs**. *Variable costs = production wages, raw materials etc.*

4) **Target-based pricing** sets the price based on the **target profit** that the firm decided they needed to make when they set their objectives. The price has to cover variable costs, fixed costs per unit and the target profit.

Market-Based Pricing uses Market Demand to work out Price

1) **Penetration pricing** is when a product has a low initial price to get into the market. As the volume of sales goes up, the price is increased. E.g. a magazine might start with a low initial price to get readers buying it.

2) **Price discrimination** is when different prices are charged for the same product — e.g. **plane tickets** vary in price depending on when you travel. Different groups of customers can be charged different prices.

3) **Price skimming** or **creaming** means starting with a high price and reducing it later. The price can go down when the product has achieved economies of scale. **High tech** goods, e.g. video cameras and digital music players, use this pricing strategy. *A product can keep a high price if it has strong brand values, a USP, or if it's meant to be seen as exclusive / luxury.*

4) **Psychological pricing** bases the price on customers' **expectation** about what to pay. For example, a high price may make people think the product is high quality. For people looking for low prices, £99.99 seems better than £100 even though it's only 1p difference.

Practice Questions

Q1 What is the formula for calculating price elasticity of demand?

Q2 If price elasticity of demand is more than 1, and there's an increase in price, what will happen to sales revenue?

Q3 Give three reasons why it can be hard to calculate price elasticity of demand.

Q4 Explain two cost-based and two market-based pricing strategies.

Exam Question

Q1 Camille Delacourt makes silver bracelets. She's considering raising the price of her product and wants to know if demand is price elastic or price inelastic. To find this out, she's increased prices from £18 to £20 for a 3-month trial period. In the 3 months before the trial started, she sold 642 bracelets. During the trial she sold 585. Calculate price elasticity of demand and say whether or not you think Camille should raise prices permanently. [6 marks]

I'm opening a really cheap bakery — it's called 'The Pricing on the Cake'

You might think this section has had way too much mathsy stuff — especially given that it's the first section of the book. Well, let me tell you...I totally agree. The good news is, the stuff on price and income elasticity really is the last of it, in this section at least. It's tricky tricky stuff though, so make sure you've really got to grips with it before you move on.

The Marketing Mix: Product

*You probably remember some of this from AS. **OCR: Marketing Option** need to read **both pages**, Edexcel just need **p.27**.*

Value Analysis makes sure that Products are Good Value for Money

1) Businesses try to make their products **good value for money** — both for **themselves** and for the **customer**.

2) **Value analysis** looks at ways of **reducing** the **costs** of **making**, **warehousing**, **distributing** and **selling** the product — these **costs** should be **reduced** as far as possible as long as they don't affect the product **quality** too much. There's no point using **expensive** screws to make a wardrobe if **cheap** ones would **do the job** just as well.

3) It's **risky** if **customers** might **notice** the **changes** and think that the **quality** of the product has **fallen**. So a firm making high quality pies might be able to use a cheaper variety of carrot, but if they **switch** from **free range** to **battery-reared chickens** it might **put** some **customers off**. It works best if the customer is unlikely to notice the change, e.g. people are unlikely to know whether beads on a beaded top were sewn on by a machine or by hand.

Products have a Life Cycle from Development to Decline

The product life cycle shows the **sales** of a product over **time**. It's useful for planning **marketing strategies**.

Development
1) The **research and development** (R&D) department **develops** the product.
2) The **marketing** department does **market research**.
3) The **costs** are **high**, and there aren't any sales yet to cover the costs.
4) New product development has a **high failure rate**. This is because there's often **not enough demand**, or because the business can't make the product **cheaply** enough to make a profit.

Introduction
1) The product is **launched**, either in one market or in several markets. It's sometimes launched with **complementary** products — e.g. the Playstation® was launched with games.
2) Businesses often **promote** the product heavily to build sales — but businesses need to make sure they've got enough **resources** and **capacity** to **meet the demand** that promotions create.
3) The **initial price** of the product may be **high** to cover **costs** of things like promotion or R&D. This is **price skimming** (see p.25).
4) Alternatively, the price can start off **low** to encourage sales. This is called **penetration pricing** (see p.25).
5) Sales go up, but the sales revenue has to pay for the high **fixed cost** of development **before** the product can make a **profit**. Businesses usually ditch products with disappointing sales at this stage.
6) There aren't many **outlets** for the new product yet, and competition is **limited**.

Growth
1) Sales grow fast. There are **new customers** and **repeat** customers.
2) **Economies of scale** mean the price of manufacturing a unit goes down the more you make, so **profits rise**.
3) The **pricing** strategy may change.
4) **Competitors** may be attracted to the market. Promotion points out **differences** from competitors.
5) The product is often **improved** or **developed**.
6) Rising sales encourage **more outlets** to stock the product.

Maturity
1) **Sales** reach a **peak** and profitability increases because the **fixed costs** of **development** have been **paid for**.
2) Sales start to go down. The price is often reduced to stimulate **demand**, which makes it less profitable.
3) At this stage, there aren't many new customers. Some products are forced out of the market.

Decline
1) The product doesn't **appeal** to consumers any more. **Sales fall** rapidly and profits decrease.
2) The product may just stay profitable if **promotional costs** are **low** enough.
3) If sales carry on falling, the product is **withdrawn** or **sold** to another business. This is called **divestment**.

 Sometimes companies can extend the life cycle by...
1) **Dropping** the **price** of the product.
2) **Increasing promotion** of the product (e.g. more advertising).
3) **Adding value** by altering the product (e.g. introducing a new flavour).
4) **Launching** the product in a **new market** (e.g. overseas).

The Marketing Mix: Product

Businesses need a *Variety* of *Products* — a *Mixed Product Portfolio*

The **product portfolio** is the **range** of different products and brands that a business holds. For example, Unilever has a massive portfolio including Marmite®, Knorr®, Domestos, Timotei, Carte d'Or® and Wall's Solero®.

> Businesses aim to have a **product portfolio** with a number of **different products**, all at **different stages** of the **product life cycle**.

The *Boston Matrix* is a model of *Portfolio Analysis*

The Boston Matrix compares a product's **market growth** with its **market share**.

> Each <u>circle</u> in the matrix represents <u>one</u> product. The <u>size</u> of each circle represents the <u>turnover</u> of the product.

1)   All **new products** are **question marks** (sometimes called **problem children** or **wildcats**) and they have a small market share and high market growth. They aren't profitable **yet** and need **heavy marketing** to give them a chance of success. A business can do various things with question marks — **brand building**, **harvesting** (maximising sales or profit in the short term) or **divestment** (selling the product off).

2)   **Stars** have high market growth and high market share — they have the best future potential. They're in their profitable **growth** phase — they're future cash cows.

3)   **Cash cows** have high market share but low market growth. They're in their **maturity** phase. They've already been promoted and they're produced in high volumes, so costs are low. Cash cows bring in plenty of **money**.

4)   **Dogs** have low market share and low market growth. They're pretty much a lost cause. The business will either harvest profit in the short term, or sell them off.

The Boston Matrix lets a business see if it has a good balanced **product portfolio**. A balanced product portfolio means that a business can use money from its **cash cows** to **invest** in its **question marks** so they can become **stars**.

The Boston Matrix **isn't infallible**. A product's **cash flow** and **profit** may be **different** from what the matrix suggests (e.g. a dog may have strong cash flow and be profitable despite falling sales).

When you use the Boston Matrix to evaluate a product portfolio in the **exam**, make sure you do it in the **context** of the **case study** in the **question**. This means looking at the **current market position** (brand image compared to other brands), the **market share** and **external factors** like the **economy**, or any **future events** mentioned in the question.

Product Differentiation means marketing products to make them *Stand Out*

1)   **Mass market** products like washing powder or pasta sauce tend to be **all the same**, more or less.

2)   They need **product differentiation** to make them stand out from the competition. **Clever marketing** and **branding** makes customers see the product as special, or particularly suited to them and their needs.

3)   Clever marketing and a firm's brand often emphasise a company's **distinctive capability** — something that the firm is particularly **good** at that can't be **reproduced** by other firms. They allow a company to get a **competitive advantage** over rival firms. High levels of quality and a reputation for innovation are also distinctive capabilities.

Practice Questions

Q1   What is value analysis?
Q2   What happens during the growth phase of the product life cycle?
Q3   What are the four types of product shown on the Boston matrix?

Exam Question

Q1   A manufacturer makes plasma screen TVs, VHS recorders, DVD players and Blu-ray™ players. Using the Boston matrix, evaluate their product portfolio.   [10 marks]

The Boston Matrix — well, that's a bit more catchy...

I'm still not sure Keanu will be keen though. The basic point of these pages is to show you that firms don't just come up with a few good product ideas and then sit back with a nice cup of tea. A company's range of products keeps changing all the time — as a new product starts to rear its head, it's a safe bet that another, older product will be packing its bags...

The Marketing Mix: Distribution

*More marketing mix. Which means, if you're doing **OCR: Marketing Option**, you'll need to learn it. Sorry.*

There are **Different Channels** of **Distribution**

Direct Selling: Manufacturer – Consumer

1) Accountants, electricians and hairdressers sell their **services** direct to the consumer.
   Direct selling is a **zero-level** channel of distribution — there are no **intermediaries**.

2) The **Internet** has made it **easier** for manufacturers to sell **direct** to the consumer.

3) Door-to-door sales, TV shopping channels, telephone sales and mail order catalogues are ways of selling direct.

4) It's more **profitable** to **sell direct** — there are no intermediaries to take a cut of the selling price.

5) Firms that sell direct (e.g. online) can offer **lower prices**, because they don't have to pay for premises or staff.

6) The fewer intermediaries in the distribution chain, the more **control** the manufacturer has over how
   the product is **promoted**, and what the **final selling price** will be.

Indirect Selling: Manufacturer – Wholesaler – Retailer – Consumer

1) This is the **traditional** distribution channel used for **fast moving consumer goods** (FMCG for short). It's a
   two-level distribution channel — there are two intermediaries between the manufacturer and the consumer.

2) It's less **hassle** to sell through **wholesalers**. Wholesalers take care of distributing the product to lots of retailers.

3) Wholesalers **break bulk** for businesses — they buy a large quantity of goods and pay for them up front, which
   increases the manufacturer's working capital.

Indirect Selling: Manufacturer – Retailer – Consumer

1) For example, **large supermarkets** buy goods direct from the manufacturer and do their **own distribution**.

Direct Selling through an agent: Manufacturer – Agent – Consumer

1) Some **mail order catalogues** (e.g. Betterware) use agents who place orders on behalf of other people and
   collect payments from them. The agent doesn't get a salary, but is paid **commission** on everything they sell.

2) Tupperware® and Jamie Oliver's Jme brand of kitchen and home products are sold by **agents** through **party
   plans** — people invite friends to their **home** and an **agent** sells the goods at the **party**.

1) In many **industries**, companies follow similar **patterns of distribution** — they use the **same channels** to distribute
   their products. E.g., office machinery companies nearly always sell direct to their customers, using salespeople.

2) **Technology** can cause **distribution patterns** to **change**. **Music** used to be sold **indirectly** through wholesalers and
   retailers but the invention of the **Internet** means that it can now be sold **direct** to the consumer in digital format.

Distribution Needs Affect a business's choice of Location

1) **Manufacturing** businesses which provide **bulky finished products** should be located near to their **customers**
   to cut down on distribution costs, e.g. bottled beer is bulky compared to the hops and barley used to make it.

2) Other companies make goods that use **bulky raw materials**. They pick locations near the source of **raw materials**
   to keep transport costs low, e.g. mineral water companies are located near the source of their water.

3) Locating in an area with a good **transport infrastructure**, e.g. near a motorway or a port, cuts distribution costs.

4) Many firms now **produce** parts or whole products **overseas**. The **growth** in **air travel** means goods can be
   transported round the world much faster, and locating abroad often allows firms to benefit from **lower labour costs**.

Physical Distribution is literally how you Move Stuff Around

1) **Physical distribution** means the **activities** involved in helping parts and goods
   move through the **distribution channel**, e.g. road, rail, ship and air transportation.

2) Most firms use **road transport** to transport goods within the UK or Europe. Transporting goods by **road** is a
   low cost option, but it causes **congestion** on motorways and has to fit round **restrictions** on drivers' working hours.

3) It's also **cheap** to transport goods by **train**. However, a lot of firms **prefer** to use **road** transport instead
   because **rail** transport is **inflexible**.

4) Goods can be transported **overseas** by **ship** or by **air**. **Shipping** is much **slower** than air transport but it's
   also much **cheaper**, so companies tend to use this method unless their product is **perishable**, e.g. food or flowers.

The Marketing Mix: Promotion

Above-the-Line Promotion is Advertising through the Media

1) Advertising uses various **media**, e.g. TV, radio or the internet. The choice of media depends partly on the **number** of **target customers** who'll **see** the ad. The aim is for the ads to be seen by as **many** of the target market as possible.

2) The **impact** of an ad is very important — especially in the "unawareness" part of the **DAGMAR** model and the "attention" part of the **AIDA** model (see p.18), which aim to **grab** your attention and make you **aware** of the brand.

3) Advertising **costs** a business **money**. The cost of an advertising campaign must be **worth it** in terms of the **extra sales** it creates. TV adverts at prime viewing times are very expensive, but they reach a lot of people.

4) **Specialist media** are aimed at people with particular interests or hobbies. They're used to selectively advertise specialist products to **niche markets**. E.g. a manufacturer of fish hooks might advertise in a monthly fly fishing magazine, instead of the Telegraph newspaper.

5) **Mass media** marketing means things like **ads** on **terrestrial TV channels** or in **national newspapers**, which can be seen by **millions** of people. It's mainly (but not always) used to advertise **mass market consumer** goods or services.

Below-the-Line promotion is Everything Else apart from advertising

1) **Sales promotions** are things like "buy one get one free" **special offers** (BOGOF), competitions, free gifts, point of sale displays, sponsorship, and trade-ins (e.g. paying for part of a new car by giving the seller your old car). Sales promotions can be aimed straight at the **customer** to **raise awareness** or **increase sales**. Manufacturers also do sales promotions aimed at the **retailer** to encourage them to **stock** more of their products.

2) **Direct mail** means **mailshots** sent to customers. Firms keep information about their customers on a database and **target** mail to particular consumer groups. Untargeted "**junk mail**" is **less effective** than direct mail.

3) **Public relations** (PR) is a firm's attempt to put out a **good message** about itself and its products or services. PR includes **press releases** sent to the media and special **promotional events**, e.g. new product launch parties.

4) **Personal selling** or **direct selling** is personal communication between a **sales person** and a customer. Personal selling includes **sales assistants** in shops as well as travelling sales people and phone sales people.

5) **Sponsorship** of **events** makes consumers aware of a firm and their products. It also gives the firm a good image.

Branding is a key aspect of Product Image

1) **Homogenous (generic)** products are the same no matter which business sells them. Brands are **unique**.

2) Firms create brands because people will pay a **premium price** and are **loyal** to them. A good brand has **benefits** for consumers that are **intangible** (hard to measure), e.g. wearing a designer dress might boost someone's confidence.

3) Brands can be **individual** products — like Sprite® or KitKat®. "Family brands," e.g. Heinz, include a **range** of items.

Real businesses Combine all Four Aspects of the Marketing Mix

1) Businesses can't just consider **one aspect** of the **marketing mix** while **ignoring** the **rest**. They have to find ways of **blending** the **four different elements** — price, product, distribution and promotion.

2) For example, **McDonald's** have followed the trend for ethical behaviour (see p.136) by making sure all the **eggs** used in their products are **free range**. They promote this through **media** which **appeal specifically** to their **target customer** (e.g. ads in BBC Good Food magazine) and sell some products at **promotional prices** on certain days of the week. A combination of **town centre** and **drive-thru restaurants** makes the product **widely available**.

Practice Questions

Q1 What is direct selling?

Q2 What is indirect selling?

Q3 Give two ways that distribution needs affect location.

Q4 Give two examples of below-the-line promotion.

Exam Question

Q1 Granny Brown is setting up a business selling knitted goods over the internet. Giving reasons for your answer, explain whether you think she should sell direct to her customers or sell via a wholesaler. [10 marks]

Someone who survives a shipwreck in one piece — a whole sailor

Finally, something to be grateful for — seven pages on the marketing mix, which you should already be familiar with. This year you need to know how to blend the different aspects together to create a successful mix, so when you're learning this stuff it's essential to keep in mind the fact that altering one aspect of the mix could have a drastic impact on the others.

Financial Objectives

*Here's where the real fun starts. Page 30 is just for **AQA**, and page 31 is for **AQA** and the **OCR: Accounting option**.*

Financial Objectives are what the business wants to Achieve

1) **Financial objectives** are **financial goals** that a business wants to achieve. Businesses usually have **specific targets** in mind, and a **specific period of time** to achieve them in. E.g. a business might have an objective to increase its profits by 10% within three years.

2) Businesses might have objectives about **return on capital employed** (**ROCE**). Remember:

$$ROCE = \frac{\text{gross profit}}{\text{capital employed}} \times 100\%$$

Return on capital employed measures how **efficiently** the business is running — it tells you how much money the business has made compared to how much money's been put into the business. A ROCE of about 20-30% is good, so if the business' ROCE is lower than that, it might aim to **increase** it. See p. 61 for more on ROCE.

3) Businesses might aim to **improve** their **cash flow**. Even **profitable** businesses can fail if they don't have enough cash to pay their debts when they're due. Businesses can improve their cash flow by getting their debtors to pay them **promptly** and using **debt factoring** (see p. 32) if payments to the business are taking a long time. Holding **less stock** and not taking more orders than the business can fulfil also improves cash flow.

4) Another financial objective might be to **minimise costs** — if the business still sells the same number of products at the same price, this will **increase** its overall **profits**. This can be done by using less expensive materials, cheaper suppliers and staff with lower wages. Businesses have to be careful that cutting costs doesn't reduce the **quality** of their products or services — otherwise sales might drop, and they'd end up with **lower profits** instead of higher profits.

5) Limited companies and PLCs might aim to **increase returns** for their **shareholders**. Businesses usually pay out around a third of their net profit to shareholders as **dividends**. To increase dividends, they can either pay out a **bigger percentage** of the net profit as dividends (but this means there's less money left to reinvest in the business) or **increase profits**.

Internal and External factors influence Financial Objectives

Businesses have to make sure that their financial objectives are **realistic** and **achievable**. There are several factors that influence a company's **ability** to **achieve** its objectives, and managers need to take these factors into account when they set financial objectives.

Internal factors influencing financial objectives

1) **The overall objectives of the business**. E.g. a company with a strong **environmental** standpoint might be more interested in minimising its carbon footprint than in maximising its profits.

2) **The status of the business**. **New** businesses might set **ambitious** targets for revenue because they're trying to grow quickly and establish themselves in the marketplace. **Established** companies might be satisfied with **smaller** increases in revenue if they're not actively trying to grow.

3) **Employees**. E.g. if a business has a **high turnover of sales staff**, an objective to dramatically increase revenue might be **unrealistic** because well-trained, experienced staff are needed to encourage customers to spend more.

External factors influencing financial objectives

1) **The availability of finance**. **Cash flow** targets might depend on how easy or difficult it is for the business to get **credit**.

2) **Competitors**. If **new competitors** enter the market, or **demand** for existing competitors' products **increases** (due to a marketing promotion or price reduction, etc), a business might set an objective to **cut costs** in order to be more competitive.

3) **The economy**. In a period of economic **boom**, businesses can set **ambitious** ROCE and profit targets. In a **downturn**, they have to set more **restrained** targets, and they might also set targets to **minimise costs**.

4) **Shareholders**. Shareholders usually want the best possible **return** on their investment — this might put pressure on businesses to set objectives to increase **profits** or **dividends**.

Sources of Finance

Businesses need Finance for Capital Expenditure and Working Capital

1) **Fixed capital** (or **capital expenditure**) means money used to buy **fixed assets**. These are things used over and over again to produce goods or services for sale — e.g. **factories** and **equipment**. Businesses need capital expenditure to **start up**, to **expand** and to **replace** worn out equipment. They must **set aside** enough **money** to stop **fixed assets** from **wearing out**, and then they can **decide** how much **money** to invest in **growth**. This is called **allocating capital expenditure**.

2) **Working capital** (or **revenue expenditure**) is the cash needed to pay for the **daily running** of a business. It's used to pay wages, suppliers, electricity/gas bills, business rates etc. The amount of working capital is predicted using the **cash flow forecast**.

3) **Fixed capital** allows a business to **grow**. **Working capital** allows a business to **survive**. All businesses need **both** types of finance.

4) You'll find **fixed capital** on the balance sheet, in the form of **fixed assets**, and the **capital** used to buy them.

5) You'll find **working capital** (**revenue expenditure**) on the profit and loss account, in the form of **expenses**.

Finance can be Internal or External

1) **Internal** finance is capital raised **within** the firm by cutting costs or putting **profits** back into the business.

2) **External** finance is capital raised **outside** the firm. Businesses can raise external capital by **selling shares**, getting an **overdraft** or getting a **loan** from a bank or a venture capitalist (see p. 32 for more).

There are Three Main Ways to raise Internal Capital

Retained profit

1) **Profit** can be retained and built up over the years for **later investment**.

2) The main **benefit** of using profit for investment is that the business doesn't have to pay **interest** on the money. **Not all businesses** can use this method though — they need to be making a good enough **profit**.

Rationalisation

1) **Rationalisation** is when managers **reorganise** the business to make it more efficient. They can do this by **selling** some of their **assets** (e.g. factories, machinery, etc) to generate capital.

2) Businesses don't need to pay **interest** on finance they raise by selling their assets.

3) The main **drawback** to selling assets is that the business **no longer owns** the asset. Also, assets like cars and computers **lose value** over time, so the business won't get back as much as it paid for them.

Squeezing working capital

1) A business can find some internal capital by **squeezing working capital**. They do this by reducing the amount of **stock** they hold, **delaying** payments to **suppliers** and **speeding up** payments from **customers**.

2) The main advantage of raising finance in this way is that it can be done **quickly**. However, the amount of capital a business can get from tightening its belt like this is **limited**.

Practice Questions

Q1 Give four examples of financial objectives.
Q2 How might a business' competitors influence its financial objectives?
Q3 What's the difference between fixed capital and working capital?

Exam Question

Q1 Discuss the advantages and disadvantages of three different methods of raising internal finance. [6 marks]

Internal finance — selling one of your kidneys...

So Liza Minnelli was right after all — money really does make the world go around. Nearly all businesses set out to make a profit, and if they can't get enough money to pay for day-to-day survival, they won't last very long at all. Make sure you're clear on the difference between fixed capital and working capital, and the ways of raising internal capital.

Sources of Finance

*Sources of finance have to be suitable for the type of business, and what the business wants to spend the finance on. Page 32 is for **AQA** and the **OCR Accounting option**, and page 33 is just for the **OCR: Accounting option**.*

External Finance can increase Working Capital in the Short Term

Businesses can use the following methods to increase **working capital** (to pay for bills, wages, etc) for a short time:

Trade credit

1) **Trade credit** is where a business negotiates a **delay** between **receiving** raw materials or stock and **paying** for them. **30 days** is a typical credit period. Larger businesses may negotiate longer periods.
2) The main advantage of trade credit is that the business gets to **keep** its money for **longer**.
3) Suppliers won't give trade credit to all businesses though — new businesses and businesses that have had trouble paying suppliers in the past probably **won't** be able to get trade credit.

Overdrafts

1) **Overdrafts** are where a bank lets a business have a negative amount of money in its bank account.
2) Overdrafts are **easy to arrange** and **flexible** — businesses can borrow as **little** or as **much** as they need (up to the overdraft limit) and they only have to pay **interest** on the amount of the overdraft they actually use.
3) The main disadvantage of overdrafts is that banks charge **high rates** of **interest** on them.

Debt factoring

1) **Debt factoring** is a service that banks and other financial institutions offer to improve cash flow. They take **unpaid invoices** off the hands of the business, and give them an instant **cash** payment (of less than 100% of the value of the invoice).
2) The **advantage** of this for businesses is that they can **instantly** get money they are owed. Also, they don't have to spend time **chasing** up customers who owe them the money, because the debt factoring company collects payment from the individual or company who should have paid the invoice.
3) The **disadvantage** of debt factoring is that the debt factoring company **keeps** some of the money as a **fee**, so the business doesn't get **all** the money it's owed.

External Finance is used for Medium-Term Needs

In order to increase their **fixed capital** for 1-5 years, businesses can take out a **bank loan**, or **lease** fixed assets:

1) **Loans** have lower interest charges than overdrafts, and are repaid in monthly instalments. The main drawback is that banks need **security** for a loan, usually in the form of **property**. If the business doesn't repay the loan, the bank can **sell** the property to get their money back.
2) **Leasing** is when a business **rents** fixed assets like cars and office equipment instead of **buying** them. Leasing means paying a smallish amount each month instead of shelling out a lot of money all in one go. Businesses can easily **upgrade** equipment or vehicles that they're leasing. In the **long run**, leasing works out **more expensive** than buying, though.

External Finance can be used for Long-Term Projects

To increase **fixed capital** over a **long** period of time (up to 25 years), businesses have the following options:

1) **Debentures** are special kinds of long-term **loan** with **low fixed interest** rates and **fixed repayment dates**. As with bank loans, the main drawback is that they're **secured** — usually against property.
2) **Grants** are money from local government and some business charities. The good thing about grants is that businesses don't have to pay them back — it's **free money**. However, businesses usually only qualify for a grant if they're creating **new jobs**, setting up in **deprived** areas or being started by **young people**.
3) A limited company can sell **shares** in the business. The advantage of this for the business is that they **don't** have to pay the money back. The disadvantage is that the shareholders **own** part of the business, so the business has to give them a share of the **profits** (called a dividend) and allow them to vote on some issues.
4) **Venture capitalists** provide capital by giving loans and by buying shares. The advantage of getting finance from a venture capitalist is that they provide **business advice** as well as cash. The disadvantage is that applying for funding from a venture capitalist is a **long** and **complicated** process. Also, selling shares to venture capitalists means that they **own** part of the business.

Sources of Finance

The source of **Finance** depends on the **Business Situation**

Businesses use **different sources** of finance depending on what they want the finance for:

New businesses

1) Start-up businesses **can't** use **internal capital** because they don't have any previous profits.
2) Entrepreneurs can finance their business with their own **savings**, but most don't have enough money.
3) Entrepreneurs who own **property** might be able to get finance through a **bank loan** or **debenture** using their house as security. Lenders will only give the owner loans if they think the business is likely to succeed, though.
4) New businesses might be able to get finance from **venture capitalists** if they have a detailed **business plan**.

Growing businesses

1) When businesses are **growing** (e.g. if they want to take on more staff or move to bigger premises), they are likely to use **retained profit** — they're probably making good profits if they want to expand.
2) **Successful businesses** that want to expand are **more likely** to be able to get finance through loans and debentures — they can show that the business has been profitable in the past, so there's less risk for the lender.
3) Limited companies and PLCs might **sell shares** to raise money for expansion.

Expanding into new areas

1) Businesses are likely to use **retained profit** to pay for expansion into **new areas** — they've probably already been making profits in their current area, and want to branch out into other areas to **increase** their profits.
2) If the business has a good **track record** of making profits, it's **less risky** for lenders than a completely new business, so they'll be more willing to lend the business money.

The **Legal Structure** of the business also affects the source of **Finance**

1) Opportunities for small businesses to raise finance are more **limited** than for large or multinational companies.
2) Sole traders and partnerships can find it hard to attract **investors** because they can't issue **shares**, so their sources of finance are mainly limited to **bank loans** or putting their **own money** into the business.
3) **Medium sized companies** could convert from a private limited company to a **public limited company**. They could then raise finance through the **stock exchange**, so they would attract more shareholders and increased investment.
4) **Large** and **multinational businesses** are usually PLCs, already listed on the Stock Exchange, often in more than one country. They would be more likely to use a mixture of **bank loans**, **rights issues** of shares (shares offered to existing shareholders at a discount), **sales of subsidiaries** and **retained profits** to fund growth.

Remember that sole traders and partnerships have unlimited liability, so the owners are responsible for all of the business' debts. Shareholders in private limited companies or PLCs have limited liability — they can only lose the money they invested in the business.

Practice Questions

Q1 State one advantage and one disadvantage of debt factoring.
Q2 What do businesses usually need to do to qualify for grants?
Q3 Which sources of finance might be appropriate for new businesses?
Q4 Why might sole traders and partnerships have trouble attracting investors?

Exam Question

Q1 Recommend three suitable sources of finance for a new business, and explain why other sources of finance would not be suitable. [6 marks]

Debt Factor would be a great name for a new reality TV show...

All this talk of sources is making me fancy a fish finger sandwich with ketchup. Or chips with gravy. Maybe now would be a good time to take a break from revision and go and make yourself a nice snack. But before you go, make sure you know everything on these pages. And you've got accounting perspective and concepts to look forward to when you get back.

Accounting Perspective & Concepts

*I don't know about you, but I reckon 'Accounting Perspective & Concepts' sounds more like something from Philosophy than Business Studies. But don't worry, it's just another page all about accountancy — phew. These pages are just for the **OCR: Accounting option**.*

All businesses need **Accounting Data** for **Decision Making**

1) In order for managers to make **informed decisions** they must have access to **accurate** and **recent** financial information. They need to know **how much** their **assets** are worth, how much they **owe**, and **when** money comes into the business or leaves the business.

> A set of final accounts contains the balance sheet, profit and loss account and cash flow statement.

2) By **law**, limited companies must produce a set of **final accounts** each year. This is made up of annual **profit and loss accounts** that detail the company's performance over a year, and a **balance sheet** that shows assets and liabilities.

3) In addition, companies produce a **cash flow statement** showing the **flow of money** in and out of the business. The data is used both for **planning** for the future and **controlling** the operations of the business.

4) The law requires businesses to give information about their finances, and present their final accounts in a particular way, to make sure they're not hiding anything. This is called the **disclosure requirement**.

Accounting Data affects All the Departments of a business

1) Information provided by the finance department is used by senior managers in order to make **decisions** about the business. The finance department affects all the other **departments**, because information provided by the finance department is used to set each department's **budget**.

2) The finance department also **monitors** the finances of each department, and **reports back** to the senior managers on how departments are **performing** — e.g. if the production department spends 75% of its budget in the first three months of the year, the finance department will make senior managers aware of the situation so that they can take steps to sort it out.

3) The finance department might have to **authorise payments** for **large amounts** of money.

4) The finance department's activities affect all the **major departments** in a business:

> 1) The **HR department** relies on the finance department to make sure that the business can afford to pay its **staff**, and that there's enough money to pay for **staff training** and **recruiting** new staff.
>
> 2) The **production department** needs the finance department to make sure that they can afford to purchase **stock** in the short-term, and that **long-term** funds are available to invest in **capital assets** like machinery.
>
> 3) The **marketing department's** activities, like advertising campaigns and free samples, are determined by the marketing **budget**. The marketing department will want to spend as much money as possible, so the finance department and marketing department need to work closely together to work out **how much** different promotional activities are likely to cost, and whether they can **afford** them or not.
>
> 4) The **sales department** relies on the finance department to keep **accurate records** of **sales** and **customer payments** so that the business can maintain a good **cash flow**.

Information Technology is used in Accounting

1) **Accounting software** allows managers to instantly call up the **financial data** they need. They can instantly see data about assets, liabilities, overheads etc.

2) Managers can run **final reports** instantly. They can check the profit and loss statement or the balance sheet **every month** at the touch of a button.

3) Computer software can work out **financial ratios** (see p.58-61) so that managers can **quickly** analyse the financial health of the business.

4) Financial and accounting software also makes it easy to manage **day-to-day** financial activity — e.g. sending out invoices and paying suppliers.

Joe had given up asking for a proper computer system.

5) It's important to make financial decisions using accurate, up-to-date information. Larger firms use **management information systems** (see p.159) that provide recent, valid data from all the departments in the firm.

Accounting Perspective & Concepts

Accounts are produced according to Seven Accounting Principles

① Going concern — assume the company will keep trading.

1) This principle assumes that a company will **continue to exist** for the **foreseeable future**.

2) If the accountant believes the company **won't** be able to continue trading, they **have** to say this in the accounts. If the business can't pay its **overheads** and its **debts**, it may be put under a different set of accounting rules and go into **administration**, or even be **liquidated**.

② Consistency — all the company's accounts must be done in the same way.

1) The company has to adopt specific **accounting policies** and use the **same** accounting policies for all its accounts. If its accounting policies **change**, the business has to make this clear.

2) This allows a user to **confidently compare** accounts from different years.

③ Realisation — recognise revenue when goods or services are sold.

1) **Revenue** is **recognised** in the accounts when a product is **sold** or a service is **performed**.

2) The transaction is realised when it **happens**, **not** when it's **paid for**, which may be weeks or months later.

④ Matching (or Accruals) — always match revenue with costs regardless of when cash changes hands.

1) Accountants should **match** the **revenue** with the **costs** involved in generating it in the **same period** — revenue and costs will be matched to show the **profit** in a set of accounts.

2) It **doesn't matter** when the **costs** were **paid for** — the **costs** involved in selling a product or service are included in the accounts when the product or service is **sold**, **not** when the costs were **incurred**.

⑤ Objectivity — accounts should be based on facts where possible, and shouldn't be biased.

1) This rule is to avoid **falsehood** and **bias** in producing final accounts. Accounts shouldn't **mislead** a user.

2) Accounts should be based on **fact** rather than opinion as much as possible. E.g. accountants should value stock at the **actual cost**, not what they **think** it might be worth if it's sold.

3) When accountants **don't** have facts, they have to use **judgement**, e.g. when estimating a future loss.

⑥ Materiality — accounts must be materially correct.

1) It's not always **practical** for accountants to check every single transaction, especially in large companies.

2) Accountants have to make sure that all **material transactions** (transactions that are likely to **influence** the user) are recorded **correctly**. The accounts should be a **true** and **fair** view of the company's performance.

⑦ Prudence (or Conservatism) — if in doubt, be cautious.

1) Accountants should always be **cautious** when valuing assets or measuring profits.

2) **Managers** can sometimes be **over-optimistic**, and prudence is designed to **balance out** this tendency. E.g. if there's doubt about whether a customer is able to pay, the accountant should make this clear.

3) If accountants are cautious, they won't **overstate** the company's financial position.

Practice Questions

Q1 Why do companies keep accounts?

Q2 How is IT used in accounting?

Q3 What is meant by "matching" in accounting terminology?

Exam Question

Q1 Explain why accounts are produced according to the principles of matching, materiality and realisation. [9 marks]

Ah yes, but there's no accounting for taste...

Accounting has a bit of a reputation for being boring, (which may well be justified, but you've still got to learn about it). There's some good stuff coming up in this section though, like budgeting, which just happens to be next. Before you move onto that, learn why accounting is important to businesses, and make sure you know all the accounting principles.

Budgeting & Variances

Budgeting's no fun at all, but most of us have to do it — and that includes businesses.
*These pages are for the **OCR: Accounting option** and **Strategic Management unit** and **WJEC**.*

A *Budget* is a *Financial Plan* that *Sets Targets*

1) **Budgets** forecast **earnings** and **spending** for the coming year. They help managers **control** their **spending**.

2) Each budget contains financial **targets** — **objectives** which help **motivate** staff and **monitor performance**.

3) The **master budget** is the **total** budget for the whole business. Each **department** also has its own budget, and the manager of that department (the **budget holder**) is responsible for making sure that the department meets its earnings targets and doesn't spend more than its expenditure budget.

The *Budget Setting* process involves *Research* and *Negotiation*

1) To set the **sales budget**, businesses **research** and **predict** how sales are going to go up and down through the year, so that they can make a good prediction of **sales revenue**.

2) To set the **expenditure budget for the production department**, businesses **research** how labour costs, raw materials costs, taxes and inflation might go up or down over the year. They can then **estimate** the **costs** of producing the volume of product that they think they're going to sell.

3) In **historical budgeting**, each year's budget is based on the **previous year's** budget. E.g. if a business expects revenue to increase by 10% compared to last year, it may increase each department's expenditure budget by 10%.

4) In **zero budgeting**, the budget is decided from scratch every year. Each **budget holder** has to say what they think the budget for their department should be, and senior managers decide how to allocate the money.

5) One department might be given a bigger **spending budget** than another, depending on what the business' **priorities** are at the time. E.g. if the business wants to focus on marketing, the marketing department might get a big expenditure budget to spend on an advertising campaign.

Budgets should be *Realistic* and *Achievable*

1) Budget targets should **stretch** the abilities of the business in order to **motivate** staff to do their best. If sales budgets are **too low**, staff don't have anything to aim for so they won't be **motivated**. If expenditure budgets are **too high**, staff won't be looking for ways to save the business money.

2) Budgets must be **achievable**. **Unrealistically** high sales budgets or low expenditure budgets will **demotivate** staff. No one likes being asked to do the **impossible**.

3) Good budgets **establish priorities**. Budget holders and staff need to know which **spending** and **sales targets** are most important. E.g. some items on the expenditure budget may be so vital that it's OK if they go over budget.

4) Budgets can be used in employee **appraisal** (see p.95). If their department has met its targets for the previous year, staff might get a bonus or some other reward.

Budgies are cute, but they're not much good at employee appraisal.

5) If the department overspends or doesn't bring in as much revenue as it is budgeted to, it **might not** be the budget holder's fault, because the budget figures are based on **estimates**. E.g. wage costs might increase more than the business predicted. **External factors** affect spending and revenue (see p. 37), so **employees** aren't always responsible for meeting or failing to meet targets.

Variance is the *Difference* between *Actual* figures and *Budget* figures

1) A **favourable variance** leads to **profits increasing**. If revenue's **more** than the budget says it's going to be, that's a favourable variance. If costs are **below** the cost predictions in the budget, that's also a favourable variance.

2) An **adverse variance** is a difference that **reduces profits**. Selling fewer items than the sales budget predicts is an adverse variance. Spending more on an advert than the marketing budget allows is an adverse variance.

3) Variances **add up**. For example, if actual sales exceed budgeted sales by £3000 and expenditure on raw materials is £2000 below budget, there's a combined **favourable variance** of £5000.

4) **Small** variances aren't a big problem, and can actually **motivate** employees. Staff try to sort out small **adverse** variances themselves (e.g. if they overspend slightly one month, they might aim to underspend by the same amount the next month). Small **favourable** variances can **motivate** staff to increase the favourable variance.

5) **Large** variances can **demotivate**. Staff don't work hard if there are large favourable variances — they **don't see the need**. If there's a large **adverse** variance, they may feel that the task is **impossible**.

Budgeting & Variances

Variances are caused by several factors — Internal and External

External factors cause variance

1) **Competitor behaviour** and changing **fashions** may increase or reduce **demand** for products.
2) Changes in the **economy** may change a company's wage bill — wages go **up** in a boom and **down** in a recession.
3) The cost of **raw materials** may go up or down.

Internal factors cause variance

1) Improving **efficiency** causes **favourable** variances. However, a business might **overestimate** the amount of money it can save by streamlining production methods. This would cause an adverse variance.
2) A business might **underestimate** the **cost** of making a change to its organisation, for example it might not take account of the cost of **training** employees to use a new computer system.
3) Changing the selling price changes **sales revenue**. A business which cuts the price of its products after it's **already** set the budget creates a **variance** for itself.
4) Internal causes of variance are a **serious concern**. They suggest that there are problems **within the business** that need sorting out (e.g. internal communication might need to be improved).

Variance Analysis means Catching variances and Fixing them

1) Businesses can either change what the **business** is doing to make it fit the budget, or change the **budget** to make it fit what the **business** is doing. This depends on whether they have a fixed or flexible budget.
   - **Fixed budgeting** means budget holders have to **stick** to their budget plans throughout the year.
   - **Flexible budgeting** allows budgets to be **altered** in response to changes in the market or economy.
2) Businesses usually have **tolerance limits** for variances — e.g. if they have a tolerance limit of 5%, they won't worry about a variance of up to 5%, but if the variance is bigger than that then they'll investigate why.
3) Businesses need to **beware** of chopping and changing the budget **too much**. Changing the budget **removes certainty** about the future financial position of the business — which removes one of the big benefits of budgets. Altering budgets can also make them **less motivational** — when staff start to expect that management will change targets instead of doing something to change performance, they don't see the point in trying any more.
4) Businesses can fix **adverse variances** by cutting production **costs**, motivating employees to **work harder** or asking suppliers for a better deal. They might change the **marketing mix** to try to increase demand for their products.
5) If a business has a **favourable variance**, they try to find out why. If it's caused by **increased productivity** in one part of the business, they'll try to **spread** the same way of working to the rest of the business. If the variance is caused by a **pessimistic budget**, they make sure that they set more **ambitious targets** next time.

Practice Questions

Q1 What's the difference between historical and zero budgeting?
Q2 How do budgets affect staff motivation?
Q3 What are variances?
Q4 Give three examples of internal factors that cause variance.

Exam Question

Q1 A business budgets £120k expenditure on wages, rent and other costs, and £270k revenue from sales. The actual costs are as follows: £80k on wages, £30k on rent and £22k on other costs. The actual sales revenue is £275k.
(a) What is the total variance? Answer on p.184. [4 marks]
(b) What does your answer suggest about the budgeting process within the business? [3 marks]

You should see the variances in my shoe budget...

All businesses need budgets to give them a good idea of how much money they'll be making, and how much money they'll be spending. When the real-life results don't quite match up to the budget, there must be something wrong with either the budget-setting process, or the actions of the business. Either way, it needs sorting out, not ignoring. Much like your revision.

Costs

The best things in life might be free, but you've got to pay for all the others. The same goes for businesses too.
*These pages are for **AQA** and the **OCR: Accounting** and **Business Production options**.*

Costs relate to **Missed Opportunities**

1) **Opportunity cost** puts a value on a business decision, based on what the business had to give up as a result.

2) Businesses must **choose** where to spend their limited finance. Managers **compare opportunity costs** when they're making their decisions. The opportunity cost of an advert halfway through an episode of X Factor might be five screenings of the same advert in the middle of another programme.

3) Each **department** is given its own **expenditure budget** (see p. 36) and has to decide what to spend its allocated money on, and what to do without. E.g. if the production department spends its expenditure budget on a new piece of machinery, it might not be able to afford to employ a new member of staff, so the **opportunity cost** to the production department of the piece of machinery is a new member of staff.

Social Costs are the **Internal** and **External Costs** of business decisions

1) Most of the **costs** involved in business transactions are paid by the **business** itself (e.g. rent, the cost of raw materials). These are known as **internal costs**. E.g. if a business decides to open a new out-of-town shopping centre, the internal costs are the cost of buying the land, building the shopping centre, paying staff, etc.

2) There can also be an **external cost** to some business decisions. External costs **aren't** just **financial** costs — they include all the **negative effects** of business decisions on people **outside** the business. E.g. the new out-of-town shopping centre might lead to increased **traffic** and **pollution** in the area, and a **longer journey time** for shoppers and employees. It could also mean that **shops** in the town centre might get less business and have to **close**, which would mean that their staff would lose their **jobs**.

Kelly's new dress had a huge social cost — her friends were too embarrassed to be seen with her.

3) **Social costs** are the **total internal** and **external costs** of a decision. Social costs take into account **all** the **financial** and **other costs** of a business decision, whoever they affect.

Businesses try to **Minimise** their **Costs**

1) A business' **profit margin** is the proportion of **revenue** from each sale that is **profit**. E.g. if a bottle of shampoo costs £1.20 to produce and sells for £3.50, the business makes a profit of £2.30 (66%) on each bottle sold.

2) Businesses can **increase** their **profit margins** by either **increasing** their **prices** or **reducing** their **costs**. Most businesses try to keep their costs as **low** as possible in order to benefit from large profit margins without putting their prices up (since this is likely to **reduce demand** for their products).

3) **Minimising costs** is particularly important for businesses operating in very **competitive markets**. They're forced to keep their prices **low** in order to compete, so the only way for them to increase their profits is by cutting costs.

4) Businesses can cut the average cost of making a product by producing in **large quantities** so that they can benefit from **economies of scale** (see p. 103). Other ways of cutting costs include switching to **cheaper suppliers** (or negotiating cheaper deals with existing suppliers), increasing **capacity utilisation** (see p. 110), cutting **staffing levels** or taking on less experienced staff who don't need to be paid as much.

Costs influence **Business Decisions**

1) Before they make a decision, businesses usually consider the **costs** involved. Businesses tend to focus on the **internal costs** (the costs the business has to pay) because they have a direct impact on the business' **profits**.

2) Cutting costs **doesn't** always mean that a business' **profits** will **increase**. If cutting costs **reduces** the **quality** of the company's products or services, it could end up causing a **fall** in **profits**. E.g. a food company might change to a cheaper type of packaging to cut costs, but if the new packaging is prone to leaking, the company's reputation could suffer and sales will probably fall.

3) When making **decisions** about which raw materials to use, which supplier to use, which staff to employ, etc, businesses **don't** just look at the cost. They also consider other **issues** depending on the company's **aims**, **culture**, etc. E.g. a health food company that prides itself on having **knowledgeable staff** to advise customers **won't** want to reduce costs by cutting back on **staff training**, because this would go against its basic aims and principles.

Costs

Costs can be Fixed or Variable, Direct or Indirect

Businesses can classify their costs as **fixed** or **variable**, and as **direct** or **indirect**.

Fixed costs

1) **Fixed costs** are costs that **don't change** with **output** — they **stay the same** regardless of how much the business produces. Even if the business doesn't produce anything at all, it still has to pay its fixed costs.

2) Fixed costs are things like **rent** on business premises, senior managers' **salaries** and the cost of new **machinery**.

Variable costs

1) **Variable costs change** depending on **output**. If output **increases**, variable costs **increase**. If output **falls**, variable costs **fall**. E.g. if you need 10 000 beads to make 100 necklaces, you'll need 20 000 beads to make 200 necklaces, so the cost of the beads will double if output doubles.

2) **Hourly wages** of staff, the cost of **raw materials** and the cost of **packaging** are all variable costs.

Direct costs

1) **Direct costs** are costs that are **directly linked** to producing products or providing services.

2) The cost of **raw materials** and the **hourly wages** of the staff who make the products / provide the service are direct costs.

3) **Direct** costs are almost always **variable**.

Indirect costs

1) **Indirect costs** (also called **overheads**) are costs that are **not directly related** to the production of goods or provision of services.

2) Business **rates** and **rent**, and the **wages** and **salaries** of staff who work for the company but **aren't** directly involved in making the product are all indirect costs.

3) **Indirect** costs are almost always **fixed**.

Louise had more than her fair share of overheads.

Practice Questions

Q1   What is an opportunity cost?

Q2   How are social costs calculated?

Q3   List three ways that businesses can minimise their costs.

Q4   Give two examples of fixed costs, and two examples of variable costs.

Q5   What's the difference between direct and indirect costs?

Exam Questions

Q1   Why do businesses need to be aware of the opportunity costs of their decisions?   [4 marks]

Q2   Outline the costs that a coffee shop is likely to incur,
        and classify them as fixed or variable and direct or indirect.   [8 marks]

Not revising this lot could cost you...

Who would have guessed there were so many different types of costs? Fixed, variable, direct, indirect, internal, external, opportunity... These pages are pretty interesting though (even if I say so myself) and not too complicated, so it shouldn't be too much of a hardship to learn everything. Don't forget the bit on p. 38 about why cutting costs isn't always a good idea.

Cost and Profit Centres

*Businesses can look at sales budgets and production budgets for the whole of the business — or they can look at one part of the business in isolation and work out how much money it's spending, and how much it's making. These pages are for **AQA**, the **OCR: Accounting option** and **WJEC**.*

Managers set Budgets for Parts of the Business — Cost and Profit Centres

1) Cost and profit centres are just a **way to work out budgets** for a particular **part** of a business. With a **cost centre**, you can set a **cost budget**, and with a profit centre, you can work out **costs** and **revenues** and set a budget for how much profit you want that part of the business to **make** over a year.

2) **Cost centres** are parts of a business that directly **incur costs**. The business can identify costs, measure them, and **monitor** them against a **mini-budget** that applies just to that part of the business.

3) **Profit centres** are parts of a business that directly **generate revenue** as well as costing money. The business can work out the **profit** or **loss** they're making by subtracting the **costs** from the **revenues**.

4) The IT department of a business is an example of a **cost centre**. Managers can work out the **costs** of IT technicians' wages and new computer upgrades. They **can't** work out the **revenue** that the IT department earns, because they **don't charge** other departments for providing IT support.

How is Hairdressing doing as a cost centre?

We're radically "trimming" costs and "restyling" price structure.

Nice.

5) A chain of shops can treat **each shop** as a **profit centre**. The business owner can work out the **profit** for each shop separately using the **costs** of stock, rent and staff wages for each shop, and the **sales revenue** for each shop.

6) Manufacturers can treat each **product line** as a profit centre. Individual **brands** can also be profit centres. You can figure out how much they cost, how much they make, and then **set a budget** based on how much you **think** they're going to cost and how much you think they're going to make next year.

Cost and profit centres have several Uses

① **Financial decision making**

1) Overall profit figures don't tell senior managers exactly **where** profits are being made. Cost and profit centres let managers **compare** the costs of different parts of the business. Then they can try to make the less cost-efficient parts **more efficient**.

2) Managers can use **cost centres** to help them **set prices** — once they know the cost, they can set the price so that they'll make a profit.

② **Organisation and control**

1) Managers can use cost and profit centre information when they want to change the **organisation** of the business. They can focus on the **profitable** areas and might get rid of unprofitable shops or products.

2) Managers can set **cost limits** and **profit targets** to coordinate staff and get them to **focus** on specific activities. They can link **pay** and **bonuses** to meeting **profit targets** and keeping costs down in each department, team or shop.

③ **Motivation**

1) Each cost or profit centre has its own budget, so **junior managers** and **employees** have the opportunity to control budgets in individual centres.

Senior managers giving junior managers the authority to make budget decisions is <u>delegation</u>. Page 86 has more on delegation.

2) **Profit share** schemes mean employees and managers within profitable profit centres can earn **bonus** payments, but this can backfire if profits aren't as good as expected — staff could end up less motivated instead of more motivated.

Example: When British Airways came under intense pressure from budget airlines, the company realised they had to **cut costs** to compete. They calculated costs, revenues, profit and loss for each **route**. Managers **closed** the **loss-making** routes and put money toward **increasing** the services on the more **profitable** routes. The marketing department were set targets intended to motivate them and generate more customers for these routes. Company performance started to improve.

Cost and Profit Centres

Businesses *Define* cost and profit centres in *Different Ways*

Depending on the type of business, cost and profit centres can be defined by:

1) **Product** — e.g. a high street **clothing** company might monitor costs and revenues for each product, so it could work out how much **profit** or **loss** different lines of clothing contributed to the business.

2) **Factory** — e.g. **car companies** use their different factories as cost and profit centres, so they know what percentage of costs and profits each factory represents to the business. This information is useful if the business needs to **downsize** — they can close the **least profitable** factories.

3) **Location** — e.g. **supermarkets** that know how much profit (as well as how much revenue) each **store** generates for the business will find it easier to choose areas with **profitable** stores for expansion.

4) **Person** — e.g. businesses with a sales force will usually monitor **each sales person** as a profit centre. Sales people are very **expensive** to employ — so a business wants to make sure none of them are **costing** the business **more** than they generate in profit.

Cost Centres must include Indirect Costs

When businesses calculate the cost of a cost centre, they have to remember to include **indirect costs** (e.g. managers' salaries and rent on a shop or factory), not just the **direct costs** that are involved in making each product (like the cost of raw materials). There's more on direct and indirect cost on p. 39.

Cost and profit centres have Advantages and Disadvantages

Advantages of cost and profit centres	Disadvantages of cost and profit centres
Managers can easily spot the successful and unsuccessful parts of the business.	Giving junior employees responsibility for setting budgets can be too much for them to handle. They'll need financial training first.
Local managers can make decisions to suit their cost or profit centre. They can set prices for the local market.	It can be hard to divide a business into cost and profit centres. Sharing out the costs of overheads like rent is particularly tricky.
Meeting targets on a local level can be more motivating than working towards a distant national target.	There's rivalry between cost and profit centres in a business. If it goes too far, it can be a problem — branches could be more concerned with beating each other's profits than with customers.

Cost and profit centres don't suit all businesses. Leaders who like to **make all the decisions** won't be happy about **delegating responsibility** for budgets. Businesses without **good junior staff** won't be able to **handle** cost and profit centres. It often isn't worth working out cost and profit centres for a business which just sells **one kind of product**.

Practice Questions

Q1 What is a cost centre?
Q2 Would the maintenance and facilities management department be a cost centre or a profit centre?
Q3 Give two reasons for using cost and profit centres.
Q4 State three ways that a business can divide its operations up into profit centres.
Q5 Give two drawbacks of using profit centres.

Exam Questions

Q1 Why might a small business owner decide not to establish cost and profit centres for their business? [6 marks]

Q2 Tanya Richards owns and manages four beauty salons, and runs each salon as a profit centre. She also has a small office where she and her assistant look after all the admin, accounting and marketing for the business.
(a) Why does Tanya run her office as a cost centre, not as a profit centre? [4 marks]
(b) To what extent might running the salons as profit centres motivate Tanya's staff? Explain your answer. [11 marks]

Need profits — go to the local profit centre...

Cost and profit centres are especially good for businesses like banks, supermarkets and manufacturers — it makes a lot of sense to divide those businesses up into individual bank branches, individual stores and individual product lines. Don't go thinking that profit centres and cost centres are opposites — it's just that you can't measure profit for a cost centre.

Standard Costs

*More costs — hurray. These pages are about how businesses can predict the cost of making individual products, and work out how accurate their predictions are. For the **OCR: Production** and **Accounting** options and **WJEC**.*

Standard Costs are the Predicted Costs for Each Unit

1) **Standard costs** (sometimes called **average costs**) are what a business expects **each unit** they produce to **cost** them. They're a bit like **budgets**, but budgets relate to **departments** and standard costs relate to **products**.

2) Businesses **predict** how much each unit will cost to make. They work out the **average cost** of the **raw materials** for one product, and add the **hourly wage** cost multiplied by the **number of hours** they expect it will take to produce each unit. They also add an estimate of the **indirect costs** involved in producing each unit — this is the **total** indirect cost, divided by the **number of products** they expect to produce.

3) In reality, some workers might take **longer** to produce one unit than others, and some raw materials might be **wasted**. **Predictions** might turn out to be **wrong** if wages or the cost of materials increase **unexpectedly**.

4) **Variance** (p. 36-37) is the difference between the **standard cost** and the **actual cost**. This can be **favourable** (costs are less than planned so there's more profit) or **adverse** (costs are more than planned).

5) **Standard costing** is usually used by businesses that produce a **large number** of the **same item**, and where the work involved in production takes the same amount of **time** for each unit (e.g. sticking labels on tins of beans in a factory). It's **not suitable** for businesses that make **one-off** products (e.g. made-to-measure wedding dresses).

Managers Interpret standard costs with Ratios

Efficiency ratio

1) The **efficiency ratio** shows whether production is **faster** or **slower** than managers **expect**.

2) To calculate it, divide the **standard hours** produced (**1 standard hour** is the number of products that workers are expected to make in **1 hour**) by the **actual number** of hours it's taken to make the products and multiply by 100%.

3) If the efficiency ratio is **more than 100%**, workers are working **faster** than managers expect, and if it's **lower than 100%** then they're working **slower** than expected.

$$\text{Efficiency ratio} = \frac{\textbf{Standard Hours Produced}}{\textbf{Actual Hours Worked}} \times \textbf{100\%}$$

standard hours = hours budgeted to make one unit × units actually made

Capacity ratio

1) The **capacity ratio** shows whether workers spend **more** or **less time** on a task than is **budgeted**. It compares the **total hours** spent on a task to the number of **hours budgeted** for it — it doesn't matter whether the employees actually **complete** the task or not, just whether they spend more or less time on it than managers have allowed.

2) It's calculated by dividing the **actual number** of hours worked by the **budgeted hours**, and multiplying by 100%.

3) A capacity ratio of **more than 100%** means that workers are spending **more time** on tasks than has been budgeted, and a capacity ratio of **less than 100%** means that not all the **available time** is used.

$$\text{Capacity ratio} = \frac{\textbf{Actual Hours Worked}}{\textbf{Budgeted Hours}} \times \textbf{100\%}$$

Production volume ratio

1) The **production volume ratio** shows how **efficiently** the budgeted time is used to produce products.

2) To calculate it, divide the **standard hours** produced by the **hours budgeted** for the project, and multiply by 100%.

3) A production volume ratio of **over 100%** means that the budgeted time is being used **effectively**, and a production volume ratio of **less than 100%** means that **less** is being **produced** in the budgeted time than managers expect.

$$\text{Production Volume ratio} = \frac{\textbf{Standard Hours Produced}}{\textbf{Budgeted Hours}} \times \textbf{100\%}$$

Full Costing adds a Percentage of the Indirect Costs to Direct Costs

1) **Full costing** is the **simplest** method of calculating costs — businesses work out the **direct costs** of making each product, and then add on a **proportion** of the **indirect costs** (overheads).

2) Indirect costs can be divided **equally** between all products, or **shared out** according to how much **revenue** each product makes, etc. E.g. if a business makes **five** different products, then the simplest way to allocate indirect costs is to allocate **20%** of the indirect costs to each product.

Cost Allocation

Absorption Costing adds a Percentage of Each Indirect Cost to the Direct Costs

1) **Absorption costing** is a bit like full costing, because it adds a **proportion** of the **indirect costs** onto the **direct cost** of each product. The main difference is that in absorption costing, each product is allocated a different percentage of **each individual indirect cost** (heating and lighting, rent, etc) rather than a percentage of **total indirect costs**.

2) E.g. **canteen costs** might be divided up according to the percentage of staff working on each product, **rent** might be shared out according to how much floor space each product requires, etc.

3) Absorption costing is more **accurate** than full costing but it takes **longer**.

4) It can also lead to **conflict** as managers argue over how they're going to allocate the overheads.

Marginal or Contribution Costing is based on Direct Cost and Selling Price

1) The **difference** between the **direct cost** per unit and the **selling price** of each unit makes a **contribution** towards paying for the **indirect costs**.

> **contribution = selling price** per unit – **direct costs** per unit

2) In **contribution costing**, once there is enough **contribution** to cover the **overheads** (indirect costs), all contribution is **profit**. The finance department works out how many **sales** the business needs to make to cover the **overheads** and start making **profit**. This figure is called the **break-even output**. See p. 54-55 for quite a bit more about contribution and break even.

The Method for allocating Fixed Costs affects Reported Profit for each product

1) Depending on how fixed costs are allocated, the same product might seem to be making either a **profit** or a **loss**.

2) E.g. Polly owns a chocolate factory. She makes **four** different flavours of chocolate bars — honey, mint, orange and banana. Her fixed costs are **£12 000**.

3) If she divides the fixed costs **equally** between the four bars, it looks like the **banana** chocolate bar is **losing** her business money.

Chocolate bar	Honey	Mint	Orange	Banana	Total
Revenue (£)	12 000	15 000	16 000	4 000	47 000
Direct costs	5 000	7 000	9 000	3 000	24 000
Fixed costs	3 000	3 000	3 000	3 000	12 000
Profit	4 000	5 000	4 000	–2 000	11 000

4) However, if she uses **contribution costing**, it's clear that the banana bar is making a **contribution** to **fixed costs**. The £4 000 revenue from the banana chocolate bar covers its £3 000 direct costs, and contributes £1 000 towards Polly's fixed costs. The total contribution is £23 000, and her fixed costs are £12 000, so her overall profit is £11 000 (as with the previous method).

Chocolate bar	Honey	Mint	Orange	Banana	Total
Revenue (£)	12 000	15 000	16 000	4 000	47 000
Direct costs	5 000	7 000	9 000	3 000	24 000
Contribution	7 000	8 000	7 000	1 000	23 000

5) Another reason why Polly might not want to stop making banana chocolate bars is that her **fixed costs** would **stay the same**, so they would be £4 000 instead of £3 000 for each of the other chocolate bars. This would make all the other chocolate bars **less profitable**. Her **overall profit** would also **go down** from £11 000 to £10 000.

Practice Questions

Q1 How are standard costs calculated?

Q2 What's the difference between full costing and absorption costing?

Exam Questions

Q1 How can the method a business uses to allocate fixed costs affect its reported profits? [4 marks]

Q2 Assess the suitability of standard costing for:
(a) a company that makes bespoke furniture.
(b) a business that manufactures ten different models of hairbrushes. [6 marks]

Absorption costing — the price of sponges...

I don't know about you, but I've had just about enough of costs after all that. All the different ways that businesses can choose to work out the cost of making products can get a bit confusing, but they're not too hard once you work out which is which. Just keep going over these pages until you're confident you know all the different names and what they all mean.

Final Accounts

*Final accounts are a little bit like an end-of-term report — they show how well (or how badly) a firm is performing. These pages are just for the **OCR: Accounting option**.*

Final Accounts are a Financial Summary of a business

Every company is required **by law** to keep accurate **financial records** in the form of final accounts for each year. The final accounts of a business consist of **three** different financial documents:

① **Profit and Loss Account**

The **profit and loss account** is a record of the performance of the business **during** the **accounting period** (usually a year). It's like a **financial history book** of a business, since it's a record of what has happened in the **past**.

② **Balance Sheet**

The **balance sheet** provides a **snapshot** of the **assets and liabilities** that a business has at the **end** of the accounting period. It has to be **signed** by a company director and then **submitted** to Companies House.

It's always summery in an accountant's world.

③ **Cash Flow Statement**

The **cash flow statement** summarises the **inflow** and **outflow** of **cash** throughout the accounting period.

Together, these documents can be used to assess the **financial position** of a business.

Final Accounts help Stakeholders make Decisions

Stakeholders use accounts to measure the **performance** of the business, and help them make decisions.

1) **Managers** use all this information to make **internal** decisions. They need to know how much the business' **assets** are worth, how much they **owe**, and when money **comes into** the business and **leaves** the business. They can use this information to decide whether to sell off some of the business' assets to pay off its debts, etc.

2) **Employees** can also use the accounts to help them decide whether the business provides good **career prospects**. If the company's accounts show that it's **struggling**, employees might be worried about losing their jobs if the business goes bust, so they might start looking for a job with a more financially stable company.

3) Existing and potential **shareholders** look at a firm's final accounts in order to make investment decisions. **Existing shareholders** look at the company's performance to see if they want to **keep investing** in the company or sell their shares. **Potential shareholders** compare the company's performance to other investment opportunities to decide which is likely to give a better return on their investment.

4) **Suppliers** use a firm's accounts to decide if they want to offer the firm **credit**. If the business isn't doing very well financially, suppliers might insist on being paid **immediately** for supplies because they're worried that they won't get paid at all if they give the business credit and it goes bust or **can't pay**. If a business' final accounts show that it's performing well, suppliers will be much more willing to offer a **credit period**.

5) **Competitors** use accounts to see how a business is doing, and to figure out what the business might do **next**. If they can **predict** what the business is going to do, they can **react** to it before it's even happened — this will save them time and help them to stay more **competitive**.

The Annual Report is a Legal Requirement for businesses

The **law** demands that **all limited liability companies** submit a set of final accounts, and that they are **checked** by independent auditors. There are **two** main reasons why businesses are required by law to do this:

1) Since **stakeholders** often use the financial records of a business to examine its performance, and **compare** this with the performance of competitors, a standard set of accounting rules needs to be used — otherwise it would be very **difficult** to truly assess the performance of a business.

2) Since businesses have to use standard **accounting rules** and have their accounts **verified**, it's difficult for them to **falsify** their accounts to make the company look as though it's performing **better** than it is.

Final Accounts

The **Annual Report** contains the **Final Accounts** and **Other Documents**

All businesses with **limited liability** are required by law to submit an **annual report** to Companies House.

As well as the **final accounts**, the annual report contains the following documents:

> Limited liability businesses include private limited companies (Ltd), public limited companies (PLC) and limited liability partnerships (LLP).

1) **Statement of Total Recognised Gains and Losses**

   This presents **additional information** that's not included in the **profit and loss account** but may have an effect on the **performance** of the business. It includes any **adjustments** from previous years and also the effects of **currency conversions** if a business has traded with foreign companies.

2) **Notes To The Accounts**

   This outlines the **accounting conventions** followed in the final accounts, so it helps to put the figures into **context**. The information contained in the notes to the accounts is used to ensure that the accounts are a **"true and fair view"** of the state of the business as required by the Companies Act 2006.

3) **The Directors' Report**

   This is a review of the business performance over the accounting period as seen through the eyes of the **directors** of the business. It's sometimes referred to as the **Chairman's Statement**. This section of the final accounts may also include additional information such as the **pay** received by the directors. It must be **signed** by either a **director** or the **company secretary**.

4) **The Auditor's Report**

   This is written by the **auditors** and includes a statement as to whether or not the annual report gives a **"true and fair view"** of the financial position of the business, as well as a comment upon the **scope** of the audit that has been carried out on the accounts. This document is **not required** for small companies, but must be signed and dated by the **auditor** where it is provided.

Under the Companies Act 2006, **small** and **medium** sized limited liability companies are not required to submit as much information to Companies House as large companies. **Sole traders** and **unlimited liability partnerships** don't have to submit an annual report at all.

Practice Questions

Q1   List the three documents that make up a company's final accounts.

Q2   Why do companies have to have their accounts independently verified?

Q3   What four documents does the annual report contain apart from the final accounts?

Q4   What kind of businesses are not required to submit an annual report to Companies House?

Exam Questions

Q1   Explain how a business' final accounts are used by its stakeholders.   [10 marks]

Q2   Explain why companies are legally required to submit final accounts and have them independently verified.   [4 marks]

It's the final accountdown...

Not really, there are still another twenty pages or so to go after this. There's still quite a bit to learn before the end of the section too, starting with this lot. You need to know all the bits that make up the final accounts and the annual report, and you also need to know who cares about all this stuff and why (the stakeholders I mean — obviously you care...).

Final Accounts: Balance Sheets

*You might have come across balance sheets at AS level, but there's loads more detail and depth for A2, so learn it all. The next three pages are for **AQA**, the **OCR: Accounting option** and **WJEC**.*

Balance Sheets are lists of Assets and Liabilities

1) Balance sheets are a **snapshot** of a firm's finances at a **fixed point in time**. They show the value of all the **assets** (the things that belong to the business, including cash in the bank) and all the **liabilities** (the money the business owes). They also show the value of all the **capital** in the business, and the source of that capital — they show where the money's **come from** as well as what's being **done** with it.

2) The **value** of the **assets** purchased **equals** the **amount of money** used to **buy** them. Balance sheets... **balance**.

Assets are things the Business Owns

1) Businesses can use **capital** to buy **assets** that will generate more revenue in the future — this is **investment**.

2) Assets provide a **financial benefit** to the business. They're given a monetary value on the balance sheet.

3) Assets can be classified as **fixed assets** or **current assets**.

4) **Fixed assets** are assets that the business is likely to keep for **more than a year**, e.g. property, land, production equipment, desks and computers. Fixed assets often lose value over time, so they're worth less and less every year. This is called **depreciation** — see p. 48 for more on depreciation.

5) **Patents** can also be classed as **fixed assets** on the balance sheet. A patent gives a business the right to use a new **invention** or **product**, and **prevents** other businesses from using the same invention or making the same product without permission for 20 years. Businesses can **sell** patents to other companies, so they are an asset on the balance sheet.

6) **Current assets** are assets that the business is likely to exchange for cash **within the accounting year**, before the next balance sheet is done. Current assets include **debtors** (companies and individuals that owe the business money) and **stock** (products, or materials that will be used to make products, that will be sold to **customers**).

7) When one business buys another, the buyer might pay more for the business than just the value of its **assets**, because it has a good **reputation**, good **location** or established **customer base**, etc. The extra money is included on the buyer's balance sheet as a **fixed asset**, called **goodwill**.

Bad Debts are debts that debtors Won't Ever Pay

1) **Ideally**, every debt owed by debtors to the business would be paid. **Unfortunately**, the **real world** isn't like that. Most debts get paid eventually, but some debtors **default** on their payments — they **don't pay up**.

2) Debts which don't get paid are called "**bad debts**". These bad debts **can't** be included on the balance sheet as an **asset** — because the business isn't going to get money for them.

3) The business **writes off** these bad debts, and puts them as an **expense** on the profit and loss account. This shows that the business has **lost money**.

> It's important to be **realistic** about bad debts.
>
> The business shouldn't be **over-optimistic** and report debts as **assets** when it's unlikely that they're ever going to be paid. On the other hand, they shouldn't be **too cautious** and write debts off as **bad debts** when they could make the debtors pay up.
>
> - Being **over-optimistic** results in an asset valuation that's **too high**.
> - Being **over-cautious** results in an asset valuation that's **too low**.

Liabilities are Debts the Business Owes

1) **Current liabilities** are **debts** which need to be paid off within a year. They include **overdrafts**, **taxes** due to be paid, money owed to **creditors** and **dividends** due to be paid to shareholders.

2) **Long-term liabilities** are debts that the business will pay off over several years, e.g. mortgages and loans.

3) All the company's **sources of capital** count as a liability, even money invested by **shareholders**. This is because if the business ceased trading, the shareholders would want their money back. Money that the owners of a **sole trader** business or a **partnership** have put into the business (the **owner's equity**) counts as a liability as well.

4) **Reserves** (retained profits, and money from any rises in the value of assets such as property) count as a **liability** because they're a **source of finance**.

> **Liabilities = where the money's from.**
> **Assets = what you've done with it.**

Final Accounts: Balance Sheets

Interpreting balance sheets — *Here's How It All Looks*

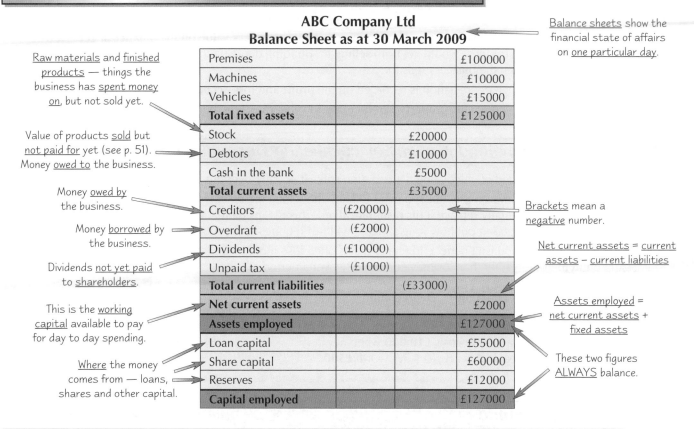

Raw materials and finished products — things the business has spent money on, but not sold yet.

Value of products sold but not paid for yet (see p. 51). Money owed to the business.

Money owed by the business.

Money borrowed by the business.

Dividends not yet paid to shareholders.

This is the working capital available to pay for day to day spending.

Where the money comes from — loans, shares and other capital.

ABC Company Ltd
Balance Sheet as at 30 March 2009

Premises		£100000
Machines		£10000
Vehicles		£15000
Total fixed assets		**£125000**
Stock	£20000	
Debtors	£10000	
Cash in the bank	£5000	
Total current assets	**£35000**	
Creditors	(£20000)	
Overdraft	(£2000)	
Dividends	(£10000)	
Unpaid tax	(£1000)	
Total current liabilities	(£33000)	
Net current assets		£2000
Assets employed		**£127000**
Loan capital		£55000
Share capital		£60000
Reserves		£12000
Capital employed		**£127000**

Balance sheets show the financial state of affairs on one particular day.

Brackets mean a negative number.

Net current assets = current assets – current liabilities

Assets employed = net current assets + fixed assets

These two figures ALWAYS balance.

Balance Sheets *show the* Short-Term Financial Status *of the* Company

1) The balance sheet shows you how much the business is **worth**.

2) **Working capital** (net current assets) is the amount of money the business has available in the short term. It's calculated by subtracting **current liabilities** from **current assets**. See p. 53 for more on working capital.

3) **Suppliers** are particularly interested in **working capital** and **liquidity**. They can look at the balance sheet to see how **liquid** the firm's assets are, as well as how much working capital the firm has. The more liquid the assets, the better the firm will be at **paying bills**. This helps them decide whether to offer the business supplies on **credit**, and how much credit to offer.

4) The balance sheet shows **sources of capital**. Ideally, **long-term loans** or **mortgages** are used to finance the purchase of fixed assets. A well managed business wouldn't borrow too much through **short-term overdrafts**, because overdrafts are an expensive way of borrowing.

> Liquidity = how easy it is to pay short-term debt (see p. 58). The liquidity of an asset is how easy it is to turn it into cash and spend it. Cash is the most liquid asset, then debtors, stock and short-term investments.

By *Comparing Balance Sheets* you can see *Long-Term Trends*

1) Comparing this year's balance sheet to previous years' accounts lets you pick out **trends** in company finances. Looking at the "bottom line" over several years shows you how the business is **growing**.

2) A **quick increase** in **fixed assets** indicates that the company has invested in property or machinery. This means that the company is investing in a **growth strategy**, which may increase their profit over the medium term — useful information for shareholders and potential shareholders, who want to see more profit.

3) Increases in **reserves** also suggest an increase in **profits** — good news for shareholders.

4) Looking at several balance sheets together also shows **trends** in how the business has **raised** its **capital**. It's risky to suddenly start **borrowing** a lot, in case interest rates rise. A company with a high value of loan capital and a relatively low value of share capital or reserves would be in trouble if the Bank of England put **interest rates** up.

Sally liked to make sure everything balanced.

Final Accounts: Balance Sheets

OCR & WJEC

Accounts reflect Assets that Depreciate — they Lose Value over Time

1)   The **drop in value** of a business asset over time is called **depreciation**.

2)   Businesses **calculate depreciation** each year to make sure that an asset's **value** on the **balance sheet** is a **true reflection** of what the business would get from **selling** it. Building depreciation into each year's accounts **stops** it hitting **all at once** when the business **sells** the asset.

3)   The **amount lost** through depreciation is recorded on the **profit and loss account** as an **expense**.

4)   Although most assets depreciate, **property** can **increase** in value over time because property prices tend to rise.

The Straight-Line method is a way of calculating Depreciation

1)   The **straight-line method** of calculating depreciation splits it equally over the life of an asset.

2)   This method is quick and simple, but you need to know how long the asset **lasts** and how much it'll be worth when you eventually replace it (its **residual value**). This means there's a **subjective** side to working out depreciation — figuring out how long an asset will last requires some subjective **human judgement**.

3)   The straight-line method isn't perfect. In reality assets often lose more value early on in their life, rather than losing value steadily over a period of time.

Straight-Line Method Equation: $\text{Depreciation per year} = \dfrac{\text{cost of asset} - \text{residual value}}{\text{useful life of asset}}$

Example: A piece of machinery costs **£10 000** when new. It's expected to last **8 years**. After 8 years, it's worth **£500**. $\text{Depreciation} = \dfrac{£10\,000 - £500}{8} = £1187.50 \text{ per year}$

OCR

The Declining-Balance method is another way of calculating Depreciation

1)   The **declining-balance method** assumes an asset depreciates by an **equal percentage** of its current worth throughout its life. This means that depreciation happens fastest in the **first year** — which is more realistic.

2)   This method is more **accurate** than the straight-line method but it's also more **complicated** and **time consuming**.

Example: An asset costs **£20 000** to buy new. It will last for **3 years**. It depreciates at **25%** per year.
After **1 year**, the depreciation is £20 000 × 25% = **£5000**, so it's worth £20 000 – £5000 = **£15 000**.
After **2 years**, the depreciation is £15 000 × 25% = **£3750**, so it's worth £15 000 – £3750 = **£11 250**.
After **3 years**, the depreciation is £11 250 × 25% = **£2812.50**, so it's worth £11 250 – £2812.50 = **£8437.50**.

There's a subjective side to this as well — an asset that's well looked
after won't depreciate as fast as one that's knocked about.

Practice Questions

Q1   Give two examples of fixed assets, and two examples of current assets.

Q2   What is goodwill?

Q3   What are bad debts?

Q4   Why is share capital classified as a liability?

Q5   Why do businesses depreciate their assets each year?

Q6   What are the two methods of calculating depreciation?

Exam Question

Q1   What can a business' balance sheet show you about its performance?   [10 marks]

All this revision's making me feel a bit unbalanced...

Balance sheets can seem weird — why are reserves liabilities when cash is an asset, for example. If you see it as where the money's from, and what the firm's done with it, you can see what goes where and why it balances. You might have to draw a balance sheet in the exam, and you need to know how to analyse them too, so make sure you're clear on it all.

Final Accounts: Profit and Loss

The profit and loss account is a pretty handy collection of financial information.
*This page is for **AQA**, the **OCR: Accounting option** and **WJEC**.*

Profit and Loss Accounts show Revenue and Expenses

1) The profit and loss account (also known as an income statement) shows how much money's been **coming into the company** (**revenue**) and how much has been **going out** (**expenses**).

2) Revenue is **sales income** from selling goods and services. This includes **cash payments** received and sales on **credit**.

> Remember that accounting follows the realisation principle (see p. 35) — sales income is recorded when the sale's made, not when the customer pays.

3) If **revenue** has **increased** by **more than** the rate of **inflation** (see p.130) since the business published its last profit and loss account, it's often a sign that the company is **healthy**.

4) Expenses are all the **costs** of the business. These are divided into **direct** and **indirect** costs, or **fixed** and **variable** costs.

5) Remember — profit and cash **aren't the same thing**. **Cash** is the actual amount of money a business has available to **spend**. That's not always the same as the **profit**, which includes any revenue or expenses that are paid on **credit** — they're included in the accounts even though the money hasn't actually been paid yet.

Profit = Revenue − Expenses *(and there are different categories of profit...)*

1) **Gross profit** is **revenue** minus **direct costs**. The direct cost of making and selling a product includes raw materials and wages of production workers, but not wages of other staff. These direct costs are called the **cost of sales** on the profit and loss account.

2) **Net profit** is **gross profit** minus **indirect costs**. Indirect costs (**overheads**) cover wages of non-production staff, advertising, office rent, rates, interest payments and depreciation (see p.39).

3) **Operating profit** takes into account all revenues and costs from **regular trading**, but not any revenues and costs from **one-off** events. It only covers activities that are likely to be **repeated** year on year. If a company's **gross profits** are **rising** but its **operating profit** is **falling**, it usually means the company is **not controlling** its **costs**.

4) **Net profit before tax** covers **all revenues and costs**, including those from **one-off events** such as the sale or purchase of another business.

5) **Net profit after tax** is what's left after corporation tax has been paid.

6) **Retained profit** is what's left from net profit after tax, once **share dividends** have been paid to shareholders.

One-off profit is Low Quality — Sustained profit is High Quality

1) Profit can be "**high quality**" or "**low quality**", depending on whether it's likely to carry on into the future.

2) Profit from **one-off events** like the sale of part of the business is considered to be **low quality**.

3) **Operating profit** is **high quality**, because it's probably going to carry on being made year on year.

4) **Shareholders** like **high quality** profit, because they want profit to continue into the future. Future profits mean future dividend payments and happy shareholders.

One-offs aren't always low quality.

The Profit and Loss Account is Three accounts in One

The profit and loss account is made up of three separate parts — the trading account, the profit and loss account, and the appropriation account.

1) The **trading account** works out **gross profit** — revenue minus direct costs.

2) The **profit and loss account** subtracts overheads (indirect costs) to work out **operating profit** and **net profit**.

3) The **appropriation account** shows what's done with profits — it's either **distributed** between shareholders, or **kept** in the business to invest in future activities. The appropriation account works out **retained profit**.

Final Accounts: Profit and Loss

*This page is for **AQA**, the **OCR: Accounting option** and **WJEC**.*

Profit and Loss Accounts calculate Profits over a period of Time

1) Profit and loss accounts should cover one whole accounting year. A profit and loss account that covers **less than 12 months** can be **misleading**. High Street retailers can generate **half their annual revenue** in the lead-up to **Christmas** — a profit and loss account ignoring this period won't give anything like an accurate picture of the business.

2) Sometimes profit and loss accounts cover a little **more** or a little **less** than a year — e.g. when a business changes its accounting year from Dec-Dec to Apr-Apr, it'll have one set of accounts that cover Dec-Apr.

3) Profit and loss accounts usually contain the **previous year's data** as well, for **easy comparison** to see what's changed. Some companies provide the previous five years' data as well. It's useful for spotting trends in turnover, costs and profits.

Here's a Reminder of what the Profit and Loss Account looks like

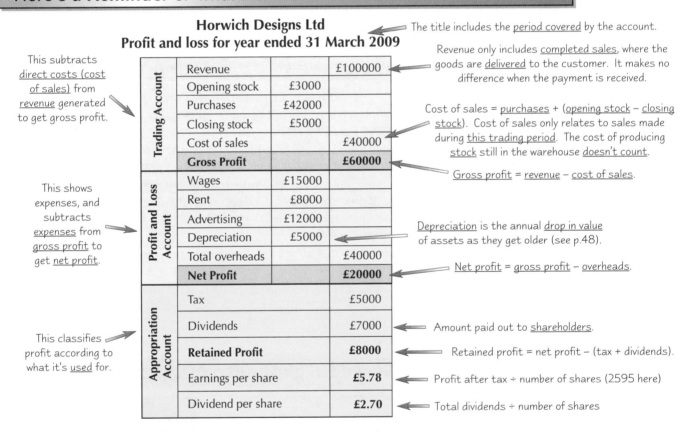

Horwich Designs Ltd
Profit and loss for year ended 31 March 2009

The title includes the period covered by the account.

Revenue only includes completed sales, where the goods are delivered to the customer. It makes no difference when the payment is received.

This subtracts direct costs (cost of sales) from revenue generated to get gross profit.

Trading Account	Revenue		£100000
	Opening stock	£3000	
	Purchases	£42000	
	Closing stock	£5000	
	Cost of sales		£40000
	Gross Profit		**£60000**
Profit and Loss Account	Wages	£15000	
	Rent	£8000	
	Advertising	£12000	
	Depreciation	£5000	
	Total overheads		£40000
	Net Profit		**£20000**
Appropriation Account	Tax		£5000
	Dividends		£7000
	Retained Profit		**£8000**
	Earnings per share		£5.78
	Dividend per share		£2.70

Cost of sales = purchases + (opening stock – closing stock). Cost of sales only relates to sales made during this trading period. The cost of producing stock still in the warehouse doesn't count.

Gross profit = revenue – cost of sales.

This shows expenses, and subtracts expenses from gross profit to get net profit.

Depreciation is the annual drop in value of assets as they get older (see p.48).

Net profit = gross profit – overheads.

This classifies profit according to what it's used for.

Amount paid out to shareholders.

Retained profit = net profit – (tax + dividends).

Profit after tax ÷ number of shares (2595 here)

Total dividends ÷ number of shares

Profit Utilisation is How a business uses its Profits

1) Businesses can use their **profits** in **two** main ways:

- they can pay **dividends** to shareholders.
- they can keep the profit in the business as **retained profit**.

2) **Shareholders** want companies to pay them **high dividends** so that they get a **good return** on their investment. If companies **don't** pay dividends to their shareholders, or pay very **low** dividends, existing shareholders might **sell** their shares and potential shareholders might invest somewhere else instead — this would cause the company's **share price** to **fall**.

3) **Retaining profit** allows the business to **spend** on things that are likely to **increase** their profits in the future — buying **fixed assets** like machinery, business premises, etc allows the business to **increase production**, which could lead to **increased revenue** and **profits** in the future.

4) Companies usually try to find a **balance** between dividends and retained profit — they pay a proportion of their profit to their **shareholders** and **reinvest** the rest in the business to fund **growth**.

Final Accounts: Cash Flow Statements

*This page is for you if you're doing the **OCR: Accounting** option.*

Cash Flow is the Movement of Cash In and Out of a business

1) The **profit and loss account** tells you what happened during the 12-month period. It records transactions that will **lead** to money **coming in** or **going out** of the business (e.g. a customer placing an order).

2) The **cash flow statement** shows the cash flow of the business during its financial year. It records how much money the business **actually paid** and **received**.

3) A **cash flow forecast** is a **prediction** of the **future** cash flow of the business. It's based on the past cash flow, and can be used by the business to **plan ahead**.

There's a Delay between Paying for Supplies and Getting Paid for Goods

1) A firm supplying its customers with goods on credit will have to **wait** to be paid for those goods.

2) While it's waiting the firm still has to pay for **overheads** and **raw materials**, so it's paying out money every month while it waits to receive money from its debtors.

3) So if a business was owed a lot by its **debtors** but didn't have any **creditors**, it could have **big profits** but not much cash available. So it's important to look at the **cash flow statement** as well as the profit and loss account.

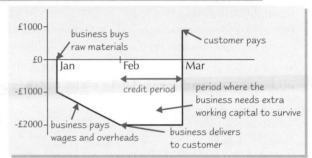

4) If the business runs out of money before its debtors pay up, and so can't pay its creditors, it will become **insolvent** (limited liability company) or **bankrupt** (sole trader or partnership).

5) A **cash flow forecast** can help the business to work out **in advance** if it's likely to be **short of cash** at certain points in the year. It can then **prepare** for that situation, for example by arranging an overdraft with the bank.

A Cash Flow Statement reports Past Cash Flow

1) A **cash flow statement** records the **total cash** coming **into** and going **out** of a business over a period of time, usually a year.

2) It shows the **total cash** that has **come into** the business through sales revenue, loans and other investment into the business, etc.

3) The cash flow statement also shows the cash that has **gone out** of the business to pay for raw materials, rent, staff wages, etc.

4) There's an example cash flow statement on the right. Businesses might break up their "cash in" and "cash out" sections into **more categories**, but cash flow statements **always** contain the figures for **total revenue, total costs, net cash flow** and **closing balance**. See p. 52 for the meanings of all the terms.

Cash in	Sales revenue	£230 000
	Loan	£40 000
	Total revenue	**£270 000**
Cash out	Rent	£60 000
	Wages	£115 000
	Other costs	£35 000
	Total costs	**£210 000**
Net annual cash flow	Net cash flow	£60 000
	Opening balance	£20 000
	Closing balance	**£80 000**

Practice Questions

Q1 Name the three accounts that make up the profit and loss account.

Q2 What are the two main ways that businesses can use their profits?

Q3 What's the difference between a cash flow statement and a cash flow forecast?

Q4 What are the four categories that cash flow statements have to contain?

Exam Question

Q1 Explain the following terms in the profit and loss account:
a) cost of sales b) opening stock c) closing stock. [4 marks]

I wish some cash would start flowing in my direction...

Profit and loss accounts and cash flow statements are both so interesting that it's hard to decide which is the most fun. Just kidding, obviously. Anyway, they might not be scintillating but they're both really useful for businesses, and you need to learn both if you're doing the OCR Accounting option. Lucky AQA and WJEC peeps only need to learn the stuff on P&L.

Cash Flow Forecasts

*Gaze into your crystal ball... this page is all about predicting the future. It's just for the **OCR: Accounting option**.*

Cash Flow Forecasts Predict when cash will Come In and Go Out

1) **Cash flow forecasts** are usually done on a **monthly** basis.

2) Managers can **predict** when they'll be short of cash, and **arrange loans** or **overdrafts** in time to avoid problems.

3) Businesses show a cash flow forecast to **financial institutions** when trying to get a loan, overdraft, or mortgage. The cash flow forecast serves as **proof of ability to pay** in the future and proof that the firm is **well managed**.

4) **Venture capitalists** like to see a cash flow forecast before investing in a business.

5) **Suppliers** offering **credit** or **hire purchase** may also expect to see a cash flow statement.

6) Businesses have to predict their cash flow based on sales predictions and predictions of costs. It's generally easier to predict costs than it is to predict sales.

Example: A new business starts up with a loan of £18 000. It sells £5000 worth of products in January, £35 000 in February, £35 000 in March and £40 000 in April. All customers are given a **one month credit period**. Wages and rent cost £15 000 each month. Other costs are £5000 in January, £8000 in February, £2000 in March and £2000 in April.

To do a cash flow forecast, draw up a table like this. Fill in the **revenue** and **costs** for each month from the data given. Add up the revenues to give **total cash in**, and the costs to give **total cash out**. Then work out each month's **cash flow**.

This shows cash coming in from <u>sales</u> and from the initial <u>start-up loan</u>. → **Cash in**

This shows <u>cash going out</u> to pay for the firm's <u>costs</u>. → **Cash out**

<u>Net cash flow = total revenue – total costs</u>. → **Net monthly cash flow**

Item	Jan	Feb	Mar	Apr
Sales revenue		£5000	£35 000	£35 000
Other revenue	£18 000			
Total revenue	**£18 000**	**£5000**	**£35 000**	**£35 000**
Wages and rent	£15 000	£15 000	£15 000	£15 000
Other costs	£5000	£8000	£2000	£2000
Total costs	**£20 000**	**£23 000**	**£17 000**	**£17 000**
Net cash flow	**(£2000)**	**(£18 000)**	**£18 000**	**£18 000**
Opening balance	NIL	(£2000)	(£20 000)	(£2000)
Closing balance	**(£2000)**	**(£20 000)**	**(£2000)**	**£16 000**

April's sales aren't included because they won't be paid for until May, by the way.

Figures in brackets are <u>negative</u>.

The business has £16 000 in the bank, but it still owes £18 000 from the start up loan.

The <u>opening balance</u> is money in the bank at the start.

<u>Closing balance = opening balance + net cash flow</u>.

The <u>closing</u> balance for <u>last month</u> is this month's opening balance.

Cash Flow Forecasts can't be 100% Accurate

1) Since cash flow forecasts predict **future** cash flow, they **won't** be completely accurate, but managers need to make them as accurate as **possible**. Cash flow forecasts predict when the business will need a **loan** to keep it afloat, so getting this wrong could result in **insolvency** or **bankruptcy**.

2) The **reliability** of any forecast **depends hugely** on the **quality** of the **data** used in its construction.

3) Cash flow forecasts are based on **assumptions** about **future sales** and **future costs**, and these need to be **realistic**. Managers are often **over optimistic** about future trading.

<u>Internal factors can change after the forecast's been made:</u>

1) **Machinery** can break down, **damaging productivity** and requiring expensive repairs.

2) Skilled **staff** may leave the company, again damaging **productivity** and **profit**.

<u>External situations can also change after the forecast has been made:</u>

1) **Suppliers** may **increase prices**, affecting **direct costs**, and possibly affecting **pricing policy** and **sales revenue**. Cash outflows will definitely be altered, and **cash inflows** may be altered if the business changes its selling prices to compensate. **Profits** will be altered by this.

2) **Competitors** may **decrease prices**, which affects **demand**. **Pricing policy** may also be affected, which has knock-on effects on **cash inflow, sales revenue** and **profit**.

3) **Technology** may advance more rapidly than planned. This may affect **market demand** and **sales revenue**, and may require money to be spent on new product development.

4) The **economy** can change. E.g. if **interest rates go up**, the **cost** of loan repayments might **increase**.

Working Capital

*If you're doing the **AQA** exam, lucky you — this page is especially for you.*

Businesses Need Enough Working Capital but not too much

Working capital = **current assets** (cash, debtors and stock) – **current liabilities** (overdraft, creditors, tax)

A business needs **working capital** for **liquidity** (a measure of its ability to **pay short-term debts**). As well as generating sales, the business must **collect money** quickly to get **working capital** to pay its liabilities. (See p.58 for liquidity ratios.)

Businesses need **just enough** working capital to pay short-term debts. They shouldn't have too much working capital. **Liquid assets** like cash and debtors are great at **paying off debts**, but lousy at **earning money** for the business. To make money, the business needs **fixed assets** that make sales possible (e.g. machinery that produces products).

Factors affecting how much working capital a business needs:

1) Businesses with **high sales volume** tend to have high cost of sales, so they need more working capital.

2) The more **credit** a business offers, the more **working capital** it needs to fend off a **cash flow crisis**.

3) The longer the **cash flow cycle/operating cycle**, the more working capital is needed. E.g. supermarkets have a short operating cycle because they don't hold stocks for long, and they don't have to wait for payment on credit.

4) **Inflation** increases the costs of wages and stock, so firms need more working capital when inflation is high.

5) When a business **expands**, it needs more working capital to avoid **overtrading**. Overtrading means producing so much that the business can't pay its suppliers before it gets the chance to be paid by its customers.

THE OPERATING CYCLE

- purchase of raw materials, cash flows out (sometimes delayed by trade credit with suppliers)
- cash → stock (raw materials)
- production, cash flows out to pay wages
- customers pay their bills, cash flows in (may be delayed by trade credit)
- debtors ← stock (finished goods)
- goods sold on credit
- goods in storage, cash flows out

Businesses must Control their Debtors and Stock

1) A business needs to control its **debtors** (people who owe money to the firm). A company which sells millions of pounds worth of goods, but doesn't make sure that **payment** has been received will have **no money coming in**.

2) Wages, loan repayments, etc. still have to be paid, so businesses have to control debtors to remain **solvent**.

3) A business needs to control the volume of its **stock** (raw materials and unsold products) to get a level that allows the business to satisfy the demands of the market.

4) A business holding **too little stock** will **lose sales** as it won't be able to supply enough goods to the market.

5) A business with **too much stock** has money tied up in stock instead of **working** for the company. It could be used to improve liquidity by paying debts, or to improve productivity by being invested in new projects.

Stock is Valued at Cost or at Net Realisable Value, whichever's Lower

Accounting conventions say that stock values must be **realisable**. The **net realisable value** is the amount the company could get by **selling** the stock in its **current state** (rather than after it's been used to make a finished product). The **realisable value** might be **lower** than the **cost value** (the amount the business **paid** for the stock). The rules are that the company must record the stock value as being the **lower** value of **cost** and **net realisable value**.

Practice Questions

Q1 List four events that might alter the cash flow of a business.

Q2 What are the disadvantages to a business of having: a) too much stock?   b) too little stock?

Exam Question Answer on p.184.

Q1 At the end of June, a business has a closing cash balance of £2500. Sales in June were worth £9500, and are expected to increase by £1500 per month for the next three months. The business gives all its customers a one month credit period. Wages and rent cost £7000 each month. Other costs are expected to total £9000 in July, £4500 in August and £5500 in September. Make a monthly cash flow forecast for the business for the next three months. [15 marks]

Is London the working capital of England...

This is about looking at the bigger picture, not just the balance sheet and the P&L account. It doesn't matter how profitable a business is over a year, if it hasn't got a good cash flow it could still end up without enough working capital to pay its bills.

Contribution and Break-Even Analysis

*Luckily, this is surprisingly straightforward. This page is for the **OCR: Accounting** and **Business Production options**. **Edexcel** people need the bottom section on contribution, but the first two sections will be useful background too.*

Break-Even *is the point where* Profit = 0 *and* Loss = 0

Definition: **Break-even** is the point where **total revenue = total costs**, so the business is making **no profit** and **no loss**. It's easy to see break even on a **graph**. Break-even graphs plot **revenue** and **total costs** against **output**. The point where revenue = total costs is the break-even point.

Example: A company has **variable costs** of **£10 per unit**, and sells each unit for **£30**. The fixed costs are **£600 000**.

Fixed costs are <u>overheads</u>, which don't vary when production is increased or decreased. <u>Variable costs</u> vary with the number of units produced. See p.39.

1) The graph shows the **variable costs** of £10 per unit as a **red line**, and the **fixed costs** of £600 000 as a horizontal **blue line**.

2) The fixed and variable costs have been added together to give **total costs**, shown as a **purple line**.

3) The revenue of £30 per unit is shown as a **green line**.

4) The point where the revenue line and the total costs line meet is the **break-even point**. It's that simple.

5) The **margin of safety** is the difference between **current output** (sales) and **break-even output**. E.g. if the firm produces 35 000 units, the margin of safety is 5000 units.

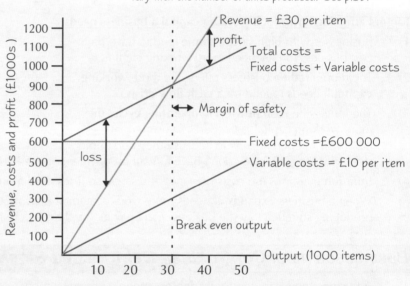

Break-Even *analysis shows what happens when* Costs *and* Prices Change

Example 1: A company has **variable costs** of **£10 per unit**, and sells each unit for **£30**. The fixed costs were **£600 000**, but they're going to rise to **£700 000** because ground rents are increasing. Break-even rises to **35 000**.

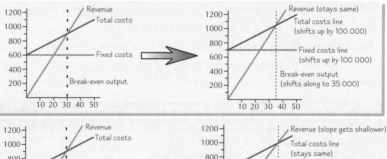

Example 2: A company has **variable costs** of **£10 per unit**, and fixed costs of **£600 000**. They're going to have to cut prices from £30 per unit to **£25 per unit**, because of increased competition. Break-even rises to **40 000**.

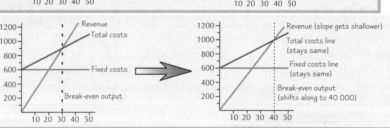

You can also Calculate Break-Even *by working out* Contribution Per Unit

1) The **contribution** that a unit makes toward the **profit** of a firm is the difference between the selling price of a product and the variable costs of making it.

> **Contribution per unit = selling price per unit − variable costs per unit**

2) Contribution is used to pay fixed costs. What's left over is profit.

3) **Break-even** is where **contribution from all sales = fixed costs**. Break-even output is fixed costs over contribution per unit:

$$\text{Break-even output} = \frac{\text{Fixed costs}}{\text{Contribution per unit}}$$

Example: A company has **variable costs** of **£10 per unit**, and sells each unit for **£30**. The fixed costs are **£600 000**.

Contribution = £20. (£30 − £10)

Break-even = 600 000 ÷ 20 = 30 000 sales

The contribution method is less fuss than the graph method, although neither method's exactly hard.

Contribution and Break-Even Analysis

*This page is for **Edexcel**, the **OCR: Accounting** and **Business Production options** and **WJEC**.*

Break-Even Analysis has Limitations

1) It assumes that the firm **sells everything** that it produces **without wastage**, which often isn't true.

2) It also assumes that **variable costs** vary in proportion to the level of output. Businesses can get **discounts** for **bulk purchases**, so their costs don't go up in direct proportion with output.

3) Break-even analysis is for **one product**. Most businesses sell **several products**, and a separate graph for each product would be needed to give an overall picture of the profitable output level. This would get **complicated**.

Contribution lets firms decide if it's Worthwhile to Accept Special Orders

Example: Mothbitten Textiles Ltd produces embroidered handbags and sells them for **£35 each**. The variable costs of producing each handbag are **£20**. A **national retailer** asks for **8000 units** at **£25 each**. The burning question is, should Mothbitten Textiles Ltd accept the order?

1) Even though the firm wouldn't make as much **profit** per item as usual, they'd still earn a **contribution** from each item. Each handbag would earn a **contribution** of **£5** (£25 price – £20 variable costs). The whole order would earn a contribution of **£40 000** (£5 × 8000).

2) Mothbitten Textiles Ltd would **probably** accept the order, as long as the **fixed costs** of producing the handbags don't go up. E.g. if the firm has to rent **extra factory space** to meet the order then fixed costs would go up. But as long as the fixed costs go up by **less than the contribution**, it's worth taking the order.

3) **Variable costs** might go up as well. Mothbitten Textiles Ltd might have to pay its workers overtime, which would increase the variable costs. This would mean that the special order would make **less contribution**.

4) Mothbitten Textiles Ltd might decide to go ahead with the order even if it doesn't make a contribution, if they reckon that exposure to a wider market will result in **higher demand** for their handbags and more sales.

Even special one-off orders at **higher** prices than usual might not be worth accepting. An order that needs to be filled very quickly could need **extra workers**, **overtime payments** and maybe **extra factory space**. It's possible that **costs** might rise by enough to make the order not worth taking.

Contribution can help a business decide what to Make

1) The decision to **delete** a product from a company's portfolio is partly based on its **contribution** to profit and the level of **output** required to **break even**. A **high break-even output** uses lots of **resources**, which could be put to better use **elsewhere** in the company. It's better to use resources where they earn contribution.

2) Other factors such as **customer goodwill** and **employee morale** should be taken into account before deciding to delete a product. Deleting a product might turn **previously loyal** customers off the whole product portfolio.

3) A **manufacturer** which assembles components into a finished item may decide to **produce** some components itself and to **buy** others in from **outside**. The decision of which to buy and which to make is based on contribution. For each component, given the fixed and variable costs of making it and the fixed costs of buying it, you can work out break-even — the amount where the costs of buying and making would be the same.

Practice Questions

Q1 Write down the equation for calculating break-even from contribution.

Q2 What happens to break-even output when (a) fixed costs rise? (b) variable costs rise? (c) the selling price rises?

Q3 Give one advantage and one disadvantage of break-even analysis.

Exam Question

Q1 Clough's make sieves at a variable cost of £3 per unit. Their fixed costs are £20 000 per year. They sell at £5 per unit. The Clough's factory is currently operating at 90% capacity.
(a) How many sieves would they have to sell to break even? Answer on p.184. [4 marks]
(b) Clough's get an order from a big retailer for 4000 sieves at £3.75 each. Why might they take the order? [8 marks]

Well, here's my two pennies' worth...

Contribution is a very useful little thing. It comes up in pricing, it's used to work out break-even, it's used to help decide whether to accept one-off orders, or whether to stop making a product. So, you ought to be able to work out contribution. Beware though, contribution calculations don't give you the final answer for special orders — there are other factors too.

Window Dressing

Window dressing is accountancy-speak for making things look better than they really are.
You know, like putting a photo with a funny caption on a boring page of business studies...
*This page is for the **OCR: Accounting option** and **WJEC**, although it's useful for the other exam boards too.*

Businesses *make their* Accounts *look better by* Window Dressing

1) The apparent strength of the final published accounts can be **legally manipulated** in various ways. This is called **window dressing**.

2) Window dressing involves working **within the rules** of accountancy, but producing accounts that show what the **accountants** and **managers** of the business want readers to see. This might not be the most accurate or useful view for **shareholders** or **potential investors**.

3) Some examples of common window dressing techniques are explained below.

It's *Easy to* Inflate *the* Value *of* Brands *and other* Intangible Assets

1) Customers may make purchase decisions based upon a brand name. This means the **brand name** has a **value**, especially if the company is ever for sale. It's an asset of the company, but it is **intangible** — it can't be picked up or touched.

2) Other intangible assets include **goodwill**, **patents**, **copyrights** and **trademarks** — non-physical possessions of the company which help the company make money.

3) Brands which have been **recently acquired** for **money** have to go on the balance sheet. Brands which have been in the company for a while **don't** go on the balance sheet. This is because the board of directors would decide on the valuation of these internal brands — and it would be far too easy to make up outrageous valuations.

4) Brands which have been **acquired** for money can **still** be **deliberately over-valued** by the business, by the simple tactic of not **depreciating** them enough. This is perfectly legal, if technically somewhat naughty.

Sale and Leaseback *is open to* Manipulation

1) A company may decide to **sell** an asset, for example its fleet of vehicles, to a leasing company and then **lease** the vehicles back for an agreed period of time.

2) The leasing company gains a customer and the company benefits from having a **lump sum payment** for the value of the assets sold to the leasing company.

3) This lump payment is an **income** for the company and it'll appear on the **profit and loss account** — so the **profit** will show an **increase**. This is great news if the natural level of profit is insufficient to meet company **objectives**.

4) There'll be **reduced fixed assets** on the balance sheet and more liquid cash, so hey presto, the **liquidity** position of the company is altered.

5) This method can't be applied every year — once you've sold some assets and leased them back you can't do the same thing to the same assets the next year.

"Now let us draw the curtains of sale and leaseback and close the shutters of overvalued brand assets..."

Businesses can *"Capitalise Expenditure"* — count Expenses *as* Fixed Assets

1) Businesses sometimes play tricks by classifying **operating expenditure** (day-to-day running expenses of the business, e.g. stationery) which count as an **expense** on the profit and loss account, as **capital expenditure** (spending on **fixed assets** like machinery), which count as an **asset** on the balance sheet).

2) Balance sheet assets look good, and can be **depreciated over several years**, which is nicer than having the expenditure hitting the profit and loss account all at once.

> **Investors** and **suppliers** use the final accounts to make **judgements** regarding a company so it's important that these people are **aware** of the methods that can be used to enhance the final figures.

Limitations of Accounts

*Accounts aren't the be-all and end-all of financial health. This page is for **AQA**, the **OCR: Accounting option** and **WJEC**.*

Accounts Don't Contain anything Non-Numerical

1) Company **accounts only** contain **financial data** about a company. This is **useful** for **potential investors**, but it **ignores** a lot of **qualitative** (non-numerical) **data** that potential investors should also take into account.

2) **Internal factors** that **don't appear** on accounts include the **quality** of staff and products, the company's **market share**, future **sales targets**, **productivity** levels, the firm's impact on the **environment** and **customer satisfaction**.

3) **External factors** such as the **economic** or **market** environment aren't reflected in the accounts either. Accounts don't tell you anything about what a **competitor** might do next, or what legislation might be passed by the government. The development of **technology**, or potential changes to the **location** of the business (e.g. a new rail link) don't appear in the accounts. You'd need to analyse all these **external factors** to see how they might affect the business (see p.156).

The Profit and Loss Account doesn't Tell All

1) The **profit and loss account** is very useful for assessing the performance of the company. It isn't the be-all and end-all, though.

2) It doesn't include any information about **external factors** such as **market demand**, which would be useful in forecasting **future turnover** and **profit**.

3) It doesn't include any information about **internal factors** such as staff morale, which would be useful in determining **productivity** and therefore **profitability**.

4) In times of **inflation**, the profit and loss account isn't so useful, because inflationary rises in price distort the true value of turnover.

5) The profit and loss account can be **deliberately distorted**, by bringing forward sales from the next trading period and including them as part of this trading period.

6) The profit and loss account can also be **window-dressed** by depreciating assets too slowly and by capitalising expenditure (see p.56).

The Balance Sheet Doesn't Tell All, either

1) The **balance sheet** is a statement about one point in the **past**, which may not help predict the **future**.

2) The balance sheet doesn't give any clues about the **market** or the **economy** that the business is trading in.

3) Balance sheets value some intangible assets (e.g. a brand recently purchased by the company), but they don't value intangible assets like **staff skill**, **staff motivation** or **management experience**.

It's best to look at the Profit and Loss Account together with the Balance Sheet

The profit and loss account and balance sheet are much stronger taken **together** than separately.

The **Directors' Report** gives more information than either, but it isn't available **outside** the company.

Practice Questions

Q1 Explain what is meant by the term 'window dressing'.
Q2 Describe two window dressing techniques.
Q3 Other than the balance sheet, describe two other sources of data that would give you a picture of a firm's financial health.

Exam Question

Q1 Analyse the value of a balance sheet to an investor considering buying shares in a football club. [12 marks]

Window dressing doesn't mean wearing clothes made from curtains...

There are lots of sneaky tricks that a business can use to show its financial position in the best possible light. But there are legal ways to do it — and that's just one reason why the published accounts on their own don't always give a complete picture. So it makes sense for investors and shareholders to get as much information as possible from other sources.

Financial Ratios

*Ratios turn final accounts into easy-to-understand numbers. You can use them to compare firms and to compare a firm's performance over time. They're for **AQA**, **Edexcel**, the **OCR: Accounting option** and **Strategic Management unit** and **WJEC**.*

Liquidity Ratios show How Much Money is available to Pay The Bills

1) A firm without enough **working capital** has poor **liquidity**. It can't **use** its assets to **pay** for things here and now.

2) The **liquidity** of an asset is how easily it can be turned into **cash** and used to **buy** things. **Cash** is **very** liquid, **fixed assets** such as **factories** are **not liquid**, and stocks and money owed by debtors are in between.

3) A business which doesn't have enough current assets to pay its liabilities when they are due is **insolvent**. They either have to quickly find the money to pay them, give up and **cease trading**, or go bankrupt.

4) **Working capital** and **liquidity** can be **improved** by decreasing stocks, speeding up collection of debts owed to the business, or slowing down payments to creditors (e.g. suppliers).

5) **Liquidity ratios** are indicators of the **solvency** of a business — its ability to pay its debts. There are **two** liquidity ratios you need to know — **acid test ratio** and **current ratio**.

The Acid Test Ratio

1) The **acid test ratio** compares **current assets (excluding stock)** to current liabilities. It shows how much of what a business owes in the short term is covered by its current assets. It doesn't include stock, because it isn't always easy to sell stock in time to pay off debts.

$$\text{Acid test ratio} = \frac{\text{Current assets} - \text{Stock}}{\text{Current liabilities}} \text{ (written as a ratio } x{:}1\text{)} \qquad \text{For example: } \frac{£30\ 000}{£32\ 000} = 0.9375{:}1$$

2) A ratio of 1:1 is ideal — it shows **both** amounts are the **same**. A value much **more** than this means the business has **money lying around** that they could use more profitably if they invested it elsewhere. A ratio of less than 1:1 means the business doesn't have **enough** current assets to **pay its bills.** A ratio of 0.8:1 shows a firm has only 80p of current assets for every £1 of current liabilities it owes. Not good...

The Current Ratio

1) The **current ratio** compares **current assets (including stock)** to current liabilities.

$$\text{Current ratio} = \frac{\text{Current assets}}{\text{Current liabilities}} \text{ (expressed as a ratio } x{:}1\text{)}$$

The current ratio is also called the working capital ratio.

2) In reality, the business probably couldn't **sell off** all its stock. It'd also need **additional capital** to **replace** stocks — the current ratio should be **higher** than 1:1 to take account of this. 1.5:1 or 2:1 is considered ideal.

3) A value much below 1.5:1 suggests a **liquidity problem** and difficulty meeting current liabilities. This is called **overtrading**. See above for **ways** that a company can **improve** its **liquidity**.

AQA & OCR

Efficiency or Performance Ratios show how Efficiently the firm is working

1) Asset Turnover Ratio = Sales Revenue ÷ Assets

$$\text{Asset Turnover ratio} = \frac{\text{Sales Revenue}}{\text{Assets}}$$

1) The asset turnover ratio shows how much **sales revenue** a business is making from its **assets**. **Fixed assets** (like **machinery**) help the business operate efficiently, and so make lots of sales (turnover), so a firm with a lot of fixed assets should have a large turnover. A low asset turnover ratio could suggest that the business **isn't** using its fixed assets **efficiently**, so they're not generating as much turnover as they should. It could also mean that the firm has **too many current assets** (e.g. its stock levels are too high).

2) What counts as a **good** asset turnover ratio depends on the type of business. E.g. manufacturing businesses will have lots of **machinery** and **stock**, so they're likely to have a **low** asset turnover ratio. Businesses that provide **services** don't usually have as many assets, so they should have a **higher** asset turnover ratio. You can tell if an asset turnover ratio is good by comparing it to **similar businesses** — comparisons across industries **don't work**.

3) Managers should **compare** the asset turnover ratio to **previous operating periods**, to see if the firm is **improving** its efficiency month after month, or year after year.

4) Businesses can improve their asset turnover ratio by **getting rid** of under-used **fixed assets**, or holding **less stock**.

5) Operating machinery to **full capacity** helps get maximum sales from fixed assets. There are **problems** with this though — machinery operating at its limit is more likely to break down and need **expensive** repairs or replacement.

Financial Ratios

2) Stock Turnover Ratio = Cost of Sales (per year) ÷ Average Stock Held

$$\text{Stock Turnover} = \frac{\text{Cost of Sales}}{\text{Cost of Average Stock Held}}$$

You need to know the value of sales at cost, i.e. what they cost the firm to make. Stock is valued at cost price, so you need sales at cost price too. You'll find cost of sales on the profit and loss account and stock held is on the balance sheet.

1) This ratio tells you **how many times** a year the business **sells all its stock**. A fruit and veg stall might sell their entire stock every day, which would give a stock turnover ratio of 365. A property developer who took 4 months to do up and sell each house would have a ratio of 3. Businesses operating **JIT production** have a **very high** ratio.

2) When you analyse this ratio, you need to judge if the business has **enough stock to fulfil orders**, but **not too much stock** to be **efficient**. Holding twice the stock needed might not be an efficient use of funds.

3) The stock turnover ratio can be improved by **holding less stock**, or by **increasing sales**. Easier said than done...

4) **Aged stock analysis** lets managers make sure that old stock gets sold before it becomes **obsolete** and **unsaleable**. It lists all stock in **age order**, so the manager can **discount** old stock and cut down orders for slow selling stock.

3) Debtor Days Ratio = Average Debtors ÷ Total Credit Sales × 365

$$\text{Debtor Days} = \frac{\text{Average Debtors}}{\text{Total Credit Sales}} \times 365$$

You'll find 'debtors' on the balance sheet as a current asset — it's the average amount of money owed to the firm by its debtors (not the average number of debtors) over the trading period. Divide it by the value of all the credit sales over the period.

1) Debtor Days is the number of days that the business has to **wait to be paid** for goods it supplies on credit.

2) It's best to have **low** debtor days, because it helps with **cash flow** and **working capital**. What makes a good debtor days ratio depends on the type of business. **Retailers** tend to get paid **straight away** unless they're offering credit on items such as TVs or fridges. **Medium size businesses** usually take **70-90 days** to get invoices paid.

3) You can **compare** debtor days ratios with previous months or years to look for **trends**. An **upward trend** may be because the business has offered **longer credit terms** to attract more customers. However, if it isn't monitored, the business may be heading for **cash flow problems**.

4) **Aged debtors analysis** lets managers **control debtor days**. Unpaid accounts are listed in order of how long they've been unpaid. The ones that are **most overdue** are **targeted** first for repayment.

5) **Asset turnover**, **stock turnover** and **debtor days** are all measures of **activity** — they tell you how **effectively** a business is using its **resources** to generate **revenue**.

4) Creditor Days Ratio = Average Creditors ÷ Total Credit Purchases × 365

$$\text{Creditor Days ratio} = \frac{\text{Average Creditors}}{\text{Total Credit Purchases}} \times 365$$

'Creditors' is a current liability on the balance sheet — it's the amount of money that the business owed to all its creditors over the trading period. Divide it by the cost of all purchases the business made on credit.

1) This is the number of days the firm takes to **pay** for goods it buys from **suppliers**.

2) You can establish a **trend** over a period of time and use this trend to analyse the efficiency of the firm. For instance, if the trend is upwards it may suggest the firm is getting into **difficulties paying** its suppliers. This might be OK, but if the suppliers get the hump and decide they want to be paid NOW, it's a **problem**.

Practice Questions

Q1 How do you work out the current ratio and acid test?

Q2 Which would have the higher stock turnover ratio, a Porsche dealer or a shoe shop?

Exam Questions

Q1 A company is owed an average of £5000 by its trade customers and sells an average of £20 000 of goods on credit each year. What can you say about its debt collection using Debtor Days analysis? [6 marks]

Q2 Comment on the efficiency of a firm that has revenue of £750 000 using £2 000 000 in assets. Last year the firm's asset turnover ratio was 25%. Is the business more or less financially efficient this year than last year? [6 marks]

Oh look, what a lot of "lovely" ratios...

Being totally honest, these ratios are a right pain in the backside to learn. There are a lot of them, and they're practically all something divided by something else, which makes them easy to mix up. Knowing these ratios can score you good marks, so take the time to learn each one, one at a time. Don't be tempted to rush this, even though it's truly, horribly tedious.

Financial Ratios

Investment ratios show the risk of investing in a business. Profitability ratios show profit margin.
*These pages are for **AQA**, **Edexcel**, the **OCR: Accounting option** and **Strategic Management unit** and **WJEC**.*

Gearing shows Where a business gets its Capital from

1) **Capital structure** is how a firm is **financed** — what proportion of its finance comes from loans, shares, retained profit, etc.

2) **Gearing** shows the **percentage** of a business' capital that comes from **long-term loans** (debt) rather than **share capital** or **reserves** (equity).

$$\text{Gearing} = \frac{\text{long-term loans}}{\text{capital employed (see p. 47)}} \times 100\%$$

Gearing is calculated using information from the lower half of a balance sheet — the part that shows where the money comes from.

3) A gearing **above 50%** shows a business is **high-geared**, **below 50%** shows it is **low-geared**.

Gearing shows how Vulnerable a business is to Changes in Interest Rates

1) The more the business is **borrowing**, the harder they'll be hit by a rise in interest rates. How much **borrowing** a business can do depends on the level of its **assets** — the more assets the business can offer as **security**, the more money it will be able to borrow.

2) This is a crude **risk assessment** that an investor can use to help decide whether to buy shares in the company. The more the firm borrows, the **more interest** it will have to pay — this may affect **profits** and the **dividend** paid to shareholders. The more the firm borrows, the more **risk** there is that the investor won't get much dividend.

> **Example:** A firm has gearing of 11% — it's low-geared.
> - This tells you that **most** long-term funds come from **shareholders**, not loans.
> - You can tell that the firm is **risk averse** — it doesn't want to run the risk of spending too much money on interest payments.
> - Because the firm doesn't have to spend its profits on interest payments, it can **withstand a fall** in profits more easily than a highly geared firm.

Looks pretty high geared to me.

High Gearing has Risks and Rewards — for both Businesses and Investors

1) The reward of **borrowing** money for the business is extra **funds** for expansion. Ideally, the loan is invested in projects or technology, which **increase profits** by more than enough to pay off the loan repayments.

2) The **risk** to the business of borrowing money is that it might not be able to afford the repayments — it might not make enough profit to pay back the loan and interest.

3) The reward (of lending money to the business) for the **investor** is **interest** or a share **dividend** (often paid out twice a year). Shareholders can sell their shares at a **profit** if the share price goes up.

4) The **risk** to the **investor** is that the business may **fail**. When a business goes into **liquidation**, the shareholders could lose most or all of their money.

5) **High gearing** can be attractive during a **growth phase**. A firm that's trying to become the market leader, and has growing profits along with a strong product portfolio, may decide to borrow heavily in order to **fund expansion** and gain a **competitive advantage**. This will **increase** the firm's **gearing**.

6) When interest rates are very **low**, high gearing is less risky because interest payments are lower. Taking out loans can be risky even when interest rates are low though, because they might **go up** later.

7) Borrowing money can help businesses to fund **growth**. During times of **growth**, there is more **profit** even after paying loan interest and repayments, so high gearing can be good for the business.

There are Various Methods of Reducing Gearing

1) Gearing can be reduced by changes to the **shareholders' funds**. The firm could decide to issue more shares or retain more of its profits, for example.

2) Businesses can also reduce gearing by **leasing** fixed assets so that they don't need to borrow money to buy them.

3) Businesses can also reduce the **risk** from gearing by borrowing via a **mortgage** that offers **lower interest payments** than a loan, or renegotiating its existing loans (borrow over a longer or shorter period or from a different bank).

Financial Ratios

Gross Profit Margin = Gross Profit ÷ Turnover × 100%

1) The **gross profit margin** measures the relationship between the profits made and the amount of sales. It's expressed as a percentage, calculated by:

$$\text{Gross Profit Margin} = \frac{\text{Gross Profit}}{\text{Turnover}} \times 100\%$$

2) What counts as a good gross profit margin depends on the **type of business**. A business with a high asset turnover (e.g. a bakery) can afford to have low gross profit margin.

Gross profit = revenue − cost of sales.
Turnover = value of sales.

3) The ratio can be **improved** by **increasing prices** or **reducing** the direct **cost of sales**.

4) Also, a business can improve its overall gross profit margin by **stopping** selling products with a **low gross profit margin**.

Net Profit Margin = Net Profit ÷ Turnover × 100%

Net profit = gross profit − indirect costs.

1) The **net profit margin** takes **overheads** (indirect costs) into account. The ratio is again expressed as a percentage:

$$\text{Net Profit Margin} = \frac{\text{Net Profit}}{\text{Turnover}} \times 100\%$$

2) It's best to have a **high** net profit margin, although it does depend on the type of business, like the gross profit margin.

3) It's useful to **compare** net profit margin with gross profit margin over a **period of time**. A business with a **declining net profit margin** compared to gross profit margin is having trouble with its **overheads**.

4) Net profit margin can be improved by **raising prices** or **lowering** cost of sales or (most importantly) **overheads**.

Return on Capital Employed (ROCE) is the most Important profitability ratio

1) The **return on capital employed** (ROCE) is considered to be the best way of analysing profitability. It's expressed as a percentage, calculated by:

$$\text{Return on Capital Employed} = \frac{\text{Operating Profit}}{\text{Capital Employed}} \times 100\%$$

2) The **ROCE** tells you how much money is **made** by the business, compared to how much money's been **put into** the business.

The operating profit is on the profit and loss account, and the capital employed is on the balance sheet. There are several ways of calculating this ratio, but this method will get you through the exam.

3) A decent **ROCE** is about **20-30%**. It's important to compare the ROCE with the Bank of England interest rate at the time.

4) ROCE can be **improved** by **paying off debt** to reduce capital employed, or by making the business more **efficient** to **increase operating profit**.

5) ROCE is just one measure of **return on investment**. Another important one is the **average rate of return** (see p.64).

Practice Questions

Q1 What's meant by "high gearing"?
Q2 Give two ways in which Return on Capital Employed can be improved.

Exam Questions

Q1 Evaluate the risks of investing in a business which has high gearing. [6 marks]

Q2 A business has sales revenue of £2 million. Its gross profit is £750 000, and its overheads are £250 000.
(a) Calculate the net profit margin. *Answer on p.184.* [3 marks]
(b) How might the business improve its net profit margin? [5 marks]

Low gearing is also helpful when driving uphill...

Oh joy of joys, it's more ratios. The exam boards sure know what makes A level students happy. You can probably guess what I'm going to say — learn the ratios carefully, don't get them mixed up, and be prepared to use them in the exam. Exam questions can ask straight out for specific ratio analysis, or you can get marks for choosing a good ratio yourself.

Shareholders' Ratios

Shareholders use ratios to see how much dividend they'll get, and to see how the business is performing.
Page 62 is for AQA and the OCR Accounting option and Strategic Management unit.
Page 63 is for AQA, Edexcel, the OCR: Accounting option and Strategic Management unit and WJEC.

Investors use Ratio Analysis to decide where to invest

1) **Investors** use several share-related financial ratios when making decisions about where to invest their money. These ratios are called **shareholders' ratios**.

2) **Dividends** are paid out to shareholders once or twice a year, out of the company's profits. **Ratios** help an investor to see the **rate of return** to expect — what proportion of its earnings a company uses to pay out in dividends.

3) Investors would also expect to see the price of their shares **increase** over time. A return on investment caused by a rise in the share price is called a **capital gain**.

4) Some investors want **short-term profits** which give them a quick return through **dividends**. Shareholders' ratios are most useful for these investors.

5) Other investors want a **long-term return** through **capital gain**. They'd want the company to invest profits in growth instead of paying them out as dividends.

What it's all about...

Dividend Per Share = Total Dividend ÷ Number of Shares

1) **Dividend per share** is usually stated at the foot of the **profit and loss** appropriation account (see p.50).

2) The amount of profit set aside for dividend payment is simply divided by the number of shares issued.

$$\text{Dividend Per Share} = \frac{\text{Total Dividend}}{\text{Number of Shares Issued}}$$

3) The resulting figure is usually expressed as a number of **pence**. Say the dividend per share is 9.5p and you own 1000 shares — you'd get a dividend cheque for £95.

4) Shareholders looking for **short-term return** want the dividend per share to be as **high** as possible. Shareholders looking for **long-term return** through capital gain might be happy with a **low** dividend per share.

5) It's pretty much OK for a company with a **low share price** to have a low dividend per share — shareholders can afford to **buy more shares** to get the dividend return they want.

6) It's the directors' decision how much profit they set aside for dividend payments, by the way. But if the shareholders don't like it, they can vote at the AGM to sack the directors and bring in a new lot.

Dividend Yield = Dividend Per Share ÷ Price Per Share × 100%

1) **Dividend yield** is a comparison between the cost of the shares and the dividend received. It's expressed as a percentage and calculated by:

$$\text{Dividend Yield} = \frac{\text{Dividend Per Share}}{\text{Price Per Share}} \times 100\%$$

2) Shareholders looking for **short-term return** want a **high dividend yield**.

3) Dividend yield and dividend per share can both be improved by increasing the proportion of profits that are paid out as dividend.

4) Dividend yield depends on share price — which can go up and down, depending on business performance.

> **Example:** Johan buys **100 shares** at **500p** each, and the dividend per share is **15p**.
>
> $$\text{Dividend Yield} = \frac{15}{500} \times 100 = 3\%$$
>
> 3% really **isn't very good** for a short-term return. If he wants short-term profit, Johan ought to be looking at **other forms of investment** to see if he could earn more profit elsewhere — e.g. a savings account at the local bank.

Dividend Cover = Net Profit ÷ Dividend Paid Out

1) **Dividend cover** allows you to see how many times a company could pay the dividend from its profits. It's calculated by:

$$\text{Dividend Cover} = \frac{\text{Net Profit After Tax}}{\text{Total Dividends}}$$

2) So, if the dividend cover is 2 then the company is paying out **half** of its earnings as an ordinary dividend. This may well be rather **attractive** to an investor.

Limitations of Ratios

Ratio Analysis has its Limitations — just like the final accounts do

All financial **ratios** compare two figures from the **accounts**, and give you a raw **number** as an answer.

Ratios don't take account of any **non-numerical factors**, so they don't provide an absolute means of assessing a company's financial health. They have several limitations that you must be able to evaluate in your exam answers:

1) **Internal strengths**, such as the quality of staff, don't appear on the accounts, so they won't come up in ratios.

2) **External factors**, such as the **economic** or **market** environment, aren't reflected in the accounts. When the market's very **competitive**, or the economy's in a **downturn**, it's OK for ratios to suffer a bit.

3) **Future changes** such as technological advances or changes in interest rates can't be predicted by the accounts, so they won't show up in the ratios.

4) Ratios only contain information about the **past** and **present**. A business which has **just started** investing for growth will have lousy ratios until the investment **pays off** — that doesn't mean it's not worth investing in.

> **Example of how ratio analysis can't predict changes in external factors**
>
> • Harry is interested in **investing** in XYZ Ltd. **Ratio analysis** indicates that XYZ is **performing strongly** and gives a **good rate of return** for the investor, so he decides to **buy 1000 shares**.
>
> • Later that day, Harry talks to Sarah, who says **new EU health and safety legislation** will **ban XYZ** from making any more of its products from next year onwards. XYZ Ltd must now either **diversify** into another product/service or **close**.
>
> • Harry doesn't feel so clever about his investment now. XYZ Ltd will need **time** and **money** to **reinvest** in a new production line so **profits will be very scarce** for the next few months. Worse still, XYZ Ltd may go **bankrupt** and he'd have shares with **no value at all**. What a nightmare.

When Comparing ratios, compare Like with Like

1) It's important to **compare** today's ratios with ratios for the same business over a period of time, to spot trends. These comparisons over time need to take account of **variable factors** — things which change over time, such as **inflation**, accounting procedures, the business activities of the firm and the market environment. These things won't always stay the same over the period that you're looking at.

2) It's also useful to compare ratios with **other businesses**, either in the same industry or in different industries. It's important to **compare like with like**. Other firms may **differ** in size, objectives and product portfolio. They may do their **accounts** differently, e.g. they may have their financial year end in a different month.

Practice Questions

Q1 Why might a shareholder not automatically want as high a dividend per share as possible?

Q2 Dividend yield is a better measure of performance than dividend per share. Why is this?

Q3 Give a brief outline of two non-numerical factors that should be taken into account when doing ratio analysis.

Q4 Why might comparisons of today's ratios with last year's ratios be misleading?

Exam Questions

Q1 Net Profit: £500 000   Profit after tax: £300 000
Dividend per share: 6p   Shares issued: 100 000
a) From the above information calculate the dividend cover. [3 marks]
b) If the share price is 300p, calculate the dividend yield. [2 marks]
Answers on p.184.

Q2 Outline two external factors that should be taken into account when analysing financial ratios. [8 marks]

Q3 Ratio analysis gives information about the past.
Discuss what value ratio analysis has in predicting future performance. [12 marks]

Limitations of ratios — well, they can't do cartwheels for starters...

It's not possible to make 100% solid conclusions from ratio analysis alone. You need to use other data from several sources alongside ratios. SWOT (p.159) analysis is a good starting point — that considers the market that the business is trading in. Also, bear in mind that using data from the past isn't always a great way to predict the future. Stuff changes.

Investment Appraisals

*Investment appraisal helps businesses decide what projects to invest in, in order to get the best, fastest, least risky return for their money. These pages are for **AQA, Edexcel**, the **OCR: Accounting option** and **WJEC**.*

Investment decisions must balance **Risk** and **Return**

1) Businesses often need to **invest** in order to achieve their **objectives** — e.g. if a firm's objective is to **increase sales** by 25% over three years, they'll need to invest in extra **staff** and **machinery** so that they can make the extra products they hope to sell.

2) Any situation where you have to **spend** money in the hope of **making** money in the future is **risky**, because there's always the possibility that you **won't** make as much money as you expect. Businesses like the **risks** to be **low** and the **return** (profit) to be **high**.

3) When companies are making strategic **decisions** about how to **invest** their money (whether to launch a new product, take on more staff, relocate their call centre, etc) they gather as much **data** as possible so that they can work out the **risk** and **reward** involved.

4) There are **two** main **questions** that businesses try to answer to enable them to make good investment decisions:

> - **how long** will it take to get back the money that they spend?
> - how much **profit** will they get from the investment?

5) There are **four methods** that businesses can use to help them **answer** these questions and decide whether investments are a good idea: **average rate of return**, **payback period calculation**, **discounted cash flow** and **internal rate of return**.

6) These **investment appraisal methods** assess how much **profit** a project is going to make, and how **fast** the money will come in. The faster money comes in, the less risk in the long run.

7) All of the methods are **useful**, but they're only as good as the **data** used to calculate them.

Average Rate of Return (ARR) compares **Yearly Profit** with **Investment**

1) **Average rate of return** (ARR — sometimes called Accounting Rate of Return) compares the **average annual profit** with the level of investment.

2) The higher the ARR, the more **favourable** the project will appear.

3) ARR is expressed as a **percentage** and calculated by:

$$\frac{\text{Average Annual Profit}}{\text{Investment}} \times 100\%$$

Example:

	Investment	Year 1	Year 2	Year 3	Year 4	Year 5
Project A	(£10M)	£4M	£5M	£6M	£7M	£5M
Project B	(£8M)	£3M	£3M	£4M	£6M	£6M

ARR!

Project A (£10M investment) has a profit of (£M) 4 + 5 + 6 + 7 + 5 - 10 = **£17M**.

Average annual profit is £17M divided by the five years = **£3.4M**

ARR = £3.4M / £10M investment x 100% = <u>34%</u>

Project B (£8M investment) has a profit of (£M) 3 + 3 + 4 + 6 + 6 - 8 = **£14M**

The pirate accountants were very fond of the average rate of return.

Average annual profit is £14M ÷ 5 years = **£2.8M**

ARR = £2.8M / £8M investment x 100% = <u>35%</u>

All other things being equal, the managers would choose project B because it has a higher ARR, just. Just. By a whisker.

Advantages of Average Rate of Return:	It's **easy to calculate** and **understand**.
	It takes account of all the project's cash flows.
Disadvantages of Average Rate of Return:	It ignores the timing of the **cash flows**.
	It ignores the **time value** of money (see next page).

Investment Appraisals

The **Future Value** of cash inflow depends on **Risk** and **Opportunity Cost**

If someone offers you £100 cash in hand now or in one year's time, you'd do best to take it **now**.
Risk and **opportunity cost** both **increase** the longer you have to wait for the money, which means
that it's **worth less**. This is called the **time value of money**.

1) There's a **risk** that the person would never pay you the £100 after a year had gone by.

2) In a year's time it'd be worth less due to **inflation**. You wouldn't be able to buy as much stuff with that £100.

3) There's an **opportunity cost** — you could **invest** the money instead of
waiting for it. A high interest account would beat the rate of inflation and
give you **even more value** than the £100 in your hand today.

4) You could invest **£100** in an account giving you **3% APR interest**,
and you'd get **£103** at the end of the year. If you invested **£97.09**
in an account giving you 3% interest you'd get **£100** at the end of
the year. So, if you assume an investment interest rate of **3%**, the value of
£100 paid to you at the **end of the year** would be the same as **£97.09 today**.

> Amount you need to invest
> to get £100 at 3% interest = $100 \times \dfrac{100}{103}$

> A payment after a year or two, or three, is **always worth less** than the **same payment** made to you **today**.

Payback measures the **Length of Time** it takes to **Get Your Money Back**

1) The **payback period** is the time it takes for the project to make enough money to pay back the initial investment.

2) The **formula** for calculating the payback period is:

$$\frac{\text{Amount invested}}{\text{Annual profit from investment}}$$

For example, a £2 million project that has an annual profit prediction of
£250,000 will reach payback in 8 years (£2 million ÷ £0.25 million = 8).

3) Managers **compare** the payback periods of different projects so that they can choose which project to go ahead
with — managers usually want to get their money back as soon as possible, so they prefer a **short payback time**.

4) Calculating the estimated payback period can be helpful, but it has disadvantages too:

Advantages of Payback Period Calculation	Disadvantages of Payback Period Calculation
1) It's **easy** to calculate and understand.	1) It **ignores cash flow** after payback.
2) It's very good for **high tech** projects (technology tends to become **obsolete** fairly quickly) or any project that might not provide **long-term** returns.	2) It **ignores** the **time value** of money.

Practice Questions

Q1 What are the two questions that businesses ask about potential investments?

Q2 Give two disadvantages of average rate of return.

Q3 What does ARR take into account that the payback period calculation doesn't?

Q4 How does risk help to explain why the value of £1000 paid in two years' time isn't the same as £1000 paid today?

Exam Questions

Answers on p.185.

Q1 A business is investing in a new product. The initial investment is £200 000. The product will generate revenue
of £100 000 per year, and costs of £60 000 per year. Calculate the average rate of return on the investment. [4 marks]

Q2 Priya owns a donut shop. She's thinking of buying a new donut-making machine, costing £5000. She estimates
that it will generate an extra profit of £1500 per year. Calculate the payback period for the new machine. [3 marks]

'Revenge of the Business Studies students 2: Payback'...

*These aren't the most interesting couple of pages in the world, but investment appraisal techniques are really useful for
businesses, and they could come in quite handy in your Business Studies exam if you get a question on them. So stick
with it until it's all practically tattooed on your brain, and then turn over for... more on investment appraisals (sorry).*

Investment Appraisals

One last page of investment appraisal calculations, and then a page about other factors that affect investment decisions.
These pages are for AQA, Edexcel, the OCR: Accounting option and WJEC.

Discounted Cash Flow allows for Inflation and Opportunity Cost

1) **Discounted cash flow** (DCF) is an investment appraisal tool that takes into account the **changing value** of money over **time** (because of **inflation** and the **opportunity cost** of not investing in something else instead).

2) It's used to calculate the **Net Present Value** (NPV) of the project. This is the amount of money the returns would be worth if you had them **now**, which is **always** less than their face value (because of inflation and lost interest).

3) The **Net Present Value** is worked out by multiplying the **cash inflow** by a **discount factor**.

4) The **discount factor** applied is based on the **rate of interest** the business could get at the bank instead of doing the project. If you have to work out NPV in an exam, you'll be **given** the **discount factors**, so you **don't** need to worry about how to work them out — phew.

5) If you end up with a **negative NPV**, that means that the business could get a better return by putting their money into a **savings account** rather than going ahead with the project. Businesses will usually only go ahead with projects with a **positive NPV** — projects that are going to **make them money**.

6) The **downsides** of DCF are that it's a bit **hard to calculate**, and that it's hard for businesses to work out what the **discount factor** ought to be. The longer the project is set to last, the harder it is to predict the discount factor.

Example: **Project A** has an initial investment of **£10M**, and **project B** has an initial investment of **£8M**.
The **expected rate of interest** is **10%**.
The discount factors are: **0.909** (year 1), **0.836** (year 2), **0.751** (year 3), **0.683** (year 4) and **0.621** (year 5).

Project A	Cash inflow	Discount Factor (10%)	Present Value
Year 1	£4M	0.909	£4M × 0.909 = £3 636 000
Year 2	£5M	0.826	£5M × 0.826 = £4 130 000
Year 3	£6M	0.751	£6M × 0.751 = £4 506 000
Year 4	£7M	0.683	£7M × 0.683 = £4 781 000
Year 5	£5M	0.621	£5M × 0.621 = £3 105 000
Total Present Value of Cash Inflows			£20 158 000
Net Present Value (total minus Investment)			-£10M = **£10 158 000**

The £27M that project A will generate is worth £20 158 000 now. Taking into account the original investment of £10M, that's a return of £10 158 000 over 5 years — 101.6%.

Project B	Cash inflow	Discount Factor (10%)	Present Value
Year 1	£3M	0.909	£3M × 0.909 = £2 727 000
Year 2	£3M	0.826	£3M × 0.826 = £2 478 000
Year 3	£4M	0.751	£4M × 0.751 = £3 004 000
Year 4	£6M	0.683	£6M × 0.683 = £4 098 000
Year 5	£6M	0.621	£6M × 0.621 = £3 726 000
Total Present Value of Cash Inflows			£16 033 000
Net Present Value (total minus Investment)			-£8M = **£8 033 000**

Project B will earn the company £22M — worth £16 033 000 now. The original investment's £8M from project B, so that's a return of 100.4%.

Working out the NPVs shows that **both** projects are **worthwhile**, because both have a **positive NPV**.
Project A gives a **slightly better** return than **project B**.

Internal Rate of Return (IRR) works out Several NPVs

1) **Internal Rate of Return** (IRR) is concerned with the **break-even rate of return** of the project.

2) It uses **DCF** to produce **several net present values** for each project, using **slightly different discount rates**, until they get an **NPV** of **zero**. An NPV of **zero** means that their money **wouldn't increase or decrease** in value — the investment would **break even**. The discount rate that gives an NPV of zero is called the **internal rate of return**.

3) Managers need to work out whether the **bank interest rates** are likely to be **higher** than the **internal rate of return** — if they are then they might as well put the money in the **bank** instead of investing it in the project.

4) Managers can also set their own "**criterion level discount rate**" which is their **minimum rate of return**. Projects which have an **internal rate of return** lower than this criterion level don't get the go-ahead.

5) Calculating the IRR is **really hard**, and there's a lot of repetition involved. It's best done by **computer**.

Advantages of Internal Rate of Return:	It allows you to set the **required rate of return**. It allows for the **time value of money**.
Disadvantages of Internal Rate of Return:	The calculation requires **computers**. Some managers find it **hard** to get their heads around it.

Investment Appraisals

Non-Numerical, Qualitative factors affect Investment Decisions

The investment decisions made by managers are based upon a wide range of numerical data and quantitative methods. Managers must also put the decisions into a **qualitative** context, based on internal factors and market uncertainty.

Business Objectives and Strategy can Influence Investment Decisions

1) An investment appraisal recommended purely on financial data **may not fit in** with the **objectives** of a firm. Many businesses will only make an investment if the project will **help them achieve** their objectives.

2) For example, a business which aims to produce **low cost products** for a large mass market (e.g. teaspoons) would be unlikely to invest **as much** in **research and development** as a high-end technology business.

3) **Human resources investment** takes away from short-term profit, so a firm with the objective of **maximising profit** for shareholder dividends would be unlikely to invest in staff development. On the other hand, a business which aims to produce **high quality**, high-tech products would invest in **skilled staff**.

Corporate Image can Influence Investment Decisions

1) **Good corporate image** brings **customer goodwill** and **loyalty** in the long term, and the firm may consider this more important than **short-term rate of return** on investment. Investment decisions that create bad publicity and damage customer loyalty will damage the bottom line in the **long term**.

2) A firm with a green, **ecologically friendly** image would avoid investments that would damage the environment. Some firms incorporate environmental costs into their investment appraisals.

Phil had spent all morning perfecting his corporate image.

Industrial Relations can Influence Investment Decisions

1) Investments which result in a **loss of jobs** may be turned down, even if they show a good rate of return.

2) **Loss of jobs** affects **staff morale**. Cost of **redundancy payments** should be factored into the decision. Trade unions may **strike** over the job losses, which would affect **productivity**. **Corporate image** may also be damaged.

There's Always Risk Involved — and Each Project Has a Risk of Failure

1) The market is an environment that has **risk** and **uncertainty** every day. **Exchange rates** may alter, **sales** may decrease/increase, **customers' tastes** may change and **competitors** may become stronger.

2) Also, **each project** has specific **risk** — a new product might not sell very well. Branching into a new market is risky and might not pay off. Every firm has a **different attitude** to **risk**.

Practice Questions

Q1 What is discounted cash flow?
Q2 How do you work out net present value?
Q3 Give one advantage and one disadvantage of IRR.
Q4 How do industrial relations influence investment decisions?

Exam Questions

Q1 Mick's Ceramics are considering investing in a new kiln. The kiln will cost £17 000, and will generate £5000 extra revenue a year for 5 years. Calculate the NPV of the project, given an interest rate of 5% and discount values of 0.952 in year 1, 0.907 in year 2, 0.864 in year 3, 0.823 in year 4 and 0.784 in year 5. [5 marks] *Answer on p.184.*

Q2 Discuss the qualitative factors that affect investment decisions. [8 marks]

Ow, my head hurts...

All these investment appraisal calculations are a bit tricky aren't they? At least you don't need to be able to work out IRR though. Just learn everything on these two pages and then that's it — the end of Accounting and Finance. Congratulations. You might need a bit of a lie down now to recover from all this accounting nonsense before you move onto the next section.

Structure of Organisations

*Structure isn't just important for architects. An organisation's structure always has an effect on the people in it. These pages are for the **OCR: People in Organisations option**, and they're good background for **AQA** too.*

Businesses can be organised by **Systems**

Organisation by systems is sometimes called organisation by departments.

narrow span of control

1) Businesses can be organised into several **departments**. Departments group jobs together by **function** (e.g. accountants work in the accountancy department), and each department is run **separately**. Organising a business in this way is called **organisation by systems**.

2) Organising a business by systems lends itself to a **tall** structure (lots of layers of hierarchy), with narrow **spans of control** (each manager supervises just a few employees).

3) Businesses can have loads of **different departments** (e.g. PR, Research & Development, etc), but some businesses just have a few. The **main four departments** are:

- The **Finance Department** looks after the money. It prepares final accounts, and does day-to-day money management, such as paying suppliers, invoicing customers, paying employee expenses.

- The **Marketing Department** looks after marketing strategy. It plans and delivers the marketing mix for all products. It knows what's selling, why, and how to make it sell more.

- The **Production Department** makes stuff. In manufacturing, this includes everything from buying raw materials to delivering finished products. Production can also mean the supply of **services**, e.g. web hosting services, editorial services, advertising design services.

- The **Human Resources Department** makes sure the business has the right number of workers with the right skills.

Organisation by **Systems** has **Benefits**

1) **Specialist** managers and workers can operate in their own **area of expertise**, without having to worry about anything else.

2) Organisation by systems tends to lead to a **rigid** structure. Everyone in the business becomes **familiar** with the structure. Everyone knows who his or her boss is.

3) Everyone knows what they need to do in order to be **promoted**. There's a clear **chain of promotion** within the department, for example from Assistant to Junior Executive to Senior Executive, etc.

Organisation by **Systems** is **Bad** for **Interdepartmental Relationships**

1) Traditional organisation by systems keeps different functions **apart**. Completely different **working patterns** and **cultures** can develop in different departments.

2) Different departments can find it hard to **share ideas** with each other. It may be that only the directors of different departments ever meet up, so there's hardly any communication between staff at lower levels.

3) If departments don't **communicate** and **work together**, this can have a negative effect on the business. E.g. if the marketing department is planning an advertising campaign that increases demand by 50% and they don't talk to the production department about it first, they might not be able to keep up with the extra demand.

4) In large organisations, there's often **rivalry** between departments. E.g. when company directors decide on departmental budgets (see p. 36), the managers of different departments might **compete** to get the most money.

Organisation by **Departments** has other **Disadvantages** too

A chain of command is a line of authority with junior staff at the bottom and directors at the top.

1) As a business grows, **chains of command** get longer, and longer, and longer. This makes decision-making take a very **long time**. Decisions are sometimes made by someone three or four links up the chain from where the decision needs to be made.

2) Senior managers can be **remote** from the factory floor or the customer-facing part of the business, which means they might make decisions that are **inappropriate** for workers and customers.

3) As a business grows, **communication chains** get longer, and communication sometimes becomes **slow** and **inefficient**. Messages can get garbled on their way up or down the chain.

Structure of Organisations

Businesses can be **Organised** on a **Product** basis

1) In businesses that produce lots of different products, each **group of products** can be run almost as a **separate business**. Each **product division** has its own director, its own marketing team, its own finance team, etc.

2) In **large** companies, separating the business in this way can **avoid** the very **tall** management structure that is typical of large businesses. Having a **flatter** management structure leads to **better communication** and gives more **responsibility** to junior members of staff, which is likely to motivate them.

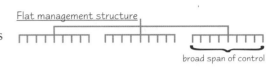
Flat management structure

broad span of control

3) A product-based structure allows managers to make decisions that are **relevant** to each product division.

4) Each division operates as a **profit centre** (see p. 40). This lets senior management compare the successes of each division, which can generate **competition**. Competition between divisions can be **healthy** or **negative**.

5) There may be **unnecessary duplication** of job roles — e.g. instead of each division having its own market research team, it might be more efficient to have just one market research department for the whole company.

6) Sometimes, product divisions are divided up into **small teams** working on **one specific product** each. These teams incorporate people from several business functions, and they tend to be **informally** organised.

> **Example — Cadbury plc**
>
> Cadbury plc is a huge company, responsible for several different **confectionery brands**, such as Cadbury, Halls, Trident® and Green & Black's®. In order to keep the business **manageable**, it is split into three sectors: **chocolate**, **gum** and **candy**. Within each sector, teams of employees might work on specific brands or products, breaking it down even further.

Organising on a **Product** basis means **Different Functions** work together

1) Within each **product division**, different business **functions** (i.e. employees with different job roles) work **together**. Production, marketing, R&D and finance functions work together to design, make and market the products.

2) Each division has **company objectives** to meet, related to each product within the division, and everyone works together to meet the objectives. This gives a sense of **common purpose**, which you don't get when the finance department, marketing department and production department are just trying to meet individual department targets.

Needs more heather.

Mmm, tastes like burning!

Or paraffin... What about paraffin?

Here we see the research and development bees in the "honeys and nectars" product division actually coming up with radical designs for new honey.

3) Organising on a product basis **forces** different functions and jobs within the business to **communicate**. Different functions have to share ideas and work practices.

4) Managers in a business organised on a product basis must be **multi-skilled**. They need to know a bit about all the areas of the business, and have a good overview of what the firm is trying to achieve.

Practice Questions

Q1 What's the difference between tall and flat management structures?

Q2 Give a disadvantage of organising on a systems basis (i.e. in departments).

Q3 What does organising by product mean?

Exam Question

Q1 Osborne Illuminations Ltd. produces a range of home lighting products, including oil lamps, electric lamps, chandeliers and candles. The business employs around 80 members of staff in various functions. The business is currently organised by systems, but the owner, Hannah, is thinking of organising on a product basis instead. Explain how she could do this and what effects it might have. [8 marks]

How can it be a tall management structure if your boss is only 5'2"...

What a nice couple of pages to ease you gently into People in Organisations. It might all seem like common sense, but make sure you learn it all properly. When you get a business case study in the exam, you need to be aware of the effects of the way the business is organised — in formal departments, in product divisions, in small teams or whatever.

Competitive Organisational Structures

Hurray, another two pages on organisational structures. It must be your lucky day.
Page 70 is just for AQA, and page 71 is for AQA, the OCR: Strategic Management unit and WJEC.

Centralised Structures keep Authority for decisions at the Top

In **centralised** organisations, all decisions are made by **senior managers** at the **top** of the business.

Advantages of centralisation

1) Business leaders have lots of **experience** of making business decisions.

2) Managers get an **overview** of the whole business, so decisions are **consistent** throughout the business.

3) Senior managers understand central **budgeting** restrictions and can make decisions to **save** the whole business **money**.

4) Senior managers can make big decisions **quickly** because they don't have to **consult** anybody else.

Disadvantages of centralisation

1) Not many people are **expert** enough to make decisions about all aspects of the business.

2) **Excluding employees** from decision-making can be **demotivating**.

3) The organisation **reacts slowly** to change, allowing its **competitors** to get ahead. This is because the senior managers who make the decisions don't spend time on the shop floor, so they're slow to notice **consumer trends**.

Decentralised Structures share out the Authority to make decisions

1) Decentralisation **shares out authority** to more **junior** employees.

2) Giving responsibility for decision-making to people below you is called **delegation** (see p. 86).

3) **National** and **multinational** firms **decentralise** decision-making, and delegate power to **regional** managers.

4) Managers have to make sure that the **work** of **all** a company's **employees** is **contributing** to the **goals** of the **business**. This can be **difficult** to achieve when a lot of **power** has been **delegated**.

Advantages of decentralisation

1) Involvement in decision-making **motivates employees**.

2) Employees can use **expert knowledge** of their sector.

3) Day-to-day decisions can be made **quickly** without having to ask senior managers.

Disadvantages of decentralisation

1) Junior employees may not have enough **experience** to make decisions.

2) **Inconsistencies** may develop between **divisions** in a business.

3) Junior employees may not be able to see the **overall situation** and needs of an organisation.

Delayering removes layers of Hierarchy

1) Delayering means **removing** parts of an organisation's hierarchy — usually a layer of managers from around the middle.

2) Delayering helps to **lower costs**. Cutting management jobs can save a lot of money in salaries. However, it can **cost businesses money** in the short term because the remaining staff might need to be **retrained** in their new roles.

3) After delayering, you get a **flatter** structure with **broader** spans of control (see p. 69).
If you **overdo** it, managers can end up **stressed** and overworked with **huge** spans of control.

4) Delayering can give junior employees **enhanced roles** with more responsibility.

5) Delayering improves communication because there are fewer layers of hierarchy for messages to pass through.

6) Some businesses use delayering as an **excuse** to cut jobs rather than to create a flatter structure.

Adapting Organisational Structures can improve Competitiveness

1) Changing the **organisational structure** of a business can make the business more **competitive**.

2) Many businesses change their structure **regularly** to keep up with the **changing demands** of the **market**.

3) Businesses might **decentralise** in **fast-changing** markets in order to **respond** to changes more quickly.
E.g. in fashion chains, each **store manager** (rather than head office) might be allowed to choose the stock for their store, because they know what **trends** the customers in their particular store are likely to be interested in.

4) The most common reason for changing the structure of a business is to **keep costs low**. If competitors keep their **prices** low, businesses might **delayer** in order to **cut costs** so that they can keep their prices **competitive**.

Competitive Organisational Structures

*This page is for **AQA**, the **OCR: Strategic Management** unit and **WJEC**.*

Flexible Working adapts working patterns to suit Employees

Flexible working is when working hours and patterns are adapted to suit the **employees**.
There are several types of flexible working, including:

1) **Part-time work** — employees work **less** than the normal number of hours. E.g. they might work 30 hours a week instead of 37.5 hours, perhaps by working four days a week instead of five.

2) **Flexi-time** — employees work **full-time hours**, but they can **decide** when to work, around fixed **core hours**. E.g. employees might have to work for 8 hours a day around the core hours of 10am to 3pm, so they could choose to work from 7.30am to 3.30pm, or 10am to 6pm, etc.

3) **Compressed hours** — employees work a set number of **hours** per week, but over **fewer days**, so they could work longer hours Monday to Thursday, and have Fridays off.

4) **Annual hours** — employees are contracted to work a certain number of **hours** over the **year**, but they have some **control** over when to work them. E.g. employees with children at school might work extra hours during term time and have more time off during school holidays.

5) **Job-sharing** — **two people** share **one job**, e.g. by working alternate weeks, or by each working on certain days of the week.

6) **Home working** — employees work from **home** instead of at the business premises.

Job-sharing doesn't have to mean sharing the same hideous fashion sense, but it helps.

Flexible working benefits **businesses** because it improves employees' **motivation**, so their **productivity** should improve.

Businesses can Outsource some of their Activities

1) **Outsourcing** (or **subcontracting**) is when businesses **contract out** some activities to other businesses (called "outsourcers") rather than doing them **in-house**. This is most common with things like finance, recruitment, advertising and IT — things that the business doesn't specialise in but sometimes needs.

2) Outsourcing can be a good idea for businesses because they benefit from the **specialised knowledge** and **economies of scale** of the businesses they outsource to. Outsourcing also means that the business doesn't have to pay for permanent staff when they're only needed occasionally, so it **reduces costs**.

3) The main **disadvantage** of outsourcing is that the business doesn't have **control** over the quality of the outsourcer's work, and if the outsourcer's work is bad, it can have a **negative effect** on the business' reputation.

Employees can be Core Workers or Peripheral Workers

1) **Core workers** are employees who are **essential** to a business, like senior managers and skilled workers. Core workers are employed on **full-time**, **permanent** contracts.

2) **Peripheral workers** are employees who **aren't essential** to a business, but that the business employs when they need to increase their staffing levels. Businesses keep their **fixed costs down** by employing peripheral workers on temporary, part-time or zero-hours contracts (so the business only gives employees hours as and when they are needed). Employing peripheral workers gives the business a lot of **flexibility**.

Practice Questions

Q1 What's the difference between centralised and decentralised structures?
Q2 List four types of flexible working, and explain what they mean.
Q3 What is a peripheral worker?

Exam Question

Q1 Christine and Bryan run a small B&B. Christine usually does the cleaning and laundry herself, but Bryan has suggested outsourcing it to a specialist cleaning company. Discuss the potential benefits and drawbacks of Bryan's idea. [4 marks]

Gymnasts are always keen on flexible working...

It's a shame you can't do a job-share for your A2 Business Studies, and just learn half the stuff. But then I guess you'd miss out on the joy of knowing the difference between centralised and decentralised structures, and ways that staff can be employed. Now all you need to do is make sure you know it all, then you can turn the page for even more knowledge.

Motivation

*Employers always want their staff to work harder, so they've come up with some motivational techniques to encourage them. These pages are for the **OCR: People in Organisations option**.*

*Motivation is what makes employees **Want** to **Work***

1) **Workers** are one of the most important **assets** of a business. Their role is to **produce** — to turn raw materials into marketable products and bring profit into the business.

2) **Managers** want employees to generate as much **profit** for the business as they can.

3) It's best if this profit is **sustainable** and **high quality** (see p.49) — which means that the workers need to be able to **keep on working** at a good level of productivity. Managers want workers to be **reliable**.

4) **Motivation** means anything that makes you **work harder** and **achieve more** than you might otherwise do. Obviously, businesses need to motivate their workers to keep productivity high.

5) Motivation is a **tough** thing to **get right**. Managers have to push workers to **produce** more, without pushing them so hard that they get **fed up** and **leave**. They have to motivate workers to produce **high quality** goods, at the same time as keeping **productivity** high.

6) **Ideally**, employees would **identify** with the **goals** of the business, and really want to do the job and do it well, just for the **love of the job**. But in the real world, a job's **just a job** to most workers — they go in at 9, work, leave at 5 and don't get wildly enthused about the company mission statement, or the departmental budget.

7) Managers have to use all kinds of **tricks** to motivate employees who aren't 100% in love with their job. These include **financial incentives** like bonuses and performance-related pay, and other incentives like staff parties, which try to **compensate** for the tedium of the job.

8) There are also **non-financial motivators** which try to make the job more **interesting** (e.g. job rotation, job enrichment and teamworking), and to make the employee feel like they **matter** (e.g. employee participation, delegation and quality circles).

9) Employees have **different personalities**, and what works to motivate one person may be useless to the person next to them. Managers have to motivate **everyone** in their team. It's best if they can tailor their motivation strategy to each employee. But this isn't always possible.

Finn never had any problems with motivation when Kim was around.

*Employees can be **Demotivated** by several factors*

1) If employees haven't been **trained** properly and don't have the **skills** and **knowledge** they need to do their job, they're unlikely to be motivated.

2) If the job is **too stressful** or employees feel that they've been given **unachievable goals**, they won't be motivated to work hard.

3) **Bad working conditions**, like rubbish pay or a horrible office, mean that employees will be demotivated.

4) **Bad managers** who are unsupportive or unfair demotivate employees.

5) Employee morale suffers when people at work **don't get on** with each other.

*Poor Motivation creates **Big Problems** for business*

1) Poor motivation can result in **low productivity**, with obvious impacts on turnover and profit.

2) Lack of motivation can result in **poor quality control**. This can damage relationships with customers.

3) Employees who aren't motivated may not bother to follow **procedures** properly. This can have serious implications for health and safety, and for quality control.

4) Poor employee morale increases **absenteeism** (sick days) and **lateness**. This costs money in **lost productivity** and in hiring **temps** or paying **overtime** to cover for absent employees.

5) **High performing employees** tend to lose morale and motivation when they feel they aren't being **recognised**, or given enough **responsibility** to make their job interesting. Their performance suffers, and they often **leave** for another job that will motivate them better. No business wants good workers to quit.

6) **Poor performing employees** who lack motivation tend to **demotivate others** — when workers see the person next to them is **lazy**, doesn't give two figs and is still in a job, they wonder why they should bother. Poor performers don't often leave because they'd find it hard to get another job.

Motivation

Managers use **Motivational Theories** to motivate employees

1) There are several **different** motivational theories — you might remember some of them from AS level. Different theories suggest different **ways** of motivating employees.

2) Motivational theories are used by managers and affect employees' lives on a **day-to-day** basis. How much they get paid, whether they work individually or as teams and even the way their office is decorated are all affected by their employer's ideas about what will motivate them to work harder.

3) The motivational theory that's used in a business depends on the **manager's** ideas about what will motivate the staff. It also depends on the **type of business** — e.g. Taylor's theories are often applied in factories.

1) **Taylor** and **Scientific Management** — people are in it for the **Money**

1) In the early 20th century, **Frederick Taylor** developed the theory of **scientific management**. It was based on the idea that workers are only motivated by **money**, and that they will do the **least** amount of **work** they can get away with.

2) Taylor developed his theories through **work-study** — watching how people work. He did **time and motion studies**, timing work activities with a **stopwatch**. This allowed him to figure out the **most efficient** way to do a job, and then make sure every single worker did it that way. He favoured **division of labour** — breaking work down into a lot of **small repetitive tasks**. This approach is called **scientific management**.

3) Taylor believed that the most **productive** workers should get paid more. He believed that financial incentives were the best way to **motivate** workers and raise **productivity**.

4) Employees didn't like scientific management. Increased productivity meant that **fewer workers** were needed — workers worried about losing their jobs.

5) There were other disadvantages, too — increased productivity could lead to a reduction in **quality**. **Supervisors** were needed to monitor efficiency and for quality control purposes. Taylor's theory also ignores the **demotivating** effect of doing very repetitive boring work.

6) Nowadays, some people see Taylor's approach as **exploitation**, but it's still used in some types of businesses, like call centres.

Example — call centres

1) Managers decide what the most efficient way to work is, and all the staff have to perform in the **same way** — it's quite common for call centre workers to have to work from a **script**. Managers often **listen in** to calls to make sure that employees are doing what they want them to.

2) The emphasis is on working **quickly** and taking as many calls as possible. Employees' calls are **timed**, and even the time they spend in the toilet might be monitored and restricted.

3) Employees carry out the same **repetitive tasks** all day.

4) Employees are rewarded with **financial bonuses** for taking lots of calls.

5) These practices mean that **productivity is high**, but customers often complain about **poor service** from call centres. This might be a result of call centre workers being **demotivated** by the **pressure** of being constantly monitored, and the **boring** and **repetitive** work.

Practice Questions

Q1 What is motivation?

Q2 Give three reasons why employees might be demotivated.

Q3 Give three examples of problems caused by poor motivation.

Exam Question

Q1 Explain how Taylor's ideas are still being used today, with reference to a particular workplace of your choice. [6 marks]

How can management be scientific if it doesn't involve Bunsen burners...

You'll have studied motivation for AS level, but there's more detail and more depth at A level. For example, you're expected to be aware of potential problems caused by poor motivation, as well as knowing about the theories. It's important to put motivation into context, and spot where it can be improved in any business case study that you get in the exam.

Motivation

I know it's a struggle, but try and motivate yourself to read two more pages on motivation.
*These pages are for the **OCR: People in Organisations option** — they continue from the previous two pages.*

2) Mayo and Human Relations — people are motivated by Social Factors

1) Elton Mayo found that people achieved more when they got **positive attention**. Mayo was doing an experiment on productivity when he found that **all** workers taking part in the experiment became more productive. He worked out that this was because they liked the **social contact** that they got from the experiments, and they liked working in a **group**.

2) Mayo thought management should **pay attention** to workers as individuals, and **involve** them in making decisions. This required a **democratic** style of management, as well as **delegation** and good **communication.**

3) He also thought that workers should **socialise** together — outside work as well as at work.

4) Many businesses have taken Mayo's ideas on board and made their workplaces more **sociable**.

> **Example — Office Angels Recruitment Consultants**
>
> 1) Office Angels was named **number 7** in the Sunday Times 100 Best Companies to Work For in 2009.
>
> 2) The company pays **attention** to **individual** employees — **85%** of staff thought that their manager **cared** about them as an **individual**.
>
> 3) **91%** of Office Angels employees also thought that their **team** was **fun** to work with.

3) Maslow's Hierarchy of Needs — people need Basics first

Abraham Maslow identified **five levels** of **needs** that employees try to achieve through work — basic physical needs, safety, social needs, self-esteem and self-actualisation.

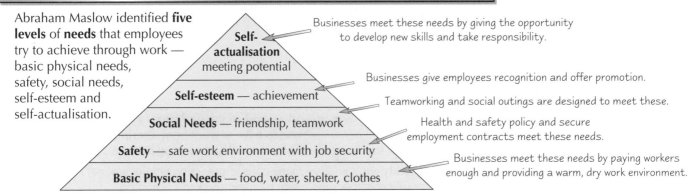

Businesses meet these needs by giving the opportunity to develop new skills and take responsibility.

Businesses give employees recognition and offer promotion.

Teamworking and social outings are designed to meet these.

Health and safety policy and secure employment contracts meet these needs.

Businesses meet these needs by paying workers enough and providing a warm, dry work environment.

Self-actualisation meeting potential
Self-esteem — achievement
Social Needs — friendship, teamwork
Safety — safe work environment with job security
Basic Physical Needs — food, water, shelter, clothes

1) According to Maslow, employees start by addressing the needs at the **bottom** of the pyramid. Once they've sorted out those needs, they can move on to the needs on the **next level** up.

2) For **employers**, this means providing employees' **basic physical needs** and then motivating them by giving them the chance to achieve **higher levels** of needs. The basic needs have to be met **first** though — employees won't be motivated by working in a team or being promoted if they're not being paid a living wage.

3) Maslow's theory recognises that employees are **individuals**, and different factors motivate them depending on their circumstances. The problem for managers is that it isn't always **obvious** which level an individual is at.

4) Herzberg's Hygiene and Motivating factors — sort out a Good Environment first

In the 1960s, Frederick Herzberg identified two groups of factors which influenced the motivation of workers:

1) **Hygiene factors** are things like good **company policy**, **supervision**, **working conditions**, **pay**, and **relations** with fellow employees. They don't motivate as such, but if they **aren't good**, workers get **dissatisfied**.

2) **Motivating factors** are things like **interesting work**, personal **achievement**, **recognition** of achievement, and scope for more **responsibility** and personal **development**. These factors **do** positively motivate workers.

3) There is a trend in modern companies to make sure that employees have a **pleasant working environment** as well as a fulfilling job. E.g. Google™ offers employees free on-site massages, an aquarium, a slide and "chill out" areas at some sites, while Innocent® provides free breakfasts, smoothies and weekly yoga classes.

Motivation

5) Drucker and Management by Objectives — companies need Clear Goals

1) Peter Drucker said that both **companies** and **managers** need to have a clear **long-term strategy**, which is broken down into **smaller goals** for the **workforce**. This method is called **Management by Objectives (MBO)**.

2) In businesses that use MBO, **senior managers** set the **objectives** for specialised **departmental managers**.

3) Drucker also said that if a business had a **clear structure**, this would lead to **better performance**.

4) One disadvantage of MBO is that it only allows **ideas** to come from the **top** of the **organisational structure**, so workers at the bottom of the hierarchy can feel **undervalued** and **demotivated**. To avoid this, companies that use MBO tend to allow **workers** at the **bottom** of the hierarchy to put forward suggestions for both **long-** and **short-term strategy**. E.g. Microsoft® holds "think weeks" several times a year, when any employee can put forward a business idea to be considered by senior management.

Example — Marks and Spencer

1) M&S has a clear long-term strategy — the company has five main objectives:
   - expand its **online** business
   - expand its **international** business
   - make sure its activities are **environmentally friendly**
   - introduce new **products** and **services** in the UK
   - increase the amount of **property** it owns in the UK

2) In order to achieve these objectives, each **store**, and each **department** within each store, has its own **smaller objectives**, set out by the management.

3) The company also has a **clear organisational structure** and hierarchy, so every employee knows their position within the business.

6) Peters' Excellence Model — employees need to be aware of a Company's Values

1) Tom **Peters** claimed that if workers were treated well, and given **autonomy** (the freedom to decide how they work), they would give **excellent performance**.

2) Peters argued that the word '**management**' should be **abandoned**, and **replaced** by '**leadership**'. The **leaders** of a company are **responsible** for **encouraging staff**.

3) He said that managers should **value workers**, but should have **high expectations** of what they can achieve.

4) He thought that management should make employees **aware** of the company's **values** and **culture**, and then delegate decision-making to employees.

Example — Procter & Gamble (P&G™)

1) At P&G™, the company that owns brands like Lenor, Olay® and Pampers®, employees are encouraged to be **creative** and **make decisions** for themselves.

2) The company emphasises "**leadership**" of employees — helping them to develop their skills — instead of "management" and telling employees what to do.

3) Employees are taught the **company values** and are expected to make decisions that **reflect** them.

4) P&G™ encourages its employees to feel and act like "**owners**" of their part of the business.

Practice Questions

Q1 What did Mayo believe was the key to employee motivation?

Q2 List the five types of needs identified by Maslow.

Q3 Which word did Peters want to be abandoned and why?

Exam Questions

| Q1 | Discuss the main similarities and differences between the approaches of Maslow and Herzberg. | [6 marks] |
| Q2 | Explain how following Drucker's "management by objectives" theory can motivate employees. | [4 marks] |

Personally I prefer ketchup to Mayo...

Businesses are really keen on motivation, but even with all these theories about how to motivate people, nobody ever seems overjoyed about the idea of going to work. Still, I wouldn't say no to a nice massage and a free smoothie right about now. This might be a good time to take a break, but come back soon for some delightful pages on leadership and management.

Leadership and Management Styles

*There are different styles of management — different ways of getting things done and different ways of dealing with people. These pages are for **AQA** and the **OCR: People in Organisations** option.*

Managers Control employees, Leaders Influence employees

1) **Managers set objectives** for their department and for the people in it.
   They **organise resources** to get the job done and **achieve** their objectives.

2) **Leaders motivate** people. They **inspire** people to do things which they wouldn't do otherwise.

3) **Managers'** power comes from their **position** — employees do what their managers tell them to do because they **have to**. **Leaders'** power comes from their **personality** — people do what their leaders tell them to do because they **want to**.

4) It's always helpful if managers have **leadership** qualities. **Managers** who are good **leaders** can **persuade** people that the decisions they make and the objectives they set are the **best** ones.

There are various different Management and Leadership Styles

1) **Authoritarian** or **autocratic** style — the **manager makes decisions** on his or her own. The manager identifies the objectives of the business and says how they're going to be achieved. It's useful when you're dealing with lots of **unskilled** workers and in **crisis management**. This method requires lots of **supervision** and monitoring — workers can't make their own decisions. An authoritarian style can **demotivate** able and intelligent workers.

2) **Paternalistic** (fatherly) style is a softer form of the autocratic style. The manager **consults** the workers before making decisions, then **explains** the decisions to them to **persuade** them that the decisions are in their interest. Paternalistic managers think that getting **involved** and caring about human relations is a **positive motivator**.

3) **Democratic** style — the manager encourages the workforce to **participate** in the decision-making process. Managers **discuss** issues with workers, **delegate responsibility** and **listen** to advice. Democratic managers have to be good communicators, and their organisations have to be good at dealing with a lot of **to and fro communication**. This management style shows managers have a lot of confidence in the workforce — which leads to increased employee **motivation**. It also takes some of the **weight** of decision making off the leader.

4) **Laissez-faire** style is a **weak** form of leadership. **Management rarely interferes** in the running of the business and the workforce is left to get on with trying to achieve the objectives of the business with minimal input and control from the top. This **hands off** style of leadership might be appropriate for a small, highly motivated team of **able** workers. For workers who need guidance, it'd be a bit of a disaster.

> In the late 1930s, Lewin, Lippitt and White carried out an **investigation** into leadership styles. Children were put into **groups** to make masks, and each group was assigned a different type of **leader** — **authoritarian**, **democratic** and **laissez-faire**.
>
> 1) In the **democratic** leader's group, the group members got on well with each other and with the leader. They were motivated, and they carried on working when the leader wasn't in the room. They produced the **best quality** masks of all the groups.
>
> 2) The group with the **authoritarian** leader **behaved badly** — some children were disruptive, and lots of children stopped working on their masks when the leader was out of the room. They produced the **most** masks, but the **quality** wasn't as good as the democratic leader's group.
>
> 3) The group with the **laissez-faire** leader was **uncooperative** and didn't work independently. They produced the **fewest** masks, and the **quality** of their masks was **low**.

Different Situations require different Management Styles

1) **Urgent** tasks need different management and leadership from **routine** tasks. Urgent tasks, like an unexpected large order coming in, may need an **authoritarian** manager to **tell** employees what to do and how to do it.

2) A **large**, **unskilled** workforce suits **authoritarian** leadership, whereas a **small**, **educated** workforce suits a **democratic** approach much better. E.g. when a business is **growing** and takes on lots of new employees, the owner might take an authoritarian approach — once the new employees are more familiar with the business, the owner can give them more responsibility and use a more democratic approach.

3) The way the organisation's been run in the **past** affects the **expectations** of the workforce, which affects how they might **respond** to leadership.

4) The **best leaders** are the ones who can **adapt** their style to suit the situation.

Leadership and Management Styles

Management is a *Balancing Act* between *"People" Needs* and *"Task" Needs*

Task needs are related to getting the **job done**. People needs are related to **morale** and **relationships**:

Examples of task needs	Examples of people needs
Meeting a **deadline**.	Feeling **appreciated** and **valued**.
Designing a **procedure** for maximum efficiency.	Feeling like **your opinion counts** in **decision making**.
Following a **procedure**.	Feeling like you **belong** in a team.
Monitoring progress towards a target.	Feeling that your effort **makes a difference** to the outcome.
Having the **physical resources** the task requires.	**Getting on** with colleagues.

1) Managers have to make sure that **task needs** and **people needs** are met.
   It can be difficult to meet **both** sets of needs at the same time.

2) Task needs are best served by a **task-oriented** approach that **monitors progress** and **rewards success**.

3) People needs are best served by a **relationship-oriented** approach that makes sure everyone's feeling **comfortable** and **confident** about the work and the work environment.

4) When **people needs** aren't met, motivation and morale **suffer** — see p.72.

Leadership is important in Managing Change

1) Businesses often need to make **changes** in order to stay **competitive**. They might change teams around, bring in new technology, move to a new location or alter their product range.

2) When businesses make changes, the employees affected by the changes are likely to be **uncomfortable** with the idea of changing, and to be **afraid** of the unknown. E.g. they might worry that they'll lose their job, that they won't see the same colleagues any more, or that their role will change and it will be too difficult for them.

3) Employees might react to the idea of change by being **demotivated** and **uncooperative**, and they might even actively **resist** the change, e.g. by going on strike.

4) Effective leadership can **avoid** the problems that can be caused by change.
   Leaders can use several methods to persuade employees to accept change:
   • leaders need to **communicate** with employees and help them **understand** why the change is necessary.
   • leaders can **retrain** employees if their job is changing, so that they feel **comfortable** in their new role.
   • leaders can **involve** employees in making decisions about how and when changes are made — this will make employees feel more **in control** and **less fearful** of the changes.

5) In times of change, **authoritarian** leadership can make employees more **fearful** of change, and they might be more likely to go on strike or resist the change in another way. **Laissez-faire** leadership can mean that employees don't have **confidence** that changes will work out well, so they won't be **supportive**. The most **suitable** forms of leadership for helping employees cope with change are the **paternalistic** and **democratic** styles.
   See p. 172-175 for more on managing change.

Practice Questions

Q1   What's the difference between a manager and a leader?

Q2   Give two examples of people needs, and two examples of task needs.

Q3   Why is leadership important when changes are happening in a business?

Exam Question

Q1   Manufacturer DCP Furniture must increase productivity by 25% by next March. Manager Sam Raynes has an easy-going, friendly attitude to his staff and likes to involve them in decision making. The managing director worries that Sam isn't up to it, and wants to replace him. Write a report advising the MD what to do.   [12 marks]

Take me to your leader...

The key to all this is being able to say what is appropriate for a particular situation — in the exam, you might get a case study of two managers with different leadership styles, and be asked to assess whose ideas are best for the situation the business is in. A lot depends on whether the situation has more "task needs" or "people needs" — they're different.

Communication

Communication is really important in business. I bet you never would've guessed that...
*These pages are for **AQA**, the **OCR: People in Organisations option** and **Strategic Management unit** and **WJEC**.*

Communication between Managers and Employees is Essential

1) The purpose of communication is to pass on **information** and **ideas**.

2) Communication **within** the business is necessary for making **plans**, giving **instructions** and **motivating** staff. Managers need to communicate goals and objectives to staff so that they know what they're meant to be doing.

3) Businesses also need to communicate with people **outside** the business, e.g. suppliers, shareholders, customers and potential customers.

Managers need to make sure that they Communicate Effectively

1) For communication to be effective, the message that's **received** should be the **same** as the message that was **sent**.

2) Good communication is **clear** and **unambiguous**. If a manager arranges a conference in Perth, Scotland, but half the people who are supposed to be there end up in Perth, Australia, communication has obviously failed.

3) Effective communication is a **two-way thing**. Managers have to tell employees what they want them to know, and they also need to listen to what their employees have to say to them.

I'll put the four candles in the post to you straight away.

There are several Categories of Communication

1) **Formal communications** are **officially endorsed** by the business. They include corporate notice boards, company newsletters, letters from managers or the HR department.

2) **Informal communications** are unofficial, e.g. gossip, emails between employees and leaked information.

3) **Vertical communication** travels **up** and **down** the hierarchy. **Authoritarian** corporate cultures often only have downward communication — but a mixture of upward and downward communication is best. **Downward** communication is used to give employees **instructions** and to **inform** them about goals and objectives. **Upward** communication is used by employees to give feedback, suggest ideas and ask for help.

4) **Horizontal (lateral)** communication occurs between staff on the **same level** within the hierarchy. Horizontal communication can be used to discuss issues and offer suggestions.

5) **Internal communication** remains within the organisation, e.g. office notice board, internal email.

6) **External communication** (e.g. websites) is aimed at **external stakeholders** like customers and suppliers.

Different Methods of Communication are suitable for different Purposes

Communication can be **verbal** (e.g. meetings), **written** (e.g. letters and emails) or **visual** (e.g. graphs and images).

1) Face-to-face **verbal communication** is the most **personal** form of communication.

2) The main **disadvantage** of verbal communication is that there's **no record** of what's been said, and different people might remember meetings or conversations differently.

3) Verbal communication is often used in **meetings** between managers and employees, especially to discuss issues that employees might have **questions** about or want to give their **opinion** on.

1) The main benefits of **written communication** are that there's a **permanent record** of it, and it can reach **lots of people** — companies can send out emails to all their employees or customers at once.

2) However, the sender doesn't know if the message has been **understood**, and they can't get instant **feedback**.

3) Written communication is also used when it's not **practical** to speak to someone in person, e.g. companies respond to customer complaints by letter or email rather than phoning or visiting them.

1) **Visual communication** can be used in **addition** to other forms of communication to make information easier to understand, e.g. companies might use graphs to show sales figures.

2) Company logos and visual adverts communicate a particular **image** of the business to the public.

Communication

Organisations face **Barriers** that **Threaten Communication**

There are seven main barriers that can prevent communication from being effective:

1) **Attitudes** — For example, the receiver may be **distracted**. The receiver may **dislike** the sender, or feel **threatened** by the communication.

2) **Intermediaries** — The **longer** the chain of communication, the more **mangled** the message can get between sender and receiver (a bit like Chinese whispers).

3) **Language barriers** — One word can mean **different things** in different cultures. Translation can **distort** meaning. **Jargon** can be confusing.

4) **No sense of purpose** — Staff who **don't understand why** they're being told something may start ignoring future messages.

Betty soon began to regret telling her boss she was fluent in Japanese.

5) **Communication overload** — If employees are **swamped** with communication, they won't be able to deal with it all. This can be a problem with emails in particular.

6) **Remoteness** — It's easy to **misinterpret** the tone of emails because of the **distance** between the sender and the receiver. In phone and face-to-face conversations, the speaker's **voice** gives you clues about how things are meant, but in emails the receiver has to guess the sender's "**tone of voice**", and it's easy to imagine that emails are meant to be rude or sarcastic when they're actually not.

7) **Group behaviour** — The way that employees behave in groups can also be **detrimental** to communication, e.g. some employees might be overbearing, making others too **afraid** to speak up in meetings, etc. There's more on group behaviour on p. 81.

Organisations can **Overcome** the **Barriers** to **Communication**

If businesses recognise the barriers to communication, they can take steps to overcome them:

1) Businesses can **encourage** face-to-face and telephone conversations, and **limit** email use, to avoid misunderstandings.

2) Managers can have **individual** meetings with employees or allow staff to give feedback **anonymously**, so that all employees can have their opinions heard.

3) Businesses can employ professional **translators** for foreign communication, so that messages get across properly.

> **Example — Phones 4U**
>
> 1) In 2003, bosses at Phones 4U estimated that **3 hours a day** were being spent on email.
>
> 2) The company **banned email** for internal communication. Head office communicated to managers and staff via the corporate **intranet**. Employees were encouraged to use the **phone** or have face-to-face **meetings**.
>
> 3) The company found that this made communication within the business much more **efficient** — there were **fewer misunderstandings**, and the volume of unnecessary information being passed around was **reduced**.

Practice Questions

Q1 What is the difference between horizontal communication and vertical communication?

Q2 Give two examples of external communication.

Q3 How can businesses avoid communication overload?

Exam Questions

Q1 Give examples of when verbal, written and visual communication are used in business, and explain the advantages and disadvantages of each method of communication. [10 marks]

Q2 Discuss the barriers to communication that businesses face. [4 marks]

Emails aren't usually meant to be rude or sarcastic...

Good communication is incredibly important in business. Managers and staff have to communicate with each other to get the job done properly. There's also communication between the business and its customers and suppliers to think about. You'll need to be able to put these facts and ideas into context if you get a question on communication in the exam.

Employer/Employee Relations

*Good employer/employee relations are plain good business sense. These pages are for the **OCR: People in Organisations option** and **Strategic Management unit**, and page 80 might be handy if you're doing **AQA** too.*

Employers and Employees need to Cooperate with each other

1) Employers and employees **need each other**.

2) **Employers** need **hard-working staff** to contribute to the production of a good or service that can be sold for a profit.

3) **Employees** need a **secure income** to support themselves and their families.

4) However, there can be **conflict** between them.

5) For example, employers would prefer to pay **lower wages** to keep **costs** down.

6) Employees want **higher wages** to improve their **standard of living**.

Nigel and Tony needed each other more than they could ever say...

The two sides must **negotiate** to reach an **acceptable compromise** on wage rates, working conditions and terms of employment. **Failure** to reach agreement could lead to a **production stoppage**, and **both parties would suffer**.

> A **successful** employer/employee relationship **maximises** the **cooperation** and **minimises** the potential for **conflict** between these two groups.

Each Employee has an Individual Relationship with their Employer

1) All employees of a company are treated as **individuals** for some purposes, such as employee appraisals. When **individual employees** negotiate with their employer about their own **working conditions**, it's known as **individual bargaining**.

2) **Individual bargaining** for **pay** means that employers can decide to pay an employee what they think he or she is **worth** to the firm. It might be **more** or **less** than other employees in the same role. This provides a financial **incentive** to the employee to work productively.

3) **Individual bargaining** is also used for things like **flexible working arrangements** — they're often based on the employee's **personal circumstances**, e.g. if an employee cares for young children or an elderly parent, the employer might allow that employee to work from home or work flexi-time.

Groups of employees have a Collective Relationship with their Employer

1) In some cases, **individuals** don't negotiate their own working arrangements or pay with their employer.

2) Negotiation is often done **collectively** by a **trade union** or **professional association**, representing a group of employees and negotiating pay and working conditions **on their behalf**. The union **bargains** for them all with their employer. This is called **collective bargaining**.

3) The result of collective bargaining for pay is a **common pay structure**, which is often called the **"going rate"** for the job. The employer can't pay anyone less than this going rate without causing trouble.

4) Employees and unions usually prefer **collective bargaining**, because it strengthens their position at the bargaining table and prevents **"divide and rule"** tactics by employers.

Collective bargaining does create some **problems**, though...

1) Having a single wage rate makes it **difficult** to **reward** variations in work **effort** between staff doing jobs with a similar rate of pay. This may **reduce** the levels of **motivation** if good staff are not recognised and rewarded.

2) In some large companies, the collectively bargained rate of pay covers employees working in **different locations** across the country. This one-wage-for-all approach doesn't recognise differences between different parts of the country — e.g. cost of living, house prices, level of unemployment, or even the wages paid by other local employers. A **variation** in wage rates to take account of these factors might be more appropriate.

Collective bargaining isn't just used for discussing pay. Employees also negotiate collectively with employers in order to come to agreements about other **working conditions**, e.g. pension contributions from employers, holiday allowance, etc.

Groups

Groups at work can be Formal or Informal

1) A **group** is made up of two or more people with a **shared purpose**.

2) **Different members** of the group will have slightly different **roles**, e.g. one person's role might be to come up with new ideas, and another's might be to lead and manage the group.

3) A **formal group** is a set of individuals brought together by a **manager** to do a specific **task** with specific **roles**.

4) **Informal groups** develop **naturally** — they can form when people work closely in formal groups. The **objectives** of informal groups and the **roles** of their members also develop naturally.

5) **Informal groups** can also be **groups of friends** within a business. People might find that they have a **common interest** with other employees in the business (e.g. a group of employees might support the same football team, or like the same kind of films).

Group Norms are the Accepted Behaviour in a group

1) When a group works together over a period of time, the members of the group begin to **expect** certain **behaviour** from each other — **group norms** are established.

2) Individuals begin to **understand** how they should **interact** with each other, how they should approach the **task** and how they can best deal with **differences** they have. E.g. one member of the group might be seen as the expert on a particular subject, so other members of the group might go to that person if they need help with it.

3) If someone in the group **doesn't follow** the group norms and fit in with the way the group normally does things, they're at risk of being **ostracised** by the rest of the group. E.g. the norm in a group at a teapot factory might be to make **30 teapots** a day. If one member of the group starts making **40 teapots** a day, other members of the group are likely to be **annoyed**, and the more efficient employee might be **excluded** from the group until they start fitting in with the group norm.

Karen knew her outfit went against the group norms at the bank, but she didn't care.

Group Norms can Help or Hinder Communication

1) Communication can become **more effective** between members of the group as they begin to understand and know each other better. They might feel more **comfortable** sharing their ideas.

2) If there is a **dominant** member in the group, other members of the group who are quiet or shy might feel too **intimidated** to say what they think.

3) **Informal roles** within a group can also **prevent** proper communication from happening. E.g. if one member of the group is seen as the "ideas" person, this might prevent others from sharing ideas they might have come up with, because they don't see it as their role. Or if they do share their ideas, the other members of the group might not be open to listening to them.

4) **Friendships** within a group can cause **communication problems** if some members of the group feel **left out**. E.g. if there are five employees in a formal group and three of them are friends outside work, the other two might feel like they won't be listened to because the three friends will decide everything between themselves.

Practice Questions

Q1 When might individual bargaining be used?

Q2 List two problems with collective bargaining.

Q3 What's the difference between a formal group and an informal group?

Exam Question

Q1 Explain what group norms are and how they affect communication within a group. [6 marks]

Formal groups — bands that dress smartly...

There's nothing startlingly new on these pages, but that doesn't mean you can skip over them. Learn why employers and employees need each other, and when businesses might use individual and collective bargaining. The stuff on groups doesn't just apply to businesses — groups of friends, sports teams and Business Studies classes all have their own norms.

Trade Unions

Some employers see trade unions as a pain in the bum, but they can come in handy when employers and employees don't quite see eye to eye. These pages are for AQA, the OCR: Strategic Management option and WJEC.

Trade Unions Negotiate with Employers on behalf of Employees

1) Trade unions act on behalf of **groups of employees** in the workforce when negotiating rates of **pay** and **working conditions** etc. with the employer.

2) By joining with others and belonging to a union an employee **strengthens** his or her **bargaining power** in a way that wouldn't be possible if he/she tried to bargain as an **individual** with the employer (see p. 80).

3) Trade unions allow employers and workers to **communicate** with each other.

4) Trade unions also give **advice** and **assistance** to **individual** employees who are having problems with their employer.

Trade unions take action in the workplace

1) Trade unions **negotiate** with employers on behalf of their members to secure fair rates of pay and/or productivity bonuses for their work.

2) Trade unions help negotiate reasonable hours of **work**, and **paid holiday** entitlement.

3) Trade unions seek to secure **safe** and civilized **working conditions**.

4) Trade unions help their members get **job security** with protection against **mistreatment**, **discrimination** and **unfair dismissal**.

Trade unions take action at a national level

1) Trade unions **put pressure on the government** to bring in legislation that serves trade union members' interests.

2) The **minimum wage** was introduced in **1998** by the government after discussions with trade unions.

3) Trade unions pushed the government to make **redundancy payments** compulsory.

4) Following demands from trade unions, the **Pension Protection Fund** was set up in April 2005 to protect the pensions of employees in private company pension schemes if their employer **goes bust**.

Trade unions take action in party politics

1) Many unions donate money to the **Labour Party** because they think its policies represent their interests.

2) In the 1970s and 80s, unions had a lot of **power** in the Labour Party. Since the **90s** they've had **less power**.

Trade Unions can influence decisions about changing Working Practices

1) When employers want to make **changes** to the **working practices** of the business (e.g. if the employer wants to reduce employees' contracted hours, or change the way it pays staff from an hourly wage to a piece rate, or vice versa), trade unions can help staff if they want to **resist** the change, e.g. by organising strikes.

2) Trade unions can also **facilitate change** by **liaising** between employers and union members, and communicating the **benefits** of the change to their members.

3) **Employees** are more likely to be **open** to change if union representatives are involved in decisions, because they **trust** trade unions to protect their interests, but may **not** trust their employers to do the same.

Trade Unions can influence decisions about changing Employment Levels

1) Trade unions stand up for employees' rights if employers want to make **redundancies**. They can negotiate with employers to persuade them to make **fewer** employees redundant, or negotiate better **redundancy payouts** for employees who are made redundant.

2) If employers are planning changes to the workforce that might **adversely affect** the current workforce, trade unions try to **prevent** these changes from taking place. E.g. if employers want to take on **cheaper** staff (e.g. foreign workers), current employees' wages could be **driven down**, or **overtime** hours might be offered to the new, cheaper workers instead of the current staff. A trade union would try to **stop** the recruitment of cheaper workers from going ahead.

3) If staffing levels are **too low** and current staff are **overworked**, trade unions can try to convince employers to take on **more staff**.

Trade Unions

There are **Different Types** of **Trade Unions**

The trade union that employees belong to can depend on what type of **job** they do, or what **industry** they work in:

Craft unions	Members of craft unions share a **common skill** but often work in **different locations**. Most of them started out as a traditional guild of craftsmen. Examples: Equity (the actors' union), the Writers' Guild of Great Britain, the PFA (Professional Footballers' Association).
Industrial unions	Members all work in the **same industry** but do a **wide range of jobs**. Their bargaining power is strong because strike action could bring production to a stop. Examples: RMT (the transport workers' union), NUM (National Union of Mineworkers).
General unions	Members range across **many different industries** in **many different occupations**. General unions tend to have a very **large number** of members. Example: Unite — a merger between TGWU (Transport & General Workers Union) and Amicus.
White-collar unions	Members work in **administration** or **non-manual occupations**. The number of **members** of this type of union is **increasing**, because more and more people are working in **white-collar jobs**. Examples: NUT (National Union of Teachers) and NUJ (National Union of Journalists).

Trade unions are particularly strong in the **public sector** (e.g. teaching and nursing) and **transport and communication** (e.g. railways and ports). There's also strong union membership in **utilities** (e.g. gas and electricity).

Cooperation with **Trade Unions** helps businesses achieve their **Objectives**

1) **Cooperation** between employers and trade unions can be **beneficial** for businesses as well as their employees.

2) Employers and union reps can **share ideas** for the benefit of everyone in the firm. If the business is profitable, it's good news for both the employers and the employees, so it's in the **interests** of the trade union to help the business achieve its objectives.

3) Trade union representatives have a lot of **knowledge** and **experience** about issues such as **employment law**, **health and safety**, **training**, etc. This knowledge can be helpful to employers, especially during periods of **change** such as a merger or if a firm is making redundancies.

Laura wasn't sure about the new uniform at first, but her union rep convinced her it was a great idea.

Practice Questions

Q1 What do trade unions do for their members?

Q2 Give two examples of ways that trade unions have influenced government policy.

Q3 How can unions influence employment levels in a company?

Q4 What's the difference between a craft union and an industrial union?

Q5 What type of workers belong to white-collar unions?

Exam Question

Q1 Snapdragon Fashion Ltd. is a medium-sized clothes retailer employing 600 people in 10 stores spread across the country. Discuss the potential advantages and disadvantages to the employer of their staff being trade union members.

[6 marks]

Detergent company employees belong to bright white-collar unions...

There's a fair old bit of detail on trade unions here. And this isn't even the last you'll hear of trade unions — there's even more over the page. Hurray. In the exam you could get asked about the pros and cons of joining a union, and what unions do for workers. You might have to comment on the ways that trade unions can help or hinder employers' plans too.

Resolution of Industrial Disputes

Industrial disputes can get pretty ugly, so businesses try to resolve them as quickly as possible.
*These pages are for **AQA**, the **OCR: Strategic Management option** and **WJEC**.*

Industrial Disputes happen when Employers and Employees Can't Agree

1) Many industrial conflicts appear on the surface to be a dispute over **wages** and **working conditions**. However, there may be **other grievances** caused by various human factors:

   • **Frustration** and **alienation** caused by **lack of communication** from managers, or frequent **changes** in work practices.
   • **Stress** and **insecurity** caused by changing work patterns and **fears of redundancy**.

2) It can be **difficult** to **express** these kinds of feelings **clearly** in an argument — so it's often **easier** to turn the dispute into one about the more **usual workplace issues**.

3) Managers who **communicate effectively** and organise their staff's work responsibilities **consistently** will have a more **motivated workforce**, who'll be less likely to start a dispute.

Industrial Action — Work to Rule, Overtime Bans and Strikes

If the trade union fails to reach an agreement with the employer through negotiation, then they can apply more pressure by taking **industrial action** to reduce production. There are various tactics used, which gradually increase pressure.

1) **Work to rule** — employees stick 100% to the terms of their **contract**. They only do the tasks that their contract **specifically** requires them to do. This usually **slows production**.

2) **Go slow** — employees simply work more **slowly**.

3) A **ban on overtime** — exactly what it says. Employees don't work **overtime** when they're **asked** to. They don't come in early or work late or work at weekends.

4) **Strike** — employees withdraw their labour and **don't go to work**. This might be a **one-day strike** to **warn** the employer that they're serious about the issue, or a more **prolonged** strike.

Collective Employment Law Controls what Unions can do

1) Unions can represent their members in discussions with the employer and ultimately call them out on strike, but this has to be done **within the law**.

2) During the **1980s** and **1990s**, the government passed a series of **laws** to control the way that **industrial relations** (negotiations between union and employer) were conducted.

3) At the time the government thought trade unions had **too much bargaining strength** in industrial relations. This pushed up **wage rates**, which in turn pushed up production costs and **prices**. This **wage and price inflation** made British goods **less competitive** in the global market.

4) "**Voluntarism**" was also common at the time — this is where an employer and the trade union(s) representing the employees at a particular workplace came up with an agreement that only applied to that particular union and/or workplace (e.g. not to strike, or to inform the employer a few days before a strike). Voluntary agreements have now been **replaced** by the **collective labour laws** brought in by the government.

5) The changes in the law **reduced** the **bargaining power** of unions. They're summarised below.

Employment Act 1980	Firms could **refuse to recognise** a union. Picketing was restricted to workers' **own place of work**.
Employment Act 1982	Trade unions could be sued. **Union-only clauses** were **banned**.
Trade Union Act 1984	Unions had to have a **secret ballot** before striking.
Employment Act 1988	Unions **couldn't punish** members who didn't strike.
Employment Act 1990	Employers could **sack** workers who went on **unofficial strike**. **Closed shop agreements** were **ended** — no one could be refused a job because they weren't in the right union.
Trade Union Reform and Employment Rights Act 1993	Unions had give employers 7 **days' notice** of strike action. Secret ballots had to be done by **post**.

Resolution of Industrial Disputes

Industrial disputes have to be **Resolved Eventually**

A **slow-down** or **stoppage** of production means less output, sales and profit for the employer. It also means **lower earnings** for the employee. Because **both parties** are suffering, they need to reach an agreement quickly.

As well as the employer and employee, **other stakeholders** suffer from lost production.

1) Local businesses suffer from the **reduced spending** of those employees.

2) **Customers** can't get the goods or services they want.

3) Other firms may rely on this firm for their raw materials or components.

4) The **firm's suppliers** suffer, especially if the firm is an important customer.

"Look, we'll have to sort it out eventually — so if you want to keep this tooth here, admit that I'm right..."

Employers and **Unions** often use **Other Organisations** to act as a **Mediator**

If the employer and union can't reach an agreement that **satisfies them both**, they might call on **another organisation** to act as **mediator** and / or **jury** to help resolve the dispute.

Industrial tribunal

This usually meets to deal with claims of **unfair dismissal** or **discrimination**. If it decides **against the employer** it may make them pay **compensation** to the employee. See p. 89 for more on industrial tribunals.

ACAS — the Advisory, Conciliation and Arbitration Service

The Advisory, Conciliation and Arbitration Service does exactly what the name says.

1) **Conciliation** — ACAS **meets both parties** in the dispute, usually separately, and tries to develop **common ground** that they can both eventually accept.

2) **Arbitration** — It can appoint an **independent arbitrator** who considers the claims and says what the outcome should be. If both sides agree, this outcome can be **legally binding**. There are two types of arbitration:

- **Compromise arbitration** is a result which lies somewhere between what the employer wants and what the employee wants. It sounds good, but the downside is that it may encourage the **union** and **employer** to adopt **extreme** first demands in order to **bias** the eventual compromise towards their position.

- **Pendulum arbitration** makes a simple choice between the competing claims — there's no compromise, and **no middle ground**. This encourages parties to adopt a more **reasonable** position to try to get the arbitrator to pick their side.

Practice Questions

Q1 Explain why disputes may not always be about pay and conditions.

Q2 List and describe the different kinds of industrial action a union might take in a dispute with an employer.

Q3 List five laws regarding trade unions that have been brought in since the 1980s, and explain how they've affected the power that trade unions have.

Q4 Explain the roles performed by ACAS in industrial disputes.

Exam Questions

Q1 "Trade union members will lose more than they gain when they enter into a dispute with an employer." Evaluate this claim.
[8 marks]

Q2 Consider a recent industrial dispute and analyse it in terms of the following: its causes, the tactics used by the union and the final settlement.
[8 marks]

I hear they've gone on strike again at the match factory...

Industrial disputes aren't much fun for anyone involved in them. It's not in the employees' best interests to be on strike for a long time — they lose pay, and damage their job prospects by damaging the industry. It's best to get things sorted ASAP. What you need to know is how disputes affect businesses and how they get resolved — through tribunals, ACAS, etc.

Employee Participation

*Obviously all businesses like their employees to participate in doing some work, but sometimes they let them get a bit more involved than that. These pages are for **AQA**, the **OCR: People in Organisations option** and **WJEC**.*

Employee Participation involves employees in Decision-Making

1) Businesses can **involve** employees in decision-making through either **consultation** or **participation**.

2) **Consultation** is when managers and employers ask employees for their **opinions** on how things should be done. It means that their input **will** be taken into account when managers make decisions, but they **won't necessarily** have any effect on the final **decision**.

3) **Employee participation** (also called **industrial democracy**) is when employees are given **responsibility** and **power** to make business decisions for themselves. Managers can **delegate** tasks to employees and give them the **freedom** to decide how to carry them out.

4) Employee participation **empowers** employees because it gives them **control** over their own working lives — they can use their initiative and creativity. Consultation **doesn't** empower employees because there's **no guarantee** that their suggestions will be acted on.

5) The work of mid 20th century **management theorists** such as Mayo, Maslow and Herzberg (see p.74) showed that **participation** could **motivate** workers. Before the 1950s, managers didn't involve employees in decision-making. They believed that it was the boss's job to make decisions, and the workers' job to follow them. Some employers are still against the idea of giving employees more responsibility because they worry that employees might make decisions that will **harm** the business.

There are different Forms of Employee Participation

Ways businesses can **introduce participation** include:

Works councils (or employee associations) discuss work issues

1) Works councils are committees made up of employee representatives and employer representatives. Employee representatives are usually **elected**.

2) They **meet regularly** to discuss **general work issues** e.g. training, new technology and methods of work.

3) The sharing of ideas and information in a relatively **relaxed** atmosphere does a lot to improve **cooperation** between workers and management.

4) Where there's **no trade union presence**, works councils take care of **collective bargaining** (see p. 80).

5) **Quality circles** are like works councils, but they only discuss **quality** issues. They meet regularly to discuss ways of improving quality. Quality circles include employees from **all levels** of the business.

6) In 1994, the EU brought in **European Works Councils** for employees of businesses based in more than one European country.

Employee shareholders have more of a stake in the business

1) Employees can buy **shares** in the business. This gives them a higher **stake** in the business, and promises financial rewards in the form of **dividends** if the business performs well.

2) Shareholders can vote at the Annual General Meeting (AGM).

3) In practice, this is actually more of a **financial motivator** than an instance of industrial democracy. There aren't usually enough employee shareholders to have any real influence at the AGM.

Autonomous (independent) work groups give employees more control

1) Managers may **delegate** responsibility and give a team more **freedom** to **plan** and carry out their own work. This improves motivation.

2) Autonomous work groups may also be able to suggest **improvements** in **working practice**.

3) Some autonomous work groups elect a **leader**, and **appoint new staff**.

4) For this to work out, the **type** of work they're doing must be **suitable**, the group must **work well together** as a team, and they must have a good **blend** of skills.

5) Even then, it doesn't always work perfectly — some individuals may not want the **hassle** of deciding their own work plans.

Employee Participation

Employers can **Encourage Participation** and **Involvement**

Employees will participate **enthusiastically** in workplace discussion and decision-making under certain conditions:

- If they feel **valued**.
- If they feel their views are **listened to** and **taken into account** in the final decision.
- If they are treated **courteously**.

Firms can organise themselves in a way that **encourages** employees to feel respected and involved.

Involving **Employees** in **Decision-Making** has **Advantages** and **Disadvantages**

Advantages of employee participation

1) Employee participation makes employees feel that they **matter** to the employer, so they are more **loyal** to the company and less likely to leave. This reduces **staff turnover** (see p. 98), which is good news for businesses.

2) Individual employees are more **highly motivated** to do their jobs well, which is likely to increase productivity.

3) Employees might have good suggestions for improving **efficiency** and **quality**.

OK, so let's decide the birdseed budget now.

What about the vote on annual migration policy?

Disadvantages of employee participation

1) It takes employees away from **immediate production** and it can be **time consuming**.

2) If it **doesn't** produce the result that employees are looking for, it may worsen their attitude to the company.

3) **Arguments** among employees, or between bosses and staff, can cause grudges and worsen industrial relations.

4) Some employees react **negatively** to being invited to participate as they consider it an **intrusion** on their time.

5) Employee participation may mean that decisions are taken by people who aren't **experts** on the subject.

6) Employee representatives on works councils etc. might be **intimidated** by having meetings with the employers, or might only be interested in **pleasing** the employers in order to get **promoted** in the future. This means that they might just **agree** with whatever the bosses say, and not really stick up for the **employees' interests** at all.

Employers need to find a **Balance** between **Empowerment** and **Control**

1) Allowing employee participation is one way of **empowering** employees — giving them **control** over their own work and allowing them to make their own **decisions**. It's good for businesses because it **motivates** staff.

2) Employers have to be careful not to empower employees **too much** though — bosses need to keep some **control** over what's going on. Otherwise, employees could make **bad decisions** that could be **catastrophic** for the business. E.g. if bank traders are given complete control over the trades they do, they could make risky decisions and end up making huge losses for the bank.

Practice Questions

Q1 What's the difference between consultation and participation?

Q2 What do works councils do?

Q3 List four disadvantages of employee participation.

Exam Question

Q1 The owner of a chain of eight restaurants claims he has no need for employee participation schemes. He says: "I am quite capable of making his own decisions, and my staff are happy to get on with their jobs and do what they are told." Write a report relevant to his situation, outlining the benefits that greater employee participation might bring, and explaining how he might go about introducing it into his business. [12 marks]

Most employees enjoy participating — but mainly in staff parties...

"Employee participation" is a bit of a weird name, but all it means is getting employees to join in with the decision making process. The key points to learn are all on these two pages, and they're pretty much exactly the same for all three exam boards — you have to know how employee participation is done, why it's good, and what problems can arise with it.

Employment Law

*Ok, time for employment law. If you've ever fancied yourself as a bit of an Ally McBeal, you've come to the right page. These pages are for **AQA**, the **OCR: People in Organisations option** and **WJEC**.*

Individual Labour Law controls what rights Employees have

1) An employee has a legal right to **fair treatment** while at work, and also while looking for employment.

2) These anti-discrimination laws **prevent** employers from **acting unfairly**, and ensure fair treatment for individuals:

Equal Pay Act (1970)	A man and woman doing the **same** or an **equivalent** job should receive the **same rate of pay**. Followed up by EU Equal Pay Directive in 1975.
Sex Discrimination Act (1975)	A person cannot be discriminated against on grounds of **gender** or **marital status** for recruitment, promotion, training or dismissal.
Race Relations Act (1976)	A person cannot be discriminated against on grounds of **colour**, **race**, **national origin**, or **ethnic origin**.
Disability Discrimination Act (1995)	The employer must make efforts to ensure that **disabled people** can be employed in that place of work (e.g installing wheelchair ramps).
The Equality Act (2006)	A person cannot be discriminated against on the grounds of their **religious** or **philosophical beliefs**, or **lack** of beliefs.

3) Anyone feeling **discriminated against** on the basis of sex, race, religion or disability can go to an **industrial tribunal** (see next page) to seek **compensation**. The tribunal listens to the arguments and makes a judgement.

The Data Protection Act gives Employees rights to Privacy

1) Businesses hold **data** about their employees and customers on **computer** and filed away on **paper** — this includes things like their date of birth, address, and bank account details. Employees wouldn't want this information getting into the wrong hands.

2) The **Data Protection Act (1998)** prevents the misuse of personal data. It says that:

Angie and Steve had been given new identities under the Date Protection Act.

- businesses **can't** obtain data **unfairly** or **illegally**.
- businesses can only use the information for the purposes it was collected for, and they **can't** use it for anything **illegal**.
- businesses **can't keep hold** of data they **don't need**.
- the data has to be **accurate** and **up-to-date**.
- businesses have to **allow people** to **see** the data that they hold about them.
- people have the right to **correct** data that's held about them if it's incorrect.
- businesses have to take measures to make sure that the data **isn't used**, **changed** or **stolen** by **unauthorised** people, or **lost** or **destroyed**.

Discrimination Laws affect All Aspects of businesses

Recruitment:

1) Employers aren't allowed to **state** in job adverts that candidates have to be a particular age, race, gender, etc. They can't use **discriminatory language**, e.g. advertising for a "waitress" excludes men.

2) Businesses are only allowed to advertise for someone of a specific age, gender, etc if it's a **genuine requirement** of the job — e.g. a female toilet attendant for ladies' toilets.

3) Businesses have to make **decisions** about who to employ without discriminating — they can't just bin all applications from women. Businesses have to be able to **justify** why they give a job to a particular candidate, in case an unsuccessful candidate takes them to a tribunal.

4) The same rules apply for **promoting** staff — employers can't make decisions based on race, religion, etc.

Pay:

1) Businesses have to give male and female employees the **same pay** for work of **equal value**.

2) Women are entitled to the same **benefits** as men too (e.g. company car).

3) If a business pays a woman less than a man, they have to be able to prove that the work the woman does is **less valuable** for the business.

Redundancies:

If businesses need to make redundancies, they **can't** deliberately select staff who are disabled, who've taken maternity leave, etc.

Employment Law

An *Employment Contract* sets out the *Conditions* of *Employment*

1) Employees are entitled to receive a **written contract** of employment within **two months** of starting work.

2) A contract of employment is a **legally-binding** agreement between the employer and the employee about what the **duties** and **rights** of the employee and the employer are. It sets out the duties of the employee (e.g. what hours they're expected to work), and what the employee can expect from the employer (e.g. what the salary is).

3) There are some **responsibilities** that are **common** to all employers and employees:

Employers' responsibilities towards employees

- Employees have the right to a **safe** working environment. The **Health and Safety at Work Act (1974)** states that the employer must ensure the working environment is **safe** (e.g. electrical equipment, moving machinery, etc must be safe). Under the **Control of Substances Hazardous to Health Regulations 2002** (COSHH), businesses also have to protect employees from the risks of any **hazardous substances**.

- In April 2009, the **European Working Time Directive** gave full-time workers the right to **28 days** of **paid holidays** per year, including bank holidays. There's also a maximum working week of **48 hours** — although in the UK an employee can **opt out** of this and work longer hours if they want to.

- Employees have the right to be **paid** at least the **national minimum wage** (see p. 96).

- Employees have the right to **paid maternity** and **paternity** leave. **Mums** get 39 weeks of paid leave (not on full pay), and can take 13 more weeks unpaid. **Dads** get up to two weeks of paid paternity leave.

Employees' responsibilities towards employers

- Employees have to **attend work** when they're supposed to, and be **on time**.
- They must be willing to carry out any **reasonable task** that's asked of them.

Employers have *Procedures* to deal with *Dismissal* and *Grievances*

OCR

1) If there's a **problem** with an employee's **conduct** (e.g. they are rude to customers), the employer can give the employee a **verbal warning**. If the warning has no effect, it's followed by three **written warnings**, after which the employee can be **dismissed**. If the employee's behaviour is **seriously bad** (e.g. being drunk at work), this is **gross misconduct** and employers can sack them without going through the normal warnings process.

2) If an employee's **performance** at work isn't up to standard, they've got to be given the chance to **improve**. If they don't improve, their employer can go through the series of warnings and eventually sack them.

3) If an employee has a **complaint** about the business, they can report their grievance to their manager, who will try to resolve it. If the issue doesn't get resolved, the employee might make a claim to an **employment tribunal**.

Employment Tribunals can settle *Disputes*

OCR

1) If employees feel that they've been treated **unfairly** by their employers (e.g. if they've suffered discrimination, been paid less than minimum wage, etc), they can make a claim to a tribunal.

See p. 84 for more on industrial disputes.

2) At a tribunal, representatives of the employer and the employee put forward their cases, and an **experienced lawyer** (sometimes a panel) decides who's in the right.

3) If the employer loses the tribunal case, they're usually ordered to pay the employee **compensation**. If it's an unfair dismissal case, they might have to give the employee their job back too.

Practice Questions

Q1 What's the purpose of the Data Protection Act?

Q2 How does the Health and Safety at Work Act protect employees?

Q3 How can employment tribunals settle disputes between employers and employees?

Exam Question

Q1 Discuss the role of anti-discrimination laws in the workplace. [15 marks]

Can tribunals settle disputes about whose turn it is to make the tea...

There's an awful lot of law to learn on these pages. Don't be too downhearted though, because it's possible to learn it all — just break it down into manageable bits and you'll be fine. This is all handy stuff to know anyway for when you get a job — if you know your rights then you can stand up to any unscrupulous employers who try to fiddle you. That'll teach 'em.

Human Resource Management (HRM)

*These pages are all about managing "human resources" — otherwise known as people. This page is for **AQA**, the **OCR: People in Organisations** option and **WJEC**. Page 91 is just for **AQA** and the **OCR People in Organisations** option.*

Human Resource Management is about Managing People

The role of Human Resource Management (HRM) is to ensure that a business achieves the **maximum benefit** from its employees at the **minimum cost**. They achieve this by:

1) Anticipating the **size** of the workforce — if the organisation is expanding they'll need more workers in the future, if it's contracting they won't need as many.

2) Deciding what **skill-level** the workforce should have, and whether staff should be employed **full-** or **part-time**.

3) Deciding **where** employees are needed if a business has several sites or branches, and **which departments** within a business require specific staff.

HRM should ensure a workforce is used appropriately, to **maximise productivity** and **minimise labour costs**:

- **too many staff** means that the business pays a **bigger wage bill** than it needs to, which **reduces profits**.
- **not enough staff** with the right skill level results in a **fall** in **productivity**, leading to a **fall in profits**.
- getting staffing levels **wrong demotivates employees** — if there are **too many** staff, employees will get **bored**, and a **shortage** of staff will result in employees feeling **stressed** and under pressure.

HRM is also responsible for maintaining **good relationships** between **employers** and **employees**.

HRM helps businesses Achieve their Objectives

There are **three** main ways that HRM helps businesses with their objectives to **increase labour effectiveness**.

See p. 98-99 for how to calculate labour effectiveness.

Reducing the rate of labour turnover

1) **Labour turnover** is the rate at which employees **leave** the company and have to be **replaced**.

2) Businesses try to keep their labour turnover rate **low**, because recruiting and training new staff is **expensive**.

3) HRM **reduces** the labour turnover rate by:
- improving the company's procedures for **recruiting** and **selecting** new staff — employing the **right person** for the right job means that they're more likely to **stay** in the job.
- improving the **relationship** between **employees** and **management** — if employees feel **valued**, they're more likely to be **loyal** to the business.

Reducing absenteeism

1) **Absenteeism** is when staff are **off work** due to **illness** or **other reasons**, including **stress** and lack of motivation.

2) HRM can combat a high absentee rate by **improving working conditions**, **improving** the **relationships** between managers and staff, and **discussing** the issue with employees who are off work frequently.

Reducing accident rates

1) **Accidents** can stop production and cause low staff morale. The business may have to pay **compensation** too.

2) The HRM department is responsible for making sure that the workplace is **safe**. They carry out regular **health and safety** checks, and make sure that **changes** are made if they are needed.

HRM has replaced the Personnel Department

1) **HRM** used to be known as the **personnel department**. Personnel had **four** tasks:
- to **recruit** staff.
- to **train** staff for a specific job.
- to oversee the **welfare** of staff.
- to manage the **termination process** (voluntary or involuntary).

2) HRM has a much **broader** role than personnel. It contributes to achieving the company's **aims** and **objectives**.

3) HRM sees employees as having **potential** and **flexibility** — ready to move positions if an opportunity arises.

4) HRM assumes that all **managers** should be monitoring their employees' **welfare**.

5) The aim of HRM is to encourage **all workers** at **all levels** to share the **same vision** and **aims**.

Human Resource Management (HRM)

HRM can be Hard or Soft

There are **two schools of thought** in human resource management — **hard HRM** and **soft HRM**.

Hard HRM	Soft HRM
1) Employees are seen as a **resource** like any other.	1) Employees are the **most important** resource.
2) Employees are hired on a **short-term basis**.	2) Employees are managed on a **long-term basis**.
3) Managers believe that employees are mainly motivated by **money**.	3) Managers motivate employees through **empowerment** and **development**.
4) Managers tend to be **Theory X** managers.	4) Managers tend to be **Theory Y** managers.
5) Appraisals are **judgemental**.	5) Appraisals are **developmental**.
6) Training is only done to meet **production** needs.	6) Training is done to meet **development** needs.

1) **Hard HRM** can be **good** for businesses because managers keep **control** of the workforce, so it's less likely that **mistakes** will be made. Since employees are seen as just another resource, it's easy for the business to **replace** them if they leave. The problems with hard HRM are that the business **doesn't** use its employees to their **full potential**, so it could be **missing out** on opportunities to increase its **profits**.

2) **Soft HRM** is likely to increase **staff morale** because employees will feel **valued**. This will make it easier to **retain** staff, and the business will also benefit from the **skills** and **experience** of its staff. Soft HRM **isn't** always **appropriate** though — employees might not be interested in **development** or **empowerment**, and soft HRM usually involves more **costs** for businesses because it encourages **investment** in employees.

Internal and External Factors influence HRM Objectives

1) The **culture** within the business influences **HRM objectives**. E.g. some businesses, like fast food restaurants, might not be worried about having a high labour turnover, so they wouldn't want HRM to spend time and money trying to reduce it.

2) The amount of **funding** available within the business and the general state of the **economy** (boom or recession) will also dictate HRM activities such as **recruitment** and **training**.

3) All UK businesses are subject to **UK** and **EU employment laws**. HRM might have to change their objectives to fit in with **new legislation**.

HRM and Other Departments have to Work Together

1) **All departments** rely on HRM to keep them **informed** about changes in employment laws so that they can **update** their **working practices** if necessary.

2) **All departments** also rely on HRM to provide them with the **staff** they need, when they need them, and to give employees the **training** they need to do their job well.

3) **HRM** rely on other departments to give them **information** that they use to **predict** workforce needs — e.g. **marketing** should tell HRM if they're planning an **advertising campaign**, as this is likely to **increase demand** for the firm's product, meaning that **more staff** will be needed to **increase output**.

Practice Questions

Q1 What are the problems of having too many staff?
Q2 Why do businesses like to keep their rate of labour turnover low?
Q3 What's the difference between personnel and HRM?
Q4 Why is it important for HRM and other departments to work together?

Exam Question

Q1 Explain the difference between hard and soft HRM and evaluate the costs and benefits of each. [10 marks]

Soft HRM is always practised in pillow factories...

HRM sounds quite tricky — you've got to make sure you've got the right kinds of staff and the right number of staff, then try to stop too many of them from leaving, and try to get them to turn up for work and leave at the end of the day in one piece. Phew. It's a bit easier to learn about it all than to actually do it, which is lucky because that's what you've got to do.

Workforce Plans

*Workforce plans are plans about, well, the workforce. These pages are just for lucky old **AQA** students.*

Workforce Planning starts with anticipating Future Staffing Needs

The **purpose** of workforce planning is to make sure that the business always has the **right number** of staff with the **right skills** to meet its needs. To do this, the HRM department predicts the firm's future staffing needs by:

- working out **how many workers** will be needed.
- deciding what kind of workforce will be needed — **skilled** or **unskilled**, **full-time** or **part-time**.
- predicting what the **staff wastage** will be — how many workers will **leave** due to retirement, dismissal, etc.

HRM departments try to predict Staff Demand and Supply

HRM departments in a business assess **what workers** will be **needed** in several ways:

1) HRM departments ask other **experienced managers** for their **opinions** and **advice**.
2) **Past statistics** are used to see if employee numbers have **risen**, **fallen** or **stayed the same**.
3) An increase or decrease in **demand** for their **product** means an increase or decrease in **need** for **workers**, so the HRM department uses the company's sales forecasts to see whether demand for the firm's products will rise, fall or stay the same.
4) HRM analyse the **current staff details** to see how many are likely to **leave** or **retire** in the near future.
5) The introduction of **new technology** and **techniques** will alter the number of workers needed.
6) HRM do an **internal staff stock take**. They look at the number of employees and their **qualities** and **skills**.

HRM also need to assess the potential **supply** of **new workers**:

1) They check the **level of unemployment** in the area to find out how many people are looking for work.
2) **Local infrastructure** is important — good housing, transport and schools can **attract** people to the area.
3) HRM departments see how many **school** and **college leavers** are seeking employment locally.
4) They see if **competitors** are recruiting a similar workforce — if there'll be **competition** for workers.

Workforce Planning includes Recruiting, Training and Retaining staff

1) When they've decided what new staff the business needs, HRM **recruit** staff. They draw up a **job description**, including the job title, the main **roles** and **responsibilities** of the job, salary, etc. They also write a **person specification**, detailing the **qualities** and **qualifications** required. HRM also decide **where** to advertise the job.
2) HRM take charge of the **selection** procedure for new staff — organising **interviews**, etc.
3) HRM organises **induction** and **training** programmes for new staff to teach them the **specific skills** they need.
4) Recruiting and training staff is **expensive**, so HRM try to **retain** staff. They can do this in various ways, including giving staff opportunities for promotion, providing social facilities, etc.

Workforce Plans are influenced by Internal and External Factors

Internal factors influencing workforce plans

1) Workforce plans have to fit in with the firm's other plans, and the overall corporate plan.
2) They must be coordinated with the marketing plan and the production plan — e.g. a plan to expand production and increase market share will require more workers and new training.
3) Changes in production style may require retraining, recruitment or moving workers to another job in the firm.

External factors influencing workforce plans

1) Employment legislation (see p. 88-89) protects employees' rights and restricts companies' ability to dismiss or transfer workers as they might like.
2) New technology might change the number of staff and the skills needed in a business, and might mean that businesses have to train their staff differently.
3) Migration has an effect on workforce planning because it alters the supply of workers — e.g. in some areas the supply of workers has increased due to immigration from new EU countries like Poland and Hungary.

Workforce Plans

There can be **Problems Implementing Workforce Plans**

1) **Collecting** and **analysing** workforce data is **time-consuming** and **expensive**, so not all businesses can afford to do it. **Recruitment** and **training** programmes are also **costly**.

2) Businesses don't always have the **resources** needed to carry out the HRM department's suggestions. E.g. there might not be anyone in the company who's **qualified** to give the training that the HRM department suggests, and managers might be reluctant to spend time **training** staff if they think that it's not a **productive** use of their time.

3) The company might **ignore** HRM's recommendations if they don't fit in with the **image** the company wants to portray. E.g. managers might choose to go ahead with a **recruitment drive** even if HRM says they **don't need** any more staff, because it will give their competitors and the public the impression that they are doing really well. For the same reason, companies are often reluctant to make employees **redundant** — they don't want to **publicise** the fact that things aren't going well.

4) **Bad relationships** between employers and employees might make it **difficult** to implement workforce plans — e.g. HRM won't be able to stop employees from **leaving** the company if they **don't get on** with their managers.

Workforce Planning can be **Useful...** or **Not Very Useful**

1) **Workforce plans** can be **useful** for businesses because they allow them to **prepare** for **changes**. E.g. it's much easier for businesses if they know **in advance** that they're going to need an extra 50 employees to cope with extra **demand**, rather than realising **too late** that they're **understaffed** and having to take on **any** employees who are available, even though they might not be qualified, and then not having time to **train** them properly.

2) **Predictions** in workforce plans **aren't** always **correct** though, so workforce planning can end up being a huge **waste of money** for businesses. E.g. HRM might believe that **extra staff** are needed because demand is going to increase by 25%, but if demand **doesn't** actually increase, the business is stuck with extra staff they **don't need**. The business will also have spent a lot of money **unnecessarily** on **recruiting** and **training** the new staff, in addition to the time and money spent **making** the inaccurate **predictions** in the first place

Workforce plans aren't much use at all if you've got them upside down.

3) Businesses need to **weigh up** the **costs** and **benefits** of workforce planning to decide whether they think it's **worthwhile** or not.

Practice Questions

Q1 What questions do HRM try to answer in order to predict the firm's future staffing needs?

Q2 Once they've decided what staff are needed, what do HRM do next?

Q3 How can a company's image affect whether it puts workforce plans into practice?

Q4 Why do some managers think workforce planning is a waste of time?

Exam Questions

Q1 Describe the main factors that influence a business' demand for workers, and the supply of workers available to them. [8 marks]

Q2 The HRM department of a large business is considering carrying out a major workforce planning exercise. Explain how they might carry out the workforce planning, and what internal and external factors they will need to take into account. [12 marks]

May the (work)force be with you...

Workforce planning is all about predicting what's going to happen in the future. Sometimes you get it right, and everything goes along swimmingly. Other times you get it wrong, and end up paying eighty people to sit and drink coffee all day. Make sure you're clear on how HRM carry out workforce planning, and the factors that can make it all go horribly wrong.

Training

*These delightful pages on training and appraisals are just for the **OCR: People in Organisations option**.*

Training can be In House or External, On-the-Job or Off-the-Job

New employees receive **induction training** to **introduce** them to the company, and to teach them the **specific skills** and **knowledge** they need for their job. **Existing employees** also need training to **update** their skills, or to learn **new** skills.

1) **In-house training** is given by **other employees** of the company.

2) **External** training is provided by people **outside** the company — e.g. colleges.

3) **On-the-job training** takes place **in the workplace**. There are several methods:

- **demonstrations** by a skilled worker.
- **work shadowing** — following and observing an experienced colleague. This is sometimes called "sitting next to Nellie".
- undergoing a period of **apprenticeship** under the supervision of a skilled worker.
- **mentoring** — a new employee is supervised by an experienced trainer.
- **job rotation**, in which the new employee experiences work in various departments within an organisation.

4) **Off-the-job training** takes place **away** from the workplace. It could include:

- **presentations** in a separate conference room or training centre, delivered by other employees or external trainers.
- attending a regular **day release course** at a local college.
- short **residential courses** at various locations.
- **visits** to relevant locations, e.g. suppliers and clients.

5) **On-the-job** training is always **in-house**, but **off-the-job** training can be either **in-house** or **external**.

Training has Benefits and Drawbacks

1) Training helps the employee to be **good** at their job. This **benefits** the employer because the employee will be **more motivated** and **more productive**, which will make the business **more profitable**.

2) However, training is **expensive** and **time-consuming**, and the **wrong** training **doesn't** benefit anyone.

Advantages of on-the-job training	
1)	It's the **cheapest** form of training.
2)	Trainees gain the **specific skills** of the job.
3)	Trainees learn about the workplace **culture**.
Disadvantages of on-the-job training	
1)	Trainers may **not** be **qualified** to train others.
2)	Trainers may **not** know **new ideas** and **techniques**.

Advantages of off-the-job training	
1)	Trainers are **qualified** to give training.
2)	Trainees get a **broader** view of their job.
Disadvantages of off-the-job training	
1)	Training might be **too general** and not specific enough to the trainee's job.
2)	It's the **most expensive** kind of training.

Training Needs Analysis identifies What Training is Needed

To avoid **wasting** time and money on **unnecessary** training, businesses can carry out **training needs analysis** (**TNA**). TNA attempts to **identify** the training **needs** of the business and the training needs of individual workers.

TNA involves finding **answers** to the following **six** questions:

1) What **skills** does the business **need** its employees to have so that it can meet its **goals**?

2) What **training** do employees need to get the required skills?

3) **Which employees** need to be trained?

4) What's the **best way** of carrying out the training?

5) Do any **changes** need to be made to the **current** training methods?

6) **Who** can provide the required training?

By answering these questions, businesses can make decisions about **what** training is needed, and **how** to carry it out.

Appraisals

Appraisals are a way of Assessing Employees' Performance

Employee appraisals are a formal way of assessing an employee's overall **performance**.
Appraisals allow employees and their managers to:

1) **Review** the employee's performance compared to **targets** and **objectives** that were set previously.

2) **Identify issues** and **concerns** relating to the employee's performance.

3) **Identify** the employee's **development** and **training needs**.

Managers can use different Methods of Appraisal

There are **three main methods** of appraisal that managers can use to assess employees' performance:

Self-assessment

Employees are given the opportunity to **write down** their thoughts about their **performance** and whether they have achieved their **targets** or **objectives**, usually in the form of a **questionnaire**.

Advantages:
* It gives the employee the opportunity to express their **opinions** and **concerns**.
* It helps managers to identify the employee's training needs.

Disadvantages:
* It's **less personal** than having a one-on-one meeting with the line manager.

Line manager appraisal

A **discussion** between the employee and their line manager is the most common form of appraisal process. Employers assume that the line manager is the best person to understand the employee's **role**, and they have **observed** the employee's performance at first hand.

Advantages:
* It allows the employee to discuss their **thoughts** and **concerns** with their manager on a **one-to-one** basis.
* The manager can identify the employee's **training needs**.

Disadvantages:
* The employee might be **too intimidated** to say what they really think.
* If the manager's **not** a **good listener**, the process won't work very well.
* Having an individual meeting with each employee is **time-consuming**.

The 360 degree method

Managers contact a variety of **sources** who have dealt with the employee (colleagues, clients, etc) and request **feedback** on the employee's performance. It's usually used in addition to a **discussion** with the line manager.

Advantages:
* It gives an **overall picture** of the employee's performance, so it's **fairer** than just the line manager's opinion.

Disadvantages:
* Collecting all the feedback is very **time-consuming**.
* The employee might feel **stressed** if they think that everyone they come into contact with is "**spying**" on them.

Practice Questions

Q1 What's the difference between in-house and external training?

Q2 Give one advantage and one disadvantage of on-the-job training.

Q3 What are the three main methods of employee appraisal?

Exam Question

Q1 Describe the purpose and process of training needs analysis. [6 marks]

Who on earth's Nellie anyway...

Presumably it's not the same Nellie who packed her trunk and said goodbye to the circus. Anyway, training and appraisals are both quite interesting, so it shouldn't be too boring to keep going over all this stuff until you're sure you know it all well enough to have it as your specialist subject on Mastermind... or at least well enough to do an A2 level exam on it.

Methods of Reward

*Interest? Fulfilment? What do they matter in comparison to cold, hard cash? This page is for **OCR: People in Organisations** option, although the **last section** is also for **WJEC**. **Page 97 is for OCR: People in Organisation** and **WJEC**.*

Time-Based Payment gives an Hourly or Weekly Wage

1) Workers who are paid a **weekly wage** get a set rate of so many **pounds per hour**. The more hours they work the more they get paid. Workers usually work a **fixed working week** of about 40 hours, and get paid more for each hour of **overtime** they work.

2) The problem with this is that there's **no incentive** for employees to work more productively — workers might even feel encouraged to **waste time** and spend longer than they need to on tasks in order to earn more money.

Monthly or Annual Salaries are another form of Time-Based Payment

1) A monthly **salary** is made up of so many **thousand pounds a year**, divided into 12 monthly payments. It isn't directly related to the number of hours — **salaried employees** work a minimum number of hours a week, and then extra hours as necessary.

2) The **advantage** of this system is that it's **easy** for everyone to **understand**. **Disadvantages** include the fact that it can lead to employees being **overworked** and that a company can't easily cut back on **labour costs** by reducing people's contracted hours if it hits bad times — it would probably need to make them redundant, instead.

3) Sometimes, salaried employees are on a **performance-related pay** scheme. If an employee's **work** is considered **above average**, they receive a **bonus** which is **higher** than the bonus received by **employees** whose work is only considered to be **average**.

Time-based methods of payment are usually used when it would be impossible to measure the productivity of each employee or when people can't control how fast they work.

Production-Based payment pays either a Piece Rate or Commission

1) Some **production workers** are paid by **piece rate** — they get paid so many pounds or pence **per finished item**. The more the worker produces, the more they get paid.

2) Sales people are usually paid **commission** — a **percentage** of the **sales** they achieve. Most sales staff get a low **basic salary** and earn commission on top of that, but some get commission only.

3) Workers can be paid a **bonus** or a **higher rate of pay** if they achieve above a **target** rate of productivity.

4) Production-based payment can **motivate** employees to work harder, and lead to increased productivity. However, **staff morale** is likely to be **low** because employees' income is uncertain. Another disadvantage of the piece rate system is that **quality** might **suffer** because workers are only interested in producing items as quickly as they can.

Businesses also Reward Employees with other Benefits

1) In addition to their weekly/monthly pay, employees may also get **fringe benefits**.

2) These include **staff discount** for company products (very common in retail), employer contributions to employee **pensions**, private **medical insurance**, health club membership, a company **car**, **profit sharing** schemes and options to buy **shares** in the company.

3) These are all **financial** rewards — they're things that can be objectively valued in terms of money. It'd cost the employees money to buy their own health insurance, gym membership, etc.

Julia valued fringe benefits.

4) Don't forget the impact of **non-financial** rewards such as praise, training, or additional responsibility.

5) Most financial benefits are liable for **income tax** — they're taxed on their "cash equivalent" which is the price it'd cost to buy them. Most benefits **can't** be used as a **tax loophole** — a way of paying someone money without them paying tax on it. However, employees don't pay tax on pension scheme contributions, and share options of less than about £3000 aren't taxed either.

Employers have to pay staff at least the Minimum Wage

1) A **national minimum wage** was introduced on 1st April 1999, to prevent workers being paid unfairly low wages.

2) The minimum wage rises in October every year. From **1st October 2009**, it will be **£5.80** for people aged 22 and over, £4.83 for people aged 18-21, and £3.57 for 16 and 17 year olds.

3) Employers who don't pay their staff enough can be **fined** up to **£5000**, and also have to **reimburse** their staff with the total amount that they've been underpaid.

WJEC JUST LEARN THIS BIT

Methods of Reward

Changing the way that staff are paid has Advantages and Disadvantages

Employers might want to change the way that they pay their staff if they think that it will **increase productivity** or **decrease** their **wage bills**.

1) Employers might want to change their employees' method of payment from an **hourly wage** to a **piece rate** or **commission** if they think it will make employees more **productive** and increase the business's **profits**. E.g. factories might switch from paying an hourly rate to a piece rate in order to encourage employees to work more quickly. This might **increase productivity**, but it also increases **pressure** on the staff, which may mean that employees don't stay in the job for long. This creates a high **staff turnover**, which is bad news for businesses — see p. 98.

2) Employees are usually **unwilling** to change their method of payment if it means they'll get paid **less** than they currently do (e.g. if staff on an hourly wage tend to do a lot of overtime, employers might decide to pay them a monthly salary instead so that they don't have to give them overtime payments). They might feel that employers are **cheating** them, which will **demotivate** them and **decrease productivity**.

3) Businesses might change **taxable benefits** for certain **benefits in kind** that are non-taxable in order to save money. E.g. employers might provide a subsidised canteen rather than a company car — that way the **value** of the benefits to the employees **stays the same**, but the benefits **cost** the employer **less**.

Labour Shortages and Surpluses affect Pay

1) When **unemployment** is **high**, workers are willing to work for **lower pay**. Labour shortages and surpluses can affect the **whole economy** or specific **industries** (e.g. if unemployment in the economy is high, there might still be a shortage of doctors — only qualified employees can do the job).

2) In jobs where there is a **shortage** of people **qualified** to do the job, employers have to offer **more money** to attract staff — when **demand** for staff is high, wages **increase** in order to **stimulate supply**.

3) When there are **plenty** of potential employees willing and able to work in a particular sector, wages and salaries will be kept **low**. The **power** of trade unions and individual employees seeking pay rises is **reduced** because it's **easy** for businesses to find employees willing to work for them for less pay.

> In the late 1990s there was a severe **shortage** of **teachers** and **trainee teachers** in the UK. In order to attract more graduates into teaching, the government **scrapped tuition fees** for graduates taking the PGCE (postgraduate certificate in education) in 2000, and brought in a scheme offering graduates a **training bursary** of **£6000** during their PGCE year to cover their living costs. Graduates in subjects with extreme shortages of teachers, like maths and modern languages, were also offered a **£4000 "golden hello"** bonus.

Practice Questions

Q1 What is a salary?
Q2 What's the difference between a piece rate and commission?
Q3 Give three examples of fringe benefits.
Q4 Why can there still be labour shortages even when unemployment is high?

Exam Question

Q1 Sue runs a small business producing hand-embroidered cushions. She produces three sizes of cushions — small, medium and large, which she sells to shops at £10, £18 and £24. She employs fifteen members of staff in her workshop and currently pays them an hourly wage of £7.20 an hour. However, she's found that some of her employees are spending up to three hours on a large cushion, which she thinks they should be able to complete in under 90 minutes. She's considering changing the method of payment to a piece rate of £4.50 for a small cushion, £8 for a medium cushion and £11 for a large cushion instead. Write a report explaining the possible effects of doing this, and explain what you think Sue should do. [8 marks]

I wonder if Gandhi got paid a peace rate...

Sorting out how to pay their staff is a bit of a minefield for businesses — they don't want to pay them more than they need to, but they've got to make sure they're paying them enough to keep them happy and working. Make sure you can weigh up the pros and cons of different payment methods in different situations, in case you get a case study in the exam.

Measuring Labour Effectiveness

*Businesses just love their calculations, don't they? Here are a few more — they're all ways of working out how effective employees are. For **Edexcel,** the **OCR: People in Organisations option** and **Strategic Management unit** and **WJEC.***

Labour Productivity measures How Much each Employee Produces

Labour productivity measures the **output per person** in a business.
It's calculated using the following formula:

Labour Productivity = $\dfrac{\text{Output per period}}{\text{Number of employees}}$

Example: A factory has 30 workers per shift working 3 shifts per day to produce 9000 DVD players per week.
Productivity = 9000 ÷ 90 workers = **100** DVD players per worker per week.

The **higher** the labour productivity, the **better** the workforce is performing. As labour productivity **increases**, labour costs per unit **fall**. This is important in **labour intensive** firms, where labour costs are a high proportion of total costs.

Ways to improve labour productivity

1) Labour productivity can be improved by **improving worker motivation** (see p.72-75).

2) **Training** can make workers more productive.

3) Labour productivity can also be improved by changing to **more efficient** methods of production (p.101) — e.g. changing from job to batch production or from batch to flow production. These gains need to be balanced against the **costs** of changing production method, and the **reduced production flexibility**.

4) Businesses can **reward** increased productivity. Paying workers using a **piece-rate** system encourages staff to produce more. Managers should take care that **quality** doesn't suffer in the process.

5) If **old** or **inefficient equipment** is reducing productivity, the business might **upgrade** their equipment.

1) Increasing labour productivity means **redundancies** and **job losses** unless sales increase.
Businesses need to **plan** for the consequences of improved productivity to avoid upsetting staff.

2) Businesses should **monitor** their labour productivity over time. When they're setting targets, they should compare their productivity to **competitors' productivity** through **benchmarking** (p.115).

3) Businesses must **balance** productivity against issues such as product **quality** and long-term worker **motivation**.

Labour Turnover measures the Proportion of Staff who Leave each year

Labour turnover measures how quickly **employees leave** the company.
It's measured using the following formula:

Labour Turnover = $\dfrac{\text{Number of staff leaving in a year}}{\text{Average number of staff employed that year}}$ x 100%

Work out part-time staff as if they were fractions of a full-time employee. Two people who each work half a week = one person working a whole week.

Example: A business has 100 full-time staff and 100 part-time staff who each work 50% of a normal week. Over a year 10 full-time and 10 part-time staff leave.
Average number of staff employed = 100 + (100 × 0.5) = **150**. **Number of staff leaving** = 10 + (10 × 0.5) = **15**.
Labour turnover = 15 ÷ 150 × 100% = **10%**.

1) The **higher** the figure, the larger the proportion of workers leaving the firm each year.

2) **External causes** of high labour turnover include changes in regional **unemployment** levels, and the growth of other local firms using staff with **similar skills**.

3) **Internal causes** of high labour turnover include poor motivation of staff, low wages, and a lack of opportunities for promotion. Staff will **join other firms** to increase their pay and job responsibilities.

4) A **poor recruitment** process which selects lousy candidates will increase labour turnover.

5) Increased **delegation, job enrichment**, higher **wages** and better **training** can reduce employee turnover.

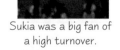

Sukia was a big fan of a high turnover.

6) Businesses need **some** labour turnover to bring new ideas in. Labour turnover of 0 means no one **ever** leaves.

7) If the rate of labour turnover in a company is **high**, HRM uses strategies to reduce it — see p. 90 for more.

Measuring Labour Effectiveness

Absenteeism is the Proportion of Time employees are Off Work

Absenteeism is measured using the following formula:

$$\text{Absenteeism} = \frac{\text{Number of staff days lost}}{\text{Total number of staff days}} \times 100\%$$

1) E.g. if a business employs **15** members of staff, and they take a total of **3** sick days in **one week**, the total number of staff days in that week is $15 \times 5 = $ **75**, and the absenteeism rate is $3 \div 75 \times 100\% = $ **4%**.

2) Low absenteeism is best, but figures need to be analysed in the **context** of each industry. For example, **police** officers might have **higher** than average figures because of the dangers and stresses of the job, while **sales** people paid on commission have **lower** rates because time off work can reduce their pay.

3) **Causes** of absenteeism include poor **working conditions**, poor **relationships** with managers and other staff, **stress** or **disillusionment** with the job, and poor **motivation**.

4) Absenteeism **increases costs**. It results in **lost opportunities**, e.g. sales enquiries left unanswered. There's also the cost of additional **wages** to cover for the absent employee — this is often expensive **overtime** pay.

5) Absenteeism increases if employees believe the firm **accepts** it as unavoidable. Some businesses require employees to fill in a **self-certification form** if they take any time off sick. Some require a **doctor's note** for anything over 7 days in a row off sick. **HRM** or line managers may **interview** absent employees on their return to work to find out why they've been absent, and to let them know that their absenteeism has been noted.

6) If worker absenteeism is very **high** the firm may consider implementing a **strategy** to improve worker motivation or working conditions. See p. 90 for more on how HRM try to reduce absenteeism.

Businesses work out How Often their employees are Late for work

1) If employees are **late** for work, **productivity decreases** because they are not working all the hours they are being paid for. This can seriously **damage** a business' **profitability**.

2) Businesses **keep track** of how often employees are late, and may take **disciplinary action** against workers who often come into work late.

3) For an individual worker, lateness can be calculated using the formula below:

$$\text{Lateness} = \frac{\text{Number of days employee is late}}{\text{Number of days}} \times 100\%$$

4) So if an employee is late **6** times in a month with **22** working days, their lateness rate is $6 \div 22 \times 100\% = $ **27.3%**.

Businesses calculate their employees' Holiday Entitlement

1) Since April 2009 workers have been legally entitled to **5.6 weeks** of paid holiday a year, including bank holidays. This means that **full-time** employees get at least **28 days** off a year — many employers offer more than this.

2) To work out how much holiday **part-time employees** are entitled to, **multiply** the number of days per week that they work by **5.6**. This will give you the number of **days** they are allowed to take as holiday. E.g. if an employee works 3 days per week, they are entitled to $5.6 \times 3 = $ 16.8 days paid holiday per year.

Practice Questions

Q1 What's the formula for measuring labour productivity?

Q2 State two possible causes of high labour turnover.

Q3 What is the annual paid holiday entitlement of a full-time employee in the UK?

Exam Questions

Q1 Explain how businesses can improve labour productivity. [4 marks]

Q2 Why do absenteeism and lateness cause problems for businesses? [4 marks]

Absenteeism — not a good strategy for coping with A2 exams...

There are loads of different ways of measuring labour effectiveness — managers might just focus on one or two, but any of them might come up in the exam, so you need to know them all. Don't forget holiday entitlement too. If you get a question on measuring labour effectiveness in the exam, putting the facts into the context of the business will get you the best marks.

Section Three — People in Organisations

Production Planning

*This section might sound complicated, but actually, it's not. 'Operations' is just a fancy word for the real reason businesses exist in the first place — to make stuff. These two pages are for **AQA** and **OCR: Business Production Option**.*

Operational Objectives are Targets set by particular Departments

A company meets its strategic objectives (p.153) by breaking them down into **smaller objectives**. These help each **individual department** know what it's supposed to be doing. Operational objectives might be linked to:

QUALITY — This type of objective is likely to involve either **maintaining** or **improving** levels of quality. For example, a company might aim to ensure that **95%** of their products last **five years** or longer, or they might aim to **reduce** the number of **customer complaints** that they get in a month.

COST — Many firms aim to **cut costs**, especially if they compete on **price**. Depending on the type of company, there are different ways of doing this. Costs can be cut in a particular **department** (e.g. HR might be asked to cut the costs of recruitment) or the costs of an individual **product** can be reduced (e.g. an airline might stop offering meals on a particular route).

VOLUME — Volume objectives often involve **increasing** the **amount** of goods or services that a company is producing. For example, a hotel might aim to have more rooms full on weeknights or a football stadium might aim to fill more seats on match days. However, a company might also set an objective to ensure that **volume** doesn't **exceed demand**, e.g. if it knows people buy fewer healthy choice ready-meals at Christmas, it might reduce production in December.

EFFICIENCY — Efficiency objectives aim to make **better use** of **resources** in order to reduce costs and increase profit. This might mean increasing **capacity utilisation** (increasing output so it's closer to the maximum amount of goods the firm could produce with current levels of staff and machinery) or taking steps to improve **labour** and **capital productivity** (how much output a particular worker or piece of machinery is capable of generating in a set time period).

INNOVATION — Companies can set their **Research & Development** (R&D) departments innovation targets, e.g. a car manufacturer might set an objective to produce the world's first pollution-free car by 2015. These objectives can be **hard** to **achieve**, as unexpected problems often occur.

ENVIRONMENT — **Pressure** from **customers** and the **government** often leads to firms setting environmental objectives, such as cutting **carbon emissions** or using a greater number of **recycled** raw materials.

Operational Objectives are influenced by Internal and External Factors

INTERNAL

- **Nature of the Product**: a computer technology firm is likely to have very different targets to a family-run bed and breakfast. The **computer technology company** is likely to focus on **innovation** whereas the **B & B** may be trying to increase its **capacity utilisation** by having lots of rooms full.
- **Availability of Resources**: many businesses would like to **increase output** but are limited by whether they have enough **resources**. For example, it won't be possible to produce 50 handpainted dolls houses in 3 days if the company only employs five carpenters.

EXTERNAL

- **Competitors' Performance**: many firms set targets in **reaction** to their **rivals' actions**. For example, if a rival gains market share, you would also probably try to increase your share of the market to make sure they don't overtake you. **Competition** from **abroad**, e.g. China, is forcing companies to set stricter **cost** and **efficiency** objectives.
- **Demand for Product**: businesses should try to make sure that **output** is not higher than **demand** (see above).
- **Changing Customer Needs**: e.g. if customers indicate that they'd like a firm to behave more ethically this can affect **cost** and **environmental** goals.

Production is all about turning Inputs into Outputs

1) Production means taking a set of **raw materials** and turning them into something the consumer **wants** or **needs**.

2) It generally refers to the **whole process** from **obtaining resources** right through to **checking** the finished product for quality and **delivering** it to the customer.

3) Production can also be used to describe a company supplying a **service**, rather than a physical product.

Production Planning

There are **Five** common **Styles** of **Production**

Job production	Production of **one-off items** by **skilled workers**.
Flow production	Mass production on a **continuous production line** with **division of labour**.
Batch production	Production of **small batches** of **identical items**.
Cell production	Production divided into **sets of tasks**, each set completed by a **work group**.
Lean production	Streamlined production with **waste at a minimum**.

It was clear the builders hadn't understood what was meant by "lean production".

1) Changing from job to batch or flow production improves **efficiency**. The cost per unit is much lower, and it's also possible to produce much **more** in the same amount of time.

2) However, flow production is **inflexible**, so the ability to tailor products to specific customer needs is lost. A niche firm with close relationships with its clients might think twice before moving away from job production.

3) Flow production can be switched to **cell production**. In cell production, each team is responsible for one unit of work, which increases motivation and engagement with the work. Cell production involves **self checking** for quality, and quality can **improve** if workers are sufficiently motivated. Changing to cell production requires **training** so that workers are **multi-skilled** enough to tackle all the tasks within their work group.

4) **Lean** production methods such as **kaizen** (see p.115) and **just-in-time** (see p.112) require changes in organisation style — usually a more **democratic management style** is needed, to encourage a sense of **cooperation** between everyone in the firm. Employees need **training** to become multi-skilled, so that production can be **flexible**.

Other Departments have an impact on **Production**

1) The **finance** department decides **how much money** can be spent on equipment and wages.

2) The **marketing** department tells the operations managers what customers want, and what they're willing to **pay** for it. Marketing will also say **when** the goods need to be produced to hit the market at the right time.

3) **Human resources management** are in charge of managing employees. They need to know how many employees are needed, what skills they need, and whether they'll need training.

4) These relationships go **both ways**. The marketing department can **ask** the production department to produce a large amount, but the production department has to say if it's **possible** or not.

Production needs to consider other **Factors** and **Decisions**

1) A business' **production method** has an effect on the **type** of **decisions** that managers are likely to make. Equally, managers can make **decisions** that have a **big impact** on the **production** department.

2) It's **hard** for some businesses to **grow** if they're committed to using **job production**.

3) If a decision is made to try to increase **market share**, a company might choose either to **increase production** or to switch **production methods** so that it can manufacture a **new product** alongside its existing range.

4) In periods of economic **downturn**, **survival** is often a company's main aim. In these periods, the company is unlikely to invest in **new machinery** or switch to **new methods**. They might consider **closing** a factory for a **few weeks** or temporarily **shutting down** certain areas of production.

5) A business that's trying to **increase** its **profitability** might well switch to **batch** or **flow** production. If it's trying to improve **cash flow**, it probably won't invest in **new capital** (machinery).

Practice Questions

Q1 What are the six types of operational objective?

Q2 Name the five different methods of production and give an advantage of each one.

Q3 How might the production department respond to a decision to try and increase market share?

Exam Question

Q1 Analyse the advantages and disadvantages to a food manufacturer of using large scale flow production. [8 marks]

Cell Production — an egg and a sperm combine to form a new cell...

Oops, no, sorry, wrong book. That's GCSE biology (which sounds more interesting, actually). The good news about the stuff on these pages is that, although it may be a bit dull, it's not that difficult. Make sure you learn the six different types of operational objective, the five production methods and the things firms have to consider when switching between them.

Production Planning

*Not only do businesses have to decide what's the best size for them to be, they also need to work out if they want more machines than people. Or more biscuits than cake. These pages are for **AQA** and **OCR: Business Production Option**.*

Businesses need to have the **Right Mix** of **People** and **Machines**

1) A successful business must have a **suitable combination** of **materials**, **machinery** and **people**. How hard it is to get this right depends on the **complexity** of the product and the number of **production stages**.

2) The **design** of the product affects the mix. For example, freshly squeezed orange juice has just one component (oranges), but a car has hundreds. The **higher** the number of **components**, the **harder** it is to get the correct mix of resources.

3) Businesses can have problems getting the right mix if there's a **shortage** of suitably skilled **labour**. For example, at the moment there's a very limited supply of **care assistants**, **geologists** and **vets**.

4) Businesses are also limited by their **finances**. Most companies would have the **latest technology** if they could **afford** it, but in reality **smaller firms** can rarely afford to keep updating their machinery on a frequent basis.

AQA ONLY

A *Capital-Intensive* firm has **Lots** of **Machinery**

1) A **capital-intensive** business uses more **machinery** and relatively few **workers**. The **car industry**, which tends to use robot-operated production lines, is one example of a capital-intensive industry.

2) **Larger** firms tend to be more **capital-intensive** than smaller companies. For example, the Morgan Motor Company produces a small number of hand-built sports cars using lots of **labour**. BMW, on the other hand, makes far greater use of **robots** and machinery.

3) A rise in the **cost** of **labour** can also cause companies to **switch** to a **capital-intensive** method of production.

Advantages of Capital-intensive Production	Disdvantages of Capital-intensive Production
Usually works out **cheaper** than manual labour in the **long-term**.	High **set-up** costs.
Machinery is often **more precise** than human workers, which might lead to more **consistent quality** levels.	If machinery **breaks down**, it can lead to long **delays**.
Machinery is able to work **24/7**.	Machines are usually only suited to one task, which makes them **inflexible**.
Machines are **easier** to **manage** than people.	If workers are worried that they might be replaced by machines, the fear of job losses can cause **motivation** to **decrease**.

AQA ONLY

A *Labour-Intensive* firm is very **People-Heavy**

1) A **labour-intensive** firm uses more **workers** and less **machinery**. For example, the **NHS** is very labour-intensive.

2) In countries where labour is relatively **cheap** (e.g. China) **labour-intensive** methods of production are common.

Advantages of Labour-intensive Production	Disadvantages of Labour-intensive Production
People are more flexible than machines and can be retrained if the company needs new skills.	It's harder to manage people than machines.
Labour-intensive methods are cheaper for small-scale production.	People can be unreliable — they may have days off through sickness.
Labour-intensive methods are also cheaper where low-cost labour is available, e.g. China and India.	People can't work without breaks or holidays.
Workers can solve any problems that arise during production and suggest ways to improve quality.	Wage increases mean that the cost of labour can increase over time. It can be difficult to forecast wage increases caused by inflation.

OCR ONLY

Specialisation means employees **Concentrate** exclusively on **One Task**

1) **Division of labour** means breaking the **production process** down into a **series** of **small**, **repetitive** tasks.

2) Over time, division of labour leads to **specialisation**. Specialisation happens when **repeating** a task over and over causes workers to become very **skilled** at that particular task.

3) **Division of labour** and **specialisation** are useful for companies because they raise **productivity**. Because workers are **skilled** at carrying out their part of the process, they become **quicker** and quicker, meaning that they are able to output **more goods** in a **shorter** period of **time**. For more on productivity, see p.108.

Production Planning

Economies of Scale mean bigger is Cheaper

Economies of scale mean that as **output increases**, the **cost** of producing **each item** goes down. **Internal** economies of scale increase efficiency **within** an individual firm. There are different types of internal economies of scale:

Technical	Technical economies of scale are related to **production**. Production methods for large volumes are often more **efficient**. Large businesses can afford to buy better, more advanced **machinery**, which might mean they need fewer staff, and wage costs will fall.
Specialisation	Specialisation economies of scale are linked to **employees**. Large businesses can employ managers with **specialist skills** and separate them out into specialised departments, which means the work is usually done more **quickly** and is of a higher **quality** than in non-specialised companies.
Purchasing	Purchasing economies of scale are to do with **discounts**. Large businesses can negotiate discounts when buying **supplies**. They can get bigger discounts and longer **credit periods** than their smaller competitors.
Financial	Financial economies of scale happen when companies **borrow money**. Large firms can borrow at **lower rates** of **interest** than smaller firms. Lenders feel **more comfortable** lending money to a big firm than a small firm.
Marketing	Marketing economies of scale are related to **promotional costs**. The cost of an ad campaign is a **fixed cost**. A business with a large output can share out the cost over more products than a business with a low output.
Risk-bearing	Risk-bearing economies of scale involve **diversification** into several different **markets** or to catering to several different **market segments**. Large firms have a greater ability to bear **risk** than their smaller competitors.

External Economies of Scale make a Whole Industry or Area more efficient

External economies of scale happen when industries are concentrated in **small geographical areas**.

1) Having an **established network of suppliers** gives economies of scale. Locating near to suppliers means firms can easily negotiate with a range of local suppliers, which tends to increase quality and reduce prices.

2) A good skilled local **labour supply** makes an industry more efficient. This is most important in industries where training is **expensive** or takes a long time. For example, software development firms in California's "Silicon Valley" know that plenty of people who are qualified to fill their vacancies **already** live within driving distance.

3) Firms located in certain areas can benefit from good **infrastructure** — e.g. an airport, a motorway or good rail links. E.g. Dublin's tourist industry had a massive boost in profits after Ryanair started **cheap flights** to Dublin.

Diseconomies of Scale — being bigger can be Bad News, too

Diseconomies of scale make unit costs of production rise as output rises. They happen because large firms are harder to manage than small ones. They're caused by poor **motivation**, poor **communication** and poor **coordination**.

1) It's important to keep all departments working towards the **same objectives**. Poor coordination makes a business **drift off course**. In a big firm, it's hard to **coordinate** activities between different departments.

2) **Communication** is harder in a big business. It can be **slow** and **difficult** to get messages to the right people, especially when there are **long chains of command**. The **amount** of information circulating in a business can increase at a faster rate than the business is actually growing.

3) It can be hard to **motivate** people in a large company. In a **small** firm, managers are in **close contact** with staff, and it's easier for people to feel like they **belong** and that they're working towards the same aims. When people **don't feel they belong**, and that there's **no point** to what they're doing, they get **demotivated**.

4) Diseconomies of scale are caused by problems with management. Strong **leadership**, **delegation** and **decentralisation** can all help **prevent diseconomies** of scale and keep costs down.

Practice Questions

Q1 Give two advantages of capital-intensive production methods and two advantages of labour-intensive methods.
Q2 What is specialisation and why is it useful?
Q3 Name three types of diseconomy of scale.

Exam Question

Q1 Explain the different types of economy of scale a business might benefit from if it takes over a rival firm. [10 marks]

Economy of scales — when snakes wear the same skin 2 years running...

Economies and diseconomies of scale are pretty important to businesses. Think of it as a balancing act (scales, balancing act — geddit?) — firms benefit from being big, but if they get too big, the balance goes wrong and their size actually ends up costing them money. It's a bit like in Goldilocks — they can be too big or too small, but they want to be just right.

Location

*Businesses have to find the optimal location — the best site their money can buy. I always like a location in town, so I can nip to the shops at lunch. These pages are for **AQA** and **OCR: Business Production** and **Strategic Management** units.*

Quantitative Factors affect choice of Location

1) Location is a big concern for most businesses. The wrong location could mean **high costs** or that potential **customers** won't notice you. Choosing the right location can be a huge **competitive advantage** (see p.162).

2) When deciding where to locate or relocate, businesses analyse the potential impact on **costs** and **revenues**. **Investment appraisal** techniques such as **payback** and **average rate of return** (see p.64-65) can be used to calculate this.

3) Factors that can be measured in **financial** terms are called quantitative factors. The quantitative factors that affect the choice of location are:

Businesses in the primary sector (e.g. mining and fishing) don't get much say in their location. They have to set up close to the natural resources that they're supplying.

Location decisions depend on distribution and supply costs

1) **Manufacturing** businesses which provide **bulky finished products** should be located near to their **customers** to cut down on distribution costs. Bulky products made from lightweight components are called "**bulk increasing**" goods.

2) Other products need **bulky raw materials** to make a **lightweight end product** — these are "**bulk decreasing**" goods. They need to be located near the source of **raw materials** to keep transport costs down.

3) A good **transport infrastructure** (see below) cuts distribution costs.

4) **Services** don't have large distribution costs. Decisions on where to locate services are based mainly on other criteria.

E.g. beer — made of water (available anywhere), plus hops and barley (low in bulk compared to the finished product). Breweries tend to be located near consumers and transport infrastructure, not near hop or barley fields.

E.g. the steel industry in South Wales. The three basic ingredients are iron ore (imported to local ports), coal and limestone (both from South Wales). The product is rolled steel, which is less bulky and can be transported by rail.

Location decisions depend on the availability and cost of resources

1) There must be a **good supply** of labour resources in the area where a business will be located.

2) The labour force must also be **suitable** — e.g. they might need to be literate, they might need special skills such as IT, technical knowledge of machinery, etc.

3) The area might need **local training facilities** for staff e.g. a college or university.

4) The area needs **facilities** such as affordable housing, suitable schooling, medical facilities, retail and leisure outlets to provide a good **standard of living** for staff.

5) Businesses can afford to pay workers less in areas where the **cost of living** is lower. To take full advantage of this, businesses need to locate **overseas** where labour costs are often lower than in the UK — see p.106.

6) Businesses also need the right land resources. They may need room for **future expansion**.

7) The **cost** of **land** and **property** for factories and business premises varies significantly from area to area — land in the London area is far more expensive than land in mid Wales, for example.

Location decisions depend on the market

1) Some businesses such as **retailers** need to locate **near to customers**, in order to catch the passing trade.

2) Businesses need to be based in locations which will **maximise their revenue**.

A good location needs an efficient and appropriate infrastructure

1) Business organisations benefit from access to **motorways**, fast **rail** links, **sea ports** and **airports**.

2) Transport infrastructure is needed for the **import of raw materials**, the **distribution of finished products**, and for **staff** to get to work.

3) Businesses also need **support services**. Most business organisations need some form of **commercial** support such as **banking**, **insurance** and **marketing** agencies.

4) They often need **technical** support such as engineering services and **IT** assistance.

Location

There are also **Qualitative Factors** involved in **Choosing** a **Location**

1) Entrepreneurs might choose to start a business near where they **live** —
e.g. Dyson™ is based in Wiltshire, near the owner and inventor's home.

2) Some places have a **good image** which suits the image of the product. High fashion works better in New York, London and Paris than in Scunthorpe or Workington — New York, London and Paris already have a fashion image.

> All these factors rarely, if ever, combine in one place to create an **ideal** location. It's more likely that the decision of where to locate a business is based on a **compromise** between different factors.

Businesses may have to **Relocate** — move facilities somewhere else

1) Established businesses sometimes have to up sticks and **move**. This may be because the firm has **grown too large** for its premises, or because **government incentives** have been withdrawn, or because taxes have risen.

2) Some firms have "**industrial inertia**"— it seems sensible for them to relocate, but other factors prevent them from doing so. For example, it might be cheaper to locate elsewhere, but moving might meaning losing an **external economy of scale** such as a good local supply of trained workers.

3) Deciding where to relocate is similar to deciding where to locate, with some **added problems**:

- Production is likely to be reduced during the move — there may be **downtime**.
- **Staff** may not **want** to move. They may need to be **paid** to relocate, especially if they have dependent family.
- Notifying **suppliers** and **customers** costs money. Updating **headed notepaper** and **brochures** costs money.

Expansion is a common reason for businesses to relocate

1) **Expansion** is another word for **growth**. There's lots more about the different types of growth on pages 168-169.

2) When a company expands, they often have more **stock**, **staff**, **machinery** and even **customers** than they had before. This means they're likely to need **extra space**.

3) Some companies can **extend** their existing premises when they expand. However, if there's a lack of **available land** or the business fails to get **planning permission** (see p.125) the business might have to **relocate** instead.

Multi-site businesses operate from **Several** different **Locations**

1) A business can expand by opening new **factories**, **offices** or **stores** whilst also remaining in their **existing premises**. This is called a multi-site location. Shops and restaurant chains often expand this way.

2) Having a multi-site location can be a good way of increasing a company's **sales** and **capacity**. It can also make it easier for companies to respond to local **market conditions**.

3) The downside of multi-site locations is that they can make **communication** harder. The business might need to be **restructured** so that it remains efficient. Multi-site businesses have a lot **more staff** than businesses operating from a single location (e.g. they might have a different manager overseeing each site) — this can lead to high **overheads**.

Multi-site locations need multi-sight managers.

Practice Questions

Q1 Identify and briefly explain three factors which affect location decisions.

Q2 Describe three problems that a company might face when relocating.

Q3 Give two disadvantages of multi-site locations.

Exam Question

Q1 One of the major decisions a business faces is where to locate a new factory. What factors would be taken into consideration in the decision-making process? [10 marks]

Expansion — not just the result of too many chocolate biscuits...

At AS-Level, the focus was on how businesses choose a location when they're starting-up. Now you need to know what factors a business needs to consider if it's thinking of changing location or opening additional premises. Luckily, start-ups and relocations aren't really all that different. All the same, there's a lot of material on these pages, so learn them well.

International Location

*Firms can locate some or all of the business abroad. This page is for **AQA**, **Edexcel** and **OCR: Business Production Option**.*

Offshoring means Moving parts of a business to Cheaper Countries

1) Increasingly, many businesses locate some of their **departments**, such as their call centres or payment processing departments, **overseas** — this is called **offshoring**.

2) The countries that firms move to most often are **China**, **India**, **Russia**, **Poland** and **Brazil**.

3) Offshoring can be a good way to **cut costs**, but it's not always good for a company's **image**. The media and trade unions often criticise companies for UK **job losses** caused by offshoring.

To everyone's surprise, staff loved the new offshore department.

Certain countries Specialise in particular Goods or Services

1) As a result of offshoring, some countries have become **specialised** in providing certain services. For example, **India** specialises in **communications** (e.g. call centres) and **IT services**.

2) If a country like India is providing a certain service to a large number of UK businesses, it **encourages** other companies to offshore that part of their business there as well. If India already has a large number of call centre providers, **prices** will probably be **competitive** and there is also likely to be a pool of suitably **trained workers**.

3) India has a **comparative advantage** over other countries that provide communication services. Because it can provide communications relatively **cheaply** and **efficiently**, it's in a **strong position** to **sell** them to other countries.

4) Specialisation does have **risks**. Workers may lose **motivation** or the size of the industry may lead to **diseconomies of scale**. There's also a risk **another country** will find a way of providing a good or service even **more efficiently**.

Locating abroad can be a way of Cutting Costs or Increasing Revenue

Locating abroad can reduce costs

1) One of the main reasons why companies choose to move production overseas is that they can often pay **foreign workers** much **lower wages** than they would have to pay their UK employees. Some companies have been accused of not paying foreign workers enough to live on — this is **unethical**.

2) The cost of **land** and **office space** also tends to be **cheaper** overseas, especially in emerging markets. For example, it's estimated that it costs around **£114** per year to rent **1m²** of office space in the **UK**. In **Malaysia**, it only costs **£38** per **m²** per year. Utilities like water and electricity might also be cheaper.

Locating abroad is a way of targeting new markets

1) Targeting new, foreign markets is one way for companies to continue to grow when their existing market **stops growing** or becomes **saturated**.

2) Relocating overseas in order to sell your products to foreign markets also helps businesses to **survive** in times of **economic downturn** or **domestic recession**.

3) Locating a firm close to the overseas market it's trying to sell to makes it easier to spot local **market trends**. This makes it less likely a company will make expensive **marketing errors** and it might even spot new market **niches**.

Locating abroad helps companies avoid trade barriers

1) Some countries create **trade barriers** in order to **protect** domestic companies from **foreign competition**. These barriers might be things like **taxes** or **restrictions** on sales of goods from abroad.

2) Locating part of a business **within** a country with trade barriers helps companies **get round** these penalties.

3) Some people also think that trade barriers protect **domestic** industries from the realities of international competition, causing them to become **inefficient**. This could mean that a **foreign** company that locates in a country with trade barriers will have a **competitive advantage**, because it's likely to be more efficient.

Improved Transport and Communication links make it easier to locate Abroad

1) In recent years, the **cost** of **air travel** has **fallen** sharply and there are many **more flights** available than there used to be. This means it is relatively **easy** for people to **travel** between overseas business locations.

2) Trading overseas has also been made easier because countries with **emerging markets** are **investing** heavily in **infrastructure**. This means that they have much better road and rail networks and ports than they had in the past. For example, in 2008, China spent 12% of its GDP on improving its infrastructure.

3) Doing business overseas has also been made easier by **technological** developments. Businesses can send messages internationally by **email** and meetings are held using **videoconferencing** — so people don't have to leave the UK.

Cost-benefit Analysis

*Cost-benefit analysis is useful for weighing up different options. This page is for **WJEC** but is also useful for **AQA** and **OCR: Business Production Option**.*

Cost-benefit Analysis finds out which is Greater — Costs or Benefits

1) **Cost-benefit analysis** involves calculating the **private** and **public costs** of a project and **weighing** them up against its **private** and **public benefits**. There's more about public costs and benefits below.

2) The basic formula for cost-benefit analysis is **social benefit – social cost**. The **social benefit** is **private benefits** and **public benefits** added together and the **social cost** is **private** and **public costs** combined.

3) This type of cost-benefit analysis is most often used by the **government** to work out the costs and benefits of a **public project**, e.g. building a new motorway, or to **rank** several projects in order of **importance**.

4) The main **advantage** of this kind of analysis is that it ensures **all costs** are **taken into account**. It also allows a **value** to be put on **positive environmental effects**, e.g. a traffic calming scheme might also reduce car emissions.

5) **Private companies** are **less likely** to use this kind of analysis because they tend to be **unwilling** to consider the **social costs** of their activities unless they're **forced** to, e.g. by government legislation. This is because trying to reduce social costs is **expensive**, and would probably result in them being **less competitive**.

6) But **private companies** do use a form of cost-benefit analysis that uses the **costs** and **revenues** shown in their final accounts. E.g. if relocating a shop to a unit in the middle of a busy high street will increase the cost of rent by £5000 a year, but takings are predicted to go up by £7000, the benefits of relocation outweigh its costs.

Cost-benefit Analysis shows whether Public Costs exceed Private Benefits

1) **Private costs** and **benefits** affect a firm directly — they're often **financial**. For example, the private cost of constructing a new shop unit might be £120 000. The **private benefit** of the new shop is the added **revenue** it will bring in.

2) **Public costs** and **benefits** are the **positive** and **negative effects** that a firm's activities have on the **outside world**. For example, **training** is a public benefit and air **pollution** is a public cost. Public costs and benefits are also called **externalities** — there's more about them on pages 138 and 140.

3) **Cost-benefit analysis** can help companies and the government work out which is **greater** — the **public cost** of something or the **private cost**. If, for example, **vaccinating** the whole population against a disease would cost **£5 million**, but the cost of **treating** the people who caught the disease would only be **£2 million**, then the government might decide it makes **more sense** to **treat** the disease, rather than to **prevent** it, despite the public cost of people **suffering** from the disease.

It can be Difficult to carry out an Accurate cost-benefit analysis

1) It's difficult to put a **financial value** on a lot of costs and benefits — e.g. it's almost impossible to know the real **monetary cost** of **pollution**. If costs and benefits are **wrongly calculated**, it might mean that a company or government makes the **wrong choice**.

   Sometimes a financial value is given to human life to make cost-benefit analysis easier. For example, if a life is worth £50 000 and a set of traffic lights will save 5 lives a year, the annual public benefit is £250 000.

2) Cost-benefit analysis might fail to **take account** of **all** the **groups** affected by a decision. For example, a new airport runway affects houseowners, workers, airlines and many more individuals. Cost-benefit analysis might not consider the impact on **everyone** who might **benefit** or **suffer** as a result of the project.

Practice Questions

Q1 Give two advantages of offshoring your IT department to a country that specialises in IT services.
Q2 Describe three advantages of locating abroad.
Q3 Give two potential problems of cost-benefit analysis.

Exam Question

Q1 Flimby council wants to build a windfarm. Explain why it would be a good idea to use cost-benefit analysis. [10 marks]

Offshoring communication — sending messages in bottles...

I don't think it's that difficult to understand why companies might like to locate abroad. After all, who wouldn't rather stare out of the window at a sunny beach rather than at a rainy, grey town centre. Make sure you learn the other advantages of international location too though, and also the stuff on cost-benefit analysis, which is a bit more complicated.

Productive Efficiency

*All these ins and outs — it's like the Hokey Cokey. P. 108 is for **OCR: Business Production Option** and p. 109 is for **WJEC**.*

Productivity measures How Good a firm is at turning Inputs into Outputs

1) **Productivity** is a way of measuring how **efficient** a business is at turning **inputs** (resources) into **output** (finished products). It's usually calculated as either labour or capital productivity.

$$\boxed{\text{Input}} \xrightarrow{\text{process}} \boxed{\text{Output}}$$

2) The business can then measure its **productive efficiency** by comparing its **productivity** over **several years** to see if it's **improving** or by looking at how its productivity compares to **productivity** in **other**, similar **firms**.

Firms measure Labour Productivity and Capital Productivity

$$\text{Labour productivity} = \frac{\text{Output per year}}{\text{Number of employees}}$$

$$\text{Capital productivity} = \frac{\text{Output per year}}{\text{Capital employed}}$$

Output is measured as the monetary value of goods produced.

Labour productivity doesn't always relate **directly** to competitiveness, or costs per unit. A business with high labour productivity might pay its workers **high wages**, which would increase its **production costs**.

Businesses can Improve their Productivity

Businesses can cut production costs

1) The **cost of materials** can be reduced, to reduce the total cost per unit.

2) The **cost of employee wages** can also be reduced.

This can reduce quality, which has a negative effect on sales.

This can reduce motivation, which lowers labour productivity.

Businesses can change production method

1) Changing from **job** to **batch** production or from **batch** to **flow** production increases efficiency.

2) Increasing the **scale** of production improves efficiency, because of **economies of scale**.

3) Switching to **lean production** improves productive efficiency. Lean production **reduces waste** to a minimum and it can also **motivate** employees to achieve more.

Businesses can change the way the workforce is managed

1) **Motivation** gets employees to work harder, and **reduces absenteeism**. See p.72-75.

2) Employees must be **trained** in the **skills** they need to do their jobs **productively** and **efficiently**.

3) **Multi-skilled** employees with broad training can be moved to **different tasks** to respond to increases in demand, and can cover for **absences**.

Training also improves motivation.

Businesses can invest in equipment

1) Employees may need **new equipment** to help them produce more, e.g. robots are used in modern car plants.

2) The **cost** of investing in new machinery may be prohibitive though.

Work Study can show where productive efficiency can be improved

1) **Work study** has two parts, **method study** and **work measurement**.

2) **Method study** examines a task and finds the most **efficient** method to use. It can cover worker motivation and ergonomic design as well as basic production methods.

3) **Work measurement** times standard tasks. It's used for **setting targets**.

Work measurement is also called time and motion study.

4) Work study is useful in finding out **where** and **how** a task can be done **more efficiently**.

5) However, managers should bear in mind that sometimes productive efficency might be affected by factors that **work study** doesn't **pick up** on — e.g. **poor management** or **dated machinery**. They need to be careful not to hold workers **responsible** for issues that are beyond their **control**.

There are Human Resource Issues with attempts to Improve Productivity

Attempts to improve productivity can be perceived by staff as a way to **wring the last drop of work** out of them without **paying** them any more.

Staff may also worry that an improvement in productivity may result in **redundancies** — if everyone's working harder, there may not be enough work to go around. The introduction of new labour-saving equipment such as robots is likely to bring redundancies, although **remaining staff** will probably be **better trained** and **better paid**.

Productive Efficiency

Outsourcing can be a way for a company to Improve Productive Efficiency

Sarah and Karl thought outsourcing was a great idea — it left them free to focus on more important activities...

1) Outsourcing is when a company pays another, **specialist** company to carry out some of its **business activities** — usually things like **IT** services or **customer service**.

2) Companies often outsource work to specialist companies located **abroad**. This is called **offshoring** — there's more about it on p.106.

3) One of the main reasons why companies outsource is to **save money**. Firms that provide outsourcing services can often do the work at much **lower cost** due to **division of labour** and **specialisation** (see p.102).

4) Companies providing outsourcing services might also have more **advanced technology** because the service they're providing is the main **focus** of their business, so they can afford to **invest** more heavily in it than the company they're working for might be able to.

5) Outsourcing firms often have greater **knowledge** and **experience** of the service they're providing.

6) It also leaves the company free to **focus** on its most important areas — such as production and developing long-term strategy.

Case study: Zurich Financial Services

Problem: Zurich is one of the biggest insurance providers in the world. In 2003, the company had around 7500 employees working in IT and 30 different computer systems. The previous year, the firm had made its biggest losses ever — $3.4 billion.

Solution: The company now outsources almost half of its IT services to specialist IT service providers like Accenture and IBM. This has reduced its number of in-house IT staff to 4000 and caused infrastructure costs to fall 45%.

Companies need to make sure they Monitor outsourced activities Closely

1) There are **disadvantages** to outsourcing too. For example, it can affect staff **motivation** if employees are concerned that outsourcing might put their **jobs** at **risk**.

2) **Communication** with **clients** can also suffer as a result of outsourcing — especially when firms outsource their call centres. Some customers don't like to think that they're speaking to a specialist call centre rather than communicating **directly** with the company. **Language barriers** can be a problem if call centres are 'offshored'.

3) The firm loses **direct control** over certain areas of the business, which can make **internal communication** slower. Sensitive **information** might be at risk of being **leaked** if its passed to external firms.

4) It takes **time** for outsourcing to be successful — it can be months before outsourced work is completely co-ordinated with the rest of the business. Firms need to **plan** for this and carefully **monitor** outsourced activities.

Practice Questions

Q1 What are the two main ways of measuring productivity?
Q2 Give four examples of things a business can do to improve productive efficiency.
Q3 Give one example of a human resource issue that might result from an attempt to improve productivity.
Q4 What is outsourcing?

Exam Questions

Q1 Calculate labour productivity for a company that outputs £4.5 million of goods per year and has 200 employees. 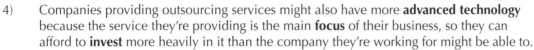 Answer on p.185. [3 marks]

Q2 Graham Green wants to do a work study in his business. Explain how he would do this, and the issues that he should bear in mind when considering the results of his study. [12 marks]

Outsource? No thanks, I prefer ketchup...

Productive efficiency is crucial — being efficient rather than inefficient has a big impact on profits. The key is to remember that productive efficiency isn't achieved by forcing staff to work like dogs — it's achieved by motivating them and teaching them how to be more efficient. You should also know why firms might get other firms to do some of their work for them.

Capacity Utilisation

Changes in capacity utilisation affect a firm's break-even point and profit levels. For **OCR: Business Production Option**.

Capacity is Maximum Output with the Resources Currently Available

1) The **capacity** of an organisation is the **maximum** output that it can produce in a given period without buying any more fixed assets — machinery, factory space, etc.
2) Capacity depends on the **number of employees** and how skilled they are.
3) Capacity depends on the kind of production **process** the business uses.
4) Capacity depends on **technology** — what **machinery** and **computer systems** a business has and the state it's in.
5) The amount of **investment** in the business is also a factor.

Capacity Utilisation is How Much Capacity is being Used

$$\text{Capacity Utilisation} = \frac{\text{Output}}{\text{Capacity}} \times 100\%$$

Capacity utilisation depends on demand.

For example: a hotel with half its rooms booked out has a capacity utilisation of 50%. A clothing factory with an output of 70 000 shirts per month and a maximum capacity of 100 000 shirts is running at 70% capacity utilisation.

Under-utilisation is Inefficient and increases Unit Costs

Low capacity utilisation is called **under-utilisation**. It's **inefficient** because it means a business is not getting as much **use** as it could out of **machines** and **facilities** that have been paid for, which causes **unit costs** to **rise**.

$$\text{Unit costs} = \text{total costs} \div \text{output}$$

You'll need to know how to calculate this in the exam.

Example: A chocolate factory's total costs are £7200 a month. In June, output was 18 000 chocolate bars, giving a unit cost of £0.40. In July, absenteeism caused output to fall to 16 000 bars, and the unit cost rose to £0.45.

1) Under-utilisation increases costs because **fixed costs** are **spread** over less **output**, so unit costs increase.
2) Higher capacity utilisation creates **economies of scale** (see p.103), which means a decrease in variable costs.
3) Operating under capacity in the **long term** can cause firms to make **big losses** and **force** them to **rationalise**.

90% Capacity Utilisation can be Better than 100% Capacity Utilisation

High capacity utilisation is better than low capacity utilisation. However, 100% capacity utilisation has **drawbacks**.

1) Businesses have to consider all their **operational targets** when they plan their capacity usage. **Cost** isn't the only thing to think about — it might not be possible to operate at 100% capacity and keep **quality** levels high.
2) The business may have to turn away potential **customers**.
3) There's no **downtime** — machines are on **all the time**. If a machine has a problem, it'll cause delays and bottlenecks as work piles up waiting for the problem to be fixed. There's no time for equipment maintenance, which can reduce the life of machinery.
4) There's no **margin of error**. Everything has to be perfect first time, which causes **stress** to managers. **Mistakes** are more likely when everyone's working flat out.
5) The business can't **temporarily increase output** for seasonal demand or one-off orders.
6) If output is greater than demand, there'll be **surplus stock** hanging about waiting to be sold. It's not good to have valuable **working capital** tied up in stock.

Businesses should plan production levels to achieve almost full capacity utilisation.

Capacity utilisation can be Increased by Reducing Capacity

1) If a business is **operating under capacity** and they think that demand isn't going to go up in the future, they need to **reduce their capacity**. This is called **rationalisation** (or **downsizing**). It's popular with large firms who want to stay competitive by cutting their production costs.
2) Businesses can reduce capacity in the **short term** by stopping **overtime** or reducing the length of the working week, allocating staff to **other work** in the business, and by not renewing **temporary contracts**.
3) Businesses can reduce capacity in the **long term** by not **replacing** staff as they retire (natural wastage), making staff **redundant**, and by **selling off** factories or equipment.
4) An area of work with low capacity utilisation can be **subcontracted out** to a specialist firm.

Capacity Utilisation

Over Capacity production means firms need More Staff working More Often

If a firm is operating near to full capacity and has a sudden increase in demand, there are methods it can use to allow it to **operate** at **over 100% capacity** for a **short** period of time.

1) Businesses can use their facilities for **more** of the **working week**. They can have staff working in **shifts** or working **overtime** on weekends and bank holidays. They can also employ **temporary** or **part-time staff**.

2) Businesses can also increase their capacity utilisation by increasing **productivity**. They can reorganise production by reallocating staff to the busiest areas of the company. In the long term, they might try to improve productivity by increasing staff **motivation**.

3) It's also possible for businesses to **sub-contract** work to other businesses in **busy periods**. **Subcontracting** is when a business pays **another business** to make a **product** on its behalf. For example, a busy architect's firm could ask another architect firm to draw up building plans on its behalf for a specific project. The **advantage** of subcontracting excess work is that it allows firms to respond to **unexpected increases in demand** without having the costs of extra staff and facilities all year round.

4) If the increased **demand** is expected to last a **long time**, firms might consider **recruiting** new staff. **Permanent** staff are **cheaper** than temporary workers in the long run.

Businesses Change capacity utilisation to match Predicted Demand

It's pointless producing more than you can sell, so companies **alter** capacity utilisation depending on **demand**.

1) Demand **changes** over time, so firms must think about demand in the **future** as well as the current demand.

2) The key to **long-term** success is planning **capacity** changes to match long-term changes in demand. Market research helps predict future demand, but it's not 100% certain. There's always an element of risk.

3) Firms should be flexible and **temporarily** increase capacity utilisation if an increase in demand isn't expected to continue in the **long term** — for example, with seasonal products like Christmas crackers, products heading towards decline in their life cycle, and one-off special orders.

4) **Long-term** solutions end up giving **lower unit costs** — as long as **predictions** of demand turn out to be **true**.

With July rapidly approaching in the Lake District, all leave was cancelled and the factory went into overdrive.

Practice Questions

Q1 Calculate capacity utilisation for a restaurant that has 65 seats but only 42 people dining each night.

Answers on p.185.

Q2 Calculate how much it costs to produce one shirt, if a factory is making 450 shirts a month and has total monthly costs of £1600.

Q3 Explain what is meant by "rationalisation".

Exam Questions

Q1 Discuss why 95% capacity utilisation is considered better for a firm than 100%. [4 marks]

Q2 Analyse how a manufacturer of fashion clothing should expand their business if recent growth has led to capacity utilisation reaching 100%. [10 marks]

No, it's not possible to run your brain at 100% capacity...

In fact, the more you learn the more information your brain can take. So, if you're struggling, have a break and a cuppa and come back and have another go a bit later. It's tricky but it should at least be vaguely familiar. You need to learn how businesses get their capacity utilisation to round about 90% or so. It doesn't just happen by chance, that's for sure.

Stock Control and Time Management

*Stock — it's not funny and it's not cool. P. 112 is for **AQA** and **OCR: Business Production Option**. P. 113 is **AQA** only.*

The value of stock a business is holding is recorded on the balance sheet (see p.47) and profit and loss account (see p.49-50).

It's **Costly** to hold lots of **Stock**

1) **Stock** is all the **raw materials** needed for making a product and the store of **finished goods** that a firm holds to supply to customers. These days firms don't tend to hold much stock — because of the **costs** involved.

2) **Storage costs** are the most **obvious cost** of holding stock. Storage costs include rent for the warehouse and also the non-obvious costs of heating, lighting, refrigeration, security etc. Don't forget those.

3) **Wastage costs** are the costs of **throwing away** useless stock. The longer a business holds stock, the more likely it is to create waste. Stock gets **physically damaged** as time goes on, and can also go **out of fashion**.

4) **Opportunity cost** is the cost of **investing** money in stock instead of **something else**. Capital tied up in stock is **unproductive** and could be used more productively elsewhere, such as financing a marketing campaign.

Stock Control aims to keep levels of stock **Just Right**

1) Most businesses try to reduce the level of stocks they're holding. The **maximum** level of stock a business wants to hold depends on the size of their warehouses, their production method and also on **opportunity cost**.

2) Businesses that use **flow production** need a **large stock** of **raw materials**, whereas **batch production** leads to large **stocks** of **work-in-progress**. **Job production** means there are **no stocks** of **finished goods** to be stored and **cell production** usually relies on **just-in-time** stock control (see below).

3) A business needs a **minimum** level of stock so that it **won't run out** of raw materials or finished goods. This minimum stock level is called **buffer stock**.

4) The **amount** of **buffer stock** needed depends on the warehouse **space** available, the kind of product (**perishable**, or something which keeps), the **rate** at which stocks are used up, and the **lead time**.

5) The **lead time** is the time it takes for goods to **arrive** after ordering them from the supplier. The **longer** the lead time, the **more buffer stocks** you need to hold — if customer demand suddenly went up, you wouldn't want to wait a long time for stocks to arrive from the supplier. A **short lead time** means you can have **small** buffer stocks and top them up as and when you need to.

Stock Control Charts help control **Stock Management**

Stock control charts allow managers to **analyse** and **control** stock over a period of time — as shown below. Have a good look at the diagram. It'll make stock control easier to understand.

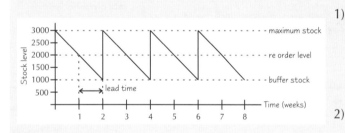

1) The **buffer stock level** is **1000 units**. The **lead time** is 1 week, and the business goes through **1000 units** each week. That means they have to **re-order** stock when they've got **2000** units left — just so they don't go below their buffer stock level. 2000 units is the **re-order level**.

2) The firm re-orders **2000 units** each time. This takes them back to their **maximum stock level** of 3000 units.

Just-In-Time (JIT) Production keeps stock levels **Very Low**

1) **Just-in-time** production aims to have as **little stock** as possible. Ideally, all raw materials come in one door, are made into products and go straight out another door — all **just in time** for delivery to customers.

2) JIT is based on very efficient stock control. **Kanban** is the JIT system of triggering **repeat orders**. When staff reach coloured kanban cards towards the end of a batch of components, they order more straight away. The **supply** of raw materials is **linked directly** to the **demand** for raw materials, and there's no need for lots of stock.

3) JIT has **advantages** — **storage costs** are reduced and **working capital control** is improved. There's **less waste** because there's less out-of-date stock lying around.

4) There are **disadvantages** — no stock means customers can't be supplied during **production strikes**. Businesses using JIT can't respond to **sudden rises** in demand. Suppliers have to be **reliable** because there isn't much stock of raw materials to keep production going.

Stock Control and Time Management

Time-based Management means companies have to be Flexible

1) Time-based management means that as well as competing on price and quality, companies can also **compete** on **time** by trying to be the **fastest** to get their product on the market. It's often used to produce **technological** items and **high fashion** clothes — areas where consumer needs change fast.

2) Time-based management depends on **flexible production facilities**, e.g. machines that can do more than one thing. For example, a fashion retailer might need a machine that can sew buttons onto coats one week and attach zips the next.

3) For time-based management to work, **effective communication** between managers and production staff is essential, so the business needs to have a culture of **trust**. Staff also need to be **multi-skilled** — so **training** is important.

Tim knew he had to get his 'real-life effect' baby ice sculpture to consumers as quick as possible — otherwise it would melt.

> **THE ADVANTAGES OF TIME-BASED MANAGEMENT ARE:**
>
> 1) It **reduces lead times** — so the cost of holding stock falls.
>
> 2) Reduced lead times also mean that **customer needs** can be satisfied **quicker**, giving the company a **competitive advantage**.
>
> 3) **Machinery** with more than one function makes it possible to offer customers a more **varied** product range.

4) However, some people have **criticised** time-based management for placing speed above **quality** — customers get a product sooner, but it might be faulty or not last as long.

Companies can also take a Time-based approach to R&D

1) The pressure of **intense international competition** and **rapidly changing technology** means that larger, multinational businesses need to come up with new, better products, **all the time**. Businesses need to use **R&D** to develop new products so that they maintain or increase their global market share.

2) The **demands** of the market **change rapidly**, and manufacturers are under pressure to **react rapidly** to meet these changing demands. New product development, like production, is squeezed into as **short** a time as possible, to get the product out to consumers as quickly as possible.

> **Example: Computer hardware and software**
> In **personal computer hardware**, as soon as one manufacturer has come out with a **new product** such as a teeny hard drive or a superfast processor, other manufacturers have to get similar products onto the market **immediately**.
>
> Computer **software** is often released before it's **really 100% ready**, and the software producer supplements the release with "**patches**" which fix any problems with the original release. This is because of the **intense time pressure**.

Practice Questions

Q1 What is meant by 'stock'?

Q2 Name two advantages of just-in-time production.

Q3 Why might a company take a time-based approach to R&D?

Exam Questions

Answer on p.185.

Q1 A suitcase shop needs 400 units of buffer stock. The lead time on new suitcases is a fortnight and the shop sells 200 suitcases a week. What is its re-order level? [4 marks]

Q2 Samuel Owen owns a women's clothes shop. A friend has recently suggested that he tries using time-based management techniques. Explain what advantages and disadvantages he might encounter if he does this. [10 marks]

Just-in-time production is a good idea — just-in-time revision isn't...

Hopefully you're reading this a good few weeks before the exam and you've got time to read and scribble until it's properly embedded in your memory. If you are tight for time though, don't panic. It's best to make sure you're really clear on topics you're already familiar with, rather than trying to learn something new. And, most importantly, get some zzzzzzz

Quality

*Quality control, quality assurance or Quality Street® — I know which I prefer. These two pages are for **AQA** and
OCR: Business Production Option.*

Quality Control and Quality Assurance are Different Things

1) It's **important** that companies produce **quality** goods. Most **customers** realise
    that **lower priced** goods won't be as **high** quality as more **expensive** ones, but
    they do expect a product to be **fit for purpose** (to do the job it's intended for).

2) There are **two** ways for a company to check it's producing goods
    of a suitable quality — **quality control** and **quality assurance**.

*Staff had taken quality assurance
to a new level — if they didn't turn
up to work, things couldn't go
wrong in the first place...*

3) **Quality control** means **checking goods** as you make them or when they arrive from suppliers
    to see if anything is wrong with them. It's often done by specially trained **quality inspectors**.

4) **Quality assurance** means introducing measures into the **production process** to try to ensure
    things don't go **wrong** in the first place. It assumes you can **prevent errors** from being made
    in the first place, rather than **eliminating faulty goods** once they've been made.

Quality Control	Quality Assurance (QA)
Assumes that errors are **unavoidable**.	Assumes that errors are **avoidable**.
Detects errors and **puts them right**.	**Prevents errors** and aims to get it **right first time**.
Quality control inspectors check other people's work, and are responsible for quality.	**Employees** check their own work. **Workers** are **responsible** for passing on good quality work to the next stage of the production process.

Quality Circles are Groups of Employees who work on quality issues

1) **Quality circles** meet a couple of times a month to discuss quality control issues.

2) They include employees from **various departments** and **all levels** of the organisation.

3) Quality circles aim to **identify** and **solve** specific quality problems that arise.

Strengths of Quality Circles	Weaknesses of Quality Circles
Quality circles can be very effective because they use the **knowledge** and **experience** of factory floor staff.	Factory floor staff might make **unrealistic** suggestions if they don't know what kind of measures the business can **afford** to introduce.
Quality circles are a good way of making staff feel involved and increasing **motivation**.	Quality circles are only useful if management actually **listen** to the suggestions and **make changes** accordingly.
Quality circles often lead to an increase in **productivity** as well as quality.	Only works if participation really is **voluntary** — staff who feel pressured into taking part are unlikely to make useful suggestions.

Total Quality Management assures Commitment To Quality

1) **Total Quality Management** (TQM) means the **whole workforce** has to be committed to quality improvements.
    The idea is to **build quality** in every department and not let quality get squeezed out. It's QA on wheels.

2) With TQM, every employee has to try to **satisfy customers** — both **external** customers
    that the business sells things to, and **internal** customers within the business.

Advantages of TQM	Disadvantages of TQM
Because all employees are involved with maintaining quality, TQM can help them to bond as a **team**.	It can take a **long time** to introduce TQM — so the company might not see immediate improvements in quality.
TQM boosts a company's **reputation** for providing quality services or products.	TQM can **demotivate staff** — it can seem like a lot of effort to think about quality in all parts of the business.
TQM usually leads to fewer **faulty** products being made — so the business creates less **waste**.	TQM is usually **expensive** to introduce — it often means investing in **training** for all employees.

Quality

Benchmarking Learns from Other Businesses

1) Benchmarking studies **other businesses** with excellent **quality standards**, and aims to **adopt** their **methods**. Companies can sometimes do this by joining benchmarking groups, where firms agree to share information about their way of doing things.

2) Businesses can **benchmark internally**, by studying similar activities in different departments.

3) It's also possible to benchmark across **different industries** — for example, an electronics manufacturer buys different raw materials than a food producer does, but the food producer might still find it useful to benchmark the **purchasing methods** and **negotiation techniques** used by the electronics company.

4) Benchmarking tends to **motivate** staff. It's more encouraging to introduce something that you've already seen being **used successfully** somewhere else than it is to introduce something completely **unknown**.

5) Another advantage is that it provides **early warnings** to businesses about **technology** or **methods** that might allow their competitors to **overtake** them.

6) One of the disadvantages of benchmarking is that the **firm** whom you're most **keen** to **benchmark** may **not** want to **share** their methods. **Competitors** are unlikely to **release** information if they're not part of a benchmarking group.

7) Another downside is that **working practices** can't always be transferred between different **corporate cultures**.

Kaizen is Japanese for Continuous Improvement

1) The **kaizen** approach means that employees should be **improving** their work slightly **all the time**, instead of making one-off improvements when management tell them to.

2) The **5 whys** are also important in kaizen. Whenever there's a problem, companies need to ask **'why?'** five times. For example, the firm's **reputation** seems to be getting worse. Managers investigate why and discover that an **unhappy customer** has talked about her poor experience. Further investigation shows that she didn't receive an order **on time**. The reason for this is that it took more than a week to **process** her order, which was due to a **lack** of **call centre staff**. Asking why there aren't enough call centre staff shows that business has **increased** 10%, but no extra staff have been **recruited**. So the real solution to the problem lies in **recruitment**, not in **PR** to improve the firm's image.

3) Workers are also responsible for keeping their equipment **clean**, their work area **tidy**, and making sure that everything is kept in the **right place**. For kaizen to work, they need to do this **every day**, not just occasionally.

4) For kaizen to work, employees at the bottom of the hierarchy have to be given some control over **decision-making** so that they can actually **implement** quality improvements.

5) Kaizen helps workers feel **involved** in quality assurance. It's also **cheap** to introduce.

6) The downside of kaizen is that, because it makes **small changes** over time, it's not great for businesses that **urgently** need to improve quality. It needs the firm to be willing to commit to the method in the **long-term**.

Practice Questions

Q1 What's the difference between quality control and quality assurance?

Q2 Describe two advantages and two disadvantages of TQM.

Q3 What is 'kaizen'?

Exam Questions

Q1 Paul Newby wants to benchmark his business against similar firms. Explain the benefits of doing this, as well as some of the problems he might encounter. [10 marks]

Q2 Bella Stevens makes table lamps. Recently a large number of customers have been returning products, saying they're unhappy with the quality. Explain how kaizen might help Bella to better understand the problem. [8 marks]

Benchmarking — the defence method favoured by lazy footballers...

It's often expensive for companies to do a really good job of monitoring quality, but it's usually worth it — if customers know you can be counted on to provide a quality product it gives you a real competitive advantage. Make sure you learn the pros and cons of these methods inside out in case you get asked to recommend a method or assess an existing one.

Research and Development

*Launching new products involves a lot of time at the drawing board. For **AQA** and **OCR: Business Production Option**.*

Research and Development comes up with New ideas, products and processes

1) Research and Development (R&D) does **technical research** to come up with new products. Many firms do some form of R&D, but businesses who want to **innovate** depend on it.

2) R&D has to turn raw ideas into **products** or **new processes**. This can take a long time.

3) R&D is **related** to market research, but they're not the same. Market research **discovers** what customers want and R&D comes up with new products to **meet** the customers' wants.

4) R&D can also be used to come up with new **production methods** — e.g. to improve productive efficiency.

Innovation can be Risky but is often the best way to make Big Profits

1) Research and Development is a very **costly** process.

2) It's also a **risky** process — it's estimated that in the **pharmaceutical** industry, only **1 in 12** new drugs **researched** are actually thought to have commercial potential and developed. Companies can end up developing something customers don't want, or they might not be able to produce the product on a large scale at a low enough cost.

3) However, market leaders normally invest in R&D. The most successful businesses have a **large portfolio** of products, **balanced** between **innovative new products** and proven older products (see p.27).

4) The ability to successfully launch a new product in the market is of great value. A company can charge a high price for its innovative product (this is called market skimming), before competitors enter the market with **similar products** at **competitive prices**. The original Sony WALKMAN® was a great example of this.

5) Being innovative can be good for a firm's **reputation** — e.g. if they've been the first to launch exciting electrical products in the past, customers will naturally go to them if they want a cutting edge digital camera or whatever.

6) Some industries are particularly **fast moving**, and need to **constantly** develop new products — e.g. the pharmaceutical industry, the microchip industry and the mobile telecommunications industry.

7) Some organisations choose not to have a specific R&D department, but instead they **adapt** and **modify** new products brought out by their **rivals**. This may be because the business is risk averse, or because its shareholders prefer profits to be paid as dividends in the short term rather than invested for the long term.

New Product Development (NPD) has Six Stages from Idea to Launch

1) Idea

The business comes up with **new ideas**, explores and **develops existing ideas** or **modifies competitors' ideas**. New ideas can come from **brainstorming** in a group, from **employee suggestions** or from **R&D department meetings**. New ideas are also discovered through **market research** finding out what consumers want, or from customers submitting requests to a firm. Businesses can sometimes also use **already patented ideas**, for a fee.

2) Analysis and Screening

The business wants to see if the product can be produced and sold at a **profit**. All aspects of the idea are investigated — whether there's a **potential market** for it or not, based on market research, whether the **technology** and **resources** exist to develop it, whether a **competitor** has an existing patent on a similar idea. At this stage, a **prototype** may be made to see what the product will be like.

3) Development

The **R&D department** develop a **working prototype**. They test it **scientifically**, and tweak the design to make the **functional** design (how it works) and **aesthetic** design (how it looks, feels — or smells and tastes if it's a food) as good as possible. This is the real "meat" of research and development.

4) Value Analysis

The business tries to make the product good **value** for money. They look at the cost of **making**, **warehousing** and **distributing** the product to make sure the whole process is **good value** — for both **business** and **consumer**.

5) Test Marketing ⟸ This is where the marketing department gets involved again.

The business sometimes sells the new product in a **limited geographical area**, and then analyses **consumer feedback** on the product, price and packaging. This allows **modifications** to be made before a wider launch.

6) Launch

A successful launch requires **enough stock** of the product to be distributed across the market. It also needs an effective **promotional campaign** in place to **persuade** retailers and consumers to buy the product.

SECTION FOUR — OPERATIONS MANAGEMENT

Research and Development

Value Analysis *finds out if the product adds enough* Value *to* Justify *its* Costs

1) **Value analysis** looks at factors which affect "**value added**" — how much the customer is prepared to **pay** for the product compared to how much it cost to **make** the product.

2) Businesses do value analysis to assess how well the product does its **job**, whether consumers like the way it **looks**, and whether they'd be prepared to pay a little more for it.

"But could we have used cheaper corks?"
This was the question that kept Elena up at night.

3) Value analysis investigates all the **costs of production** to see whether they could be reduced. For example, maybe cheaper materials or cheaper processes could be used.

4) Value analysis has been blamed for reduction in **quality** — cheaper materials and cheaper labour sometimes create a **tatty product** or one that **wears out** quite quickly.

5) However, some people argue that most customers will **replace** their laptop computer after 5 years whether it's **worn out** or **not**, so there's no equipping it with a battery that lasts 50 years. Supplying a battery with a 5 year lifespan is an **effective response** to **market research** — it means the company is meeting customer needs exactly.

Innovation *affects what goes on in* Other Departments

FINANCE

1) R&D for innovative products is **expensive**, so the finance department might need to raise extra **working capital** to pay for it. For more about ways of raising finance, see pages 31-33.

2) Innovation in **production methods** might mean that finance has to spend a lot on new **capital** (machinery). New machinery is expensive, but tends to make companies more **cost-effective** in the **long-term**.

MARKETING

1) Companies might **increase** the amount of **market research** they do when researching an innovative idea — the risks and costs are high, so they need to be absolutely sure customers want or need the product.

2) An innovative product can lead to big changes in the **marketing mix**. For example, marketing will often use a different **pricing strategy** (usually skimming) for an innovative product. Promotional activities are affected too — there's often a lot of **PR** (public relations) activity when a radically new product is launched as everyone wants to feature it in their newspaper or on their TV show.

HUMAN RESOURCES

1) Innovation can mean there's a change in **staffing needs** — if a company suddenly decides to focus heavily on R&D they might need more **skilled staff**.

2) HR need to make sure that the business has the right **culture** for innovation to be successful. In a culture where staff are **scared** of the consequences of **failing** (e.g. that it might lead to dismissal), workers are unlikely to want to take risks. It's the job of HR to find ways of **encouraging** employees to take **risks**, e.g. by **rewarding** people who try **new things**, even if they don't work.

Practice Questions

Q1 What's meant by "research and development"?
Q2 Give two reasons why R&D is risky.
Q3 What is value analysis?
Q4 Give two ways that R&D can affect the marketing department.

Exam Question

Q1 Explain why it is important to invest in research and development. [10 marks]

R&D — not to be confused with R&B, which can also be fast-moving...

Hey, all those amazing new products have to come from somewhere. Just think, there are research and development eggheads beavering away as we speak, to come up with something utterly amazing that we'll all rush out to buy. Of course, it could turn out to be yet another shampoo for colour treated hair, or yet another web publishing tool. Yippee.

Controlling Operations

*Only **OCR: Business Production Option** people need p. 118. Luckily, there aren't many words because of that big picture.*

Gantt Charts help Control Operations

1) A business must make sure it carries out marketing, production and sales processes in the **correct order**.

2) Gantt charts have horizontal bars which represent the **duration** of each individual task in a complex operation. The tasks are arranged to show which tasks can be done at the **same time**.

Example: This simple Gantt chart shows the things that a business must do before it can open a new shop.

Task	Week 1	2	3	4	5	6	7	8	9	10	11	12	13	14	15	16	17	18	19	20
Market research	■	■	■																	
Obtaining premises				■	■															
Planning permission						■	■	■	■											
Shopfitting										■	■	■	■	■	■	■	■	■	■	
Recruiting workers					■	■	■	■												
Training workers										■	■	■	■	■						
Unpacking stock																■	■	■	■	
Grand opening																				■

1) The **length** of each bar represents the **time** that a task takes.

2) The chart helps to schedule the events. Some tasks can take place **simultaneously**, while other tasks are dependent upon another task getting finished first.

3) So... in this example the firm can begin to **start shopfitting** in **week 10** once planning permission has been granted to use the premises as a shop. Shopfitting takes 10 weeks, therefore the chart shows that the new shop can't open until **week 20**.

There are Several Advantages to using Gantt Charts

1) They show at a glance whether a project or production line is **on schedule**.

2) If it's falling behind, more resources can be allocated. This means operations can be **controlled** more efficiently.

3) The graphical format is **easy to understand**. It's a good way for managers to communicate what needs to be done to the rest of a team.

4) For Gantt charts to be effective, managers need to remember to **update** them if anything changes.

5) One **disadvantage** of Gantt charts is that they don't show how one activity being **delayed** will affect all the **other activities** on the chart. For example, it doesn't make clear how a delay obtaining premises affects recruitment.

6) For very **complex projects** with lots and lots (30+) of **different activities**, **critical path analysis** is often used as an **alternative** to Gantt charts.

Practice Questions

Q1 What does the length of a horizontal bar on a Gantt chart show?

Q2 Give two advantages of using Gantt charts to control operations.

Answer on p.185.

Exam Question

Q1 Mr Snowdon is relaunching his shop for the winter season. It takes a week to buy stock, and two weeks to repaint the changing rooms. Planning the launch party takes three weeks, and staff training takes four weeks. Making the window displays takes another fortnight. Buying stock, repainting the changing rooms and planning the launch party can all be done simultaneously. The staff can't be trained until the stock arrives and the window displays can't be done until the staff are trained. Draw a Gantt chart to show Mr Snowdon's schedule. [6 marks]

I prefer Cant charts — as in, I cant possibly do that until a week on Friday...

Actually, Gantt charts are great. They show you all the different bits of a project and exactly when you need to start each one. I might even start using them to organise my personal life. Which reminds me... another advantage of Gantt charts is that you can normally draw one up in a basic spreadsheet program — so you could even have a go at making your own.

Critical Path Analysis

*Critical Path Analysis is used to find the most cost-effective way of doing a complex project. You need to learn the stuff on the next three pages **no matter which board** you're doing.*

Critical Path Analysis works out the Quickest Way to Finish a Set Of Tasks

Critical Path Analysis (CPA) identifies the most **efficient** and **cost-effective** way of completing a complex project — i.e. a project made up of a series of activities.

1) The various activities which together will make up the project are **identified**, and the **order** or **sequence** of these activities is identified.

2) The **duration** (how long each activity will take) is **estimated**.

> *For large, complicated projects made up of tens of steps, computer programs are used to construct the network.*

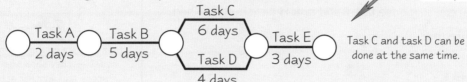

> *CPA is sometimes just called 'network analysis'.*

Task C and task D can be done at the same time.

3) These factors are then arranged as a **network** or graph, showing the whole project from start to finish, and showing which tasks happen at the same time.

4) The **shortest time** required to get from start to finish is identified. The sequence of tasks which have to be done one after another with **no gaps in between**, to get the project done as fast as possible, is called the **critical path**. Activities on the critical path are called **critical activities** — if they're delayed, the **whole project** is delayed.

Critical Paths include Start Times, Finishing Times and Float Time

1) **EST** = **earliest start time**, in number of days since the start of the project. An activity can't start until the activity before it has been completed — e.g. you can't ice a cake before it's baked. EST is worked out by **adding** the **duration** of the **previous activity** to its **EST**. The EST of the first activity is always 0.

> E.g. a business needs a sign for the door. The sign needs to be **constructed** (3 days), **painted** (2 days), left to **dry** (4 days) and then **hung** (1 day).
> So, the EST of drying is: $0 + 3 + 2 = 5$

2) **EFT** = **earliest finishing time**. It's the time that an activity will **finish** if it's **started** at the **earliest start time**. You can work out the EFT for an activity by **adding** its **duration** (in days here) to its **EST**.

> Using the same example, the EFT of drying is: $5 + 4 = 9$

3) **LFT** = **latest finishing time**. This is the **latest** time by which the activity can be completed without **holding up** the **next activity**. It's calculated by **subtracting** the **duration** of the activity from the **LFT** of the **next task** — you have to work out the LFTs by **working backwards** from the **end** of the project.

> If the business needs the sign to be hung by the end of **day 14**, the LFT of **painting is: $14 - 1 - 4 = 9$**

4) **LST** = **latest start time**. It's the **latest** time an activity can be **started** and still be **finished** by its **LFT**. To calculate LST, **subtract** the **duration** of the activity from its **LFT**.

> The LST of **painting** in the example above is: $9 - 2 = 7$

5) **Float time** is the **spare time** available for an activity. Only **non-critical** activities have **float time**.

- **Free float** is the length of **time** you can **delay** an individual **activity** for without **affecting** the **EST** of the **next** activity. You can work it out by:

> EST (next activity) − duration (this activity) − EST (of this activity) = **free float**

- **Total float time** is the length of **time** you can **delay** a **path** of **activities** for without **affecting** the **finish** time for the **overall project**. You can work it out by:

> LFT (this activity) − duration (this activity) − EST (this activity) = **total float time**

Critical Path Analysis

Here's an *Example* of *Critical Path Analysis*

A project is made up of **nine separate tasks** — A to I:

- **Task A** takes **4 days** to complete and can be done at the same time as **task G** (5 days).
- **Task B** (7 days) and **task C** (9 days) can be done at the **same time** once **task A** is finished.
- **Task D** (6 days) can start once **task B** is completed.
- **Task E** (5 days) can start once **task B** and **task C** have **both** finished. **Task E** can be done at the **same time** as **task D**.
- **Task F** (3 days) can start once **task D** and **task E** have both finished.
- **Task H** (7 days) can start once **task G** has finished.
- **Task I** (4 days) can start once **task F** and **task H** have both finished.

Guide to Nodes

Number of node.

Earliest start time of next activity.

Latest finish time of previous activity.

The circles on the network are called nodes — they show where one activity stops and another activity begins.

The network looks like this:

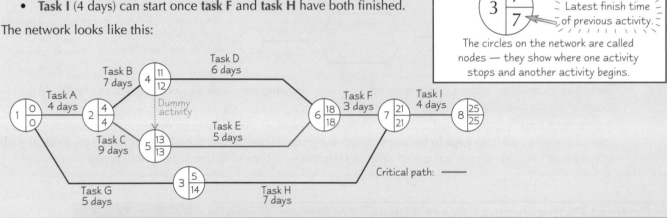

1) The **critical path** (in red) is task **A** (4 days) then task **C** (9 days), task **E** (5 days), task **F** (3 days) and finally task **I** (4 days). If you add up the time taken to do each task, it shows that the project takes **25 days** in total. The EST and LFT of task I in the final node are both 25 days.

2) You can work out the **ESTs** of all the tasks by working **forwards** from the start of the project, and then work out the **LFTs** of the tasks by working backwards from the end of the project.

3) In each node on the **critical path**, the EST equals the LFT. For nodes that are off the critical path, the EST and LFT are **different**.

4) **Task B** and **task D** both have a total **float time** of 1 day, and **task G** and **task H** have a total float time of 9 days. These tasks are **non-critical activities** — if there is a **delay** in starting them, it's still possible to complete the project **on time**. E.g. if task G starts on day 5 instead of day 0, it will still be completed before its latest finishing time. If **critical tasks** start **late** or take **longer** than they're expected to, the project **can't** be completed on time.

> There is a **dummy activity** between node 4 and node 5. A **dummy activity** is an **imaginary activity** — it just shows that one activity is **dependent** on another. In the example, the dummy activity shows that **task E can't start** until **task B** and **task C** have **both** finished. **Without** the dummy activity it would look as though **task E** was only dependent on **task C**, but having only **one node** between tasks B and C and tasks D and E would imply that **task D** was dependent on **both task B** and **task C**, instead of just **task B**.

Critical Path Analysis is used for *Scheduling* and *Allocating Resources*

1) Critical path analysis is used when **planning** a **complicated project**, such as the launch of a new product or building a new office block.

2) It allows companies to work out when they'll need **resources** to be **available**, e.g. that a certain **machine** will need to be **free** on Friday or that **raw materials** will need to be **ordered** so they arrive on day 25 of a project.

3) In many cases, it's possible to **shorten** the **critical path** by allocating **additional resources** to an activity. For example, sewing buttons onto a batch of jumpers might be expected to take 5 days, but if the company hired extra machinists, it might be possible to reduce that to 3 days.

4) Some **resources** can be **switched** between activities — e.g. multi-skilled staff can be moved from construction to painting. It's easier to switch resources between activities if the firm has **flexible production facilities** (see p.113).

5) Critical path analysis also helps managers with **strategic decision-making**. Knowing the **latest finish time** of a project makes it easier to decide when to launch an **ad campaign** or when to schedule a **launch party**.

Critical Path Analysis

Critical Path Analysis has several Advantages

1) CPA identifies the **critical activities** (activities on the critical path), which need to be supervised closely, to make sure they meet their deadlines.

2) Labour resources can be transferred from activities with **float time** to **critical activities**, to make sure that deadlines are met.

3) CPA allows managers to operate **just-in-time** production. **Resources** such as raw materials, labour and equipment can be employed efficiently from the **earliest start time**, instead of hanging around waiting to be needed. This saves on the **storage costs** and opportunity costs of stock holding, and **improves liquidity**.

4) Critical path analysis helps firms forecast their **cash flow** — it gives definite earliest start times when cash will need to be spent on raw materials, which allows the firm to predict its liquidity.

5) Critical path analysis finds the shortest time possible for completing a complex project. This can give a competitive advantage. It's an important element of **time-based management**.

6) It's an excellent **visual aid** to communications, because it shows at a glance which steps take place at the **same time**, and which have any **float time**.

7) Critical path analysis forces managers to think about the **activities** involved in the project. Without the **systematic approach** of critical path analysis, something might be forgotten.

8) CPA can be used to review progress on **individual tasks**, e.g. if a task overruns its float time or total float time you can see if it will delay the overall project or just the next activity. If there are changes and modifications to the progress of the project, the critical path can be **updated** as the project goes on.

Critical Path Analysis has Disadvantages as well

1) Critical path analysis relies on **estimates** of how long each task will take. If these aren't accurate, the whole analysis will be inaccurate.

2) Unless **critical activities** are identified and supervised closely, there'll be **delays** to the whole project. Critical path analysis can sometimes put **excessive pressure** on managers to **meet deadlines**.

3) Managers must make changes to the CPA once they know that delays are likely. Otherwise, it'll be inaccurate.

4) Constructing the CPA will require a significant amount of **planning** and **time**.

5) Critical path analysis sets **tight deadlines**, especially for critical activities. It's tempting for employees to **cut corners** in the rush to meet deadlines. **Quality** can suffer.

6) Critical path analysis can't tell you anything about **costs** — or anything about **how good** the project is.

Practice Questions

Q1 What is meant by the "critical path"?
Q2 What do the initials EST and LST mean?
Q3 Explain the term "total float time".
Q4 Give two advantages to managers of using critical path analysis.

Exam Questions

Q1 A project contains six separate activities. Activity A must be completed first, and it has an estimated duration of eight days. Activities B, C and D can take place at the same time — B takes four days, C six days and D four days. E can only be started once B, C and D are completed and will take seven days. Once E is completed, F and G can take place at the same time — F taking three days and G five days.
Answer on p.185.
(a) construct a critical path analysis from this data. [5 marks]
(b) Mark in the critical path and state the minimum number of days the project will take to complete. [2 marks]
(c) what are the float times at B and F? [2 marks]

Q2 What is the purpose of a critical path analysis? Identify and explain three advantages and three disadvantages of employing this technique. [14 marks]

What did the critical path say — "get your badly-dressed self off my gravel"...

To be honest, this is hard to learn from scratch. Once you've got a diagram to show the order of tasks in a project, and which ones can be done simultaneously, you can figure out where there's some spare time. Remember that you work out EST by working forwards from the start date, and you work out LFT by going backwards from the end date.

External Constraints on Production

External factors affect businesses (e.g. laws, availability of resources, market size). Businesses also have an effect on their external environment — they need to be aware of this and control the amount of waste they create and energy they use. Page 122 is for OCR: Business Production Option and page 123 is for OCR: Business Production Option and WJEC.

There are External Constraints on Production

Businesses face production constraints they **can't control**, because they're **external**. These might include:

1) **Market size**. There's no point in producing 1000 units if you know that last year there were only 300 sold in the whole of the market.

2) **Supply chain**. A business must be aware of what its **suppliers** are capable of supplying them with. There's no point in filling 2000 bottles with cola if your supplier can only provide you with 1000 bottle tops.

3) **Competition**. No business operates in isolation — everyone's got competitors, and each business must keep an eye on what the competition is doing. Competitor actions may affect the **number of units** that need to be produced, or **what product** needs to be produced.

4) **The law**. Some aspects of production are controlled by law. There's much more about this on p.124-125.

5) **Public Relations**. Businesses try to avoid doing things that'll give them a **bad press**. Environmental damage, or ethical problems such as the use of child labour or testing on animals can give a business a bad name.

What do you mean, we can't produce a billion units of deadly radioactive lemonade in a year? How about a million — the production line would handle a million units, right?

Ethics and Production

- A firm looking to **reduce costs** as much as possible would use the **cheapest labour** possible and make sure its workers worked the **longest hours** possible, with the **least** possible **health and safety** and **employment rights**. Moving production to some less economically developed countries (LEDCs) can achieve this.

- This kind of behaviour is often seen to be **unethical**, which can affect a company's **image**. For this reason, most companies try to behave ethically, e.g. by paying fair wages and investing in measures to improve health and safety, even though it might make production more expensive.

- Ethical considerations aren't limited to production in LEDCs. Switching to **24-hour production** could be seen as forcing workers to accept non-family-friendly **night shifts**.

- There's lots **more** about how ethical issues affect businesses on p.136.

Resource Management *means trying to use resources in the Best Way*

1) Businesses use lots of different resources. **Raw materials** count as resources and so do **machinery** and **staff**. Firms should try to use resources as efficiently as possible — this is called **optimising** the use of resources.

2) Obviously, it makes **financial sense** to avoid wasting resources. Not using what you've paid for really wrecks those precious **cost-per-unit** ratios. Wasting resources also has **social** and **opportunity costs** (see opposite).

3) It makes long-term sense to use resources **sustainably**. Completely **running out** of a resource would be bad news. Also, as resources **run low**, their **price rises** (supply and price are linked, remember), increasing **costs**.

> For example, as **oil supplies** start to dip, the **price of oil** will **go up**, and it'll keep going up. Producing goods made from crude oil, such as **plastics**, will become more **expensive**. **Transporting** goods will also get more expensive, which will **increase costs** for pretty much every business out there.

4) A business can find out if it's using resources sustainably by doing a **green audit** (sometimes called an environmental audit).

5) **Green audits** assess whether the firm is meeting **legal requirements** for environmental protection, and whether it's meeting its own **green targets** for things like carbon dioxide emissions, amount of cardboard recycled, amount of waste discharged into waterways, etc. You can do a green audit for the **whole business** or for a particular **product** or **department**. There's more about them on p.138.

6) Making the most of capital and human resources doesn't just mean running machines **24/7** and trying to **force** workers to be more **productive**. **Machines** tend to **last longer** if they're **switched off** occasionally, kept **clean** and regularly **serviced**. Getting the **best** from **employees** might mean taking steps to increase **motivation** or making work a nice place to be in order to reduce **labour turnover**.

External Constraints on Production

You can get rid of waste by *Burying* it, *Burning* it or *Recycling* it

1) **Landfill** means getting rid of rubbish by **burying** it on special sites. Most rubbish in the UK is disposed of this way. The advantage of this method is that it's **easy** and **cheap** (although businesses do have to pay special **taxes** on landfill waste). The **disadvantages** are that landfill sites produce large amounts of **methane**, a greenhouse gas which causes **global warming**, and that the UK is rapidly running out of **space** to bury rubbish.

2) **Incineration** is when waste is **burnt**. Many people think it's more **environmentally friendly** than landfill, because the **gases** released during burning can now be **cleaned** before they're released into the atmosphere (although some people are worried that the clean gas might still have negative effects on people's **health**). Other disadvantages are that incinerators are **ugly** (so people campaign against them being built) and there are still very **few** incinerators in the UK.

3) **Recycling** is the most **environmentally friendly** way for businesses to get rid of waste. Not everything can be recycled, but a lot of stuff can — **paper**, **glass**, **metals** and **plastic**, for example. Businesses can also recycle **resources** used in the **production process** by **cleaning** them and then either using them again or releasing them back into the environment. **Water** is often recycled this way.

4) Businesses can also try to **reduce** the **amount** of waste. **Lean production** techniques aim to reduce waste to an absolute bare minimum — mainly in order to reduce **opportunity costs** and increase **productive efficiency**. The benefits to **society** and the **environment** are a happy knock-on effect.

Good *Waste Management* can increase *Efficiency* and *Profits*

Effective **resource management** will involve good **waste management**. It's in the interests of a business to minimise waste, since **more waste** means **more costs per unit**. These costs can take a number of forms:

1) **Financial costs.** The most **obvious** cost involved in throwing away resources is the money that's been spent on **purchasing** them. Ensuring that the production process **makes the most** of every raw material used means that the costs are minimised.

2) **Opportunity costs.** The money that has paid for the wasted materials could have been used **elsewhere** in the business.

> Waste disposal is an ethical issue. For example, it's unethical for a business to dump its waste in landfill without considering the impact it has on the environment.

3) **Social costs.** Waste has to be handled and managed and this imposes costs on **society**. For example, waste that's disposed of in **landfill sites** may be an **eyesore** to the local community.

4) **Environmental costs.** These include **air pollution** from incinerating waste, **water pollution** from discharging it into rivers and **groundwater pollution** from burying it.

Practice Questions

Q1 Name one external factor that might affect how many goods a business produces, and explain how it might affect production.

Q2 What is resource management?

Q3 Name three ways of getting rid of waste.

Q4 Give three examples of the costs of waste.

Exam Questions

Q1 Snazzyplazzy Ltd is a food packaging company that produces a lot of plastic waste. Analyse how the company might be able to reduce the amount of waste it sends to landfill. [10 marks]

Q2 "Effective waste management is as important to a business as effective human resource management." Evaluate this statement, using examples to justify your views. [16 marks]

I tried to find a waste joke, but they were all rubbish...

Production departments have had a lot more issues to consider as firms have become more ethical. Not only do they have to worry about the stuff they've always had to worry about, like their suppliers and the law, but they also need to think about how they're treating workers and whether they're using resources efficiently. And lots to think about means lots to learn...

Production and the Law

*There are a number of laws that affect the production of goods, and so any business that's involved in production must be aware of their implications. These pages are for **AQA** and **OCR: Business Production Option**.*

The Law protects Customers and Consumers

The Trade Descriptions Act (1968)

This law ensures that businesses don't **mislead** consumers with **false descriptions** on **packaging** or **advertising materials**.

The Sale of Goods Act (1979)

1) This Act sets out the main **rights** of customers when making a purchase.

2) It's been updated by the **Sale and Supply of Goods Act (1994)**, and the **Sale and Supply of Goods to Consumers Regulations (2002)**. Together, these laws mean that goods must be **fit for their purpose** and of **satisfactory quality**.

The Consumer Protection Act (1987)

1) This Act says that **new consumer goods** must be **safe**.

2) Along with this law, there are **regulations** governing things like **furniture fire safety** — all new products made after the regulations came into effect have to conform to the regulations. Manufacturers had to **change the materials** they used for sofa and chair cushions, and this incurred costs.

The Food Safety Act (1990)

1) Under this Act producers must ensure that foodstuffs are **not harmful**.

2) If any **part** of a batch of food is considered unfit for human consumption, then the whole lot is unfit, and it all has to be **destroyed**. This has serious implications for cost and revenue.

3) Foods must also not be **labelled** in a **misleading** way. The **Food Labelling Regulations** of 1996 say:
   - Food must be labelled with a **descriptive name** and a list of **ingredients**.
   - Labels can only claim "low in fat" or "high in vitamins" if the food meets **set standards**.
   - You can only claim that a food has **health benefits**, e.g. "lowers cholesterol", if it's been **scientifically proven** to do so.
   - Food labels must also have a **Best Before** or **Use By** date, and should say how to store the food.

4) The Act also requires that workers **handling food** should be trained in **basic food hygiene**.

The Law protects the Community and the Environment

1) Industries which release waste into the **water** or **land** are regulated by the **Environment Agency**. Businesses have to change their production processes to reduce pollution, or risk heavy fines.

2) Light industrial processes which only release pollution into the **air** are regulated by **local authorities**. Businesses must get **authorisation** from the local council before carrying out processes which create **smoke** or make **noise**. **Environmental health** officers can force factories to **stop making noise** at night, if it's disturbing **local residents**.

3) Here are some examples of specific laws:

   - The EU directive on **Waste Electrical and Electronic Equipment (WEEE)** forces businesses to increase **recycling** of waste electrical and electronic equipment, much of which previously ended up in landfill sites. From August 2005, manufacturers have increased responsibility for ensuring that goods such as computers, TVs and VCRs are recycled once they've come to the end of their useful life.

   - The **Landfill Tax** was introduced in 1996 as a punitive tax to **reduce the amount of waste** being dumped into **landfill** sites.

   - The **EU Packaging Waste Directive** forces businesses to increase the recycling of packaging. There are targets for the % of wood, paper, glass and plastic that must be recycled.

The Law protects Workers

1) **Employment law** covers things like ensuring people are **recruited** fairly and have a certain amount of **job security**. It's covered in much more detail on p.88-89.

2) **Health and safety** law makes sure people don't have to work in **dangerous** conditions. See p.89 for more on this.

Production and the Law

The **Law** says **Where** companies can and can't **Build** factories

1) There are laws which prevent businesses from **building** wherever they want to or from **extending** their existing premises without **permission**. These are called **planning laws**.

2) A business that's planning to build new premises has to submit a **form** to the **local authority** saying exactly what it wants to do. The local authority then has a **meeting** and decides whether or not to give the business **planning permission**.

3) If a business builds **without** planning permission, they'll be asked to apply for **permission** even if they've already **completed** the work. If they don't get permission, the council can force them to **take** the building **down**.

Vicarious Liability means it's all the *Employer's Responsibility*

1) Workers are also protected by **vicarious liability**. This means that an **employer** will normally be **liable** for any act committed by an employee in the normal course of their job.

2) The idea of vicarious liability has **serious implications** for businesses. Imagine a situation where a lorry driver has loaded his vehicle incorrectly. When he's on the road the load comes loose, and causes an accident. The **employer** will be responsible for paying **compensation** to any people injured as a result of the accident.

Companies are *Punished* if they *Break* the *Law*

"What do you mean I broke health and safety law so I won't be getting any presents?"

1) If a company breaks the law then the **local council** can step in to **penalise** them. **Fines** are the most common penalty — for example, if a company is convicted in a magistrates'- court of not having complied with the **Trade Descriptions Act** they can be fined up to **£5000** per offence.

2) **Inspectors** check that restaurants and cafés aren't breaking **food safety** laws. If a business is preparing food in a way that isn't hygienic, they'll be given a **deadline** by which they have to **improve standards**. If the standards of hygiene are **really bad**, they can **close** the business **down** for a certain number of **weeks** or **months**.

3) The penalties for breaking **health and safety** law were made tougher in 2008. The maximum **fines** have **gone up** and, in cases where somebody has **died** as a result of **serious neglect** or the law being broken **repeatedly**, it's possible for the person responsible to be sent to **prison**.

New Laws cost *Money*

1) The introduction of a new law might mean that manufacturers have to **change** their **production processes**.

2) Changing production processes costs money. There may be **reduced productivity** during changeover if a firm has to **stop production** while new **machinery** is **installed** and **workers** are **retrained**. It's also possible that the new processes won't be as **efficient** as the old ones or that new materials required by law may be **more expensive**.

Practice Questions

Q1 What does the Trade Descriptions Act prevent businesses from doing?

Q2 Give two examples of European Directives that affect manufacturers.

Q3 How do inspectors enforce food safety laws?

Q4 Name three effects that the introduction of a new law might have on a business.

Exam Questions

Q1 Clare McFadden is planning to open a teashop. Explain the impact that the Food Safety Act is likely to have on her business. [8 marks]

Q2 Bob Stevens runs a construction firm. One of his employees erected some scaffolding incorrectly and it collapsed, injuring 3 people. Explain what is meant by vicarious liability and how it might affect Bob. [6 marks]

I fought the law and the law took my profits and stopped me from trading...

Most businesses comply with the law, so it's unlikely you'll ever see health inspectors shut down your favourite restaurant cos' of cockroaches. Sadly, there'll always be some firms who try to get away with endangering employees, cheating customers and selling dangerous tat. The law's there to make sure that all firms obey the rules, or face the costs.

Technology

*It's all about technology these days. Technology is the reason why things are quicker and more exciting and why nobody reads books any more. Oh, wait, this is a book...anyway, these pages are for **AQA** and **OCR: Business Production Option**.*

Production Methods have Changed as a result of new Technology

1) Production technology is changing all the time. New technology tends to make production **faster**, more **efficient** and more **accurate**. It also makes **innovation** easier.

2) **Computer-aided design** (CAD) uses computers to design new products, or make alterations to existing products. CAD produces 3D mock-ups on screen — managers don't have to wait for the product to roll off the production line before they know what it will look like. This can also be useful for **marketing** things like new kitchens.

3) **Computer-aided manufacture** (CAM) uses computers to produce a product, usually involving **robots** or 'computer-numerically controlled' (**CNC**) machines — machine tools which form a material into a finished product from a computer design. CAM is often combined with the CAD process — products are designed on computer, and the design data fed straight into the production machine. This is called **CAD/CAM**.

4) Computers make **stock control** easier. Holding stock information in a database makes it much easier to monitor when you need to order new stock. In retailing this is often combined with **Electronic Point of Sale (EPOS)** systems that rely on barcodes to record which products are being purchased by customers. This means stocks can be re-ordered automatically. Having a good stock control system makes it easier for companies such as supermarkets and big retailers to move to a **just-in-time** supply system (see p.112).

5) New technology can also improve **quality control**. For example, in 2008, **Cadbury** introduced a new system which allows them to test **more** product samples for **harmful bacteria** in a **shorter** amount of **time**.

Robots do the Boring, Repetitive bits of production

1) **Robots** are mostly used to replace human staff for **tasks** which are **dangerous**, **repetitive** or **boring**.

2) **Factories** and **production plants** often use **automated pickers** to take goods from the production line and pack them into boxes. It's usually **cheaper** and **faster** for robots to do this job instead of humans.

Susie wasn't actually a big, orange robot. A bad spray tan had just made her look like one.

Case study: Ocado

Traditional Method: Most supermarkets that offer internet shopping use shopfloor workers to pick goods from stores, load them into vans and deliver them to customers. Accuracy rates are usually roughly 90%.

New Method: Ocado uses remote-controlled machines to guide human workers to the right product, so they pick goods more accurately. Accuracy levels have been shown to be much higher, at around 99%.

Marketing has Changed as a result of new Technology

1) Many companies now use **technology** to gather **information** about the **lifestyles** of their **customers** and the **products** that they **buy** or are likely to buy. This helps them to make sure that **promotions** are **targeting** the right people and stand the best chance of causing **sales** to **increase**.

2) Lots of supermarkets offer **loyalty cards** which give customers money back according to how much they spend. One **benefit** for the supermarket is that it allows them to form a **database** of customer names and addresses which they can then use to create **mailing lists** for **direct marketing** campaigns.

3) **Loyalty cards** also tell the supermarkets what **products** a particular customer is **buying**. This means they can send out **offers** which **relate** to the kind of products that the person buys **most often**.

4) **Social networking websites** are another way that businesses can use technology to find out more about customer likes and dislikes. People who use these sites often list information about themselves, including the type of **music** they like, where they go on **holiday**, what **car** they drive etc. Companies who advertise on these sites can make their adverts visible only to the people who are **likely** to **buy** their product — this is **cheaper** and more **effective** than targeting everyone who uses the website. **Search engines** like Google™ often use **targeted advertising** — they show adverts that are **relevant** to the topic the user searched for.

5) New technology has also made it easier to extend a product's life cycle using an **extension strategy**. For example, **Apple®** have harnessed new technology which allows them to extend the life of the **iPod classic™** by increasing its **memory** and simplifying its **controls** and **software**.

Technology

New Technology can cause the Culture of a Business to Change

1) Developments in **communication technology** have had a big impact on business culture. For example, a small business with a close-knit team that are used to face-to-face contact might find that employees become **demotivated** if they're encouraged to communicate more by **email**. On the other hand, email has been a good thing for businesses because it allows messages to be sent with **speed** and **ease**.

2) **Flexi-working** has also been made much easier by technology — **remote access** means employees can now access their work computer from their home PC.

3) Many businesses have **software** which allows companies to **monitor** exactly what employees are doing on their computers. This might increase **productivity**, but there's a big risk that **trust** between employee and employer could break down if the employee feels they're being **watched** the whole time.

4) A firm that switches to **automated** production processes might find that employees lose the desire to be **creative** and help with **problem-solving**. Making them responsible for **quality assurance** (see p.114) can help with this.

5) Developments in technology can encourage firms to be more **innovative**. If a firm is going to pursue a **diversification** strategy (see p.3), the culture of the business will need to encourage **risk-taking**.

New Technology isn't Always a Good Thing

1) A new piece of **CAM** equipment or a new computer system doesn't automatically make the **design** process **faster** or **cheaper**. Equally, just because a product is designed using an **advanced computer system** does not guarantee it will be a **success** in the market place — the customer still needs to **want** the product.

2) It can be difficult to **integrate** new technology with existing machines. The business might be less **efficient** during the time that it takes to **coordinate** multiple systems.

3) The **initial cost** of installing new technology is usually very high. The business needs to look carefully at the impact that buying new technology will have on its **cash flow** (see p.51). The good news is that up-to-date machinery usually makes a business more **cost-effective** in the **long-term**.

4) New technology often requires workers to be **retrained**. Training can be **expensive** and it also has **opportunity costs**, e.g. the workers could be producing goods in the time it takes to train them.

5) New technology can mean that the business doesn't need as many workers. This might mean that workers need to be **retrained** and moved to **other departments** or it might lead to **redundancies**. Redundancies often have a **demotivating** effect on remaining staff. Trade unions in the car industry have been very resistant to automation because it reduces labour requirements.

6) New technology can affect the level of **customer service** a firm is able to provide. **Automated telephone switchboards** and **answering machines** are **cheaper** than telephone operators but many customers don't like listening to a machine and would rather deal directly with a **person**.

Practice Questions

Q1 What are CAD and CAM technologies?
Q2 Describe three ways that technology can affect the culture of a business.
Q3 Give two potential disadvantages to a business of introducing new technology.

Exam Questions

Q1 Discuss the impact that new technology might have on the activities of a company's marketing department. [12 marks]

Q2 "Adopting new technology is always beneficial to the long-term success of a business." Discuss. [14 marks]

Computer says no...

Technology is a great thing for businesses, it really is. It's just that sometimes it has an annoying habit of crashing at really crucial moments. That's just one of its many disadvantages — make sure you learn the others on this page too. If your brain just doesn't seem to want to store the information, why not turn it off, wait ten seconds, then turn it back on again.

Economic Growth

*This section is all about how the outside world makes its mark on businesses. It starts with how economic growth affects businesses and governments. Page 128 is for **AQA** and **all OCR students**, page 129 is for **AQA**, **OCR** and **WJEC**.*

GDP (Gross Domestic Product) indicates the Size of a Nation's Economy

GDP is the **total market value** of **goods** and **services** produced **by** a nation **within** that nation during a period of time.

GDP = total **consumer spending** + business **investment** + **government spending** + the value of **exports** − the value of **imports**.

GDP is calculated in **real terms**, i.e. by ignoring **inflation**.

Economic Growth is the Increase in Size of a nation's Economy

1) Economic growth is an **increase** in the nation's production of **goods** and **services**.

2) It's measured as the **rate of increase in GDP** (Gross Domestic Product).

3) Economic growth means the same thing as "an increase in **economic activity**" — growth means there's **more demand** in the economy and **more output** to meet that demand.

Economic Growth is determined by Resources and Productivity

1) The **growth potential** of an economy depends on the **amount** and **quality** of economic **resources** available — e.g. labour and fixed assets.

Quantity and quality of labour	**Quantity** of labour depends on **population size and age**, and on its **gender** composition (e.g. if lots of the female population are of childbearing age then they may not be available to work). The **quality** of labour is the level of **education and training** that workers have reached. **High quality** of labour enables an economy to **grow faster**.
Investment	**Investment** increases the amount of **productive assets** (machinery etc. used for production). For the **value** of productive assets to **grow**, the **level of investment** in productive assets has to be greater than the amount of **depreciation** (the amount by which machines wear out) during the year.

2) Economic growth also depends on **productivity** — how hard the nation is willing to work.

3) **Governments** can encourage **short-term** growth by cutting taxes and interest rates (see p.130-131). This encourages businesses to borrow money and invest it in production. It also encourages consumers to borrow money and spend it on goods, which increases demand in the economy.

4) These days, economists tend to think it's better to **encourage steady growth** by using "supply-side policies". There's more on these on p.133.

Economic Growth has Mainly Positive Effects for business and government

Economic **growth** means an increase in **national income**, which is good news.

Individual Businesses

1) On the whole, **growth** in GDP means **higher revenues** and higher **profitability** for **businesses**.

2) Economic growth gives the potential for **economies of scale**.

3) Sustained growth increases **confidence** and helps businesses **plan** for the future.

4) Economic growth affects the type of **strategic decisions** that a business makes. In periods of sustained growth senior managers might decide to **expand** the business, launch **new products** or try to break into **new markets**.

5) On the down side, fast growth may cause **shortages** of raw materials and skilled labour.

Governments

1) **Higher revenue** encourages investment in new projects, which creates jobs. This is good for the government — there's less need to pay welfare benefits.

2) Growth also enables the government to earn **increased revenues** through **taxes**.

3) Very high rates of growth are usually followed by **recession**. Governments try to avoid this boom-and-bust situation by keeping growth at a **sustainable level**.

It appears someone's gone a bit wild with the fertiliser.

Economic Growth

The **Business Cycle** is a regular pattern of **Growth** and **Recession**

1) In a **recovery** or upswing, **production increases**, and **employment** increases. People have more money to spend.

2) In a **boom**, production levels are high. As production reaches **maximum capacity**, there are **shortages**, and price increases. Shortages of skilled labour mean **wages rise**.

3) In a **recession** incomes start to go down, and **demand** goes down. Business **confidence** is reduced.

4) In a **slump**, production is at a **low**. Businesses close factories and there are a lot of **redundancies**. **Unemployment** is **high**. A lot of businesses become **insolvent** or **bankrupt**.

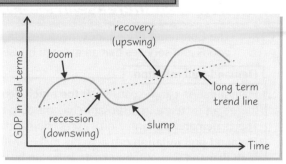

5) How much a business is **affected** by the business cycle depends on the **income elasticity of demand** of its products (see p.24). Businesses selling **income elastic** goods such as luxury holidays find that demand shoots **up** in a **recovery**, and dives **down** in a **recession**. Firms selling **income inelastic** goods such as staple foods **aren't affected** all that much by the business cycle.

> Income elasticity of demand = extent to which demand depends on customer income.

Businesses deal with **Changes** in **Economic Activity Locally** and **Globally**

1) During **booms**, businesses can **raise prices**. This increases profitability, and it slows down demand a bit. Businesses may have to increase prices to cover their own costs if there are wage rises due to shortages of labour.

2) In a long lasting boom, businesses **invest** in **production** facilities to increase capacity. They may come out with **new products** to take advantage of increased consumer income.

3) During **recessions**, businesses can make workers **redundant** to **save wage costs** and **increase capacity utilisation**.

4) During a **local recession**, businesses can **market** their goods elsewhere in the country — a local shop could go mail-order. In a **national recession**, businesses can **market** their products **overseas**.

5) When the national recession or slump lasts a long time, some businesses choose to **relocate** abroad.

6) In general, **global upswings** provide growth opportunities for **everyone**, and **global recessions** are bad for **everyone**.

Supply and **Demand** can **Vary Seasonally**

1) As well as cyclical variations in demand caused by the business cycle, there are **yearly variations** in **demand** and **supply**. This is called **seasonality**.

2) **Weather** and **holidays** such as Christmas produce variations in **demand**. For example, **Christmas** creates high demand for **toys**. Hot weather creates demand for ice lollies, paddling pools and air conditioning units.

3) They can also cause variations in **supply** — there are more strawberries available in summer, for example.

4) It's impossible to avoid seasonality. Businesses must have **strategies** to deal with it. After Christmas, demand for retail goods drops, so shops **cut prices** (the **January sales**) to artificially boost demand, and get rid of stock.

5) Food producers can cope with seasonality in supply by **preserving food** — e.g. by canning or freeze-drying.

Practice Questions

Q1 What is economic growth and how is it measured?

Q2 What are the effects of economic growth on governments?

Q3 What happens to production during a boom period?

Exam Question

Q1 Discuss the negative effects to a business of rapid economic growth. [12 marks]

Tip for the January sales — if it's beige (or yellow), don't buy it...

Trust me, they don't suit anybody. Growth in the national economy is a good thing for businesses. The problems start when growth is too fast — production can't keep up, and a pleasant period of growth swings round into an unpleasant recession. Learn the whys and wherefores of the business cycle, and learn a couple of things that firms do to cope with it.

Economic Variables

*Pages 130-131 are for **AQA**, **OCR** & **WJEC**. Page 132 is for **AQA** & **OCR** but **not WJEC** — they don't do unemployment.*

Inflation is an Increase in the Price of Goods and Services

1) The **Consumer Price Index** measures UK inflation — it tracks the prices of hundreds of goods and services that an average household would buy. There are **two types** of inflation:

Demand-pull inflation

High inflation can be caused by **too much demand** (more than the economy can supply) — it happens when there's an increase in disposable income so people buy more and companies can't supply goods quick enough. This is **demand-pull** inflation. Excess demand when the economy is near its full capacity is called **overheating**. **Demand-pull inflation** can actually make **profit margins** go **up**. Businesses can put up prices in response to **high demand** without their **costs** going up by as much.

Cost-push inflation

Rises in inflation can be due to **rising costs** pushing up **prices** — this is **cost-push** inflation. **Wage rises** can make prices go up — especially if productivity isn't rising. **Cost-push inflation** can make **profit margins** go **down** if businesses decide not to put up their prices.

The Bank of England has to keep the inflation rate within a target range set by the Government.

2) When inflation is **high**, spending goes **up** temporarily — people rush to buy more before prices go up even more. If **wages** don't go up in line with inflation, spending goes **down** as people can afford less.

3) **Expectations** of inflation can make inflation worse. A business which expects its **suppliers** to put their prices up will put its **own** prices up to cover increased costs. Employees' expectations of rising prices makes them demand **higher wages**, so prices go up. This is the **wage-price spiral** — it's a big cause of cost-push inflation.

4) When inflation in the UK is high, it makes UK **exports** expensive abroad. UK businesses become **less competitive**. When inflation in the UK is low, UK businesses have a competitive advantage.

Inflation affects Business Strategy

It's harder to plan when inflation is high. Businesses need stable prices to be able to make accurate sales forecasts.

1) Companies producing **premium goods** are the **most** likely to be **affected** by inflation because if customers have less to spend they start to look at **alternative products**. Manufacturers of premium products can react by **reducing prices** (although they have to be careful not to reduce them so far that the product loses its premium image) or by investing heavily in **advertising**.

2) Periods of high inflation can be a **good time** for firms to **expand** — if **interest rates** are **lower** than the rate of **inflation** it's **cheap** for them to **borrow money** to invest in **new premises** or **machinery**.

Deflation is a Decrease in the Price of Goods and Services

1) **Deflation** is the **opposite** of inflation — it's when there's **not enough demand** so companies **reduce** their **prices**.

2) Deflation causes a **fall** in **productivity** because companies won't keep endlessly supplying the market with goods that nobody wants. **Lower productivity** usually means firms don't need as many workers — so deflation often leads to a **rise** in **unemployment**. This makes **demand drop** further and causes firms to **lower prices** even more.

Interest is the Price Paid for Borrowing Money

1) Interest rates show the **cost of borrowing**. A **fall** in the interest rate **increases** businesses' levels of activity — it's **cheaper** for them to borrow money to invest. A **rise** in interest rates makes firms **decrease** their activity, because it's **more expensive** to borrow money to invest.

2) Interest rates affect **consumer spending**. High interest rates mean most consumers have less money to spend. People with existing **borrowing** like **mortgages** have to pay more money back in **interest**, and many people also **save more money** because they get a better rate of return on it, so market **demand** goes down.

3) The effect of interest rates on demand depends on the **product**. Products that require **borrowing** (e.g. cars, houses, new kitchens and high-end consumer electronics) are more **sensitive** to interest rate changes. When interest rates go up significantly, firms change strategy to diversify away from these goods and into cheaper ones.

4) Firms compare **UK** and **foreign** interest rates. When the UK interest rate is high or volatile, firms tend to expand into **other countries** with low, stable interest rates, as it's **cheaper** to borrow money there to invest in expansion.

5) When **interest rates** are **high**, **foreign investors** want to **save money** in **UK** banks. To do this, they **buy British pounds**, which boosts demand for the currency and makes the **exchange rate go up**, affecting **imports** and **exports**. When **interest rates** are **low**, investors prefer to invest abroad, so they **sell** their pounds and the **exchange rate falls**.

Economic Variables

Exchange Rate is the Value of One Currency in terms of Another Currency

1) Exchange rates affect the amount of **foreign trade**.

   - When the exchange rate is **high** (e.g. more euros to the pound), UK **exports** are relatively **expensive** in Europe and **imports** into the UK are relatively **cheap** for Brits. A **strong pound** is **bad** for UK exporters because their goods aren't competitively priced abroad.

   - When the exchange rate is **low** (e.g. **fewer euros** to the **pound**), UK **exports** are relatively **cheap** for foreigners (which is **good** for UK **exporters**) and **imports** into the UK are relatively **expensive** for Brits.

2) A **strong pound** and **cheaper imports** mean **lower costs** for UK businesses importing raw materials from abroad, but they're bad news for UK manufacturers who export goods abroad.

3) When a rise in the value of the pound is predicted, a business might decide to move its **production** abroad. The business can also consider **importing** the **raw material** from abroad.

4) **Cheaper exports** should lead to increased **demand** and therefore higher **output**.

"Today's exchange rate is two sheep to the goat."

Exchange Rate Fluctuations create Uncertainty

1) For example, a UK manufacturer agrees a contract to sell to France, and agrees to be paid in **euros**. After the deal is made, the pound rises in value against the euro. The euro payment in the contract is now worth **fewer pounds** than before, so the UK manufacturer makes **less profit** from the contract than predicted.

2) Let's say that the UK manufacturer insists on being paid in **pounds**. When the pound rises in value, the goods are more expensive in euro terms for the French firm. They put the **selling price** up to compensate. The increase in price reduces **demand** for the goods, and there may be **less revenue** than predicted.

Some manufacturers based in the UK and **exporting to the EU** are considering **relocating** to **Euro zone** countries, so that their costs are in Euros — the same currency their customers pay in. They may also decide to pay UK suppliers in Euros, again to keep costs in the same currency that their customers pay them. See p.150 for more on the Euro.

Taxation Rates affect Economic Activity

1) **Individuals** are taxed on their **income**. Businesses are taxed on their **profits** — sole traders and partnerships pay **income tax**, and limited companies pay **corporation tax**. These taxes are **direct taxes**.

2) Businesses also pay **business rate** tax based on the **value** of their **premises**. The rate is the same all over the country. However, because **property values** are generally **higher** in the **South** than in the North, **businesses** in the **South** generally end up **paying more**. This can **reduce** their **competitiveness**.

3) There are also **indirect taxes on spending**, e.g. VAT, taxes on pollution, tax on tobacco and tax on alcohol.

4) A business' **local competitiveness** can be affected by **local taxes** such as **congestion charges**. E.g. if a bakery is located within a congestion charge zone and customers can buy bread from another bakery that they don't have to pay to get to, they're more likely to go to the other bakery instead.

5) **High** tax rates **discourage** individuals from **spending**, and businesses from **expanding**. Increasing income tax **reduces spending power**, **cuts demand** and **lowers economic activity**.

6) The effect of a tax cut or tax rise depends on the **income elasticity** of the good or service. Rises in income tax hit **luxury goods** (e.g. luxury new kitchen appliances) harder than **staple goods** (e.g. petrol or bread).

The Labour Market is the Supply and Demand of Workers

Labour is a very important **resource** for businesses. How much labour is available depends on the labour market.

1) The **labour market** is made up of all the people who are available to work (e.g. people over 16 who are looking for a job) and all the employers who are advertising vacancies.

2) The **supply of labour** is linked to **wage rates**. As wages rise, the **supply** of labour is also likely to **rise** — higher wages **attract workers** from other industries and those who are currently unemployed.

3) Wages also affect **demand** for labour. Increasing wages increases the **cost of production**. This raises the **price** of products, which reduces **demand** for those goods. As demand for goods falls, demand for labour **decreases**. The demand for labour also **falls** when labour can be substituted by a **cheaper alternative** e.g. machinery.

4) **Changes** in the labour market can force firms to **relocate** or start **offshoring**. For more on this see p.105 and p.106.

OCR ONLY

Economic Variables

This page is for AQA and OCR.

Unemployment is measured by the number of People Seeking Work

1) Unemployment is measured by the number of jobless people who are
a) **available** for work and b) **actively seeking jobs**.

2) There are five main **types** of unemployment.

> **Structural** unemployment is due to changes in the structure of the economy, e.g. a **decline** in a **major industry** such as coal mining. When structural unemployment is concentrated in a particular region of the country it's called **regional unemployment**.
>
> **Frictional** unemployment is temporary, caused by the delay between **losing** one job and **getting** another.
>
> **Cyclical** (demand deficient) unemployment is due to a **downturn** in the business cycle, e.g. a lack of **demand** for labour because production has decreased and businesses are trying to cut costs.
>
> **Seasonal** unemployment is due to the **season**, e.g. ice cream sellers in the winter.

3) High unemployment can affect **sales**. Producers of **luxury** goods are badly affected by **cyclical** unemployment. Businesses producing **essentials** aren't affected all that much unless people can easily switch to cheaper brands.

4) **Structural** and **regional** unemployment affects **local** businesses — unemployed people in the area have little money to spend.

5) When unemployment is **high**, businesses can hire staff easily. There's a good **supply** of labour, so businesses won't have to pay **high wages**. People in work will be extra **productive** to protect their job.

6) If unemployment is **structural** or **regional**, it's not all that easy to hire staff. Unemployed workers often aren't in the **right place** or the **right industry** for the jobs that are out there. They need **training**.

7) The government has various ways of trying to reduce unemployment. There's more about them on the next page.

Low Unemployment is linked to Skills Shortages

Skills shortages are bad news for most businesses, but good news for recruitment consultants.

1) As well as a labour surplus or shortage, you can also have a **skills surplus** or **shortage**.

2) There are **shortages** of skilled labour in many industries.

3) Skills shortages are solved by **training**, but training is **expensive**. Governments can help by providing **training schemes** and pushing colleges to offer **vocational** (job-related) courses and qualifications. Businesses who invest in training can find that competitors **poach** employees once they're trained.

4) Businesses can get round skills shortages by investing in labour saving **machinery** — in other words, switching from labour-intensive production to **capital-intensive** production.

5) Businesses can also get round skills shortages by **relocating production** or service provision **abroad** where there are plenty of skilled workers.

6) It's possible to have **too many** skilled workers in a particular industry— this is a **skills surplus**. It can lead to high **unemployment** in a particular industry if workers aren't willing to accept lower-paid unskilled jobs.

7) **Shortages** and **surpluses** of skills can be caused by having **too few** or **too many workers** in the country. To work out if the working population has grown or shrunk, you **subtract** the number of **people** who've **left** the **UK** from the number of people who've **come** to live in the UK. This is net migration. If there are **lots of jobs** it's better if there's **more immigration** (people arriving) than emigration (people leaving). If jobs are scarce, the reverse is true.

Practice Questions

Q1 Explain what is meant by 'inflation' and 'deflation'.

Q2 Give one example of a local tax that can affect a business' competitiveness.

Q3 Name the five types of unemployment and briefly explain what each one means.

Exam Question

> Q1 Jemmy McDougal sells Scottish smoked salmon to catering companies in the US and Canada. She's noticed that the pound has been very strong in recent months. Explain the impact this is likely to have on her firm and why. [10 marks]

Structural unemployment — when buildings can't find work...

Personally, I think this chapter's quite interesting — it gives you a feel for how companies actually operate in the real world. They have to be on the look out for changes in all kinds of factors and they need to know what they'll do if interest rates suddenly shoot up. Think of it like juggling — businesses have to keep all the balls in the air if they want to be successful.

Government Policy

Politics — you love it really. **Pages 133-134** are for **AQA, WJEC, OCR** and **Edexcel**, *page 135 is for* **WJEC** *and* **Edexcel**.

The Government plays Four Roles in the Economy

1) The government **provides** services like education, healthcare and defence.
2) The government **supports** businesses and individuals with things like tax credits and subsidies.
3) The government is a **legislator** — it makes laws and regulations (e.g. health and safety).
4) The government is a **consumer** — it buys products and services.

Not that kind of role play...

Monetary Policy controls the Interest Rate

Monetary policy means **tweaking the interest rate** to control **inflation** and **exchange rates**. Monetary policy aims to:

1) Control **inflation**.
2) Control the overall rate of **economic growth**.
3) Manage **unemployment** levels (e.g. if interest rates are low, people have more money to spend and increased demand leads to a rise in production).
4) Influence **foreign exchange rates**.

Even though the Bank of England sets interest rates independently, the Bank of England Monetary Policy Committee bears the government's fiscal policy in mind when it makes its decisions.

Altering the **interest rate** has an impact on **business activity** — see p.130 for more on this.

Fiscal Policy changes Taxes and Spending to Heat or Cool the Economy

1) **Fiscal policy** does **two** things — it sets **tax rates**, and it sets the amount of **government spending**.
2) **Raising taxes** cools the economy down, and cutting taxes heats it up — **low rates of tax** give businesses more profit, and **encourage business activity** like expansion and new start-ups.

- It's fairly easy to predict the effects of a change in **direct taxation**. Raising **income tax** reduces consumer spending, and reduces business output.
- **Indirect taxation** is a bit harder to predict. Increases in **VAT** cut consumer spending, but **raise inflation**.

3) **Government spending** on social services, health, education etc. also heats up the economy.

- Changing government expenditure on **welfare benefits** has a **quick** impact on the economy, because poorer people who receive benefits will change their spending habits straight away.
- Government spending on **infrastructure** such as roads has a **slower** effect on the economy.

4) **Fiscal policy** is really about the **balance** between tax and spending. The Chancellor of the Exchequer decides what the balance is going to be in the yearly Budget.

Fiscal Policy	When it's done	How it's done	Change in government borrowing	The effect it has
Expansionary fiscal policy	Economic slowdown / high unemployment	Cutting taxes and/or Raising spending	Government **borrowing increases** (or government **surplus decreases**)	**Demand** for goods and services **increases**
Contractionary fiscal policy	Production at 100% capacity / risk of high inflation	Raising taxes and/or Cutting spending	Government **borrowing decreases** (or government **surplus increases**)	**Demand** for goods and services **decreases**

5) Expansionary fiscal policy helps to **lower unemployment**. **Cutting taxes** gives people **more to spend** and increased **state consumption** boosts **production** and creates **jobs**. It can cause **inflation** though, so it needs to be monitored.

Supply-side Policies encourage Growth in the Market

Supply-side policies are policies that aim to help **markets work freely**. They attempt to **reduce unemployment** and **increase output** and the **supply** of **labour**. They work by:

1) **Privatisation** (see p.134) and **deregulation** (opening up a market, e.g. parcel delivery, to new competitors).
2) **Encouraging international trade** (e.g. by setting up trade agreements like the European Single Market).
3) **Promoting entrepreneurship** by offering loans to new businesses.
4) **Lowering corporation tax** to attract investors from outside the country and encourage growth.
5) **Decreasing income tax** (people are more motivated to work when they keep a larger proportion of their wages).
6) **Cutting benefits** and **spending** more on **training**.

Government Policy

Nationalisation is Government Ownership and Control of Businesses

1) **Nationalisation** means taking businesses into **government ownership**. It's a risky move because it usually creates a **legally protected monopoly**. This means there's a lack of competition, which can lead to inefficiency and poor quality. Nationalised industries often don't make much profit.

2) Despite the problems with nationalisation, sometimes it **makes sense** for **certain industries** to be nationalised — usually when they supply **essential public services** or **goods**. That's why the **NHS** and the **Royal Mail** are state-run.

Privatisation is when State-Owned Business are sold to Private Investors

1) In the 1980s many state-owned firms were sold into the private sector to **improve efficiency** and make a **profit**. Examples include **British Telecom**, **British Gas**, **British Steel**, the **water** companies and the **electricity** distributors.

Benefits of privatisation	Drawbacks of privatisation
Privatisation **promotes competition**, which **increases efficiency**, and offers **better quality** products at **lower prices**.	**Some** privatised companies have **raised prices** and **cut quality** to **exploit** consumers — especially if they're effectively a **monopoly**.
The **government** made a big **profit** from privatisation. This helped the government to **cut taxes** and **reduce its borrowing**, which in turn **encourages business activity**.	Privatised companies tend to have **lots of shareholders** — often **private citizens** holding just a few shares. Shareholders tend to look for **quick profit** at the expense of **long term strategy**.

This profit is one-off profit — the privatisation can't be repeated.

2) Some industries are **natural monopolies** — for example, you wouldn't have several sets of rail tracks from one city to another. When privatising a natural monopoly like the **railways**, the government needs to build in regulations to prevent the new owners from exploiting their position and raising prices or cutting quality.

Case study: Railtrack

Privatisation: The UK government privatised the railways, and placed them under the control of Railtrack. Railtrack was effectively a monopoly, with train operating companies as its customers.

Regulation: The government set up the Office of the Rail Regulator (ORR) to keep an eye on Railtrack. The ORR had to make sure that Railtrack did not allow its commercial interest to get in the way of public standards and safety.

The State is a Consumer — it uses Goods and Services

1) The state **buys products** and **services** just like individuals do. For example, if the government is planning to build a new motorway it will need to pay a road construction company to do the work. For **some products**, e.g. drugs, the **state** is the **biggest consumer**.

2) **Depending** on the **government** to buy your product can be **risky**. For example, if your company makes submarines and the government cuts defence spending, there might not be any **other market** for your product. This often leads to **regional unemployment**.

"And the Prime Minister will have the steak and chips..."

Intervention vs Laissez-Faire — whether governments Interfere in the economy

1) The idea of **laissez-faire** means that **governments don't interfere** in the economy. The idea of **interventionism** means they **do** get involved.

2) Governments **intervene** by charging **taxes**, passing **laws** which affect business, providing **public services** and taking part in the economy as a **consumer**. They also provide **subsidies** — payments to certain essential industries (e.g. farming), to help pay for the costs of production and ensure the business is making a reasonable income.

3) Governments that take a **laissez-faire** approach **dismantle** existing regulations that **constrain** business, abolish wage controls and **reduce taxation rates**.

Some governments are more likely to intervene than others. Traditionally, Conservative governments intervene less than Labour governments. There's more on government intervention on p.133.

Arguments for Laissez-faire	Arguments for Intervention
Intervention raises costs and makes businesses less efficient and less profitable.	Governments need to step in to make sure there's fair competition in the market.
Allowing businesses to cut wages makes them more competitive.	Totally free, profit-driven markets usually have social and environmental costs.
Encourages businesses to behave responsibly, rather than relying on the state to bail them out.	Subsidies help pay for the costs of production and ensure that businesses are making a reasonable income.

Government Policy

Businesses are affected by *Political Issues* at *Home* and *Abroad*

Domestic political changes affect business, because they usually trigger change to **economic policy**. Political **change abroad** can also create **opportunities** by opening up **new markets** (e.g. China, India) and **threats**, e.g. if the EU creates new **taxes** which apply to businesses.

MILITARY CONFLICT

1) **War** is one **political change** that has a big impact on businesses.

2) For companies that produce **military supplies** (uniforms, tanks, aircraft etc.) there's a big **increase** in **demand** for their products.

3) But for a lot of firms it creates **big threats** — the war in Iraq led to big rises in the **price** of **crude oil**, which **increased** companies' **transport costs**. War can also mean that companies have to **replan** their **shipping** and **flight routes** to avoid conflict zones and they might have to **stop trading** with a country that's at war.

4) **Terrorism** is also a **threat** — **tourism** in America suffered after the September 11th attacks.

GLOBAL WARMING

1) The responses of governments around the world to global warming can create threats for businesses (there's more on this below) but it also creates a lot of **opportunities** for **innovation** and **new product development**.

2) For example, if the US government begins to encourage Americans to **switch** to **renewable energy** sources, it **benefits companies** that are already producing or doing R&D for **environmentally friendly products** such as **hybrid cars** and **biofuels**.

Government Policies create *Opportunities* and *Threats* for businesses

Government **policies** have a big effect on businesses — sometimes a change in policy is a **good** thing for business and sometimes it creates a real **risk**.

1) **Carbon rationing** is one of the policies the government is considering for **fighting climate change**. Currently, the UK is part of the **EU's 'Emissions Trading Scheme'** but this only affects **businesses** which give out a **lot** of **carbon**, e.g. oil refineries, power stations, food, drink and car producers and metal, glass and paper processing plants. If a scheme was introduced to ration businesses' carbon use, businesses would be set a **limit** on the amount of **carbon** they can produce and if they **exceeded** this limit they would have to **buy credit** from companies which were **not using** their **full allowance**.

2) Some people think that it would be **impossible** to introduce a carbon rationing scheme that was **fair** to everyone. This might mean that **larger businesses** would have an unfair **competitiveness advantage**. Their **finances** are **not** as **limited** as those of smaller businesses so they would easily be able to buy more carbon rations if they needed them. On the plus side, it might encourage businesses to switch to **new** lower carbon **production methods** or develop new **products** (see above for more on this).

3) **Privatisation** and **nationalisation** also have an impact on business activity — see p.134 for more on this.

Practice Questions

Q1 What are the four roles that the government plays in the economy?

Q2 How do supply-side policies work?

Q3 Give two advantages and two disadvantages of privatisation.

Q4 What is the difference between intervention and a 'laissez-faire' approach to the economy.

Q5 Explain the impact on businesses when the UK is at war.

Q6 Why would it be difficult to introduce a fair carbon-rationing scheme?

Exam Question

Q1 Assess the impact that it would have on businesses and the risks they might face if the Chancellor of the Exchequer announced a contractionary fiscal policy. [10 marks]

Political change — what's left over from government spending...

There's a lot of material to cover on these pages, but stick with it — this stuff has the power to make or break businesses. The key point to learn is that not everyone agrees about how involved the government should be — some people find government intervention reassuring, other people just think they should keep their hands off. Which is better? You decide...

Social and Environmental Influences

*Social and environmental concerns affect business. These three pages are so good, **everybody** needs to learn them.*

Businesses *have to* Respond *to* Social Changes

"Ooh yes, since we've been watching Jamie, we love a bit of lemongrass..."

1) The **structure** of the UK **population** changes over time in terms of **age**, **sex** and **race** — this is **demographic change**.

2) Demographic change is important to businesses because it has an **impact** on the **workforce**. The UK has an **ageing population**, which means that the number of people **available to work** (those aged 16-65) is **falling**. It's a bad thing if businesses **can't find** enough **workers** to fill all their vacancies, because it makes them **inefficient**.

3) However, the **ageing population** also creates **opportunities** for some firms, such as mobility scooter manufacturers and private healthcare providers. Retired people often travel a lot — so it's good news for holiday companies, too.

4) **Consumer tastes** are another thing that **change** over time. In recent years lots more people have started watching cookery programmes, so **supermarkets** stock far more **exotic ingredients** than they used to. Another example is the switch from CD to MP3 players, which means that companies now supply **music** for **download**.

Changes *in* Employment Patterns *means* Businesses *have to be more* Flexible

In recent years, the concept of **work-life balance** has become more important and businesses have had to adapt to give workers more **choice** over **where**, **when** and **how** they work. Two of the most common ways of doing this are:

1) **Flexible working** gives employees more **choice** about **when** they work and **how many hours** they do — it's popular with **mums** who have to fit their working hours round **childcare**. It's good for **reducing absenteeism** and increases a company's **choice** of **potential employees**, but can **increase administration** costs.

2) **Homeworking**, unsurprisingly, means **working from home**. New **technology** like **remote access** has made it far more common. Like flexible working, it **reduces labour turnover** and **absenteeism**, but it can be hard to **monitor** employees' **performance**. Also, not being in a social working environment can cause **worker morale** to **drop**.

Case study: BT

Objective: BT recognises that a lot of its workforce have responsibility for either a child or an ageing parent. It aims to help staff fit work around their caring duties.

Solution: The firm used its broadband technology to help introduce flexible working. In 2008, 71% of BT's employees were on some kind of flexible scheme. The company says flexible working has increased productivity by 20%.

Business Ethics *help businesses make* Socially Responsible Decisions

1) In recent years, **trends** have led many firms to consider whether their **behaviour** is **ethical**. Not everyone **agrees** on what's ethical and what's not. For example, most people **agree** that **child labour** is **unethical**, but **opinions differ** on whether it's **unethical** to **sell cigarettes** even though they cause cancer.

Morals are personal beliefs about what is right and wrong. Ethics are rules which say what is acceptable behaviour for members of a group. Business ethics are about doing the "right thing".

2) In the UK, one of the ethical issues that manufacturing businesses have to consider is the **balance** between **capital** and **labour**. It might be most efficient for them to replace some of their workforce with machines, but many people think that this is **unethical** if it leads to high numbers of **redundancies**.

3) Ethical behaviour can affect **profit**, e.g. if it means paying **suppliers** a **higher price**. However, it has **positive effects** too — behaving ethically **attracts customers** who **approve** of this approach. It can be a **unique selling point**, particularly in retail (e.g. The Body Shop® products, Co-op's fairtrade chocolate etc). Ethics can be **good PR**.

4) Growth objectives can also be affected by ethical behaviour. For example, a company producing fairtrade clothes is unlikely to be producing goods as quickly as a non-fairtrade company would, so the time it takes to build up stock might prevent it from expanding rapidly.

5) Businesses might also try to accommodate their employees' **spiritual needs**. This might mean providing separate **kitchen facilities** for employees with **religious dietary needs** or providing a quiet **place** to **pray**.

> **Sweatshops**
>
> Sweatshops are a big ethical issue currently. A sweatshop is a **factory** (usually overseas) where workers are forced to work **long hours** in **poor** and **unsafe conditions** for **low pay**. Some firms, e.g. **Marks and Spencer**, have **voluntarily promised** not to buy from suppliers who use sweatshops, but many **other companies** either still **use** them or have only **stopped** following **pressure** (e.g. boycotting) from **customers**. Another problem is that some companies aren't very good at **checking up** on the behaviour of their **suppliers**.

Social and Environmental Influences

Social Responsibility means being responsible towards the Whole of Society

1) Corporate social responsibility (CSR) is the **voluntary** role of business in looking after **society** and the environment.

2) Businesses have special responsibility to their **stakeholders** — everyone who's affected by the business, e.g. **employees**, **suppliers**, **creditors**, **customers**, **shareholders** and local **communities**.

Employees

1) Every firm has **legal responsibilities** to its staff. ⟵ Examples — providing a safe work environment, not discriminating based on race or gender, giving lunch breaks and paid holiday. See p.88-89.

2) Firms have a responsibility to **train** employees.

3) Firms can **choose** to give their employees a better deal than the bare legal minimum. Firms that operate internationally can **choose** to give workers abroad similar rights to workers in the UK.

Suppliers

1) It's not in a firm's best interest to treat their **suppliers** badly. For good results, be **honest** and **pay** on time.

2) Firms can build **long-term relationships** with suppliers — e.g. by offering **long-term exclusive supply contracts** and placing **regular orders**. A good relationship makes it more likely that the supplier will pull all the stops out to deliver **fast service** when it's really needed.

3) There's also a responsibility to the rest of **society** to choose suppliers who don't **exploit** their workers or **pollute** excessively. Firms may not see this as worthwhile, **unless** customers care enough to **boycott** the product.

Customers

1) Firms who treat their **customers** well can build up **customer goodwill**. Good customer service, good quality products and reasonable prices all encourage **customer loyalty** and **repeat business**.

2) Customers are more and more willing to **complain** when firms don't treat them well. Customers can even **campaign against** firms who disappoint, and **persuade** other people **not to buy** their goods and services.

Local Community

1) Firms can be responsible to the local community by keeping **jobs secure**, and using **local suppliers**.

2) They can also avoid **noise pollution**, **air pollution** and excess **traffic** on local roads.

3) Businesses can **earn goodwill** by making **charity** donations or **sponsoring** schools, leisure centres, parks etc.

Some people claim that it's **unethical** to produce certain types of product, e.g. tobacco and weapons, and that the companies who make these things only behave in a **socially responsible** way because it distracts the consumer and acts as a form of **positive PR**. These people tend to think that **government regulations** and **laws** are the only real way of getting businesses to behave responsibly.

Here are Two corporate social responsibility Case Studies

Case studies: The Coca-Cola Company & Cadbury

- **The Coca-Cola Company's** corporate social responsibility policy covers **four areas** — **employees**, the **environment**, the **community** and **customers**. The company's social goals include **reducing** the amount of **water** it takes to produce each litre of Coke®, helping consumers make healthy choices by having a **product portfolio** which is **36%** low sugar or **sugar free** and using **flexible working** to help **women** reach senior positions.

- **Cadbury** have **CSR targets** to meet by **2010**. These include **sustainably sourcing** half of their **raw materials**, ensuring all packaging is recyclable or biodegrable and donating **1%** of their **pre-tax profit** to **community** projects.

Being Socially Responsible has an impact on the Decision-making process

1) Traditionally, the **decision-making process** put the **needs** of **shareholders first** — which meant that the business was concerned with its **profits** above all else.

2) Corporate social responsibility means that the **needs of other stakeholders** also have to be **considered** during the decision-making process. E.g. a company that makes chocolate bars for children might put some stuff on the website about the importance of healthy eating and being active.

3) In reality though, it can be **hard** to take into account the needs of all shareholders. If a company has promised to **invest** in a **local school** for the next **5 years** but its **profits fall** sharply, it has to decide which is more important — keeping **shareholders happy** or the need to **behave ethically**.

Social and Environmental Influences

Business Activity can be Harmful to the Environment

1) Businesses pollute the environment through **production** processes, through **traffic pollution** caused by **transporting** raw materials and finished goods, through **dumping waste** in waterways and seas, and through **burying** or **burning waste**. **Packaging** creates a large amount of **landfill** waste.

2) Businesses also damage the environment through **unsustainable resource management** — e.g. cutting down rainforest for mining developments, building on greenfield sites.

3) The **Environment Act (1995)** set up the **Environment Agency**, which coordinates pollution control. Businesses can't release dangerous substances into waterways or the air without a **permit** from the Environment Agency. There are also a lot of EU directives relating to pollution.

4) Most environmental costs are **external costs**, i.e. they affect society, not the business itself. External costs include health issues caused by air pollution, the greenhouse effect and acid rain.

5) The government **fines** businesses who pollute more than a certain level. Pollution control is also done by **taxation**. This means that pollution has **internal financial costs.**

6) Many businesses now try to **minimise** the **impact** they have on the environment. One way they can do this is to ensure that their activities are **sustainable**, e.g. **replacing resources** as they use them. This might mean **cleaning waste water** before it's pumped back into rivers and lakes, **planting new trees** to replace trees that are cut down for timber or making sure that **overfishing** doesn't cause certain species to die out altogether.

Environmental Auditing shows how a firm is affecting the Environment

1) An environmental audit is a review of the **environmental effects** of the firm's activities. It assesses whether the firm is meeting legal environmental protection requirements, and whether it's meeting its own **targets**. Environmental audits show businesses where they need to **change** their **waste management** practices.

2) For example, one of the environmental costs of business activity is the emission of **greenhouse gases**. A business which has decided to **reduce** the amount of **greenhouse gases** emitted into the atmosphere would set a clear **objective** for reducing emissions and **check their progress** towards this objective through an **environmental audit**.

3) Environmental audits only work if a company has something to **compare** its **waste output** to (e.g. **legal requirements** or **company policy**) and if it knows what **action** will be taken to reduce the amount of waste if it's too high. Firms aiming to reduce their waste output over time need to keep **accurate records** of waste levels.

Companies need to be Aware of Positive and Negative Externalities

OCR & EDEXCEL ONLY

1) **Positive externalities** (also called **external benefits**) are the **positive effects** that a **firm's activities** have on the **outside world**. If a construction company builds an upmarket housing estate, it's likely to attract high income families. This creates a positive externality because those families spend money in local shops etc. **Training** is another example of a positive externality — it benefits companies who employ the trained workers in the future.

2) **Negative externalities** are things like **pollution** and the **health issues** caused by certain products, e.g. cigarettes. They're a **cost** to society.

3) **Positive** and **negative** externalities can cause **problems** if they lead to **market failure** — more on this on p.140.

Practice Questions

Q1 What is demographic change? What are its positive and negative effects on businesses?
Q2 How does ethical behaviour affect profit?
Q3 What does corporate social responsibility mean?
Q4 Give two examples of ways that businesses can behave responsibly towards the local community.
Q5 Give two examples of ways that businesses can make their activities sustainable.

Exam Question

Q1 Evaluate the following statement: "Profit should be a higher priority than social responsibility for businesses." [9 marks]

CSR — just a new TV crime series....

Corporate social responsibility has become far more important over the last 20 years — lots of consumers worry about the way the products they buy were made. Some firms take these concerns very seriously and try to make sure their behaviour is ethical, others don't care much at all. Learn to spot examples of firms behaving in a socially responsible way...

The Competitive Environment

*The competitive environment — a standalone page for **AQA**, **OCR** and **Edexcel**.*

Market Structure affects Strategy and Competitive Behaviour

1) **Perfect competition** is where all firms compete on an **equal** basis — their **products** are near-enough **identical** and it's **easy** for businesses to **come** and **go** from the market. In this environment, the consumer has lots of sellers to choose between and can easily find out who's offering the best price, so they get **high quality** products for **low prices**. Perfect competition often leads to **low profit margins** so firms try to keep **costs low** and focus on **efficiency**.

2) A **monopoly** is where one business has **complete control** over its market. There's **no** competition. Since there are no alternatives, if the consumer **needs** the product, the monopoly can charge whatever **price** it wants. But although monopolies are **very powerful**, they can be **inefficient** and **don't** often **innovate**. In the UK, the Competition Commission treats any firm with over 25% market share as a monopoly and can stop monopolies from occurring.

3) **Monopolistic competition** is when there are a lot of businesses in the same market but their products are sufficiently **different** for competition to **not** be based just on price — consumers choose based on how closely the product matches their needs, so the company's focus should be on making their **product** stand out.

4) In an **oligopoly**, a **small** number of **large** firms dominate a market, and charge **similar prices**. If the consumer **needs** the product, they must pay this price. Firms in an oligopoly focus more on **marketing** and **brand image**.

5) Businesses have to **rethink** their **strategies** if a **new competitor** enters the market. For example, if a high street music retailer launches a music download website, existing online music retailers might either have to **lower** their **prices**, invest in a fresh **marketing campaign** or **diversify** into new areas (e.g. film downloads).

6) A **dominant business** is the **strongest business** in a particular market. If a new dominant business enters the market then the **strategies** of its **competitors** will **change** based on the **decisions** made by the **dominant business**. E.g. if the dominant business decides to charge £300 for its product rival firms will generally charge slightly less. Equally, if the dominant firm starts researching new technology, its competitors usually end up doing the same.

Companies are affected by how Powerful their Customers and Suppliers are

1) The **amount** that **people spend** in shops is mostly determined by their **disposable income**. If people have **less disposable income** (e.g. in an economic downturn) then they will **spend less**. If a large proportion of consumers reduce their spending, then **retailers** start to **reduce prices** in order to shift their stock.

2) If a **supplier gains power** in a market, then they are able to command **higher prices**. For example, PC manufacturers nearly all buy software from **Microsoft®** because most people are already using Microsoft® products and it's important to consumers that their computer is compatible with other people's.

Sometimes it's Better for companies to Cooperate rather than Compete

1) In certain situations it is **beneficial** for businesses to **cooperate** with each other, rather than try to compete. This is because **competition** can cause **resources** to be **wasted** as firms try to outdo each other.

It's often difficult for firms to switch from competing to cooperating.

2) Firms might cooperate to benefit from **economies of scale**, to **compete** more effectively with **rivals**, to **improve quality** or access to **new technology**, to break into **new markets** or to **speed up R&D**.

3) A **good example** of cooperation is the **Blu-Ray™ Disc Association**, which includes companies such as Sony, Philips, Panasonic, TDK and Warner Bros. These companies **worked together** to develop **Blu-ray™ technology**, cutting **research** and **development** time and costs. Also, when companies agree to use the same technology in this way it takes much **longer** for the technology to become **obsolete**.

Practice Questions

Q1   What is monopolistic competition?

Q2   Give four reasons why companies might choose to cooperate rather than compete.

Exam Question

Q1   Carryme TV are now the dominant firm in the portable TV market. Analyse how their competitors might react. [8 marks]

What did the competitive environment say? 'I'm greener than you are...'

Ooh, a bonus top tip. We've gone from businesses playing nice on the last two pages to the scary world of monopolies where it's not so much survival of the fittest as survival of the most terrifyingly huge. Learn how businesses cope when more powerful rivals arrive on the scene and why it's sometimes a good idea for them to join forces for the common good...

Market Failure

Here are two one-page topics to round off this section. **This page is for OCR and Edexcel, page 141 is for WJEC.**

Market Failure *is when* Free Market *supply and demand* Don't Apply

1) Free markets are supposed to **allocate resources** efficiently by the process of supply and demand. Ideally, if there's **demand** for a good, there'll be **supply** to meet it — and supply and demand dictate the **price** of the good.

2) **Market failure** occurs when free markets **don't** deliver an ideal **allocation of resources** (they produce too much or too little of a product) or when letting people **act independently** doesn't result in the greatest **benefits** for **society**.

Market Failure *can have several* Causes

The 'goods' that cause market failure aren't necessarily products — they can also be services.

Externalities:

1) **Negative externalities** (see p.138) cause market failure if the negative **side effects** of a firm's **production process** **outweigh** the **advantage** of having the **finished product**. For example, if a company makes wooden tables and workers are having **breathing problems** because of the sawdust created by the machinery, the **cost** of providing **healthcare** for the affected workers might be **greater** than the **benefits** created by the **item** they're making.

2) **Positive externalities** (see p.138) cause market failure because goods tend to be **underprovided** if they cause unintentional positive **social** side effects which **outweigh** private benefits. For example, wild land is useful for **flood control** and **biodiversity**. However, the land owner is usually more interested in its financial value and might make more **profit** if they sell it for **farming**. Not enough land is left wild, which leads to market failure.

Public goods:

Monopolies (see p.139) can also cause market failure when they let prices get too high or underproduce goods.

1) Goods and services that aren't supplied by a **free market** because it's **difficult** to keep **non-buyers** from using them are called public goods. E.g. **everyone** would benefit from a private police force which arrested criminals, even if they **didn't subscribe** to the service.

2) They're **not used up** by consumers — one person benefiting from the police service doesn't stop someone else benefiting from it. It's impossible to sell public goods to several individuals one at a time.

3) The **private sector** won't get involved with this type of good because it **can't make** a **financial profit** from it.

Merit goods and **demerit goods:**

1) **Merit goods** are goods that are beneficial to society but which people probably **wouldn't use** enough if the price was set by a totally **free market** (e.g. health or education) — so private firms wouldn't make a **profit** from them.

2) **Demerit goods** (e.g. alcohol and cigarettes) are goods which people would probably use **too much** of if the price was set by a totally **free market**. A bit like negative externalities, the social costs of dealing with the side effects of demerit goods is greater than the profits they generate.

3) Merit and demerit goods cause market failure because of **imperfect information** — the market doesn't provide **enough information** for **consumers** to **fully understand** the **risks** or **benefits** associated with a product. **Information failure** can happen if the **seller** of a product or service has more **information** than the **buyer**, or **vice versa**. E.g. if a used car dealer doesn't tell a customer that a car's engine is failing, it's information failure.

Labour market failure: **structural unemployment** is a kind of market failure. Redundant workers have **skills** which aren't needed by employers, and they **don't** have the skills which are needed. Labour **resources** therefore sit **idle**.

Governments *Intervene to Prevent Market Failure*

1) Market failure caused by demerit goods or negative externalities can be prevented using **fiscal policy** (usually introducing indirect taxes) to alter levels of **demand**, as long as the goods are **price elastic**. For example, **cigarette taxes** reduce demand. **Pollution taxes** correct negative externalities.

2) In theory, **monetary policy** can also **decrease demand** for **demerit goods** as **higher interest rates** mean people have **less to spend** on non-essential items. However, it only works if **demerit goods** are **income elastic**, e.g. fine wine.

3) Market failure caused by merit or demerit goods or information failure is prevented by governments intervening to provide **better information** — e.g. compulsory health warnings on cigarettes help people make **informed choices**.

4) The government **subsidises** or directly **provides** merit and **public goods**. **Training** prevents **labour market** failure.

5) Businesses have **corporate strategies** for dealing with **market failure**. **Mergers** can allow firms to **internalise negative externalities** — e.g. a food packaging company might be creating waste that's polluting local rivers and affecting the fishing company that supply fish to be packaged. If the two firms merge, they'll be forced to find a solution that suits both companies, so the negative externality will no longer be a problem.

Pressure Groups

Pressure Groups try to Influence government policies and business decisions

1) The aim of all pressure groups is to influence the people who have the power to make decisions.

2) There are **environmental** pressure groups such as Greenpeace and Friends of the Earth, **consumer** pressure groups such as the Consumers' Association, **animal welfare** pressure groups such as the RSPCA and BUAV, **human rights** pressure groups such as Amnesty International and Liberty, **business interest** pressure groups such as the CBI (Confederation of British Industry) — and all **trade unions** are pressure groups as well.

3) Pressure groups use different methods to influence business policy:

The CBI lobby the government to make laws more favourable to businesses.

Lobbying	Pressure groups discuss issues with **business decision makers** and **political decision makers**, to try to **influence** their thinking.
Direct action	Pressure groups organise **direct protests** against specific businesses (e.g. **boycotts** of Nestlé® products, **blockades** of Shell petrol stations).
Publicity	Pressure groups try to make the **public** more **aware** of the issues. Consumers may **choose not to buy** a product which they think causes **social** or **environmental problems**.
Petitions	Petitions (lists of signatures) **prove** that people **agree** with the point of view of the pressure group.
Legal Action	Pressure groups can fight the firm through the **courts**, if they believe that the business is acting **illegally**.

Lobbying Politicians takes time

1) The aim of lobbying is to get politicians to word policies and laws the way you'd like them to be. It takes time for a pressure group to **win politicians around** to their point of view.

2) The first step for any pressure group is to put forward their issues and concerns to the lawmakers. Pressure groups do this by **writing letters** and holding **meetings**, and providing analysis and information.

3) Politicians are more likely to change the law if they think the new law will have **public support**, so it's important for pressure groups to do **publicity** campaigning at the **same time** as lobbying.

Direct Action against Businesses can be Very Powerful

1) Businesses hate **negative publicity**. Direct protests by pressure groups bring unwanted publicity for the businesses, which may result in lower sales, or loss of reputation.

2) Direct action can take the form of a **picketing** protest outside a factory or shop, an **organised boycott** of a product, or even illegal **violent direct action** such as damage to property.

3) Businesses weigh up the **costs** and **benefits** of giving in to direct action. They're more likely to give in when there's **widespread public support** for the pressure group, where the market is **competitive** enough that a boycott would hurt, and where their **public image** is seriously damaged by the protest.

Practice Questions

Q1 What are merit goods and demerit goods?

Q2 What can governments do to deal with market failure caused by externalities?

Q3 Why do pressure groups lobby politicians?

Q4 Give an example of legal direct action.

Exam Questions

Q1 Analyse the government's policy of taxing tobacco products, in terms of market failure and action to prevent it. [9 marks]

Q2 Evaluate the methods that Greenpeace might use to stop supermarkets selling GM products. [12 marks]

Lobbying politicians — harassing them in the hallway...

When I go to the supermarket, and they're all out of tomato soup, is that market failure, I wonder? Well, no, not really — market failure is when the private market as a whole can't make supply and demand match up. Learn the different types of market failure, and what governments do to sort it out. The pressure group topic is a bit more straightforward, luckily.

International Markets

Trading in lots of different countries sounds like fun, but there's quite a lot to it.
*These pages are for **AQA**, **Edexcel**, **WJEC** and **OCR: Strategic Management** unit.*

Gina was very pleased
with her latest purchase
from the globe market.

Globalisation is the creation of a Global Market

1) **Globalisation** is when businesses operate in lots of **countries** all over the world.

2) Globalisation means that companies can be **based** anywhere in the world, and can **buy** from and **sell** to any countries in the world.

3) Globalisation has **increased** over the last few decades — huge multinational **brands** like McDonalds and Coca-Cola® can be found almost **anywhere** in the world.

4) The **internet** has encouraged globalisation because it allows businesses to transfer data between countries very quickly and cheaply.

Trading Internationally offers businesses Benefits

1) Firms can **increase** their **market size** by selling existing products to **new countries** — the bigger the market, the more they're likely to sell and the higher their **revenue** will be. E.g. supermarkets like Tesco have nearly saturated the UK market, but they can still increase the size of their market by opening stores in other countries, like China.

2) They can **extend** the **life cycle** of their products by launching them in **new countries** as the product enters **maturity** in its home market or if **foreign competitors** begin to gain market share in the UK. This is common with cars — businesses can sell models that are old-fashioned in the UK to developing countries like India.

3) Businesses can **reduce costs** by getting their **raw materials** from countries with the **cheapest** prices.

4) They can also **manufacture components** in **overseas** countries where labour is cheaper, before putting the final product together in the UK. This is called **global sourcing**.

5) **Relocating** factories, etc to **developing countries** with lower wage rates than the UK also **reduces costs**.

6) **International growth** leads to **economies of scale**, which reduces the cost per item of products.

7) If the UK economy is in **recession**, businesses can secure revenue by **exporting** to a **growing economy**.

Businesses look for Opportunities in Developing Markets

1) Because **developing markets** are usually many years **behind** developed economies, products that appear old in a developed economy can be offered as **new** in a developing economy.

2) This means firms are able to **lengthen** the **product life cycle** and **increase** sales **revenues** for existing products.

3) Developing economies like Brazil, India, China and Russia represent significant opportunities for businesses in developed countries because of their **large populations** and recent **economic growth**. E.g. many **tobacco manufacturers** based in developed economies have experienced recent **growth** by launching old established brands in developing markets, although many people consider this **unethical** (see next page).

Political Changes can make international trade Easier or Harder

1) **Tariffs** (import taxes) **discourage** international trade. **Removing** or **reducing** tariffs between countries makes international trade **easier** and **cheaper**. Since the **World Trade Organisation** was set up in 1995 to encourage international trade, the proportion of imports worldwide that are **tariff-free** has risen to more than **50%**.

2) **Quotas** are **limits** on **imports** that one country places on another. Countries sometimes use quotas as a way of trying to **protect** their own economies and jobs — this is called a **protectionist policy**. **Removing** (or **reducing** the number of) quotas between countries **encourages** international trade.

3) Since the **UK** joined the **European Union** in 1973, British **exports** to EU countries have **increased** because there are **no quotas** or **tariffs** within the EU. **Imports** from other EU countries to Britain have also **increased**. EU countries also **manufacture** to increasingly **common standards**, which makes trade more **straightforward**.

4) **Trade** between **euro zone** countries has also **increased** in recent years. It has been made easier by the **common currency**, the euro. There's more about how the euro affects trade between euro zone countries on p. 150.

5) **Trading blocs** are when groups of countries agree to **remove trade barriers** (e.g. tariffs) between them. E.g. MERCOSUR (Brazil, Argentina, Paraguay, Uruguay and Venezuela) is a South American trading bloc. Trading blocs make trade between **member countries easier**, but **discourage** trade between the bloc countries and **other countries**.

6) **Trade embargoes ban trade** with a particular country. E.g. the USA has had an embargo against Cuba since 1962.

International Markets

International Trade involves Ethical Considerations

1) **International trade** offers businesses lots of opportunities to **make money** — **selling** their products **abroad** can increase their **turnover** by increasing the size of their market, and **buying raw materials abroad** or relocating **production** abroad can **cut costs**. However, there are also **ethical factors** involved in international trade, and businesses need to consider these when they make decisions about trading internationally.

2) Some companies with factories abroad might **exploit foreign workers** to cut their costs (see p. 146). This kind of behaviour is very unethical, and can lead to consumers **boycotting** the company if its unethical practices come to light.

3) Businesses might take into account the **damage** that their activities might do to the **environment**. Getting **raw materials** from abroad is often **cheaper**, but **transporting** them from one country to another, often by plane, causes **pollution**. **Distributing** finished products to other countries also causes **pollution**. E.g. around 95% of the fruit sold in the UK comes from other countries, even though most of it could be produced in the UK.

4) **Tobacco companies** can make huge profits by selling **cigarettes** in **developing countries**, but many people think that this is unethical because people in developing countries often **don't know** about the **health risks** associated with smoking, so they can't make an **informed decision** about whether or not to smoke. Also, people in developing countries often **earn very little**, and cigarettes are **expensive** in comparison with their income, so if they get **addicted** to smoking they end up spending a **large proportion** of their **income** on cigarettes. Smoking-related **illnesses** can also **overwhelm** the **health system** of developing countries.

5) **Weapons manufacturers** can make money by selling **missiles** and other **weapons** abroad, but selling weapons to **oppressive regimes** or countries that are seen as a **security threat** is unethical. Governments place **restrictions** on which countries companies can sell weapons to.

There are Other Issues involved in International Trade

1) Businesses have to pay to **transport** the goods they want to buy from, or distribute to, other countries. Transporting goods **internationally** can be very **expensive**.

2) Businesses have to make sure that they're **aware of** and **follow** the **laws** of the countries they operate in — they can't just assume that employment laws, etc, will be the same everywhere. They also have to comply with all **customs laws** — e.g. some products, like fresh fruit, can't be transported across international boundaries without permits.

3) Businesses trading internationally will have **higher** business **travel costs** as employees will need to travel to the various locations the business trades in. Travel costs can be reduced by the use of ICT such as email, telephone conferencing and video conferencing.

Harry's boss was keen to keep staff travel costs as low as possible.

4) Trading in **foreign-speaking** countries increases **costs** (e.g. **translations** might be needed).

5) Fluctuations in **exchange rates** make the cost of international trade **unpredictable**, so it's difficult for businesses to accurately **forecast** revenue and profits.

Practice Questions

Q1 What is globalisation?

Q2 What are: a) tariffs? b) quotas? c) trading blocs?

Q3 How does international trade affect the environment?

Q4 Why does trading in foreign-speaking countries increase costs?

Exam Question

Q1 Explain how international trade can extend the life cycle of a product. [4 marks]

I always thought an embargo was some kind of embarrassing illness...

Globalisation's quite an interesting one — some people hate the fact that city centres around the world are all starting to look alike, while other people find it comforting that wherever they are in the world, they can always find a McDonalds or a Starbucks. Whatever you think about it, you need to learn all the issues affecting businesses that trade in other countries.

Global Strategy

*Global strategy is all about how to take over the world. Or at least how to sell your products all over the world. These pages are for **Edexcel**, **WJEC** and **OCR**.*

Global Strategy means selling the Same Product in Different Countries

1) A **global strategy** is a **plan** to coordinate business activities in different parts of the **world**, so that the **same product** is sold in the **same way** all over the world. **Control** is **centralised** (see p. 70), so all the decisions are made in the original country.

2) A **global strategy** leads to **global brands** that are recognised in many different countries, like BMW, Disney, Microsoft®, Mercedes-Benz and Apple®.

3) Businesses gain **economies of scale** by using a global strategy. It allows them to use the same tried and tested product ideas in each country. E.g. BMW sells the same cars all over the world.

4) **Global marketing strategy** means that a business uses the **same promotional message** in every country. This **reduces** their **marketing costs** because they don't have to spend time and money coming up with new advertising campaigns, slogans, etc. for each country — they can just use one they prepared earlier.

5) A global strategy will only work if customers' **needs and wants** in the different countries the business trades in are the **same**. Global strategy doesn't take into account the **social** and **cultural differences** between countries, so there's a risk that there might be **no demand** for the product in other countries.

Global Localisation means Adapting Products for Each Country

1) **Global localisation** is when a business operates in many **different countries**, but **adapts** its products, marketing activities, and working practices to reflect the **culture** and **society** of each country it operates in.

2) Businesses also **balance** their **resource investments** — they allocate **different levels** of **resources** to countries depending on how **big** the **market** is, e.g. you don't need huge warehouses in a country where not many products are distributed.

"Ambassador, with these baked beans you are really spoiling us."

2) Businesses can **alter** their **products** to suit international tastes. E.g. McDonalds adapts its menu in each country to reflect local tastes — Hindus don't eat beef, so McDonalds in India sells the lamb "Maharaja Mac™" instead of the "Big Mac®".

3) Businesses can sell the **same products** but **market** them **differently** in different countries to suit the local market. E.g. Baked beans are a budget food in the UK, but in Russia they're seen as a delicacy, so Heinz market their baked beans as a luxury product in Russia.

4) Businesses check that their **brand names** and **logos** aren't **offensive** or linked to a **negative meaning** in different languages or cultures. E.g. Bimbo® is a best-selling brand of bread in many Spanish-speaking countries, but it would probably be less popular in the UK.

5) Businesspeople need to be aware of **local customs** in different countries so that they don't **offend** potential clients — e.g. in the UK lunch or dinner meetings to discuss business are popular, but Mexicans believe that business should never be discussed during mealtimes. Some businesses employ **agents** from the country they want to do business in so that they can **avoid** language difficulties and culture clashes.

Takeovers and Mergers can help businesses to Expand Internationally

1) **International takeovers** and **mergers** allow a business trading in one country to take over or join with a business that already has **experience** and **expertise** in a **different country**.

2) The main **benefit** of growth through international mergers and takeovers is that they allow a business to grow at a very **fast** rate. The business doesn't need to go through the slow process of **establishing itself** in a new country because the company it takes over or merges with will already be **well known** and will have an established name and reputation. E.g. Vodafone grew internationally by buying several smaller competitors in other countries. This helped Vodafone grow very rapidly, as with each takeover they acquired lots of new customers as well as established networks and masts.

3) International takeovers and mergers can **reduce** the **risk of failure** because the staff from the business that's been bought out have **knowledge** of the **local market** and **local culture**.

4) The main **problem** with international takeovers and mergers is that they can lead to **management problems** if the businesses keep operating as **independent businesses** instead of as parts of the same company. To avoid these problems, the company might send a team of employees to **manage** a company it has taken over and make sure that things are done the way they want. See p. 170 for more on the issues involved in takeovers and mergers.

Global Marketing

Global marketing helps businesses to create a global demand for their products.
*This page is for **Edexcel**, **WJEC** and the **OCR Strategic Management** unit.*

Global Niche Marketing *targets* Niche Markets *in* Several Countries

1) **Global niche marketing** involves marketing to **defined market segments** across different countries.

2) Because niche marketing targets a **small segment** of the market, there is only a **small** pool of **potential domestic customers** for the product. The only way to increase the pool of potential customers for a niche product is to increase the total size of the **market** — businesses can do this by **expanding abroad**.

3) Businesses recognise that there are **similar segments of society** with similar needs in different countries, so they can market the **same product** to niches within various countries.

4) **Global market niches** can be defined by many variables including **income**, **age** and **gender**. E.g. people with high levels of disposable income generally desire luxury goods and will pay a premium for goods that reflect a lifestyle others aspire to. This is the same in many countries. **Aspirational goods** represent an important and growing global niche market. Many multinational businesses target high earning professionals in various developed countries.

5) Global niche marketing is more **complex** than developing a **general global brand** because the business has to **identify** segments of their market with similar **needs** and **wants** in different countries, and then launch a coordinated marketing strategy targeting the identified niche in several countries.

6) Successful niche marketing on a global scale is very **hard to achieve** because of the cultural and geographical differences that need to be overcome. Many businesses **underestimate** how hard it is to sell successfully to a defined niche in a second country after successfully selling to that niche in their own market.

The number of Global Brands is Increasing

1) **International broadcasting** allows people to watch **television programmes** from different countries. This can create **international demand** for items in many countries. US brands like Levi's® and Coca-Cola® became popular in developing countries like India and China partly because they advertised on popular TV channels like MTV.

2) The **internet** also allows companies to market and sell their products internationally. Businesses can **sell** their products **internationally** but avoid the **expense** of setting up in foreign countries by advertising their products on **foreign websites** and offering **overseas shipping**. This allows them to create a global brand but avoids the **risk** that comes with setting up a business abroad.

Practice Questions

Q1 Why might businesses alter their brand names in different countries?

Q2 Explain how international takeovers and mergers help to reduce the risk of failure.

Q3 What is global niche marketing?

Q4 How does television help to create global brands?

Q5 How can businesses use the internet to create a global brand?

Exam Questions

Q1 Explain the difference between global strategy and global localisation. [4 marks]

Q2 To what extent do you agree with the statement that if a product is popular and sells well in one country, it will be popular and sell well in another country? [6 marks]

Global localisation? Surely that's an oxymoron or something...

These pages are quite nice aren't they? I especially liked the bit about Bimbo® bread — hee hee. And I quite fancy trying a Maharajah Mac™ too — they sound quite nice. Anyway, just keep reading over all this lovely stuff until you've got it all nicely tattooed on your brain. Hmm... brain tattooes — I wonder if there's a global market niche for that...

Multinationals

*Multinationals are businesses that are based in more than one country. A bit like those annoying celebrities who have holiday homes in various exotic locations. Multinationals aren't quite as glamorous though I'm afraid. These pages are for **Edexcel**, **AQA** and **WJEC**.*

Multinationals *are located in* More Than One Country

1) A **multinational company** is a business that **locates** its factories, call centres, etc. outside the country its **head office** is based in.

2) Locating some parts of the business **abroad** means that multinationals are able to produce products in the most **cost-effective locations** — this has increased the overall level of **international trade**.

3) Many multinational organisations relocate parts of the business to **developing countries** like India, where **labour** is **cheaper** and other **costs** are also **lower**.

4) Some of the largest multinationals now have **annual turnovers larger** than the **GDP** (gross domestic product — a country's total income) of some countries. This means these businesses have a lot of **economic power**.

Multinationals *can* Benefit Developing Countries

1) Multinationals **increase employment opportunities** for the local population in the countries they locate in.

2) Multinationals **increase** the local **standard of living**. Although they get paid less than workers in developed countries, the employees of multinationals in developing countries often receive **better pay and conditions** than employees of **local companies** in the developing country.

3) **Inward investment** into the host country increases because multinationals **spend money** on building the **factories** and **infrastructure** (roads, etc) that they need. This is called **foreign direct investment** (FDI).

4) Multinationals cause **economic growth** in the countries they locate in. The GDP of the host country increases as a result of **additional spending** in the economy on things like increased travel into the area and demand for hotel rooms from visiting businesspeople.

5) Multinationals locating in developing countries will **pay taxes** to the **local government**. This results in increased **government income**, which might be spent on projects such as **schools** and **hospitals**. Payments by multinationals to local governments might include:
   - taxes on the **purchase of land**,
   - taxes on **profits** they make,
   - taxes on the **wages** of local employees,
   - taxes on products **exported** abroad.

6) **Ethical multinationals** try to benefit the countries they locate in by paying **fair wages** rather than exploiting workers. This **increases costs**, but if businesses highlight the fact that they trade ethically then consumers may be willing to pay slightly higher prices for their products.

7) Many multinational companies are increasingly committed to **Corporate Social Responsibility** (CSR) in developing nations, so **exploitation** is **less common** than it used to be.

Multinationals *might* Exploit Developing Countries

1) Some multinational businesses may **exploit developing countries** in order to **maximise** their **profits**.

2) Some multinationals base their production in countries with **low wages** to **reduce** their **costs**. They might set up **sweatshops** — factories where employees work long hours in difficult and sometimes dangerous conditions for minimal payment.

3) A multinational might locate in a country with **less strict employment laws** in order to reduce costs by employing **child labour**, making employees work **long shifts**, or not providing the correct **safety equipment**.

Confusing 'sweatshop' and 'sweetshop' when you're looking for a job could have disastrous consequences.

4) Multinationals sometimes sell **products** which **don't** quite **meet** EU or American **safety standards** to developing countries.

5) A multinational might extract large quantities of **unsustainable natural resources** such as oil, gas or minerals. It might also fail to redevelop the landscape when there's no more to extract. In a developed country a company would be required to **minimise** its **environmental impact**, but in some developing countries, **environmental laws** are **less strict**, and multinationals might take advantage of this.

6) The **governments** of developing countries might **overlook unlawful behaviour** by multinational businesses because they **rely** on the **tax income** they generate, so they won't want the business to relocate away from their country.

Multinationals

Multinationals also locate in **Developed Countries**

1) Many multinationals also locate in other **developed countries**. They might set up factories in the countries they **sell** their products to in order to keep their **distribution costs low**.

2) Producing products in the country where they're sold also helps companies to **avoid** some **taxes**. Many global multinationals **manufacture** and **sell** their products within the **European Union** (EU) to avoid paying the **import tax** for non-EU products imported into the EU. E.g. Toyota and Honda both manufacture cars in the UK for distribution within the EU.

3) Multinationals can **sell** items from one **part of the business** to another, **manipulating** the **price** in order to make all the **profits** appear to belong in a country with very **low tax rates**. This is called **transfer pricing**. E.g. if a multinational **produces** its products in a country with a **high rate of tax** on profits, it can **sell** the products to another part of the business for a very **low price** — this means that they **avoid** paying tax in the first country. Transfer pricing **reduces** the amount of **tax** a multinational corporation pays but might **conflict** with any **Corporate Social Responsibility** (CSR) code they have.

Multinationals are subject to **Political, Economic** and **Legal Restraints**

1) Because multinational corporations operate in many different countries, each with its own laws, governments sometimes **coordinate** their approaches to control and manage the activities of multinationals. E.g. the **European Union** has tried to **standardise employment laws** such as Equal Opportunities and Health & Safety standards to ensure that multinational corporations within the EU have to meet **minimum standards** wherever they locate. This is known as **harmonisation**.

2) **Governments** sometimes use **protectionist policies** like **tariffs** and **quotas** to protect their own economies. See p. 142 for more on how governments can create **barriers to trade**.

3) **Pressure groups** sometimes try to **influence government policy** on multinational organisations. They try to persuade governments to put **tighter controls** on how multinationals from one country operate in **other countries** (e.g. to stop multinationals from using child labour in foreign countries).

Not that kind of legal restraint...

Practice Questions

Q1 What is a multinational?
Q2 State three ways in which multinationals might exploit developing countries.
Q3 Why might a multinational locate in a developed country?
Q4 What is transfer pricing?
Q5 What is harmonisation?

Exam Questions

Q1 Describe the main advantages to developing countries of having multinationals located there. [6 marks]

Q2 To what extent do you agree with the statement that "multinationals who locate manufacturing plants in developing countries in order to avoid more stringent Health & Safety laws that exist in their own countries are above the law"? [4 marks]

"No sultana limit" — a weird anagram of "multinationals"...

You've probably noticed that most location decisions for multinationals are based on one thing — money. You need to learn why companies locate parts of the business in developed or developing countries (it almost always comes down to saving money one way or another). You also need to know the benefits and drawbacks of this for developing countries.

The World Economy

*The world economy used to be dominated by the EU and the USA, but lately some other countries have been emerging as economic powers. These pages are just for **Edexcel**.*

The **Indian** and **Chinese Economies** have **Developed Rapidly**

The **Indian** and **Chinese** economies have grown very quickly in recent times. Businesses based in these countries are now competing with other multinationals to be **world leaders** in many sectors.

How China became a global economic power

1) Chinese industry used to be controlled by a **command economy**. A command economy means that **economic decisions** (e.g. what large businesses should produce) are made centrally by the **government**. It's different to a **market economy**, where **businesses** decide what to produce (through market research, etc.).

2) Chinese businesses used to be more **bureaucratic** and **slower to respond** to changing customer demands than UK businesses, because decisions came from government officials who had **very little knowledge** of what consumers wanted.

3) In 1978 the Chinese government implemented **economic reforms** to **expand** and **modernise** their **manufacturing economy**. This involved giving businesses **more control** over their own activities.

4) By 2005, **70**% of China's GDP (gross domestic product — see p. 128) was generated in the **private sector**. Only **30**% came from the **public sector**, which is dominated by about 200 very large corporations. They concentrate their activities on utilities and manufacturing.

5) **Services** and **manufacturing** are becoming increasingly **important** to the Chinese economy. Farming now represents only around 11% of China's economic activity, while the **manufacturing industry** accounts for almost **half** of China's economic activity and **services** account for about **40%.**

6) **Multinationals** are attracted to China because Chinese factories have **low wage rates**, which makes them very **cost effective** when producing standard items using mass manufacturing methods.

7) In 2007 China became the **second-largest exporting country** in the world (behind Germany) with exports worth $1218 billion. **8.7**% of all global exports come from China – almost three times more than the UK's annual exports total.

How India became a global economic power

1) Since 1991, the Indian government has worked hard to establish a **market economy** and **encourage international trade**.

2) The Indian economy has grown at a **faster rate** since 2000 than most **developed economies** in the western world. The Indian economy has even **overtaken** some developed economies in terms of **GDP**.

3) By 2007 the Indian economy was growing at **9**% per year, much **faster** than any **developed nation** and at the same rate as **China**.

4) Today the Indian economy is still very **diverse**. **Agriculture** is very important in rural areas but the **manufacturing** and **service** sectors (e.g. international **call centres**) have developed in urban areas.

5) Traditional **exports** from India include spices, rice, tea and fish. More recently, Indian businesses have earned their money exporting **call centre services** and **software development expertise**.

The **Indian** and **Chinese Economies** are likely to **Keep Growing**

1) China and India are likely to **remain competitive** because of their **low wage rates**, which mean that they can provide goods and services to companies in other countries for much less than it would cost the company to organise these activities themselves. This means their economies are likely to grow further.

2) In **India**, young people are being **trained** to go into business. Cities like Delhi now have large universities that specialise in **business** and **management courses** to train the next generation of global **business leaders**.

3) The main factors that might **prevent growth** in **India** are:
   • Its **infrastructure** (roads, etc) **isn't very good**.
   • India has an adult **literacy rate** of only around **60%** — this **cuts down** the potential pool of employees.

4) The main factors that might **prevent growth** in **China** are:
   • **Fewer** Chinese people than Indian people speak **English**, so China can't compete in the **call-centre** market.
   • China's **universities aren't as good** as India's for training future business leaders.

The World Economy

India and *China* offer *Opportunities* for *UK Businesses...*

1) In 1999 **China** signed an agreement with the **World Trade Organisation** (WTO) to **remove** protectionist **barriers** to international trade. In 2001, it became a **member** of the WTO. As a result China no longer prevents imports from Western businesses in sectors such as banking and telecommunications, so UK businesses have more **opportunities** to **export** their products to China.

2) As **India's income** has increased, its **imports** have also increased, meaning that UK businesses have more opportunity to export their products to India.

3) **China** has a rapidly **increasing population**, so there is a huge pool of **potential customers** there. **India** also has a very **large population**. They are both **huge markets** that can be very **profitable** for UK businesses if they manage to create **demand** for their products there.

4) UK businesses can **reduce** their **costs** by **outsourcing manufacturing** to China or India, and having their **call centres** in India. E.g. average annual call centre salaries in the UK are about **£15 000**, compared with around **£2000** in India, so using Indian call centres can drastically reduce a business' costs and enable it to keep its **prices low** and stay **competitive**.

5) Recent **economic growth** has produced many **millionaires** and even **billionaires** in China and India, so there's a lot of potential for UK companies selling **luxury products** to be very successful there.

... but it can be **Difficult** *for* **UK Businesses** *to trade with* **India** *and* **China**

1) Despite the recent economic growth, many people in China are still **very poor**. Although China has one of the world's largest economies in terms of GDP, its **GDP per person** is **below average**. In India around **25%** of people are **below** the **poverty line**. This means that the **number** of **potential customers** for any product is **reduced**.

2) The **Indian government** has put **restrictions** on **foreign businesses** investing in Indian companies. This trade barrier makes it **more difficult** for UK businesses to break into the Indian market.

3) **Language** and **cultural barriers** can prevent UK businesses from trading with India and China. These barriers are particularly difficult to overcome in **China** — in India more people speak English, and the culture is more similar to UK culture because it's a former UK colony.

India's trade barriers made Paul's job much more difficult.

4) China and India both use **different currencies** to the UK (the yuan in China and the rupee in India), so UK businesses are **vulnerable** to changes in currency values. A **strong pound** makes **British exports more expensive** abroad, which would **reduce demand** for products from UK companies in India and China.

Practice Questions

Q1 Why were Chinese businesses previously slow to respond to market changes?

Q2 Why do lots of multinational companies use China as a location for manufacturing?

Q3 What are India's main exports at the moment?

Q4 Why has importing to China been easier for UK businesses since 1999?

Q5 Why might companies that specialise in luxury products be interested in the Indian and Chinese markets?

Exam Questions

Q1 Discuss whether economic growth in China and India is likely to continue or not. [4 marks]

Q2 Explain why trading with China and India is an attractive prospect for UK companies, and describe the barriers to trade that UK companies face in those countries. [8 marks]

Global economic powers are ok, but I'd still prefer super powers...

It's pretty strange to think that a few years ago India and China weren't very big players economy-wise, and now they're taking the world by storm. Makes you wonder which countries will be "global economic powers" in another few years. Anyway, once you've learned everything on these pages you're almost at the end of the section — just two pages to go.

The European Union

*The EU is a union of 27 independent countries, with a population of over 495 million — bigger than the US and Japan put together. So it's a pretty big deal. For **AQA**, **Edexcel**, the **OCR: Strategic Management** unit and **WJEC**.*

The EU is a **Single Market** — **Trade** between member states is **Easy**

1) There are very few **trade barriers** between EU member states — this is called the Single Market. Businesses don't pay **tax** when they **import** goods from other EU countries. The EU provides easy export opportunities for UK firms.

2) The EU has **customs union**, which means the **same customs duties** apply to all goods entering the area irrespective of which country they come from, and which country they're going to.

3) The Single Market **smooths out price differences** between member states. **Producers** can look for the **highest selling price** within the EU, and consumers can look for the **lowest purchase price** within the EU. When the price in part of the EU is high, producers flood that area with their product, driving down prices. Low prices attract more buyers to the market, pushing prices up.

4) There's freedom of movement within the EU for all **raw materials**, **finished goods** and **workers**. EU citizens can work in any country of the EU.

5) A common **EU competition law** controls anti-competitive activities — e.g. setting up a **monopoly**.

6) There are **common policies** on **product regulation** as well.

The **Growth** of the **EU** has increased **Business Opportunities**

1) Whenever the EU expands, the **size of the market** available to an EU-based producer increases. Businesses can enjoy **increased sales** and take advantage of **economies of scale**.

2) The EU collectively has **more political whack** than its member states. For example, the EU can negotiate any trade dispute with the USA on equal terms. This increases competitiveness.

3) **Production costs** are **low** in the **new EU countries** that joined in 2004 (Poland, Hungary, etc) and 2007 (Romania and Bulgaria). Businesses can locate production facilities there to increase their competitiveness.

Increased **Competition** in the EU can be a **Threat**

1) The expansion of the EU brings **businesses** from **new member states** into the market.

2) There's **increased competition** in industries where new member states like Hungary and Poland have an advantage — e.g. **manufacturing** and **agriculture**. This threatens UK manufacturers and farmers.

3) **High tech** UK businesses keep their **competitive advantage**.

4) Increased competition may also hurt **inefficient** producers in the new member states, who were previously serving protected national markets.

Ian found that the best way to deal with the competition was just to trip them all up.

The **Euro** is the **Common Currency** of **Most** EU countries

The euro became the **common currency** of 11 EU member states in **1999**. They stopped using their old currencies completely in **2002**. These countries are commonly called the **eurozone**. More countries have joined the eurozone since the euro was first introduced, and there are now **16** eurozone countries. The **UK isn't** part of the eurozone — there are **benefits** and **drawbacks** to not being a member:

Benefits of keeping the pound	Drawbacks of keeping the pound
The UK still has power over its **interest rates**. For countries in the eurozone, the **European Central Bank** sets the interest rates, which causes problems if different countries have different **economic situations** (e.g. if inflation is high, higher interest rates are needed to control it).	1) **Changing money** on the foreign exchange market **costs money**. A common currency would **reduce transaction costs** between businesses in the UK and eurozone countries. 2) It's harder to **compare prices** when they're not in the same currency. 3) UK businesses exporting abroad face the **uncertainty** of fluctuating exchange rates. When the **pound rises** in value against the euro, UK exporters **lose** international competitiveness because their goods are more **expensive** for eurozone countries. Eurozone businesses don't have the uncertainty of constantly changing exchange rates.

The European Union

It's **Difficult** for businesses to come up with **Pan-European Strategy**

1) It's easy for businesses to think of the EU as a big single market, with the same rules and regulations throughout. In reality, it's tricky to come up with a **pan-European strategy** — one that works all over Europe.

2) There are still **cultural differences** between countries, and lots of **different languages**, so EU businesses need to market products in different ways to suit **different countries**.

3) Having to do lots of marketing campaigns for one product **reduces economies of scale**.

4) There are also still **legal** differences between EU countries.

EU Institutions pass **Laws** which affect **Business**

EU laws are divided into **four main categories**:

Most EU laws are directives.

1) **Regulations** are **binding laws** that apply to **all** EU citizens as soon as they're passed.

2) **Directives** tell **member-state** governments to **pass a law** that meets a specific objective — e.g. reducing working time to 48 hours per week, or reducing pollution. It's up to member-state governments how to word the law. Some member governments make **strict** laws in response to EU directives, while others are more slack.

3) **Decisions** are **binding laws** that apply to a **specific country** or a **specific business**.

4) **Recommendations** aren't really laws at all, because they're **not legally binding**.

The European Commission and the Council of Ministers decide on policies and laws

1) The **European Commission** puts forward new laws. The EU Commission is **appointed**, not elected.

2) The Council of Ministers **decides** whether or not to bring in **new laws** suggested by the Commission. It's made up of **government ministers** from **each member state**.

There's one commissioner from each member state.

The European Parliament is involved in making new laws

1) The European Parliament is **directly elected**, so it gives some democratic legitimacy to European law.

2) Most decisions on new EU laws are made **jointly** by the Council of Ministers and the European Parliament.

The European Central Bank (ECB) controls the euro

1) The **ECB** decides monetary policy (i.e. it sets interest rates) in the eurozone.

2) Only the eurozone countries have a say in the running of the bank.

The European Court of Justice interprets EU law

1) The European Court of Justice makes sure that **EU law** is applied in line with the **Treaty of Rome** — the treaty that says how the EU must be run.

2) It also sorts out disputes between member states.

3) The decisions of the court take precedence over the laws of each member state.

Practice Questions

Q1 Give an example of a benefit to business of the EU Single Market.

Q2 Give one benefit to business if the UK adopted the euro.

Q3 What is an EU directive?

Exam Questions

Q1 Analyse the ways in which a Welsh toy manufacturer would be affected if the UK decided to adopt the euro. [10 marks]

Q2 "The bureaucrats in Brussels can't change the way I run my business."
Do you agree with this statement? Justify your answer. [6 Marks]

The Single Market's the place to go if you're looking for love...

The EU is a big deal for businesses — as the Single Market grows, there's more opportunity for easy importing and exporting. The EU is also another source of laws and regulations that businesses have to follow. Whether you're generally pro-Europe or anti-Europe doesn't change the fact that you need to revise both these pages to be prepared for the exam.

Using Objectives and Strategies

Ooh, a whole section on objectives and strategies — you lucky thing.
*These pages are for **AQA**, **Edexcel**, the **OCR: Strategic Management** unit and **WJEC**.*

Functional Objectives contribute to the Company's Corporate Objectives

1) All businesses have **objectives**. Objectives are things that the business wants to **achieve**.
   Corporate objectives are general objectives that refer to the business as a **whole**,
   e.g. an objective to become the first-choice supplier of ready meals for UK supermarkets.

2) Setting corporate objectives is fairly **straightforward** for a sole trader or partnership business —
   the owner or owners know what they are trying to achieve. The planning process for a **limited
   company** is usually more **complicated** because the managers and directors have to make
   decisions on behalf of the shareholders.

3) **Functional objectives** (sometimes called **departmental objectives**) are the objectives of each
   department. E.g. to increase sales per salesperson from 10 to 13 orders a day within the next 2
   years is a sales objective, and to increase the net profit margin from 15% to 22% within the next
   2 years is a financial objective.

4) Businesses need to set **functional objectives** that will help them **achieve** their **corporate
   objectives**. E.g. in order to achieve a corporate objective of becoming the first-choice supplier
   for UK supermarkets, the production department would need to produce high quality products,
   the sales department would have to achieve certain sales levels, the finance department would
   have to arrange appropriate prices and payment terms, etc.

Business Always involves Risk

1) All businesses have to take some **risks**. Developing **coordinated objectives** between the
   departments of a business **reduces the risks** of failure, but it **can't** remove risk completely.

2) Some business objectives are very **high risk** but if they are successful bring **high rewards**.
   E.g. **borrowing** large amounts of capital in order to **grow quickly** in an emerging market
   could be considered a **high-risk**, **high-reward** objective.

3) Businesses often try to **reduce risk**. They can do this through careful **planning** and **research**.

4) Managers and business leaders can attempt to work out the likely impact
   of **quantifiable** risks (risks that can be **measured**) based on the likelihood
   of them occurring and the estimated effect these events might have.

5) **Decision trees** (See p. 160-161) can help managers to **quantify** risk.

6) Some risks **can't** be anticipated — they are **unquantifiable**.
   Unquantifiable risks have to be dealt with by managers as they happen.

7) **Contingency planning** sets out how a business should **react** to an
   unexpected situation or disaster — see p. 157. It doesn't reduce the level
   of risk associated with business, but planning for unexpected disasters
   can **reduce the impact** that they have on the business if they do happen.

A stampeding bull is just one of the risks that businesses don't usually plan for.

Functional Objectives are used to form Strategies

1) A **strategy** is a **plan of action** developed to achieve an objective.

2) **Corporate strategies** are developed to achieve **corporate objectives**. These can involve **several departments**.

3) **Functional strategies** are developed to achieve **functional objectives**. Each department has its own functional
   objectives, so functional strategies only involve **one department**.

4) A **strategic gap** is when the results from the strategy that has been developed **aren't** expected to **achieve** the
   stated **objective**. E.g. if the objective is to increase sales by **10%**, and the strategy is to use a TV advertising
   campaign, which is only expected to increase demand by **8%**, there's a **strategic gap**. When a strategic gap is
   identified managers must either **alter the objective** or develop more **supporting strategies** — e.g. they could
   do a 2-for-1 promotion in addition to the advertising campaign to increase demand further.

Using Objectives and Strategies

Objectives can be Strategic or Tactical

1) **Strategic objectives** are the **medium-term goals** of the business as a whole. They help businesses to achieve their overall **corporate objectives**.

2) **Tactical objectives** are **short-term functional objectives**. Businesses have to meet their **tactical objectives** in order to meet their **strategic objectives**. E.g. if a business has a **strategic objective** to increase sales by 5% in one year, the production department might set a **tactical objective** to increase output per person from 200 units to 210 units per month, in order to produce the extra products that the business intends to sell.

3) **Senior managers** set the **strategic objectives** for the business, but **departmental managers** decide on their own tactics to make sure that those strategic objectives are met. E.g. the marketing manager might arrange a promotion if it doesn't look as though the strategic objective to increase sales by 5% is likely to be met.

Roberto wasn't really bothered about tactics or strategies — he just really liked the outfit.

Objectives should be Specific, Measurable, Agreed, Realistic and Timely

To be effective, an objective should be 'SMART' — specific, measurable, agreed, realistic and timely.

Specific	**Vague objectives** like "to improve quality" **don't** really tell staff what they're supposed to be aiming for. Making them more **specific**, e.g. "to reduce the number of items produced that have defects", means that the business is more likely to **achieve** them.
Measurable	If the objective **isn't measurable**, the business **won't know** if it's achieved it or not. E.g. "to increase turnover by 5%" is a measurable objective, but "to increase turnover" is vague.
Agreed	Everyone who's going to be involved in **achieving** the objective needs to **know** about it and **agree** to it. E.g. if the objective is to increase sales, the sales manager and salespeople will all need to agree to it.
Realistic	There's no point setting objectives that are **too ambitious**, e.g. tripling sales within 12 months, or achieving a 95% market share. **Impossible objectives** just **demotivate** staff.
Timely	There should be a **specific timeframe** that the objective has to be achieved in. E.g. the objective might be to increase turnover by 5% within 12 months. If there's **no time limit**, staff won't see the objective as **urgent** — they might think they don't need to worry about achieving it because as long as it gets done at some time in the future then it doesn't matter.

Practice Questions

Q1 What's the difference between corporate objectives and functional objectives?
Q2 What is an unquantifiable risk?
Q3 What are tactical objectives?
Q4 What does SMART stand for in the term 'SMART objectives'?

Exam Question

Q1 Low-cost airlines have experienced rapid growth in recent years. How important are corporate objectives and strategy likely to have been in contributing to this success? [8 marks]

This all seems pretty DUMB to me...

Lots to learn here — don't go skipping over it to get to the more exciting things like... er... decision trees and stuff. If you don't learn this basic stuff then you don't stand much of a chance of understanding the rest of the section. So stick with corporate strategies, strategic gaps, SMART objectives and all the rest until you know it better than the back of your hand.

Corporate Aims and Objectives

*Businesses can't get very far if they don't know what they want to achieve — that's where corporate aims and objectives come in. These pages are for **AQA**, **Edexcel**, the **OCR: Strategic Management** unit and **WJEC**.*

The Aims and Objectives of For-profit businesses are mainly Financial

1) Setting **objectives** help businesses achieve their **aims**. The **main aim** of most businesses is to make a **profit**.

2) **New businesses** that are currently making a loss might aim to become **profitable**. Established businesses that are already profitable might want to **increase** their profits (e.g. by 10% within three years).

3) Businesses might also want to increase their **market share**. E.g. a company that makes perfumes might aim to have a 20% share of the perfume market.

4) Businesses might aim to **expand geographically**. E.g. a business with four sandwich shops in Hull might aim to open other sandwich shops in cities around Yorkshire, and a successful UK clothes retailer might aim to expand into Europe or the USA.

5) Businesses might also aim to **expand** their **product range**. A business that makes toys might expand into organising children's parties, or a pizza restaurant might start offering pasta dishes too. Companies like Virgin have successfully expanded into areas completely unrelated to each other, like travel, music and cosmetics.

Sally needed to work on her corporate aim.

Not-for-profit businesses have different Aims and Objectives

1) **Not-for-profit** businesses **aren't** set up to make a profit. They have other aims, usually to **benefit society** in some way (e.g. by providing affordable housing, buying toys for children in hospitals).

2) **Social enterprises** are normal businesses with a **social objective**. The business **trades** and **makes profit** like any other business, but its profits are used to pay for its **social activities**. E.g. all the profits from the bottled water company One Water are used to build water pumps in villages in Africa.

3) **Charities** exist to raise money for **good causes**. They raise money through donations, sponsored events, shops, etc. The government treats charities differently from normal businesses — charities don't have to pay all the **taxes** that other businesses do, they can use **volunteers** as staff, and they get a discount on **rent**.

4) **Mutual organisations** like building societies aim to offer their customers the best possible **value** on products and services. **Profits** are **reinvested** into the business in order to **reduce prices** — that means that building societies can often offer higher savings rates and lower loan rates than banks, because they don't have to pay any of their profits to shareholders.

Different Stakeholders have Different Objectives

1) Businesses have a lot of different **stakeholders** — groups that are **connected** with the business in some way. Stakeholders include employees, shareholders, customers, suppliers, etc. Stakeholders all have their own **objectives**, which are often **conflicting**:

- **Shareholders** usually want high **dividends** and a high **share price**.
- **Employees** want good **pay** and **working conditions**.
- **Suppliers** want to be paid a **fair price**, and be paid **on time**.
- **Customers** want the best possible **quality** at the lowest possible **price**.
- Local **residents** want the business to create **jobs**, and not to **pollute** or damage the local area.

2) Many businesses are mainly interested in keeping their **shareholders** happy. In order to achieve high share prices and dividends, the business would have to maximise its profits, and wouldn't be able to reinvest money into the business for expansion.

3) Businesses have to strike a **balance** to try and keep all their stakeholders as happy as possible. E.g. a business might cut costs in order to increase its profits if it's trying to keep its shareholders happy, but if this reduces the quality of the products, customers won't be happy and will stop buying products from the business — so the plan will **backfire**.

Corporate Aims and Objectives

Mission Statements give Clues to corporate culture

1) **Mission statements** are written **descriptions** of corporate objectives. They set out what the business does, and why they do it. Mission statements are intended to make all **stakeholders** aware of the corporate objectives, and to **encourage** all employees to **work towards** them.

2) Mission statements usually state the **purpose** of the business (e.g. "to make the best chocolate in the UK"), its **values** (e.g. "to pay a fair price to our suppliers"), its **standards** (e.g. "to treat customers with respect at all times") and its **strategy** (e.g. "to have a 20% share of the UK chocolate market within 10 years").

3) Mission statements give clues about the company's **culture** (see p. 166-167). For example, a mission statement that mentions ethics and principles gives a big hint that the corporate culture is focused on ethical practice as well as profitability.

4) Some mission statements **explicitly** state what the business believes its corporate culture is. After a short statement of corporate aim and vision for the future, there may be a **statement of shared beliefs**, e.g. "We believe in providing outstanding service to customers", "We believe that we gain strength through our diversity".

5) Businesses can have underlying cultures within **departments**, known as **subcultures**. For example, a design department might be relaxed, whereas the head of sales might run a very tight ship. One benefit of a mission statement is to try and **prevent** this by creating a **unifying**, visible culture for all employees to **identify** with.

6) **Changing** the mission statement can help change corporate culture.

There are Advantages and Disadvantages to having a Mission Statement

Advantages

1) Mission statements can give **staff** a sense of **shared purpose**, and encourage them to work towards **common goals** — having the cooperation of all the staff makes it more likely that a business will achieve its aims.

2) A mission statement gives **consumers** a clearer idea of the company's **values**. This allows consumers to choose companies whose values match theirs.

Disadvantages

1) Companies sometimes use mission statements to try and create good **public relations** for themselves rather than to state their **actual aims**. E.g. a company might say in its mission statement that it is committed to protecting the **environment** just to encourage more consumers to use its products. Companies **don't** have to **prove** that what they say about themselves in their mission statement is accurate, so they can say what they think consumers want to hear, without having to do anything about it.

2) Since mission statements are only a **few lines** long, and the aims and values of a business are usually quite **complex**, it's almost **impossible** for a mission statement to sum up what an organisation is all about. That's why some companies choose not to produce one.

Practice Questions

Q1 Give three examples of objectives that a for-profit business might have.

Q2 What is the difference between a charity, a social enterprise and a mutual organisation?

Q3 List three stakeholder groups and their main objectives.

Exam Question

Q1 Explain what a mission statement is, and discuss why some businesses have mission statements and others choose not to.

[8 marks]

Mission Statement Impossible — I think I saw that at the cinema...

Ok, so it might not be the most exciting part of Business Studies, but this is really important stuff. The stuff about mission statements is quite good anyway — you can just imagine the scene in the boardroom: "Your mission, if you choose to accept it, is to provide quality sofas and dining furniture." Anyway, your mission is to get these two pages learnt.

Corporate Plans

*Once businesses have decided on their corporate objectives and strategy, they write it all up in a nice corporate plan. These pages are for **AQA**, **Edexcel**, **WJEC** and the **OCR: Strategic Management** unit.*

Businesses make **Corporate Plans** which set out their overall **Strategy**

1) Corporate plans set out the **corporate objectives** for the business as a whole, and set out the **overall strategy** the business will use to reach its objectives.

Corporate plans are sometimes called 'strategic plans'.

2) For example, a corporate plan lays out **how** the business intends to **survive**, whether the business intends to **grow**, and **how** it might go about growing.

3) The corporate planning process involves several stages:

> 1) Senior managers decide on the long-term **corporate objectives** of the business.
>
> 2) They research the **market** to identify **opportunities** and **threats** to the business.
>
> 3) They look at **each department** to identify the **strengths** and **weaknesses** of the business.
>
> 4) They develop **strategies** to achieve the corporate objectives, focusing on the external **opportunities** and the internal **strengths** of the business.
>
> 5) They **review** each strategy and make any **adjustments** that are necessary.

4) The corporate plan will also include an outline of **functional objectives** for each department. The details of the functional objectives are decided by the managers of each department.

5) The **purpose** of having a corporate plan is to make sure that all the parts of the business are **working together** towards the **same goal**. Businesses are much more likely to achieve their objectives this way.

External Factors can affect a business' Corporate Plan

The **external factors** that can affect a corporate plan are:

1) **Political and legal factors**
   New laws can affect businesses. E.g. the ban on smoking in public places could be a **threat** to restaurants, because it might discourage smokers from eating out. On the other hand, it created an **opportunity** for restaurants to grow by targeting **families**, who might be more willing to eat in restaurants because of the smoking ban.

2) **Economic factors**
   Customers' **spending habits** are affected by **economic factors**. High interest rates, low GDP, high unemployment and high inflation all mean that consumers have **less money** to spend, which is a threat to businesses. When interest rates, inflation and unemployment are low, and GDP is high, consumers will have **more disposable income**.

3) **Social factors**
   Businesses need to consider migration patterns, an ageing population, etc.

4) **Technological factors**
   Trends like the popularity of internet shopping and the availability of new machinery affect businesses.

5) **Environmental factors**
   Customers are starting to consider the **environment** more, so businesses have to take things like **pollution** and the use of carrier bags into account when they make plans.

Internal Factors can also affect the Corporate Plan

1) **Skilled** and **motivated staff** help businesses to **achieve** their **objectives**. If staff are **unskilled** and **unmotivated**, this **limits** the plans that businesses can make.

2) Businesses also need to take into account how **good** their **products** are — it's hard to increase **sales** if there's no **demand** for your products.

3) The business' **finances** affect their **corporate plan** — e.g. poor cash flow restricts the plans that the business can make.

4) **Production capacity** can also limit the plans a business can make — e.g. if a business can't increase output, there's no point in trying to increase demand.

With a product like liver and kidney milkshake, achieving sales objectives is tricky.

Corporate Plans

Contingency Plans prepare for Out Of The Ordinary Events

1) Corporate plans include **contingency plans** — planning what to do if something **unexpected** happens.

2) Contingency planning can help a business **respond** to lots of different types of **crisis**, such as:
   - **Faulty** or **dangerous products**.
   - A **hostile takeover bid**.
   - A **fire** that destroys a factory.
   - **Bad news** or **PR** in local papers.
   - A sudden **change in demand** for products caused by competitor activity or an economic crisis.
   - An **overseas** factory having to be shut down because it doesn't comply with **foreign law**.
   - **Lost** or **corrupt data** caused by computer network problems.

3) For example, most businesses have a **contingency plan** in case of **IT** disasters. They might take **backups** of their data at the end of each day. Some of these backups must be **stored off-site** — otherwise if there was a fire at the site, all the data would be **lost**, even the backups. That would be very expensive.

4) Businesses **can't** plan for **every unforeseen event**. Some adverse events are hard to plan for. Contingency planning is very **expensive**, so it's not worthwhile to plan for every single thing that could possibly go wrong. Managers have to decide **how likely** a particular adverse event is to happen, and how **badly** it would damage the business if it did happen.

> **Crisis management** is when an unexpected situation **occurs**, and a business has to respond.
> - It's **less effective** if managers haven't carried out **contingency planning** — they're **not prepared** so they have to make **snap decisions** about what to do. If they've done contingency planning then they've already decided what to do in that situation, which makes crisis management **much more straightforward**.
> - Managers need to **act quickly** and **decisively** to **limit** the amount of **damage** caused. This is best achieved through **strong leadership**, e.g. an autocratic leader (see p. 76).

Corporate Plans can Help and Hinder businesses

1) Corporate plans can be **helpful** because they give the business a **clear direction**, and everyone working for the business knows what they're trying to achieve.

2) Corporate planning is also helpful because it makes managers think about the **strengths** and **weaknesses** of the business, and its **external threats** and **opportunities**. This helps managers to spot ways to **improve** the business that they might not have noticed otherwise.

3) The **drawback** of having a corporate plan is that it can **restrict** the business' **flexibility** — employees might think that they have to follow the corporate plan even if the situation has **changed** since it was made, or if they can think of a **better way** of doing things.

Practice Questions

Q1 What is included in a corporate plan?
Q2 List two external factors and two internal factors that affect corporate plans.
Q3 Give three examples of situations that a business might have a contingency plan for.
Q4 What's the difference between contingency planning and crisis management?

Exam Question

Q1 Discuss the extent to which corporate plans are helpful for businesses. [6 marks]

What's your contingency plan for falling down a well on the way to the exam...

Any of this stuff about corporate plans could come up in your exam, so make sure you're clear on what it's all about. You need to know what corporate plans are, the internal and external factors that affect them, and their pros and cons for businesses. Don't leave out the best bit — contingency plans and crisis management. I love a good crisis.

Decision-Making Models

*Ah, decisions, decisions... These pages are for **AQA**, the **OCR: Strategic Management** unit and **WJEC**.*

Decision-Making is essential for Planning

A plan is a **collection of decisions** about what to do. Without decision-making, you can't make a plan.
There are **three types** of decisions that businesses have to make — **strategic**, **tactical** and **operational**.

Strategic decisions

1) These are **long-term** decisions affecting the **general direction** of the business. They are made to help the business achieve its **long term aims**.

2) Strategic decisions are usually **expensive**, so they are **high-risk** decisions. It's not always obvious whether the business made the right decision until a long time **after** they make it. E.g. in 2001 Marks & Spencer opened its first 'Simply Food' stores in the UK. Launching the stores was **expensive**, and M&S would have lost a lot of money if they had failed. However, the 'Simply Food' stores have proved **successful** and there are now **more than 300** branches in the UK, so the strategic decision seems to have been a good one.

3) Strategic decisions are usually taken by the **owners** or **directors** of a business.

Tactical decisions

1) These are **medium-term** decisions that are made **after the strategic decisions** have been agreed. E.g. Marks & Spencer's decisions about the **exact location** of 'Simply Food' shops was a **tactical decision**.

2) It's usually much **easier** to predict the **impact** of tactical decisions than strategic decisions.

3) Tactical decisions are usually taken by the **senior managers** of a business.

Operational decisions

1) These are **routine decisions** that are taken on a **daily** basis, e.g. store managers at Tesco decide how many checkouts to open at different times of the day.

2) Operational decisions are usually taken by **middle** or **junior managers**.

Decisions can be made Scientifically — or based on Gut Feeling

1) Scientific decision-making means **collecting** data, **analysing** it to arrive at a **conclusion** (or decision) and then **testing** that decision to see if it works. It allows businesses to predict the outcomes of complex decisions. The **alternative** to the scientific approach is **inspired guesswork** based on **experience** or **gut reaction**.

Tony's gut feeling told him it was nearly time for dinner.

2) There are three common scientific decision-making **techniques**:

   • **Break-even analysis** shows how much businesses need to **sell** to cover their **costs**.

   • **Investment appraisal techniques** help managers predict which **capital investment project** will give them the most favourable **financial return**.

   • **Decision trees** allow managers to **quantify** the likely **financial impact** of alternative decisions based on the **probability** of different events occurring.

3) Scientific decision-making is **costly** and **time-consuming**, but it **reduces** the risk of making **expensive mistakes**.

4) The **type** of problem influences how managers make decisions. **Routine problems** can be handled with an experience-based approach. **Unfamiliar** problems and **big decisions** need research and analysis.

Several Factors influence Decision-Making

1) **Pressure groups** sometimes try to influence decisions, e.g. by using the threat of **bad publicity** to persuade decision-makers to make decisions in the interest of the pressure group.

2) **Corporate culture** (see p. 166-167) also influences decision-making. A business with a **risk-taking culture** will encourage people to take **risky decisions** if the potential **rewards** are **high**. A firm with a more **conservative** culture will **discourage risk taking**, e.g. by not promoting people whose decisions have led to costly mistakes in the past.

3) The business' **stakeholders** also try to influence decisions — e.g. **shareholders** might not want businesses to make risky decisions, because they won't want to **lose money** on their investment.

4) The firm's **ethics** (see p.136) have an effect too — e.g. they might decide not to switch to a cheaper supplier if that supplier is less environmentally aware than their current supplier.

5) **Resource availability** is also a factor — the business might not plan to grow if there's a **shortage** of local **labour**.

Decision-Making Models

Management Information Systems and ICT help managers make Decisions

1) **Management information systems** (MIS) are the **computerised systems** in a business that **gather** and **analyse information** for managers to use when making their decisions.

2) The types of data stored and analysed by management information systems are:
   - **Marketing and sales** data (e.g. sales levels for each product, number of sales made by each salesperson)
   - **Production** data (e.g. output levels, quality standards)
   - **HRM** data (e.g. employee turnover)

3) If managers receive **too much data** from their management information system, they become **overwhelmed** when trying to make decisions. This is **information overload**. Businesses need to focus on the **quality** rather than the **quantity** of data that a management information system can produce.

4) Using **ICT** can also help improve decision-making in many ways. Computer programs allow businesses to **plan** for various costing and pricing decisions. ICT also helps make **forecasts** more **accurate** — e.g. managers can use computer programs to analyse data trends in order to extrapolate graphs into the future.

Businesses use SWOT Analysis to make decisions about their Future

1) A **SWOT analysis** is a four-factor model that details the **strengths**, **weaknesses**, **opportunities** and **threats** facing a business — this helps managers to develop business strategies.

2) The **strengths** and **weaknesses** of each department are **internal** factors that the business **can control**.

3) The **opportunities** and **threats** relate to market conditions, so they are **beyond the control** of the business. The business has to **understand** them in order to react appropriately.

4) **External factors** that might pose opportunities or threats include political, economic, social, technological and environmental factors (see p. 156).

> **Example:** Margaret and Sheila run a small **tea shop** in the centre of Harrogate. In 2007 they won an **award** in a local newspaper for "the best toasted teacake in North Yorkshire". The tea shop only seats **22 customers**, but Margaret and Sheila have decided not to move to bigger premises because their current **location**, on a main shopping street, attracts **passing trade**. Instead, Sheila has suggested that they start selling **takeaway** drinks and cakes to take advantage of their popularity. Margaret and Sheila are concerned about reports that a big **coffee shop chain** is planning to open a branch close to their tea room. Margaret has suggested **cutting their prices**, which are fairly high, but Sheila doesn't think that competing on price is a good idea, as they don't have the same **economies of scale** as a large chain.
>
> | | |
> |---|---|
> | **Strengths:** | Good reputation, good location, good quality products. |
> | **Weaknesses:** | Small premises, lack of economies of scale. |
> | **Opportunities:** | Selling takeaways could increase their market size. |
> | **Threats:** | Possibility of new competitor with lower prices. |

OCR & WJEC

Practice Questions

Q1 What is the main advantage of using scientific decision-making rather than 'gut feeling'.

Q2 What does MIS stand for?

Q3 What four things does SWOT analysis tell managers about the business?

Exam Question

Q1 Explain the difference between strategic, tactical and operational decisions. [6 marks]

When you can't decide, just ask a model — they know a lot...

Decision-making models can help with any business decision, whether it's to do with marketing, production, human resources or whatever. SWOT is the basic one-size-fits-all way of working out what the situation is — after that, managers still have to come up with the best plan. Experience can be extremely useful alongside the scientific approach.

Decision Trees

Decision trees are a bit like Magic 8-Balls® — they help with decision making.
*These pages are for **Edexcel**, the **OCR: Strategic Management** unit and **WJEC**.*

Decision Tree Analysis *combines* Probability *and* Expected Benefit

1) When businesses make decisions (e.g. whether to open a new outlet, whether to develop a new product to add to their range), they **know** what the **cost** will be, but often the **outcome isn't certain**.

2) **Probability** is the **likelihood** of an event occurring. Managers often **don't know** how likely it is that an outcome will happen, so they make a **subjective estimate** based on **experience** or **past data**.

3) Probability is usually expressed as a **decimal** in decision trees — e.g. 0.6 for a 60% probability. The probability of an event **happening** and the probability of it **not happening** have to add up to 1 (certainty).

4) **Expected Monetary Value (EMV)** is the **probability** of an event occurring, **multiplied** by the **benefit** the business can expect to gain. E.g. an advertising campaign will increase revenue by £200 000 if it is successful. The campaign has an estimated 0.7 chance of success. If it fails (with a probability of 0.3) it might only make £20 000. The expected monetary value is therefore 0.7 × 200 000 + 0.3 × 20 000 = £146 000.

Learn these Features *of* Decision Trees

1) A **square** (a **decision node**) represents a **decision point**.

2) **Circles** (or **event nodes**) mark where there are **alternative outcomes**, which are shown by **lines** (called **branches**) coming out of the node.

3) The **decimals** on the lines are the **probabilities** of each event occurring.

4) The **values in £s** represent the **income** to the business if that outcome happens.

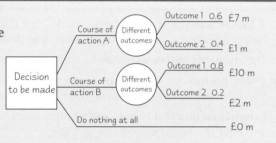

Decision Trees *show which* Course Of Action *is probably* Best

1) When creating a decision tree, managers first identify which courses of action are open to the business.

2) They outline the **possible results** of each course of action.

3) They assign **probabilities** to each of the results, estimating the probabilities they don't know.

4) The next step is to **calculate** the "**expected monetary values**" (EMV) of each result.

5) Managers should choose the course of action with the **highest expected monetary value**.

Example — decision tree for launching a new chocolate bar

A confectionery business wants to launch a new chocolate bar.

1) With a **market research** budget of **£15K** the chance of a **successful launch** is estimated at **0.75**. **Without** market research the chance is estimated at **0.5**.

2) A **successful** launch would earn a revenue of **£100K** — but if it **failed**, revenue would be **£20K** at best.

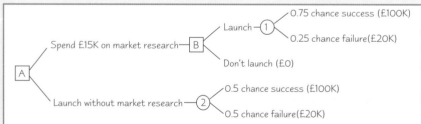

Calculate EMVs for each event node by multiplying the benefit by the probability:

Node 1: (£100K × 0.75) + (20K × 0.25) =
£75K + £5K = **£80K**

Node 2: (£100K × 0.5) + (20K × 0.5) =
£50K + £10K = **£60K**

A To decide whether **market research** is worthwhile, take off the **cost** of market research from the expected **value** of launching **after** market research. This works out as £80K – £15K = **£65K**. Compare this amount with the expected value of launching **without** research (**£60K**). This shows that doing market research is **worthwhile**.

B The decision at square B is whether to **launch** at all. Compare the **expected value** of the launch (**£80K**) with **not launching** (**£0**). This shows that after market research, it's best to **go ahead** with the launch.

So the course of action with the **highest** EMV is to **launch** the new chocolate bar **after** carrying out **market research**.

Decision Trees

Decision Trees have Advantages...

1) Decision-tree analysis makes managers **work out** and **think about** the **probability** of each outcome, and the **potential payoff** of each outcome. Managers have to come up with real numerical values for these — much better than vague statements like "this will increase sales".

2) Decision trees are a nice **visual representation** of the potential outcomes of a decision.

3) Decision trees allow managers to compare options **quantitatively** and **objectively**, rather than going for the fashionable option or the option they thought of first.

4) Decision trees are useful in **familiar situations** where the business has enough experience to make **accurate** estimates of **probabilities** and **benefits**.

Stay small. The expected benefit from growth is lower than you think.

...and Disadvantages

1) Decision trees are **quantitative** — i.e. they're based on numbers and ignore non-numerical **qualitative data**. **Qualitative data** includes things like the **employees' opinions** about business decisions, and businesses should take qualitative data into account before deciding on a course of action.

2) **Probabilities** are very hard to **predict accurately**. **Estimated payoffs** are also assumed to be accurate — in real life things may work out differently. If either of these estimates are based on **dodgy** information, the decision is **flawed** too.

3) In reality there's a **wider range** of potential **outcomes** than the decision tree suggests. For example, a new marketing campaign might increase sales for a shorter period than predicted — the decision tree might only allow for success or failure, not for short-term success versus long-term success.

Practice Questions

Q1 Explain the difference between the circles and the squares on a decision tree.

Q2 Outline the stages used in decision tree construction.

Q3 Define expected monetary value and say how it's calculated.

Q4 Give one disadvantage of decision-tree analysis.

Exam Questions

Q1 Cruse plc is a multinational business that maintains electronic defence systems . It has won a contract to overhaul the electronics on an ex-Royal Navy submarine. Three other submarines require similar work in the next four years but Cruse plc does not have the current capacity to complete these contracts in the time available. To win the subsequent contracts Cruse has three options: increase capacity, use existing resources but take longer, or subcontract two-thirds of the work. Expected outcomes are as follows:

Option	Outcomes	Probability	Profit (£m)
Increase existing capacity	Success	0.4	700
	Slight success	0.5	400
	Failure	0.1	-100
Use existing capacity	Success	0.4	400
	Slight success	0.3	200
	Failure	0.3	-30
Subcontract	Success	1	300

Answer on p.185

(a) On the basis of the information given, construct a decision tree for this problem and label it showing probabilities and forecast pay-offs. [8 marks]

(b) Calculate the expected value for each option. Advise Cruse as to the best option. [14 marks]

(c) Assess the usefulness of constructing a decision tree in this case. [6 marks]

(d) Discuss other factors which Cruse plc might consider when taking the decision. [14 marks]

Decision tree, decision tree, your branches green delight us...

Decision trees are a really nifty way of working out what the best option is, when a manager is faced with an important decision. It's based on the potential benefit if things work out well, and the likelihood of it working out well or badly. Practise working your way through a few decision trees to get the hang of it — don't leave it all until the day of the exam.

Porter and Generic Strategy

*Once upon a time there was a chap called Michael Porter, who was what you'd call a business guru. He came up with a few ideas about strategy. Page 162 is for **Edexcel**, page 163 is for **Edexcel, OCR: Strategic Management** and **WJEC**.*

Businesses' *Distinctive Capabilities* give them a *Competitive Advantage*

1) A business' **distinctive capabilities** are the **skills** and **knowledge** within the business that can't be **copied** by its competitors, or that would be very difficult to copy. Distinctive capabilities can be in any area of the business — technology, marketing etc.

2) The distinctive capabilities of a business give it its **competitive advantage**.

3) Porter identified **two** main ways that a business can get an **advantage** over its competitors:

Cost advantage

1) A business can get a **competitive advantage** by selling a similar **product** at lower cost than its rivals.

2) **Low-cost airlines** like EasyJet and Ryanair use a "no frills" strategy to keep their costs at a **minimum** — they use cheaper airports like Luton and cut out travel agents' fees by using online booking.

Differentiation advantage

1) Selling **better products** at the same or a slightly higher price creates a **competitive advantage**.

2) Offering a product that consumers see as **different** from competitors' products can make consumers think it's **better**. This is called **product differentiation**.

Porter suggested *Three Generic Strategies* to *Gain Advantage*

Cost Leadership

1) **Cost leadership** strategy calls for the **lowest cost of production** for a given level of quality.

2) In a **price war**, the firm can maintain profitability while the competition suffers losses.

3) If prices **decline**, the firm can stay profitable because of its low costs.

4) A very **broad market** is needed for this strategy — preferably a **global** market, with huge production facilities to take advantage of **economies of scale**.

Differentiation

1) **Differentiation** strategy requires a product with **unique attributes** which consumers value, so that they **perceive** it to be **better** than rival products.

2) The value added by uniqueness allows the business to charge a **premium price**.

3) Risks include **imitation** by competitors and **changes** in **consumer tastes**.

Focus

1) **Focus** strategy concentrates on a **narrow** market **segment** to achieve **either** cost advantage or differentiation.

2) A firm using this strategy usually has **loyal customers**, which makes it very hard for other firms to compete.

Porter's Strategic Matrix shows a business' *Competitive Strategy*

1) Porter's **strategic matrix** shows the **generic strategy** used by a business, based on its competitive strategy and its market scope.

2) Any business can be placed onto the matrix if you know whether it's aimed at a **broad** or **narrow market**, and whether it offers **cheaper** products than competitors or **unique**, **quality** products. E.g. in the jewellery market, Accessorize sells products to a broad market at relatively low prices, so it would be placed in the **cost leadership** segment of the matrix. Tiffany & Co. sells high-quality products at premium prices, focusing on a narrow market, so it would fit into the **differentiation and focus** segment.

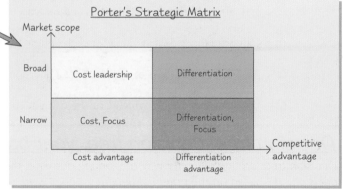

Porter's Strategic Matrix

Market scope	Cost advantage	Differentiation advantage
Broad	Cost leadership	Differentiation
Narrow	Cost, Focus	Differentiation, Focus

Competitive advantage →

Porter and Generic Strategy

Porter's *Five Forces Model* shows *Influences* on an industry

Porter's **Five Forces model** shows an industry being influenced by **five competitive forces**. It analyses the state of the market and helps managers figure out the **best strategy** to gain competitive advantage in that **particular market**.

① Barriers to entry — how easy it is for new firms to enter the market

1) New entrants to the market will want to compete by selling similar products — it's in the **interests** of existing firms in the market to make it **hard** for new firms to get in.
2) **High start-up costs** (e.g. **expensive equipment**) might deter new firms from entering the market.
3) **Patents**, **trade marks** and **licensing** make it hard for new entrants to sell similar products.
4) Established businesses may control **distribution channels**, making it hard for new entrants to sell.

② Buyer power — buyers want products at as low a price as possible

1) **Buyers** have **more power** when there are **few buyers** and many sellers.
2) Buyers have **more power** when products are **standardised** — it's easier for firms to charge a premium price for differentiated goods and services.
3) Firms with **power** over their supplier can **buy the supplier out** — this is "**backwards vertical integration**".
4) A supplier's **main customer** can **negotiate special deals** and lower prices.

Remember, this lot applies to business customers, wholesalers and retailers, not just Joe Public.

③ Supplier power — suppliers want to get as high a price as possible

1) **Suppliers** have **more power** when there are **few suppliers** and lots of firms buying from them.
2) Businesses can try to tie buyers into **long-term contracts**.
3) Suppliers with power over their buyers can **forward integrate** — e.g. by setting up their own **retail outlets** or **buying** the retailers they supply to.

④ Threat of substitutes — how likely it is that consumers will buy an alternative product

1) The **willingness** of customers to substitute is a factor affecting competitiveness.
2) Relative **price** and **quality** are important — buyers are unlikely to change to a poor value substitute product.
3) There may be a **cost** associated with **switching** brand — e.g. if you wanted to switch to a different brand of printer cartridges, you'd probably need to buy a new printer. Firms try to make it **expensive** for buyers to get **substitutes**, e.g. mobile phone customers have to sign 12- or 18-month contracts.

⑤ Rivalry within the industry — how much competition there is

Businesses with high fixed costs don't want production to sit idle.

1) Rivalry is **intense** in a market with lots of **equally sized competitors**.
2) Industries with **high fixed costs** are **competitive**. Firms cut prices to raise demand and use up their capacity.
3) Industries producing **standardised** goods (e.g. steel, milk, flour) have **intense** rivalry.
4) Rivalry is also **intense** in **young industries** where competitors are following **growth strategies**.

Practice Questions

Q1 What's meant by the terms "distinctive capability" and "competitive advantage"?
Q2 Describe Porter's generic strategies.
Q3 What are the five forces in Porter's five forces model?

Exam Questions

Q1 Describe how a generic differentiation strategy allows a business to pursue competitive advantage. [6 marks]

Q2 Evaluate how useful Porter's Five Forces model can be to a business manager. [10 marks]

Porter conveniently ignores the force of gravity...

... which isn't a luxury most of us have. Darn pesky gravity, making things fall down. Anyway, the Five Forces model is a rather useful tool to analyse the market and see where threats and opportunities are. Porter also came up with three generic strategies which can be adapted to suit absolutely any business — and don't forget the lovely strategic matrix too.

Strategy

*Managers have to decide on strategies and then figure out how to improve them if they're not working. Sounds a bit too much like hard work to me... These pages are for **Edexcel** and **OCR: Strategic Management**.*

Strategy is the way in which Objectives are achieved

1) Business decisions must fit in with **corporate objectives**. Objectives must be **measurable** — vague objectives are useless, and don't help managers make decisions that move the business forward.

2) **Short-term plans**, known as **tactical plans**, contain precise, detailed and measurable ways to achieve objectives. This level of planning is done by **middle managers** and supervisors.

3) **Long-term plans** to achieve **strategic objectives** are not as detailed or measurable. The longer the timescale of the plan, the less certain the outcome can be. Long-term plans are drawn up by **senior management**. They're also known as **strategic** or **corporate plans**. See p. 156 for more on strategic plans.

4) Objectives provide **direction** and **unity of purpose**, and allow managers to **measure performance**. For example, a measurable objective set by **senior management** may be to increase **market share** by 15% within 3 years. This **target** can be used to control and measure the activities of junior managers. Market share is **checked** periodically to make sure things are on track.

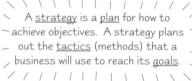

A **strategy** is a **plan** for how to achieve objectives. A strategy plans out the **tactics** (methods) that a business will use to reach its **goals**.

5) The objectives of a firm's **stakeholders** influence the firm's own corporate objectives. For example, **shareholders** might have an objective of quick return on investment — the firm might aim to please the shareholders by having an objective of **profit maximisation**.

Successful Implementation of a plan requires Motivation and Communication

1) Successful implementation of a strategic plan relies on the **people** employed by the company.

2) Senior managers must **communicate the intentions** of the strategic plan clearly to all sections of the business, so that everyone knows what they're supposed to be doing. There should be as few **barriers to communication** as possible. Chains of communication shouldn't be too long. Communication overload should be avoided. See p.78-79 for more on communication.

3) **Middle** and **junior managers** are very important in **interpreting** the plan into the day-to-day actions of their different departments and sections.

4) It's important that everyone is **motivated** to push forward with the strategy — everyone from the top of the organisation to the bottom needs to know what's in it for them.

Implementing a strategy could mean Changes have to be made

1) A new strategy may require **different ways of working**. This could involve **retraining**, which might be costly, or take a long time. Not all staff can be trained at once.

2) It might also mean that changes need to be made to the company's **physical resources**. It may need to **relocate** to a different location, increase or reduce the amount of **stock** it holds, or invest heavily in new **machinery**.

3) **Financial resources** are also affected by new strategies. For example, if a business invests heavily in new machinery, it'll have **less working capital** (see p.31) available for the day-to-day running of the business.

Valerie's view of the new customer service strategy had taken a sudden downturn.

4) **Mistakes** can occur during the transition period, and these can affect relations with customers. Customers may **resent** a change in the way they're dealt with, unless it's clearly loads better than the old way.

5) A new strategy might mean making some **staff redundant**.

6) Staff might have to change their **attitude** towards their work. They might have to work **harder**, or **longer** hours, or **shorter** hours, or be more **customer-service** orientated.

7) The management structure might need to be **altered** — departments could be split up, or merged, or moved to another senior manager's control. This can **cause friction** between managers.

All the above changes can have an effect on the **morale** and **motivation** of employees.

Good managers can implement change in a way that doesn't seriously hack off their staff (see p. 172-175) — which of course means that staff will put their weight behind the new strategy faster.

Strategy

Strategies must be continually Checked and Reviewed

1) The managers who devise a strategy must **monitor** its **effectiveness**. They need to **constantly monitor** whether all parts of the firm (marketing, production, HR, etc) are **meeting** their targets. If they're not, it's crucial to find out **why**.

2) Short- and long-term plans include a series of **planning horizons**. This is the timescale within which each target will be met. At the end of each planning horizon **actual** performance is measured against the **targets** in the plan.

3) Results don't always meet expectations. A **difference** between a strategic target and reality is called a **strategic gap**. Managers **analyse** the gap to see **why** there's a difference between the target and reality, and take **corrective action**.

Businesses use Various Techniques to Monitor how the strategy is going

Businesses use **market analysis** and **management information systems** to work out the **starting point** for the strategy — and then to monitor progress towards marketing and production **targets**.

Market analysis shows if assumptions about the **market** are correct.

1) Firms use both primary and secondary **market research** to check how the strategy is proceeding.

2) They **audit sales levels**, concentrating particularly on the **target markets**. If a strategic gap appears then the business will want to know why. There's more on strategic gaps on p.152.

Management information systems provide most of the information.

1) **Management information systems** are computer systems that constantly **collect** and **process** routine financial, stock and production data, to give a picture of the **current state** of the business. This data is used to see if the business is on course to meet its **objectives**.

2) Managers use **mathematical techniques** such as moving averages and scatter graphs to interpret the data.

> See p.159 for more about management information systems.

Businesses set and monitor **financial objectives** using **budgets** — see p. 36.

Even the Best Laid Plans can Go Wrong

The business environment **changes** all the time. External and internal changes can mean a good plan isn't good any more.

1) Changes in **technology** can make a product **obsolete**, or **increase the productivity** of **competitors**.

2) **Consumer tastes** can change **quickly**, which reduces the length of the product life cycle.

3) Improvements in **communications** systems can benefit competitors. Businesses may feel forced to make changes to keep up with competitors — e.g. by **outsourcing** customer services to India or other low labour cost countries.

Practice Questions

Q1 Give two differences between long-term and short-term plans, other than "one's long-term and one's short-term".
Q2 Give three examples of changes that might need to be made when a new strategy is being implemented?
Q3 What is a planning horizon?
Q4 What is a strategic gap?
Q5 Describe three external or internal factors that could affect the success of a strategic plan.

Exam Questions

Q1 Margaret is responsible for ensuring that all departmental managers and supervisory staff in Hooz Electricals Ltd. understand the company's plan to become the most successful company in their market. The customer service target is to answer 95% of calls in a target time. Six months into the implementation phase the following figures for two customer service supervisors are:
Supervisor A: 98% of calls answered within target time.
Supervisor B: 85% of calls answered within target time.
Explain why Margaret's implementation strategy may be working with one supervisor and not another. [8 marks]

Q2 Discuss the changes that might have to be made in a business when a new strategy is implemented. [6 marks]

Strategy! When the feeling's gone and you can't go on it's strategy...

A lot of this topic is common sense — obviously implementing a new strategy is going to rock the boat, and obviously it makes sense to check up on a strategy and see if it's working or not. It is good to have it all spelled out like this though, because then if a question on strategy comes up in the exam, you'll be able to answer it without batting an eyelid.

Corporate Culture

*Corporate culture isn't about going to the opera or reading Dostoevsky novels — it's to do with a company's values. These pages are for **AQA, Edexcel**, the **OCR: Strategic Management** unit and **WJEC**.*

Corporate Culture is the Way a business Does Things

1) **Corporate culture** is the way that a business does things, and the way that people in the business expect things to be done. It shapes the **expectations** and **attitudes** of staff and managers.

2) Because corporate culture **affects staff behaviour** and how they make decisions, it has an effect on planning, objective setting and strategy.

3) Corporate culture is **created** and **reinforced** by company **rules**, **managerial attitudes** and behaviour, **recruitment** policies that recruit people who "fit in", **reward** systems (e.g. how bonuses are calculated and allocated), etc.

4) A company's culture can be **identified** by looking at its **heroes** (people who exemplify the company's values), the **stories** that are told repeatedly within the company, **symbols** (like staff mottoes and sayings) that represent the company's values, and the **ceremonies** (such as office parties) that the business holds.

Corporate Culture can be Strong or Weak

Strong culture
Corporate culture is strong when employees **believe** in the corporate values of the company. Having a strong corporate culture has several advantages:

- Employees need **less supervision**, because their behaviour will naturally tend to fit in with the company's values.
- Staff are more **loyal** to the business, so **staff turnover** is lower.
- It increases employees' **motivation**, so they work more productively.

Weak culture
Weak culture is where the employees of a company **don't** share the company's values, and have to be **forced** to comply with them (e.g. through **company policies**).

There are Four Main Types of Corporate Culture

Charles Handy identified the following **four types** of corporate culture in 1993:

1) **Power culture** — organisations where decision-making authority is limited to a **small number** of people — perhaps just **one person**.

2) In these businesses, objectives reflect the wishes of the person at the **top**.

1) **Role culture** — **bureaucratic** firms where authority is defined by job title.

2) These organisations tend to **avoid risk** for fear of failure, so they develop **cautious** aims and objectives.

3) The danger here is that overcautious companies can lose out in the long run, especially in **new** or **expanding** markets where strategies need to be developed and implemented quickly. Organisations with role culture often fail to **exploit opportunities** before their competitors do.

1) **Person culture** — loose organisations of individual workers, usually **professional partnerships** such as solicitors.

2) The objectives of these firms will be defined by the **personal ambitions** of the individuals involved. The firms have to ensure that the individuals actually have **common goals**.

1) **Task culture** places an emphasis on getting specific **tasks** done.

2) Task culture gets **small teams** together to work on a project, then disbands them. There may be **conflict** between teams for resources and budgets. It can be confusing if a firm has too many products or **projects**.

3) This culture supports objectives which are based around **products** (e.g. make Product X the market leader).

4) Task cultures respond well to **management by objectives**. Management by objectives translates corporate objectives into **specific targets** for each **department** and for each **individual employee**.

In addition to Handy's models, **Stephen McGuire** identified another model of corporate culture in 2003 — **entrepreneurial culture**. In entrepreneurial cultures, employees are encouraged to look for **new ways** of bringing **revenue** into the company. **Innovation** and **creativity** are valued.

Corporate Culture

Managers might want to Change the Corporate Culture

There are two main reasons why the managers of a business might want to change the corporate culture :

1) The corporate culture of a business depends on the **preferences** of its **leaders**. When a new manager joins a business, they might change it to make it more **similar** to businesses they have worked in **before**. E.g. if a manager who is used to working in a business with a role culture starts working in a business with a task culture, they might force the business to adopt a role culture because that is what they are used to.

2) A business might change its culture in order to be more **competitive**. E.g. businesses with a **power culture** can be **slow** to spot ways to **save money**, or more **efficient** ways of working, so adopting an **entrepreneurial culture** where all the staff are constantly looking for ways to **improve** the business could make the business more **competitive**.

Changing the Corporate Culture can be Difficult

1) Employees usually **resist** any kind of change (see p. 173), including changes in **corporate culture**. Employees who have worked for the business for a long time are **especially likely** to resist changes to the corporate culture, because they have been used to one way of working for a long time.

2) Changing corporate culture means changing the **attitudes** and **behaviour** of staff, so it's much more **complicated** than changing things like pricing structure. E.g. the managers of a clothes retailer might want to introduce a more **customer-focused** culture, but bringing in loyalty cards and generous refund policies **won't** achieve that if staff are **rude** to the customers.

3) Changing the corporate culture can also be very **expensive**. It might involve buying new **equipment**, changing **office layout**, or changing the company **logo** or **motto** on stationery, advertising, etc. This means that businesses can't always afford to change their culture, as much as they would like to.

Corporate Culture is Important for the Stakeholders of the business

The **corporate culture** of a business affects its **staff**, **customers** and **shareholders**:

<u>Staff</u>
Culture affects the **motivation** of the employees. E.g. a **power culture** or **role culture** can **demotivate** creative staff who can see ways to **improve** things but don't have the **power** to put changes into practice.

<u>Customers</u>
Corporate culture affects **customers' loyalty** to a business. Businesses with a **customer-focused** culture are more likely to have loyal customers.

<u>Shareholders</u>
The level of **risk** that businesses take depends on their corporate culture. Shareholders might get **low returns** on their investment if they invest in a company with a **low-risk culture**, whereas investing in a company with a **high-risk culture** gives shareholders the possibility of **high returns**, but there's also the risk that they'll **lose money**.

Practice Questions

Q1   What is corporate culture?

Q2   Describe the power culture, and its approach to setting objectives.

Q3   Why is changing corporate culture difficult?

Exam Question

Q1   Explain the importance of corporate culture for the stakeholders of a business.   [6 marks]

Corporate Culture Club — an 80s tribute band formed by executives...

This stuff on corporate culture's pretty interesting I reckon. Remember that the corporate culture of a business affects all sorts of things — from whether or not they take financial risks, to whether they have office parties. When you get a case study, look for clues about the corporate culture of the business — it can tell you a lot about what's happening and why.

Growth

*Growth causes a lot of changes to a business. Most businesses are keen to grow, but growth can bring problems too (like having to buy a whole new wardrobe for a start). These pages are for **Edexcel**, **WJEC** and **OCR: Production** option.*

Organic Growth *is when a business* Grows Naturally

Allison had experienced a lot of organic growth.

1) To see if a business is growing, you need to know what **size** it was in the first place. Business size is usually **measured** either by **revenue** (see p.49) or **number of employees**.

2) If a business is **successful**, it will **grow naturally** — demand for the company's products grows, so they produce more, they sell more, profits increase, and they have more money to spend on marketing to increase demand for their products further.

3) This kind of growth, when an **existing** business expands as a result of its success, is known as **organic growth** (it's sometimes called internal growth too).

4) Businesses that grow organically are often able to **finance** their growth (more machinery, bigger premises, more staff, etc) by **reinvesting profits** into the business. If they need **external finance**, it's **easier** to get hold of if they can demonstrate that they've been successful in the past.

5) Organic growth is **slower** and **more gradual** than external growth (i.e. mergers and takeovers — see p. 170), which means that it's easier for the company to **adapt** to growth.

Businesses *might* Decide Not *to Grow*

Businesses usually want to grow because bigger companies benefit from larger **economies of scale**, a bigger market share, etc. However, business owners may choose to **restrict** growth for the following reasons:

1) They may want to **maintain the culture** of a small business.

2) If the business **"overmarkets"** their products they could let customers down — the productive, administrative or distributive capacity may not be enough to handle the **increased demand**.

3) The business will become more **complicated** to manage as it gets bigger.

4) Growth requires the business to **secure additional financial resources**, which can be complicated.

5) They may not want to put too much **strain** on their **cash flow** position.

Internal Finance *for* Growth *comes from* Profits *or* Owners' Capital

1) Sources of finance for growth depend on the **amount of capital** needed to implement the strategic growth plan. If the amount required is within the firm's own resources then expansion can be **funded internally**.

2) **Retained profits** are where the firm **reinvests** its profits back into its activities. This may work well as a firm expands from small to medium-sized, but the funding available at any one time could be **too limited**.

3) **Owners' capital** is another source of **growth funding**. If the owners of the firm have the resources they could agree to **increase** their investment into the company. This source of funding is also **limited**.

4) In most cases, firms need some **external investment** to fund their growth.

The way External Funding *is raised depends on* Original Size *and* Ambitions

1) It can be much **easier** for **large** or **established companies** to attract **investment** to fund growth than it is for small businesses. Investors are more likely to invest in businesses that are already **successful** because they can expect a good **return** on their investment. Investing in newer businesses can be risky because the business might fail and the investor could **lose** their money.

2) **Smaller businesses** can raise finance through **bank loans**, but banks and other investors might be **unwilling** to lend the business money until it has proved it can be **profitable**. This means that small businesses might only be able to get hold of **small amounts** of investment, which can be a problem if they have **ambitious** plans for growth.

3) Businesses can apply for **regional aid grants** if the expansion involves providing substantial additional employment in **deprived** areas. These grants can be useful to **smaller** businesses that might have trouble getting hold of funding from other sources.

4) Becoming a **PLC** allows businesses to raise **large amounts** of finance for growth by selling shares on the stock exchange. Investing in PLCs is **attractive** for investors because shares in PLCs are much more **liquid** than shares in other types of businesses (i.e. they can be turned into cash easily). Becoming a PLC is only an option for **established medium** and **large** businesses though.

Growth

Growing Businesses must manage their Cash Flow particularly carefully

1) Just like at any other time, during a period of growth and investment it's essential that there are funds available to pay for the current **day-to-day expenses** of the business.

2) Fast growth increases the risk of **overtrading**. Increased **demand** means the business needs to buy more raw materials and employ more people. This **reduces** the amount of **working capital** available to pay the bills, and the business runs the risk that they'll go bust before they have the chance to get paid by their customers.

3) Firms might need **additional borrowing** to manage their working capital. Interest payments from loans add to the **cost** of the growth, which makes growth **less profitable** for the firm than it would be otherwise.

Growing in Size brings its Own Problems

1) When a company changes from a **private limited company (Ltd)** to a **public limited company (PLC)**, the original owners won't find it so easy to maintain **control**, as they'll be responsible to a wider range of **shareholders**.

2) Once a company becomes a **PLC** then it's more open to being **taken over**. Anyone with sufficient resources could buy its shares in sufficient quantities to take a **controlling interest**.

3) Becoming a **PLC** can make managers more **short-termist**. Shareholders often want a **quick return** on investment through **dividend** payments, so they're **unlikely** to favour investment in **long-term projects**.

4) The process of **floating** the business on the **stock market** is **expensive** and **complicated**. The business has to employ a **merchant bank** to apply for a stock market listing and handle the share offer for them. They'd need to use some of the finance raised to **fund** this.

5) When companies **expand overseas** they need to be familiar with the **commercial law** of the host country. They need to know the **employment regulations**, deal with the problems involved in carrying out transactions in **other currencies**, and comply with any regulations which cover the **product specifications** for those markets. Companies operating abroad may also have to deal with **different languages** and **cultures**.

6) Large companies can suffer from **diseconomies of scale** (see p. 103). Diseconomies of scale are when the business grows so much that the **cost** of producing each unit **rises**. E.g. the more employees a business has, the more supervisors and managers are needed — they get paid more than shop-floor workers, but don't actually produce anything. This means that the business' **wage bills** increase, but **output** doesn't.

7) Businesses have to avoid growing so much that they **dominate** their market and become a **monopoly** (see p. 139) — this is bad for consumers because it restricts choice, and companies can be penalised by the **Competition Commission** if they're found to be **damaging competition** in a market.

Businesses may become Smaller — this is called Retrenchment

1) Businesses can choose to become smaller if they are suffering from **diseconomies of scale**.

2) They can **retrench** if they've lost focus. Doing too many different activities makes it hard to stay competitive.

3) Businesses can be forced to get smaller if they're **forced out of a market** by a larger competitor. They can also be forced to stop making some types of product by changes in **consumer taste**.

4) Also, changes in the **economy** such as recession or high interest rates may force a business to downsize.

Practice Questions

Q1 What is organic growth?
Q2 Give three reasons why a business might choose not to grow.
Q3 Why is it important to manage cash flow during a transition period?
Q4 What is retrenchment?

Exam Question

Q1 Discuss the advantages and disadvantages of growth for small businesses. [8 marks]

Could a fertiliser business ever choose not to promote growth...

Growth might seem like a pretty straightforward topic, but there's a fair amount to learn on these pages. Make sure you learn the reasons why businesses might want to grow or stay small. It's not just a case of "to grow or not to grow" either — there's organic growth, finance and cash flow to think about too. Don't forget that businesses can retrench as well as grow.

Change in Ownership

Changes in ownership of businesses can occur for several reasons and in several ways. For **Edexcel** *and* **WJEC**.

Changes of Ownership can be Takeovers or Mergers

Watch out with these terms, because they're often used incorrectly.

1) The definition of a **takeover** is when one business buys enough shares in another, so that they have more than 50% of the total shares. This is called a **controlling interest**, and it means the buyer will always win in a vote of all shareholders.

2) A **merger** happens when two companies **join together** to form **one company**. They might keep the name of one of the original companies, or come up with a new name. The **shares** of the merged company are **transferred** to the shareholders of the old companies.

Takeovers can be Agreed or Hostile

1) **Hostile takeovers** happen when one **public limited company (PLC)** buys a **majority** of the shares in **another** PLC against the will of the directors of that company. It can do this because the shares of PLCs are **traded** on the stock exchange and **anyone** can buy them. The company will encourage existing shareholders to sell them the shares by offering a **premium** — more than the shares are actually worth.

2) **Agreed takeovers** happen when shareholders or other types of owners such as sole traders **agree** that they'll sell the business to someone else. This is usually because the owners believe it would benefit the **survival** of the business.

There are Many Reasons why companies Take Over or Merge With others

1) Some businesses decide to **diversify** and buy **existing** businesses operating in the market they want to **enter**. They **gain** from the **experience** of those employed by the businesses they buy, so they can make **profits** faster.

2) They may want to buy out companies that **operate in the same market** so that they can **reduce** the amount of **competition** that they face.

3) Other companies will want to **extend** their market in the **same industry** but in **other countries**. E.g. T-Mobile (a German mobile phone operator) bought One-2-One (a British mobile phone operator).

4) Some businesses make profits from "**asset stripping**". They buy poorly performing businesses **cheaply** and then sell off the assets at a profit. The land on which the original business had its factory may be more valuable as building land, and could be **sold off** by the buyer at a nice profit.

5) Two large companies in the same industry may merge so that both could benefit from increased **economies of scale**. This is called **corporate integration**. In the car industry, companies such as Ford, Peugeot, BMW, and General Motors have bought out car manufacturers overseas. They can **switch production** from country to country where **labour costs** may be lower but the **expertise** already exists.

Takeovers and Mergers can be Horizontal, Vertical or Conglomerate

1) **Horizontal integration** happens when a firm buys out another firm in the **same industry**. It's the **most common** type of takeover or merger. It **reduces** the **competition** in the market. For example, the Morrisons supermarket chain bought out Safeway to extend its branch network and reduce competition.

2) **Vertical integration** occurs when a firm merges with or takes over another in the same industry but at a **different stage of the production process**, e.g. a retailer taking over its supplier.

3) Vertical integration can be **forward** or **backward**.

> **Backward vertical integration** is when a business buys its supplier. This allows them to **control production** of their supplies so they can be sure that supplies won't be **disrupted**.
>
> **Forward vertical integration** is when a manufacturer buys the **outlets** where its products are sold. This allows them **direct access** to the retail market. They can then **control** what is sold and exclude competitors' brands.

4) **Conglomerate mergers** are between **unrelated** firms — they aren't competitors of each other, and they aren't each other's supplier or customer. **Pure conglomerate mergers** are between totally unrelated firms. **Product extension mergers** are between firms making **related products** (e.g. hairbrushes and hairspray). **Geographic market extension mergers** are between firms in the same industry, but competing in **different geographic markets**.

Change in Ownership

Takeovers can be Buy-Ins or Buy-Outs

1) When the owners of the company want to **close** a division because it **no longer fits** in with its **strategic** plan (e.g. when a retailer no longer wants to own its suppliers) the managers of that division may buy it. This is called a **management buy-out**.

2) **Management buy-ins** are similar to management buy-outs, but managers from **outside** the business buy into it. This often happens when a business goes into **liquidation.**

3) **Private equity buy-outs** are when private equity firms take over a company using their **clients' money**.

Taking Over other businesses is Not Risk Free

1) There can be **tension** between the staff of businesses that have been merged as they try to **establish** their **status** in the new organisation.

2) It will take **time** for staff to **learn** new procedures — **mistakes** could lead to **poor customer service**.

3) Some parts of the new organisation may need to be sold off or closed. This could mean additional **redundancy costs**, which will **reduce profitability**.

4) When one business buys another, it takes on all the **liabilities** of the other business — this could include things like **compensation claims** for long-term disabilities suffered by **ex-employees** of the other business.

5) The **Competition Commission** investigate whether the proposed merger will **restrict competition** in the marketplace. If this is found to be the case the government can **stop** the takeover taking place or place **restrictions** on it. The finance used to **plan** a merger or takeover would then be **wasted**.

6) If a takeover is part of a **diversification strategy**, the purchasing business will have **limited experience** in the new industry and it will take time to **learn** how it works. Mistakes would **reduce profitability**.

Demergers are when companies Split Up

1) **Demergers** are the **opposite** of mergers — instead of two businesses joining together, a business **splits** into two (or more) parts, e.g. when a company sells off part of its business.

2) Demergers can happen when a company **takes over** another company, but things **don't go to plan**. For example if it doesn't get the **economies of scale** it expects, or if a company has taken over its supplier but can't run the business **profitably** enough because it doesn't have the right expertise. Managers demerge the businesses so that they can **focus** on their **original business**.

3) Demergers can happen if there's a **recession** or economic downturn — most companies **borrow** money to fund takeovers, and in a downturn they might want to **reduce** their debt or their repayments, so they **sell off** the part of the business they acquired previously.

They seemed happy, but within three years they'd demerged.

Practice Questions

Q1 When would you consider a takeover to be "hostile"?

Q2 What's the difference between a takeover and a merger?

Q3 What's the difference between a management buy-out and a management buy-in?

Q4 What is a demerger?

Exam Question

Q1 A high street fashion retailer is concerned that the overall group profits are falling, yet turnover is up. The Board of Directors receive a report from their management consultants which indicates that the problem is one of rising costs. There have been delays in receiving deliveries from suppliers through delays at the supplier's factories. After some discussion the Board decides that they should buy two of their suppliers, both of which are small PLCs.

a) What form of integration is this proposal an example of? [2 marks]

b) Why do you believe that the Board took this decision? [4 marks]

c) Evaluate the risks involved in taking this approach. [8 marks]

Buy-in, buy-out, shake it all about...

There are quite a few different terms to learn on these pages — mergers, demergers, buy-ins, buy-outs, horizontal integration, vertical integration... Try not to get too bogged down with it all — all the terms are quite descriptive, so you'll probably find they're not too hard to remember once you get going. Just don't have nightmares about hostile takeovers.

Managing Change

Businesses have to take care to manage change so that it goes smoothly.
*These pages are for **AQA**, the **OCR: Strategic Management** unit and **WJEC**.*

Change can be caused by Several Factors

When the business **environment** changes, managers must **change** the way the business is run to suit the new **circumstances** — they might change **staffing levels**, **location** or **product range** or start **spending** more on **research and development**, staff **training** and **new machinery**. The **key factors** that cause firms to make changes are:

1) A change in the size of the business. If the business increases in size, then more employees, more machinery, bigger premises, etc. might be needed to cope with the need to increase output. If the business retrenches (becomes smaller — see p. 169), they will probably need to reduce staff numbers and machinery.

2) A change in ownership. After a takeover or merger has happened, the new owners might have different ideas about how the business should be run, so they are likely to make changes.

3) The availability of new technology. Businesses might change their production methods if new technology makes production faster or cheaper or means their current machinery no longer matches their needs. New technology can also lead to shorter product life cycles — companies have to adapt to this to make sure their competitors don't start taking their market share.

4) Changes in consumer demand. If consumer tastes change, the business might need to alter its product range to fit in with changing demand.

5) Poor performance. For example, changes need to be made if a business isn't achieving predicted profit levels.

6) Changes in legislation. Changes in the law can affect the way businesses are run.

Change can be either Planned or Unplanned

1) Change in business can be **planned change** — part of a **strategy** decided by management. E.g. a clothes business might plan to expand its market abroad, so opening shops in other countries would be a planned change.

2) **Unplanned change** can occur after some **disaster** or other unexpected event which is **outside** the firm's control, such as a **fire** at a **supplier's warehouse**, or the launch of a **rival** product.

Change can be Incremental, Catastrophic or somewhere In Between

Incremental change is gradual

1) It's usually the result of a **strategic plan** being put in place.

2) Managers decide a **timescale** for the necessary changes and then **timetable strategies** for achieving them (e.g. training, closures, product development, promotional activities and all that sort of thing).

Catastrophic change is sudden

1) Management of catastrophic change forces firms to suddenly do things in a way that they might not normally do. They may have to **close or sell off subsidiary companies**, spend heavily on **promotions** to raise customer confidence or **totally restructure** the way the firm's organised.

2) When you think of catastrophic change, you usually think of a **sudden negative event** that destroys a lot of stock or makes it useless (e.g. a product is found to be dangerous and taken off the shelves), or makes a whole lot of customers suddenly go elsewhere (e.g. a rival brings out a competing product). It's also possible for **customer demand** to **increase** and force the company to expand even though it wasn't planning to.

Changes in the **law** can be **incremental** or **catastrophic**. Sometimes, the government gives businesses **plenty of notice** that they're going to change the law, so that businesses can **plan ahead** for the change and put a strategy in place to implement the change. Sometimes governments change the law **suddenly**, e.g. in response to a health scare.

Businesses can be Prepared for Catastrophic Change

1) Even catastrophic change can be planned for, up to a point. Businesses may have thought up **contingency plans** in advance — they'll have thought up various "what if?" scenarios, and made plans to cope with them. These contingency plans help them keep on **supplying customers** with the minimum of disruption.

2) For example, IT businesses (e.g. web hosts) may have **backup systems** in different geographical areas, so they can keep on running if something happens to their main location. Businesses might have a contingency plan for who would take over if one of the directors **died**, etc.

Managing Change

A few *Factors* make *Change Difficult*

1) Change usually **costs** a lot of money — buying new equipment, changing location and retraining staff are all **expensive**. If businesses don't have, or can't get hold of, enough finance, they **won't be able** to make changes.

2) Changes are unlikely to be successful if managers don't have much **experience** of managing change.

3) **Staff resistance** also makes change more difficult.

Any Change in business operations is *Unsettling* for *Employees*

1) Employees naturally **resist change**. Change is **uncomfortable** and **stressful** for people for several reasons:

> 1) When **restructuring** is part of the change process, employees might be worried that they'll be made **redundant**, or that they'll lose their **status** in the company.
>
> 2) Staff will be worried about having to take a **pay cut**, or that their **conditions** might change (e.g. longer working hours).
>
> 3) Change can lead to employees having the wrong skills (a **skills mismatch**). However, employees may not want to learn **new routines** or skills because this may take them outside their "**comfort zone**".
>
> 4) Staff working in teams develop **good working relationships**. These could be broken up.

Ben had been resisting changes in fashion since 1992.

2) Employees might react to the idea of change by being **demotivated** and **uncooperative**, and they might even actively **resist** the change, e.g. by going on strike. See p. 84 for more on industrial action.

Lewin came up with a *Three-step Model* for *Change*

OCR

1) There's a **conflict** in business between the **pressures** on companies to **change** (e.g. new technology, changes in consumer tastes — see previous page), and the employees' **resistance** to change.

2) According to Lewin, when businesses want to make changes, they can either **increase** the pressures for change, or **reduce** the pressures to keep things as they are. They can also use a **combination** of these techniques.

3) Lewin thought that the most **successful** method for bringing about change was to **reduce** the pressures to keep things the **same** — he thought that this method would give a smoother transformation than increasing the pressure for change. He put forward a **three-step model** for bringing about change:

① **Unfreezing** — Businesses **reduce** the pressures to keep things the same.

② **Moving** — Businesses **make** the necessary **changes**. Employees are likely to feel some **stress** and **confusion** during this stage.

③ **Refreezing** — The **new way** of doing things becomes **normal** and employees feel as **comfortable** as they did before the changes were made.

Practice Questions

Q1 Give one example each of planned and unplanned change.

Q2 Give an example of a catastrophic change.

Q3 Give three reasons why employees might resist change.

Q4 List the three steps in Lewin's model of change.

Exam Question

Q1 Discuss the main reasons for change, and the barriers businesses face when they implement changes. [12 marks]

Letting a friend perm your hair is a recipe for a catastrophic change...

Change is a fact of life, and a fact of business too. In general, people prefer stability — change is stressful, and the bigger the change, the more stressful it is. Managers need to be aware of this when they're planning to move their offices or bring in new equipment or new ways of working. And you need to be aware of it for your delightful A2 Business Studies exam.

Managing Change

*You're probably ready for a change from all this learning about change. Well don't worry, because you're almost at the end of Section 7 now — phew. These last two pages are for **AQA**, the **OCR: Strategic Management** unit and **WJEC**.*

Managers need **Strategies** to **Overcome Resistance** to change

1) The most **successful changes** happen when all employees have opportunities to be **fully consulted**.

2) Staff don't like being kept **in the dark**. They cope better when they have **information** about what's going on. **Lack of information** can lead to rumour and **distrust** of management's **intentions**, which affects **motivation** and **morale**.

See p. 173 for more on employees' feelings towards change.

3) Employees also don't like to feel **powerless**. They cope better when they're given the opportunity to **have their say**, and **influence decisions** in some way.

> There are **two strategies** commonly used by managers to overcome resistance:
>
> 1) Everyone who may be affected by the change is expected to **become involved** at the **planning stage**. This helps them to understand **why change** is necessary. When a decision needs to be taken, all employees affected have an opportunity to **comment** on the proposal, **suggest** changes and eventually reach an **agreement**. This is easier to achieve when change is incremental but more difficult at times of crisis. This strategy is used by **democratic** managers.
>
> 2) All staff affected by change are kept **informed** at each stage of the process, but don't get the chance to become involved in planning the change. Managers try to **persuade** employees that the changes are a good idea. This is the strategy that **paternalistic** managers use.

Project Champions and **Project Groups** can help change **Succeed**

1) A **project champion** is a manager within the company whose role is to **encourage** employees to **support** changes. They do this by being **enthusiastic** about the changes, and trying to spread their enthusiasm among the staff. They explain to people why they think the changes are a **good idea**, and what the **benefits** will be. This makes employees feel more **positive** about the changes.

2) **Project groups** are groups of **employees** who are involved in the change process. They might be involved in making **decisions** about the changes, or they might just sit in on **meetings** so that they're kept **informed** about what's going on. Other employees are likely to be **less suspicious** of changes when a project group is involved, because they know that they're getting the full picture of what's going on, rather than just hearing what managers want them to know.

Being the project champion was ok, but what Jon really wanted was a pay rise.

Teamwork and **Motivation** can help to **Achieve Change**

1) Employees are usually **resistant** to changes at work (see p. 173). But if change is **managed well**, businesses can get the staff on their side, which will make the whole process a lot **easier**.

2) Staff who want to **avoid** change can cause a lot of **trouble** for businesses — times of change are already difficult for businesses because there's a lot to organise and adjust to, but if staff are uncooperative then implementing changes becomes almost **impossible**. E.g. if a business wants to bring in a new, more efficient, system for taking orders but staff refuse to use it or deliberately make mistakes, the business will be in a **worse position** than it was to start with. If staff go on **strike** then no work will get done at all.

3) On the other hand, if managers can **motivate** employees using the techniques described above, changes will happen much more smoothly, because staff will be **committed** to making the changes successful, so they'll be willing to do whatever they need to do to make it work.

4) When all the employees in a business work **together** as a team, there's a much greater chance that the changes will work than if some of the employees are **resisting** the changes or trying to make things go wrong.

Managing Change

The way businesses manage **Change** depends on their **Corporate Culture**

Company culture (see p. 166) has a big impact on the way companies handle change, and whether staff are **open** to change or **resistant** to it:

Task culture
Staff working in a company with a task culture are likely to be **comfortable** with change because they are used to **changing teams** often and working with a variety of people. This means that they are likely to be **less resistant** to change in general.

Power culture
All the **decisions** are made by **one** person or **a few** people at the **top** of the business. This means that employees are likely to be **more resistant** to change, because they don't have the opportunity to give their **opinions** on what changes should and shouldn't be made. They might also be resistant to changes because they don't have enough **faith** in senior managers who they feel are **out of touch** with the day-to-day activities of the business.

Role culture
In companies with a role culture, **decisions** come from **senior managers**, so employees don't have the opportunity to be involved in the decision-making process. Change is also quite **rare** in companies with a role culture because they **avoid** taking risks and trying new things, so employees are likely to resist any changes that are brought in because they're **not used** to things changing.

Entrepreneurial culture
Change is a big part of entrepreneurial culture, and **all employees** are responsible for coming up with ideas to **improve** how the business is run. If employees are encouraged to be **creative** and **innovative**, they are likely to be much more **open** to change, especially when changes are made based on their suggestions.

Person culture
Change in businesses with a person culture can only happen when the **goals** of each person in the business change. **Decisions** are made **jointly**, so employees are likely to be **comfortable** with changes that are made because they have agreed to them.

Involving Employees in change Reduces their Resistance

Employees are likely to be more open to change if they are **involved** in planning changes, and kept **informed** about how changes are progressing (see p. 174). The **two main ways** of involving employees in the change process are through **total quality management** and **kaizen**.

1) **Total quality management** (TQM) is a process where **every worker** is **responsible** for the quality of the product produced. By encouraging and giving workers responsibility for the task in hand they are often **less resistant** to change when it comes. It may have been one of the **workers** on the factory floor who spotted a change that could be made to improve quality. See p. 114 for more on TQM.

2) **Kaizen groups** promote **continuous improvement** and so when workers meet to discuss **improvements** that can be made, they are **expecting** change to happen, and are **open** to it. See p. 115 for more on kaizen.

Practice Questions

Q1 What are the two main strategies that managers can use to overcome resistance to change?
Q2 What is a project champion?
Q3 How does total quality management reduce employees' resistance to change?

Exam Question

Q1 Explain how corporate culture affects how changes are made, and whether they are successful. [8 marks]

We are the (project) champions...

Yep, you've done it. That's the last page of the last section in the book (except for the handy maths and exams tips that are up next). Before you get too excited and start jumping up and down on the furniture and singing with joy at the top of your voice, make sure you know everything really well — project champions, corporate culture, and all the rest. The end.

Maths Bits

You need to understand a bit about maths if you want to do well in Business Studies. These pages are for everyone.

Businesses work out **Percentage Changes** in figures

1) Businesses work out **percentage increases** or **decreases** in sales, revenue, profit, etc. so that they can see how the business' performance is **progressing** over time. Percentage changes can show **trends** in performance.

2) The **formula** for calculating percentage change is ⟹

$$\text{Percentage change} = \frac{\text{new figure} - \text{previous figure}}{\text{previous figure}} \times 100$$

3) E.g. if a company's profits have gone up from £20 000 to £23 000, this is a percentage increase of (23 000 − 20 000) ÷ 20 000 × 100% = 15%.

4) It's important not to **underestimate** large changes in figures even if they only produce a **small percentage change**. E.g. a fall in revenue of £1 million shouldn't be overlooked even if it only works out as a 2% decrease.

Index Numbers show **Changes** in data over time

1) **Index numbers** are a way of showing **changes** in revenue, profits, etc. over a period of time.

2) The **earliest figure** is the **base figure** — the value of the base figure is set at **100**. The rest of the figures are shown **relative** to the base figure — this is done by **dividing** each figure by the **base figure** and then **multiplying** by **100**.

3) The main **advantage** of index numbers is that they make it easy to see **trends** within the business.

Year	Total revenue	Revenue index (2005 = 100)
2005	£35 200	100
2006	£38 700	110
2007	£43 200	123
2008	£56 600	161

base figure

Graphs can display **Data Clearly**

1) It can sometimes be difficult to get a clear picture of what's happening in a business just by looking at the figures.

2) Displaying data in **graphs** and **charts** makes it easy to **understand** without wading through pages of figures.

3) **Bar charts** and **line graphs** make **trends** in data more obvious. They can also be used to **compare** sets of data (e.g. a company's sales figures can be plotted against its competitors', or against its own sales figures from previous years).

4) **Pie charts** are useful for showing **market share**, or for showing what proportion of a company's sales come from each of its products.

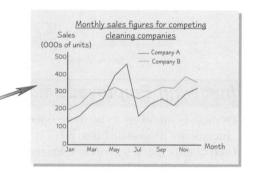

Graphs can sometimes be **Misleading**

1) Graphs are a **useful** way of displaying data, but they can sometimes give a **false impression** of what's going on.

2) If you're given a graph in an exam, keep an eye out for axes that don't start at **zero** — they can make differences look much bigger than they really are. If you're comparing graphs, check that they both use the same **scale**.

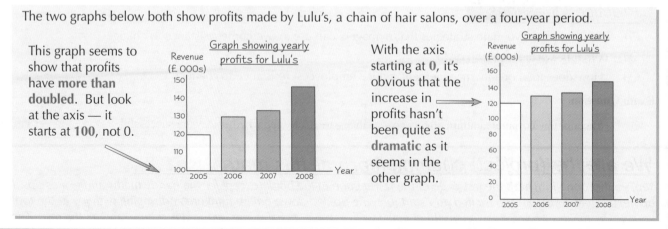

The two graphs below both show profits made by Lulu's, a chain of hair salons, over a four-year period.

This graph seems to show that profits have **more than doubled**. But look at the axis — it starts at **100**, not 0.

With the axis starting at **0**, it's obvious that the increase in profits hasn't been quite as **dramatic** as it seems in the other graph.

Maths Bits

The **Mean** is the **Average Value** in a set of data

1) The **mean** is the **sum** of all the **values** in a data set divided by the **number of values** in the set.

2) It's calculated using the following formula:

$$\text{Mean} = \frac{\text{total amount}}{\text{number of values}}$$

> Anna is thinking of opening a restaurant. She wants to know if there's enough **demand** for a new restaurant in her town, so she asks five people **how often** they eat out on average per month. The results are: 3, 2, 12, 8 and 10.
>
> The **mean** is: $\dfrac{3 + 2 + 12 + 8 + 10}{5} = 7$.

3) The **median** is the **middle value** in a set of data when all the numbers are listed in **order** from lowest to highest.

4) The **mode** is the **most common** value in a data set.

> In the following set of data: 4, 5, 7, 10, 11, 12, 12, 13, 16
> - the **median** is **11**, the 5th value out of 9. If there's an **even** number of values, you take the **mean** of the two middle numbers to get the median.
> - the **mode** is **12**, because it's the only number that appears more than once.

Standard Deviation shows how Spread Out values are around the Mean

1) **Standard deviation** is used to measure the **distribution** of values around the **mean**. A **low** standard deviation means that all the data is **clustered** around the mean, and a **high** standard deviation means that the data is **spread out** a lot.

2) The **formula** for standard deviation looks pretty scary, but it's actually quite straightforward when you know what all the **symbols** stand for:

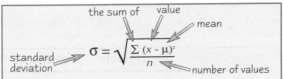

$$\sigma = \sqrt{\frac{\Sigma (x - \mu)^2}{n}}$$

standard deviation — the sum of — value — mean — number of values

> Anna can work out the **standard deviation** of her data about how often people eat out. She already knows that the **mean** is 7 (see above), so she takes **7 off** each value, **squares** the results and **adds** them all together, then **divides** the total by 5 (the number of values) and takes the **square root** of the result. This is shown in the table:
>
> | x | 3 | 2 | 12 | 8 | 10 | | |
> |---|---|---|---|---|---|---|---|
> | $x-\mu$ | -4 | -5 | 5 | 1 | 3 | sum | SD |
> | $(x-\mu)^2$ | 16 | 25 | 25 | 1 | 9 | 76 | 3.9 |
>
> Anna could do similar market research in **other towns** and work out the standard deviation to see if people's eating-out habits are **more varied** (a standard deviation of more than 3.9), or **more similar** to each other (a standard deviation of less than 3.9) than in her town. See p. 16 for more on standard deviation.

Practice Questions

Q1 How are percentage changes worked out?

Q2 What do index numbers show?

Q3 What's the formula for standard deviation?

Exam Question

Q1 Discuss the ways that graphs can be used by businesses. [4 marks]

It's a bit "mean" to make you learn all this maths, isn't it...

You might have thought that you left maths behind after GCSE, but here it is, popping up again like a long lost friend/ bad penny. Even if you hate maths, you still need to know these few bits because you're more than likely going to have to analyse a graph or some figures in the exam. So learn it all and then you've just got 'Do Well in Your Exam' left. Hurray.

Do Well in Your A2 Exam

These pages tell you what the actual exams will be like — so it won't be too much of a surprise on the day. You don't need to learn this stuff as such, but it's worth making sure you understand it no matter which board you're doing.

You get marks for **AO1 (showing knowledge)** and **AO2 (applying knowledge)**

AO1 and **AO2** questions usually start with words like "**Show**", "**Calculate**", or "**Explain why**".

AO1

1) **AO1** marks are for **content** and **knowledge**.

2) You'll only get about **2 marks** for this, whether the question is a short one worth 2 marks, a shortish one worth 6 marks or a long one worth 15 marks. At A2 level, they assume you know what most **basic business terms** mean.

AO2

1) **AO2** marks are for **applying** your **knowledge** to a **situation** — e.g. thinking about the type of ownership of the business in the question, the product or service it's selling, the type of market it's in.

2) You usually get **2-3 marks** for this as well.

You get marks for **AO3 (analysis)** and **AO4 (evaluation)**

AO3 questions usually start with words like "**Analyse**", "**Examine**" or "**Consider**".

AO3

1) **AO3** marks are for **analysis** — thinking about benefits, drawbacks, causes, effects and limitations.

2) Use your knowledge to **explain** your answer and **give reasons**.

3) With data, say what the figures **mean**, what might have **caused** them and what the **consequences** might be.

4) Write about **context** — e.g. compare a business' situation with the industry as a whole, or with a competitor.

AO4 questions usually start with words like "**Evaluate**", "**Discuss**", or "**To what extent**".

AO4

1) **AO4** marks are for **evaluation** — using your **judgement**.

2) Give **two sides** of an argument, and say which you think is **strongest**. Consider **advantages** and **disadvantages** and weigh them up.

3) You don't need a definite answer. You can point out that it depends on various factors — as long as you say what the factors are, and say why the right choice depends on those factors. Use your **judgement** to say what the **most important factors** are.

4) Relate your answer to the **business** described in the **question** and to the **situation** in the question. Give reasons **why** the business would make a particular decision, and how and why the particular circumstances might **affect** their **decision**.

"I might...maybe...we'll see" — there are some situations in life where it is important to give a definite answer.

The **Marks** are **Shared Out** differently by **Different Exam Boards**

1) For **AQA**, and **Edexcel** questions worth up to **6 marks**, all the skills are marked **separately**.

2) For example, an **evaluation** question has some marks for **content**, some for **application**, some for **analysis** and some for **evaluation**. You can **lose marks** for poor content, application and analysis. If you evaluate possible pros and cons **without** specifically stating the **obvious facts**, and specifically **relating** them to the **actual business situation** in the question, you'll **lose out**.

---

1) With **OCR**, **WJEC** and **Edexcel extended answer** questions the mark scheme is like a **ladder** with **AO1** skills at the **bottom** and **AO4** skills at the **top**. You get marks according to how far up the ladder you get.

2) For example, in an **evaluation** question worth **11 marks**, you can get **1-2 marks** for only giving **content**, **3-5 marks** for **applying knowledge** but not analysing, and **6-7 marks** for **analysis** but no evaluation. Even if you struggle with the evaluation bit, you can still get **8 marks**. A really **good evaluation** will get you the **full 11 marks**.

Do Well in Your A2 Exam

A2 Material is Based on AS Material — your AS Work is Relevant

Even though you're taking the A2 exams, you'll still be expected to **use information** from the AS course:

1) As **background knowledge** to help you **apply knowledge**, and **analyse** and **evaluate** business decisions.

2) In the "**synoptic**" papers which test knowledge from the AS part of the course as well as the A2 part. Depending on your **exam board**, you might have to do a **fully synoptic** paper, or one that has **some specific questions** and **some synoptic questions**. There's more about synoptic papers below.

Synoptic questions test Everything you've Learnt in the last Two Years

Both the papers you did at AS-Level, and most of the A2 papers, are based on **specific topics**, which means you can pretty much tell what the examiners are going to ask you about. As part of the A2, you'll sit at least one **synoptic paper** which tests your knowledge of **everything** you've learnt since the **beginning** of **AS**. It sounds **hard**, but it doesn't have to be, as long as you remember these things:

1) The synoptic paper is a great chance for you to show the examiner just **how much** you **know**. You **choose** what material to include in your answer, so it's a good opportunity to **focus** on the bits of the course you were **good at** or **enjoyed**.

2) However, you can only focus on issues that are **relevant** to the question. Don't go on and on about motivation if it's not at all **related** to what you're being asked. The best way to get **high marks** is to always clearly **link** what you're talking about back to the **original question**.

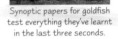

Synoptic papers for goldfish test everything they've learnt in the last three seconds.

3) **Practise** linking ideas together. You don't need to write whole essays when you're revising. Just try to get a big supply of **practice questions** and give yourself **15 minutes** to scribble down all the things you can think of that are linked to the question. It's a good idea to get used to spotting all the **different factors** that are involved when a business makes a **decision**. There's an **example** of a synoptic question essay plan below:

Balance sheet might be more important to certain groups of stakeholders than others, e.g. shareholders.

Government is a stakeholder — they'll want to know that laws (e.g. minimum wage) aren't being broken to achieve high levels of profit. This information isn't on the balance sheet.

"The balance sheet is the only thing stakeholders need to look at to get a good picture of a company's activities." Discuss.

Don't forget to include a conclusion at the end of your essay.

The business plan and the company's corporate objectives are important because they show future plans as well as current position.

Corporate Social Responsibility Policy — CSR could have an impact on long-term profitability. Many companies have a written CSR document which stakeholders could look at alongside balance sheet.

You get marks for Quality of Written Communication

Jotting down a quick essay plan will help.

1) You have to write a **well-structured essay**, not a list of bullet points.

2) You need to use **specialist vocabulary** when it's appropriate, so it's worth **learning** some of the **fancy terms** used in this book (check out the glossary for the ones you really need to know).

3) Write **neatly** enough for the examiner to be able to read it and use good **spelling**, **grammar** and **punctuation**. Out of the whole paper, you only get **2** or **3** marks for written communication — but remember that if the examiner can't **read** or **understand** your writing, you won't get the **other marks** either.

Make sure you thoroughly revise Words and Concepts you often get Mixed-Up

Everybody has certain topics they find it **difficult** to get their head around. The important thing is to spend **extra time** revising the bits you find really **tricky**, rather than concentrating on the things you find easy and hoping the tough stuff doesn't come up. It might also be helpful to **check** you're absolutely clear on the **difference** between these **frequently confused terms**.

Price and **cost**	**Interest** rate and **exchange** rate
Productivity and **productive efficiency**	**Migration** and **net migration**
Liquidation and **bankruptcy**	**Differentiation** and **diversification**
Quota and **stratified** sampling	**Value added** and **mark up**

Do Well in Your AQA Exam

*This page is all about how to do well in AQA exams. So don't bother reading it if you're not doing **AQA**.*

There are two **Exam Units** at A2

1) There are **two examinations** at A2 — **units 3** and **4** which are each worth **25%** of the total A level marks. Each exam lasts **1 hour 45 minutes** and has a total of **80 marks**.

2) **Unit 3** is called **Strategies for Success**. It's a **synoptic** paper based on an **unseen case study**. It has about four **extended answer** questions worth between **10** and **34** marks. It focuses on **functional objectives** and **strategy**, **financial strategies** and **accounts**, **marketing strategies**, **operating strategies** and **human resource** strategies. You'll be expected to show knowledge of the material you covered at **AS Level** too.

3) **Unit 4** is called **The Business Environment and Managing Change**. It has **two** parts and is also **synoptic**, although the focus of the paper is on **corporate aims** and **objectives**, **assessing change** in the business environment and how businesses can **manage change**. **Section A** is based on **pre-released research tasks** that you'll have covered in the run-up to the exam — these tasks should give you a pretty good idea of the kind of questions that might come up. **Section B** contains a choice of three long essay questions. You must answer **one question** which is worth **40 marks**.

Here's an **Example Answer** to give you some tips:

> Malvern Holdings manufactures electronic components for domestic appliances. The company has recently received some large orders after a successful marketing campaign. To meet these orders it must increase its capacity and replace existing machines with new technology. Analyse the benefits to Malvern Holdings of using critical path analysis to meet these large orders. (10 marks)

1 mark (AO2) — applies knowledge to Malvern Holdings.

1 mark (AO1) — understands the term 'critical path analysis'.

Critical path analysis is a tool used by firms to work out the quickest way of doing things. Before Malvern Holdings can get the products to their customers it needs to increase the size of its factory and replace existing machinery, CPA will help them do this in the quickest way by identifying the critical path. This will not only allow them to satisfy customers orders but give them an advantage over their competitors.

1 mark (AO3) — analyses disadvantages of CPA.

By using a CPA managers at Malvern Holdings can establish which activities can take place at the same time. For instance, Malvern Holdings may be able to order raw materials whilst improvements to the factory are taking place. There is a risk though that managers may have wrongly estimated the time needed to do each activity and orders could be late to customers.

2 marks (AO2) — refers to Malvern Holdings.

1 mark (AO1) — shows knowledge of CPA and cash flow.

CPA can also help firms forecast their cash flow, it gives earliest start times when cash will be needed and may also indicate when they are likely to receive inflows of cash. This will help the firm avoid cash flow problems.

Relating this knowledge to the question would score more marks.

2 marks (AO2 and AO3) — analyses benefits of just-in-time production for Malvern Holdings.

Given the number of orders that Malvern Holdings has received for its products it may have to adopt a just-in-time production system. Resources used to produce the components such as raw materials and labour can be employed at the earliest start time, instead of hanging around and waiting to be needed. This will reduce both storage and opportunity costs. This may be especially important for the firm as the successful marketing campaign is likely to have cost them a large sum of money.

The conclusion is weak — it doesn't fit in well with the answer and doesn't show evaluation.

There are of course lots of problems with CPA. The earliest start and latest finish times are estimates made by managers. There is a risk these could be inaccurate and therefore the whole CPA will be incorrect. Once a CPA has been constructed it is important that the process is then supervised. If it is not, delays may occur and customers lacking satisfaction.

This is a good answer and would get about **8** out of **10 marks**. It examines a range of points **relevant** to Malvern Holdings, but the answer is **let down** by a **weak conclusion**. **More evaluation** would improve the answer.

Do Well in Your Edexcel Exam

*This page is all about how to do well in **Edexcel** exams.*

There are two **Exam Units** at A2

1) There are **two exams** at A2 — **units 3** and **4a** which are each worth **25%** of the total A level marks. Each exam lasts **90 minutes** and has a total of **80 marks**. Both exams are **synoptic**.

2) **Unit 3** is a **two-section** exam called **International Business**. Section A is based on data and usually has around 4 questions each worth between 6 and 12 marks. Section B has questions based on a case study and is worth 45 marks.

3) **Unit 4a** is called **Making Business Decisions**. It tests your knowledge of **corporate objectives** and **strategy**, **competitiveness**, **managing risk**, **change** and **external influences** on businesses. Like Unit 3, it has **two sections**. Section A contains 6 **short-answer questions** based on previously **unseen** data and is worth **30 marks**. Section B consists of a 'decision-making report'. You have to read the report and then answer a **two-part question** worth **50 marks** in total. Edexcel release details about the context of the case study a year in advance, so you'll have some **idea** of what the report's going to be about **before** you go into the exam.

Here's an **Example Answer** to give you some tips:

> Evaluate the benefits of reduced global protectionist measures for UK manufacturing firms. (12 marks)

1 mark (A01) — understands the term 'protectionism'.

2 marks (A02) — applies knowledge of protectionism to the question.

1 mark (A02) — applies knowledge of manufacturing costs to the question.

This conclusion is weak — it doesn't add any new information and it's very vague.

Protectionism is way in which governments can protect their domestic firms from overseas competition; methods could include tariffs and quotas. With reduced protectionist measures this means freer trade across the globe that has benefits to both consumers and producers.

With the onset of reduced protectionist measures UK manufacturing firms now have a much larger market place to sell their products to and therefore a greater number of consumers to buy their products. With a larger market place UK firms may now be able to increase their scale of production, this may bring cost savings through economies of scale, and average cost per unit may fall. The fact that they can now produce each product at a lower cost may mean that they can charge a lower price and therefore become more competitive in a global market place. UK manufacturing firms though have suffered as a result of freer trade. Aside from a greater number of customers there are also a greater number of competitors. UK firms have faced competition from firms in India and China who can produce at lower costs, often due to the cheap wages paid to workers, and thus charge a lower price.

With greater levels of trade comes a greater availability of resources that UK firms can use in their manufacturing process. Firms may be able to source their inputs at a lower price than they are currently paying. As with the previous point this may mean that UK manufacturing firms can compete with lower priced products with overseas firms. There is a risk though that these inputs are susceptible to other factors such as changes in exchange rates, which in the future could actually make these inputs more expensive, if the pound fell in value

UK manufacturing firms can greatly benefit from reduced protectionist measures but there are some problems that may result.

Defining protectionism and giving examples of protectionist strategies is a good start.

2 marks (A03) — analyses the effects of an increased market size.

1 mark (A02) — applies knowledge of international economies to the question.

3 marks (A02, A03, A04) — applies knowledge of exchange rates and analyses their effect on business' costs, evaluating the effects with reference to the question.

This is a good answer, but the conclusion lets it down. It would get about **10** out of **12 marks**. The answer starts off well with a good **definition** of protectionism, and analyses some of the **benefits** and **drawbacks** of protectionist measures. Showing more **evaluation** in the conclusion would pick up more marks.

Do Well in Your OCR Exam

*This page is all about how to do well in **OCR** exams. So don't bother reading it if you're not doing **OCR**.*

There are **Two Exam Modules** at A2 — **One Compulsory** and **One Choice**

1) If you're studying **OCR**, the first of your two exams at A2 is on a subject of your (or your teacher's) **choice**. The modules available are **Marketing**, **Accounting**, **People in Organisations** or **Business Production**.

2) This module is worth **20%** of your total A Level. It's examined in a **2 hour** exam. The exam paper is based on an **unseen case study** and contains **6 questions**. The **final question** on this paper is a **synoptic** question, so it'll test everything you've learnt since the beginning of AS, as well as the material you've been taught for this module. There are **60 marks** available overall.

3) The second module is **compulsory**, so everyone has to sit it. It's called **Strategic Management** and is worth **30%** of the overall A Level. This exam also lasts **2 hours**, but the paper is worth **90 marks** in total. You'll have to answer **4 questions** on a **case study** you'll have **seen before** the exam.   One of the questions will have a maths-type element, and you'll be expected to do some **calculations**. The entire paper is **synoptic** — so make sure you revise **everything**. You'll have a copy of the case study in the exam, but it's a good idea to make sure you **know the material** well before you go into the exam so that you don't **waste time** looking for the information you need. Reading the case study can give you **clues** about the **questions** that might come up.

Here's an **Example Answer** to give you some tips:

> Sumo Bike is a Japanese manufacturer of scooters and motorcycles. It set up a UK manufacturing plant in the early 1990s, but is considering relocating the factory abroad due to high overhead costs and low productivity in the UK plant. Discuss the extent to which the different external stakeholder groups might be able to influence whether or not the UK factory remains open. (18 marks)

Defining terms at the beginning of your answer is ok, but it's better to show your knowledge by applying it to the question.

Stakeholders is the name given to the different groups of people who are affected by the actions of a business. They can be separated into two groups; internal, e.g. staff, and external, e.g. customers.

1 mark (AO1) — understands the term 'stakeholder'.

If the suppliers are also UK based firms then the loss of a customer will concern them. However, their influence will depend on whether they supply other factories owned by Sumo Bike; if they only supply the UK factory they may have little influence.

2 marks (AO3) — bases analysis on the real-world situation.

Don't be afraid to make assumptions if information isn't provided.

If the UK is a major market for the firm's products then any negative publicity could have a negative impact on sales, so customers may be able to influence Sumo Bike's decision. Customers have become more ethically aware in recent years, so they may object, although in reality, it is likely that many customers will not be too interested in where the product is made, and so will have little influence.

1 mark (AO4) — evaluates theoretical ideas in a real-world context.

4 marks (AO2) — identifies four relevant external stakeholder groups.

Assuming Sumo Bike employs people who live near the factory, the local community is also a stakeholder and is likely to be upset at potential job losses. The community is unlikely to be very powerful by itself, but it could hold protests or similar in an attempt to get the government involved.

1 mark (AO3) — says how stakeholder can influence business.

1 mark (AO2) — applies knowledge of government intervention in business.

The government is also a stakeholder in the business. The fact that Sumo Bike is a Japanese company which has invested in the UK and created jobs will be welcomed by the government. As such, they are likely to apply pressure to the firm to ensure that the UK factory remains open. The government may be willing to negotiate grants or other incentives to keep the factory open to prevent the political damage that job losses can create.

2 marks (AO4) — draws a sensible conclusion.

1 mark (AO3) — analyses reasons for not intervening.

Given the situation that Sumo Bike finds itself in, it is likely that the most influential stakeholder group would potentially be the government. However, if there is little political will to keep the UK factory open, say because there are plenty of other jobs in the area where the factory is situated, then the government could quite easily have little influence.

This is a clear conclusion that answers the question.

This is a fairly good answer and would get about **13** out of **18 marks** since it considers a number of **different stakeholders** of the business, and refers to the **situation** described in the **question**. The answer could be improved by going into **more depth** in explaining **how** stakeholder groups influence the business — e.g. "suppliers might influence Rava's decision because they could refuse to supply its other factories if it closes the UK factory".

Do Well in Your WJEC Exam

*Ah, last but not least — how to do well if you're doing **WJEC exams**. Don't bother reading if you're not doing **WJEC**, cos it'll be no help at all.*

There are two **Exam Units** at A2

1) A2 is made up of **two exams**, each lasting **two hours**. Each **exam** is worth **25%** of the total **A Level**.

2) The first exam is called **Business Decision-Making**. It's worth **60 marks** in total and requires you to answer around five **compulsory** questions about an **unseen case study**. This paper tests you on the stuff you learnt as part of **Unit BS3** and also at **AS Level**.

3) The second paper is called **Business Strategy and Practice**. It's also worth **60 marks** and is divided into **two sections**.

4) The **first section** is worth **40 marks** and tests you on the material you learnt in **Unit BS4**. It consists of **short answer** and **problem-solving questions**. The questions are based on previously **unseen** data.

5) The **second section** lets you choose **one** of three **synoptic essays** which are designed to test everything you've learnt since the beginning of AS Level. Section 2 is worth **20 marks**.

Here's an **Example Answer** to give you some tips:

> Ready Mealz is a manufacturer of high quality ready meals. It does not sell to consumers using its own name, but instead provides own-brand products for most of the major supermarket chains. Evaluate the extent to which Ready Mealz is affected by the environmental issue of recycling. (10 marks)

1 mark (A01) — understands what pressure groups are.

Recycling is really important today and it is an external factor that no business can afford to ignore. Pressure groups often oppose businesses which do not encourage recycling, and pressure groups can create bad publicity for such businesses. This is a particularly important point for Ready Mealz, since they do not produce products under their own brand-name. Instead they produce own-label products. This means that it is their customers (the supermarkets) who will receive the bad publicity from the pressure groups, which may mean that supermarkets look for alternative suppliers.

It's good to relate the answer to the information provided in the question

1 mark (A02) — applies knowledge of pressure groups to the question.

2 marks (A03) — analyses the ways in which the company can use recycling to its advantage.

The current focus upon waste and recycling should be seen as an opportunity by Ready Mealz in terms of marketing. By ensuring that their packaging is recyclable they can provide themselves with an opportunity to promote this within their marketing materials. It should certainly be made quite prominent on the products themselves.

As a manufacturer there is a legal requirement that Ready Mealz minimise the packaging requirements of their products. It is in the interest of the business to comply with this, to avoid fines. They could even use recycled materials to produce their packaging, which could also be used as a marketing tool.

1 mark (A02) — applies knowledge of business laws to the question.

2 marks (A03) — analyses recycling in terms of finance and marketing.

In conclusion it is clear that a manufacturer such as Ready Mealz is affected in a number of ways by the issue of recycling, but with careful management this issue can be turned into one that provides a number of positives for the firm.

Summarising your ideas is a good idea, but make sure you don't just repeat what you've already said.

This is a reasonably good answer and would get about **7** out of **10 marks**. It considers a number of **different impacts** on the **marketing** of the business, and also considers the **relationship** between the business and its customers. However, the conclusion doesn't really **add anything** to the answer, and the answer **doesn't** get any marks for **evaluation**.

To improve the answer, the student could consider the **financial implications** of recycling and the importance of **corporate social responsibility** and **business ethics**. A **clearer evaluation**, outlining the potential **consequences** of not taking recycling seriously, would also be helpful — e.g. "consumers are increasingly environmentally aware, and might avoid using products from companies that don't recycle".

Answers to the Numerical Questions

Section One — Marketing

Page 9 — Exam Questions

Q1   Market share = sales ÷ total market size x 100%
Market share = 985 000 ÷ 5 000 000 x 100% = 19.7%
[1 mark for formula, 1 mark for working and 1 mark for final correct answer]

Page 11 — Exam Questions

Q1(a)

Year	Quarter	Sales revenue (thousand £s)	4 quarter moving total	8 quarter moving total	Quarterly moving average
2006	1	630			
	2	567			
	3	552	2427	4845	605.63
	4	678	2418	4847	605.88
2007	1	621	2429	4849	606.13
	2	578	2420	4762	595.25
	3	543	2342	4665	583.13
	4	600	2323	4618	577.25
2008	1	602	2295	4549	568.63
	2	550	2254	4468	558.50
	3	502	2214	4415	551.88
	4	560	2201		
2009	1	589			

[14 marks]

(b)

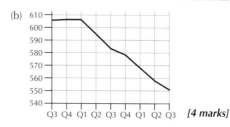

[4 marks]

Page 13 — Practice Questions

Q2

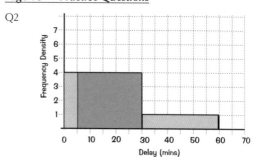

Page 17 — Exam Questions

Q1   Mean = (20+18+14+12+24)÷5 = 17.6 *[1 mark]*

Standard deviation formula: $\sigma = \sqrt{\dfrac{\sum (x - \mu)^2}{n}}$ *[1 mark]*

Squares of difference between each figure and the mean:
[1 mark for calculating x-µ terms, 1 mark for calculating (x-µ)² terms]

x	x–µ	(x–µ)²
20	2.4	5.76
18	0.4	0.16
14	-3.6	12.96
12	-5.6	31.36
24	6.4	40.96

Sum of (x-µ)² = 91.2. *[1 mark]*
Divide by number of observations to give variance: 91.2÷5 = 18.24 *[1 mark]*
Take square root to give standard deviation = 4.27 *[1 mark for working and 1 mark for final correct answer for standard deviation]*

Q2   99.7% = 3SD either side of the mean.   *[1 mark]*
Mean = 40 minutes   1SD = 7 minutes   *[2 marks]*
3SD = 7 × 3 = 21   *[1 mark]*
Minimum Delivery time = 40 – 21 = 19 minutes   *[1 mark]*
Maximum Delivery time = 40 + 21 = 61 minutes   *[1 mark]*

Page 25 — Exam questions

Q1   PED = % change in demand ÷ % change in price
[1 mark]
% change in demand = (585 – 642) ÷ 642 x 100%
= -8.9% decrease *[1 mark]*
% change in price = (20 – 18) ÷ 18 x 100%
= 11.1% increase *[1 mark]*
PED = -8.9 ÷ 11.1 *[1 mark]*
= -0.80 *[1 mark]*
PED is less than one, so product is price inelastic.
Camille should raise prices. *[1 mark]*

Section Two — Accounting and Finance

Page 37 — Exam Questions

Q1 (a)   Total expenditure = £80k + £30k + £22k = £132k. *[1 mark]*
Variance on expenditure = £12k(A). *[1 mark]*
Variance on sales revenue = £5k(F). *[1 mark]*
Total variance = £12k – £5k = £7k(A). *[1 mark]*

Page 53 — Exam Questions

Q1

	Item	Jul	Aug	Sep
Cash in	Sales revenue	£9500	£11 000	£12 500
	Other revenue			
	Total revenue	**£9500**	**£11 000**	**£12 500**
Cash out	Wages and rent	£7000	£7000	£7000
	Other costs	£9000	£4500	£5500
	Total costs	**£16 000**	**£11 500**	**£12 500**
Net monthly cash flow	Net cash flow	(£6500)	(£500)	£0
	Opening balance	£2500	(£4000)	(£4500)
	Closing balance	**(£4000)**	**(£4500)**	**(£4500)**

[15 marks]

[3 marks for correct sales revenue figures, 3 marks for calculating total costs correctly, 3 marks for calculating net cash flow correctly, 3 marks each for correct opening and closing balances.]

Page 55 — Exam Questions

Q1 (a)   Contribution = selling price – variable costs per unit *[1 mark]*
Contribution = £5 – £3 = £2 *[1 mark]*
Break-even output = fixed costs ÷ contribution *[1 mark]*
Break-even output = £20 000 ÷ £2 = 10 000 units per year
[1 mark]

Page 61 — Exam Questions

Q2 (a)   Net profit margin = net profit ÷ turnover ×100% *[1 mark]*
Net profit margin = (£750 000 – £250 000) ÷ £2 000 000 × 100%
= 25% *[1 mark for working, 1 mark for answer.]*

Page 63 — Exam Questions

Q1 (a)   Dividend cover = net profit after tax ÷ total dividends *[1 mark]*
= £300 000 ÷ (6p × 100 000) = £300 000 ÷ £6000 = 50
[1 mark for working, 1 mark for answer.]

(b)   Dividend Yield = dividend per share ÷ price per share × 100%
= 6p ÷ 300p × 100% = 2%
[1 mark for working, 1 mark for answer.]

Answers to the Numerical Questions

Page 65 — Exam Questions

Q1 ARR = (average annual profit ÷ investment) × 100% *[1 mark]*
Average annual profit = £100 000 − £60 000 = £40 000 *[1 mark]*
ARR = £40 000 ÷ £200 000 × 100% = 20% *[1 mark for working, 1 mark for answer.]*

Q2 Payback = amount invested ÷ annual profit from investment *[1 mark]*
Payback = £5000 ÷ £1500 = 3.33 years (or 3 years and 4 months)
[1 mark for working, 1 mark for answer.]

Page 67 — Exam Questions

Q1

	Cash inflow	Discount Value (5%)	Present Value
Year 1	£5K	0.952	£5K × 0.952 = £4760
Year 2	£5K	0.907	£5K × 0.907 = £4535
Year 3	£5K	0.864	£5K × 0.864 = £4320
Year 4	£5K	0.823	£5K × 0.823 = £4115
Year 5	£5K	0.784	£5K × 0.784 = £3920
Total Present Value of Cash Inflows			£21650
Net Present Value (total minus Investment)		-£17K =	**£4650**

[2 marks for calculating all present values correctly, 1 mark for calculating 2-4 present values correctly] [1 mark for adding present values correctly] [1 mark for working of net present value calculation, 1 mark for answer of £4650]

Section Four — Operations Management

Page 109 — Exam Questions

Q1 Labour productivity = output per year ÷ no. of employees *[1 mark]*
Labour productivity = 4 500 000 ÷ 200 *[1 mark]*
= £22 500 per employee *[1 mark]*

Page 111 — Practice Questions

Q1 Capacity utilisation = output ÷ capacity x 100%
42 ÷ 65 x 100% = 65% (to nearest whole percentage).

Q2 Unit cost = total costs ÷ output
£1600 ÷ 450 = £3.56

Page 113 — Exam Questions

Q1 Buffer stock = 400 units, company supplies 200 units
a week, lead time = 2 weeks *[1 mark]*
200 x 2 = 400 *[1 mark]*
Re-order level = 400 + 400 = 800 units *[2 marks]*

Page 118 — Exam Questions

Q1

Task	Week						
	1	2	3	4	5	6	7
Buying stock	▓						
Painting changing rooms	▓	▓					
Planning launch party	▓	▓					
Staff training		▓	▓	▓			
Window displays						▓	▓

[1 mark for drawing the chart correctly, 1 mark for each activity correctly shaded in on the chart.]

Page 121 — Exam Questions

Q1 (a)

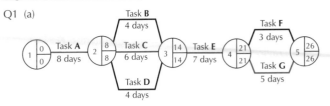

[3 marks for putting (A), (B, C and D), (E), and (F and G) in the right order. 2 marks for one error. 1 mark for 2 errors], [1 mark for B, C and D as simultaneous], [1 mark for F and G as simultaneous].

(b) *[1 mark for the critical path — it's a thick pink line on the diagram] [1 mark for the total time — 26 days]*

(c) *Float times for B and F are both 2 days. [1 mark for each]*

Page 161 — Exam Questions

Q1

(a)

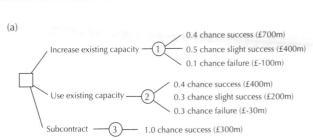

[1 mark for each correctly labelled probability and payoff]

(b) *Expected value at 1: £280m + £200m − £10m = £470m [1 mark for each correct value, 1 mark for adding them correctly]. Expected value at 2: £160m + £60m − £9m = £211m. [1 mark for each correct value, 1 mark for adding them correctly] Expected value at 3: £300m [1 mark]. Choosing and explaining the best option [4 marks].*

Glossary

Acas The Advisory, Conciliation and Arbitration Service, which acts as a mediator in industrial disputes and aims to improve employment relations.

AIDA Stands for Awareness (or Attention), Interest, Desire, Action. A marketing tool which helps make sure promotions actually persuade people to buy.

Ansoff's Matrix Shows the strategies that a firm can use to expand, according to how risky they are.

asset Anything that a business owns.

balance sheet A snapshot of a firm's finances at a fixed time.

break-even analysis Identifies the point where a company's total revenues equal their total costs.

budget Forecasts future earnings and future spending.

business cycle The regular pattern of growth and recession in the economy.

capital A company's finances or resources (land, premises and machinery).

cash flow Money that comes into and goes out of a firm.

competition policy Government policy to prevent anti-competitive behaviour by businesses, such as the formation of monopolies.

competitive advantage The way that a company offers customers better value than competitors do — generally either lower prices or more product features.

consistency The accounting principle of keeping methods of calculating and recording financial data consistent over time.

contingency plan A plan for when something goes wrong.

corporate culture The way a business does things — it affects the attitudes and expectations of employees.

corporate objectives The goals of the whole business.

corporate plan Sets out the business' corporate objectives and the strategy the business will use to achieve them.

corporate social responsibility (CSR) When a business' objectives consider the needs of all its stakeholders, not just shareholders.

cost centre Part of a business that directly incurs costs.

cost-benefit analysis Assessing the financial and social costs of an activity and its financial and social benefits.

critical path analysis Works out the most efficient and cost-effective way to finish a set of tasks.

DAGMAR (Defining Advertising Goals for Measured Advertising Results) A method for improving the effectiveness of advertising.

deflation Decrease in the price of goods and services.

Delphi method Forecasting method based on the consensus of a panel of experts.

depreciation Losing value over time — fixed assets often depreciate.

distinctive capability The competitive advantage that makes one firm stand out from another.

diversification Expanding to produce new products or enter new markets.

division of labour Breaking a job down into small, repetitive tasks.

economic growth Increase in the amount of goods and services that a country produces. Measured in rate of increase of gross domestic product (GDP).

elasticity of demand Shows the relationship between changes in price and demand for a product or service.

emerging market A country with rapid economic growth.

ethical Morally and professionally acceptable.

exchange rate The value of one currency in terms of another.

final accounts A company's balance sheet, profit and loss account and cash flow statement at the end of the financial year.

fiscal policy Government policy that sets tax rates and government spending.

fixed assets Things businesses keep long-term or use repeatedly — e.g. property, equipment, land, computers.

fixed costs Costs that stay the same — no matter how much or how little a firm produces.

forecasting Trying to predict what will happen in the future.

functional objectives The objectives of individual departments.

Gantt chart Shows all the activities needed to complete a project with their start and finish times.

gearing The proportion of a business financed through debt rather than equity or reserves.

GDP (gross domestic product) The total value of goods and services produced by a country, in the country, over a year.

globalisation The breakdown of traditional national boundaries with the growth of communications, transport and global organisations and businesses.

going concern The accounting principle of assuming that a firm's activities will continue into the foreseeable future.

green audit Independent check on the environmental impact of a firm's activities. Also called an environmental audit.

Human Development Index (HDI) Ranks countries according to GDP, literacy levels and life expectancy.

Human Resource Management (HRM) Looks after all the people aspects of a business — like recruitment and training.

industrial democracy Allowing the workforce to have some input into an organisation's decision-making process.

inflation The increase in the price of goods and services.

interest rate Shows the cost of borrowing.

just-in-time (JIT) production Manufacturing process which operates with very small amounts of stock.

kaizen Japanese for "continuous improvement", an approach used to improve quality control and efficiency.

lean production Techniques that aim to reduce waste to an absolute minimum (e.g. JIT production).

liabilities Debts a business owes.

liquidity How easily assets can be turned into cash.

management buy-in When managers from outside a company take control of it by buying up its shares.

management buy-out When the managers of a business buy the shares back from shareholders.

market analysis Finding out about the market you're operating in, e.g. its size, growth, classification and who has what share.

market classification Identifying a market's characteristics (by geography, seasonality, etc).

market failure What happens when supply and demand don't allocate resources efficiently.

market growth When demand for a product or service increases.

market research Finding out about customers, markets and competitors.

Glossary

market segmentation Identifying the different types of customer in a market, e.g. by gender or spending power.

market share The percentage of sales in a particular market that belong to a particular company or brand.

marketing mix The four Ps firms use to market their goods / services — price, product, promotion and place (distribution).

matching The accounting principle of recognising the revenue and the costs involved in a transaction in the same period.

materiality The accounting principle of focusing on important transactions in the accounts in order to give a fair impression of the company's performance.

merger Where two companies agree they should join together into one business.

mission statement A written description of a company's corporate objectives.

monetary policy Government policy that controls the interest rate.

monopoly Where one firm controls most or all of the market share.

motivation Anything that makes you work harder and achieve more than normal.

moving average A way of finding trends in a set of data over time by smoothing out cyclical and seasonal variations.

multinational A business with its headquarters in one country and bases in other countries.

nationalisation When the government takes over the running of a private company or an industry.

objective A medium- to long-term target.

objectivity The accounting principle of not allowing bias or personal opinion to influence accounts.

offshoring When a firm has one or several of its activities carried out abroad.

operations management Planning and monitoring business operations to ensure they're as efficient as possible.

opportunity cost The idea that money or time spent doing one thing is likely to mean missing out on doing something else.

organic growth When a business grows naturally.

outsourcing When a firm has one or several of its activities carried out by another, specialist company.

PEST analysis Used to analyse external opportunities and threats — looks at political, economic, social and technological issues.

Porter's Five Forces Analysis Method of assessing how to gain a competitive advantage in a market.

Porter's Strategic Matrix Identifies where a brand sits in the market, e.g. according to price and market scope.

privatisation Selling publicly-owned companies to private individuals and firms.

productive efficiency How good a company is at turning inputs into outputs.

profit and loss account Statement showing how much money's gone into and out of a company over a period of time. Also called an income statement.

profit centre Part of a firm that directly generates revenue.

protectionism When a country tries to protect its own companies by making it harder for foreign companies to trade in that country.

prudence Belief that accountants should be cautious in their assumptions when drawing up accounts.

qualitative forecasting Non-scientific method of predicting sales of a product, e.g. using intuition or hunches.

quantitative forecasting Predicting future sales using mathematical calculations.

realisation The accounting principle that revenue is recorded after a service or product is delivered to a customer, not when they pay for it.

return on capital employed (ROCE) Shows you how much money is made by the business compared to how much money's been put into the business.

SMART objectives Objectives which are Specific, Measurable, Agreed, Realistic and doable within a certain Time period.

social benefit Internal benefits + external benefits

social cost Internal costs + external costs

specialisation Breaking a job into smaller tasks so that workers become expert at their given task.

stakeholders Everyone affected by a business including workers, shareholders, customers and the public.

standard cost The average target cost of producing an item.

strategy A plan for achieving objectives.

subsidy Money paid by the government to certain industries to keep the costs of production down.

supply-side policies Government policies that aim to allow markets to work as freely as possible.

sustainability How long a production process can continue, bearing in mind its impact on resources like oil.

SWOT analysis A method of assessing a business' current situation — looks at the Strengths, Weaknesses, Opportunities and Threats facing the firm.

takeover Where one firm buys over 50% of the shares of another firm, giving them the controlling interest.

tariff Tax paid on an imported product.

time series analysis (TSA) Recording data on a graph over time to help identify trends.

trade barrier Measures such as tariffs or quotas that make it more difficult for foreign goods to enter a country.

trade unions Groups that act on behalf of groups of employees in negotiations with employers.

trading bloc A group of countries that trade freely with each other.

training needs analysis (TNA) A way of improving training by identifying gaps between workers' skills and a business' needs.

value analysis Identifying ways of lowering the cost of making a product.

variable costs Costs that vary, depending on how much business the firm does.

vicarious liability Where an employer is responsible for any act committed by an employee during the normal course of their job.

waste management Keeping levels of waste as low as possible and within legal limits.

working capital Money available for day-to-day spending.

Index

Index